DATE DUE

MAR 25 1995	
APR 0 8 1995	
NOV 2 8 1995	
FEB . 7 1998	
OCT 2 8 1998	

BRODART   Cat. No. 23-221

THE DEBATE
OVER
CHILD CARE
1969–1990

THE DEBATE
OVER
CHILD CARE
1969–1990

A Sociohistorical Analysis

ABBIE GORDON KLEIN

State University of New York Press

Published by
State University of New York Press, Albany

©1992 State University of New York

For information, address State University of New York Press,
State University Plaza, Albany, N.Y., 12246

Production by Marilyn P. Semerad
Marketing by Fran Keneston

Library of Congress Cataloging-in-Publication Data

Klein, Abbie Gordon, 1954-
    The debate over child care, 1969-1990: a sociohistorical analysis
/ Abbie Gordon Klein.
        p.   cm. — (SUNY series in issues in child care)
    Includes bibliographical references (p.   ) and index.
    ISBN 0-7914-0975-9 (cloth)
    1. Child care services—United States.   I. Title.   II. Series.
HQ778.7.U6K58   1992
362.7'1—dc20   91-13640
                                                           CIP

10 9 8 7 6 5 4 3 2 1

For Jonathan, Francesca, and Isabel

CONTENTS

Part II. The Kindergarten Debate

Part III. Conclusion

Acknowledgments

I found the motivation for the research leading to this book when I was student teaching at Grosvenor House Day Care Center on Manhattan's Upper West Side. I worked with the most dedicated people. Ursula Foster, as teacher, and Ellen Dublin, as administrator, provided the children a highly nurturing environment despite limited resources.

I was there only a brief time, but something of Grosvenor House has stayed with me all these years. I remember the children, especially Pauline, Jerry, Jamal, and Jose. I have always felt that the children of Grosvenor House deserved—that all children of America deserve—more attention and better care. I set out to discover the reasons why our young people are not in the forefront of our lives but instead tucked away in hard-to-find corners.

Many individuals gave selflessly of themselves as I attempted to answer research queries. I am indebted to those who contributed to the content of the text by thoughtfully answering questions and offering information. I thank the individuals who chose to remain anonymous and those who were never identified by name, including the numerous librarians who secured key pieces of information for me.

Specific people facilitated the development of the book, and I would like to express my gratitude to them. Each of the following contributed in a unique way to my work: Harriet Alger, Helen Blank, Marian Blum, Patrick Canan, Lisa Carr, Abba Cohen, Abby J. Cohen, Cathy Dillon, Matia Finn-Stevenson, Margery Freeman, Isabelle Garcia, John Gehan, Judith Golub, Molly Guth, Greg Humphrey, Syd Johnson, Bill Krupman, Victor Krupman, Barbara Kurtz, Karen Linkins, Ann Muscari, Joe Nyitray, Maribeth Oakes, Oralia Puente, and Donna Santman. Thanks, too, to the Charles Reiley Armington Research Program on Values in Children and the Columbus Jewish Foundation, for research support.

Colleagues also nurtured ideas underlying the work, particularly, Arthur Blum, Michael Grossberg, and Alvin Schorr. I thank my editor, Carola Sautter, for giving voice to my ideas and the production team, adeptly headed by Marilyn

Semerad, for transforming those ideas into print. The technical support of
Gnomi Schrift Gouldin, Leah Gilbert, Ron Gilbert, Jonathan Klein, Mark
Kmetzko, and Jennifer Waters was most appreciated.

I extend my heartfelt appreciation to Jonathan Gordon for his contribution
to Chapter 4. His legal insight was extremely beneficial and his collegiality
welcome.

My family steadfastly stood by me as the months turned into years and I am
most grateful for their support. I thank my parents, Evy and Larry Gordon, for
giving their granddaughters the highest-quality care at all times and for never
wavering in their encouragement. They have given much of themselves to this
project.

Millie Amaddio merits recognition for her loving care of my daughters.
Further, I am grateful to all the teachers who provided excellent care of my
children over the last few years.

My husband, Jonathan, and children, Francesca and Isabel, deserve the
highest accolades for sharing the writing experience; it demanded extraordinary
patience and understanding on their part. This book is dedicated to Francesca
and Isabel with the hope that they will parent in a more caring and supportive
society.

I dedicate the book to Jonathan for innumerable reasons. In essence, the
book exists because of him. I cherish his generosity of spirit and fortitude. He
has my love, admiration, and gratitude.

List of Acronyms

BNA:	Bureau of National Affairs
CCAC:	Child Care Action Campaign
CCDBG:	Child Care and Development Block Grant
CCEP:	Child Care Employee Project
CDF:	Children's Defense Fund
CLASP:	Center for Law and Social Policy
CLUW:	Coalition of Labor Union Women
CRS:	Congressional Research Service
CQA:	Congressional Quarterly Almanac
CQW:	Congressional Quarterly Weekly
CWLA:	Child Welfare League of America
DSG:	Democratic Study Group
FSA:	Family Support Act
IKU:	International Kindergarten Union
NAEYC:	National Association for the Education of Young Children
NASBE:	National Association of State Boards of Education
NBCDI:	National Black Child Development Institute
NCJW:	National Council of Jewish Women
NKA:	National Kindergarten Association
NRC:	National Research Council
OBRA:	Omnibus Budget Reconciliation Act of 1990
SEIU:	Services Employees International Union

PART I

THE CONTEMPORARY DEBATE

1. Introduction

"Children can't wait! Children can't wait!" So rang the rallying cry of the 17,000 children's advocates gathered at the October 1989 national conference of the National Association for the Education of Young Children in Atlanta, Georgia. "Children can't wait! Children can't wait!" The attendees were advocating an increased federal role in the provision of child care services, a major issue in then-pending congressional legislation.

But children persistently wait in American politics. Generations of children have lingered on waiting lists. For years they have lingered in supervised, but substandard child care settings and in unsupervised, informal arrangements. They continue to linger to this day. Nevertheless, the collective cries of "Children can't wait! Children can't wait!" symbolized a turning point in the national response to children's needs and foretold the unraveling of a tumultuous congressional debate that had begun years earlier.

Those cries of an awakened movement for children heralded the attention of Congress and the president. Thousands of newly recruited children's advocates across the nation rejoiced at the passage of the landmark child care legislation signed by President Bush on November 5, 1990. The Omnibus Budget Reconciliation Act of 1990 (PL 101-508), with its far-reaching tax component and subchapters, the Child Care and Development Block Grant and Child Care Entitlement Grant, signified the culmination of twenty years of waiting for comprehensive child care legislation to pass through Congress and receive a presidential endorsement. The celebrated act is the product of sophisticated coalition politics, specifically three years of concerted lobbying efforts by a formidable alliance of diverse organizations known as the Alliance for Better Child Care. The passage of the Child Care and Development Block Grant (CCDBG, or the Child Care Act) is an unprecedented victory for children's advocates, all the more monumental because of the heated political strife surrounding the formulation of the legislation. Although the act is acclaimed as an example of milestone legislation, it also is perceived as Janus–faced. Optimists find hope in the creation of a foundation from which to build future legislation; pessimists despair over the many compromises that were implemented and the constitutional issues that remain unresolved.

The Child Care Act of 1990 evolved in a markedly American fashion of incremental steps and pragmatic political decisions. The new legislation responded to a social problem that had escalated so dramatically over the past twenty years that congressional action was inevitable. The care of children while parents work had become a major issue affecting a significant majority of families with children of preschool and school age. An upsurge in the number of mothers employed outside of the home in the last twenty-five years has created a pressing need for new forms of child care arrangements. The traditional mode of care, that of the mother staying at home, is no longer typical as more mothers of young children participate in the labor force.

In 1976, women composed 40 percent of the labor force; whereas, it is projected that by the year 2000, women will compose 47 percent (Fullerton 1989, 3). Citing the Bureau of Labor Statistics 1988 report, the Select Committee on Children, Youth, and Families noted various trends in their report, *Children and Families: Key Trends in the 1980s* (1988). In particular, the committee recognized that the majority of American families rely on two incomes and that employed mothers are the norm:

In March 1988, 65 percent of all women with children under 18, 73.3 percent of mothers with school-age children 6–17, 56.1 percent of mothers with preschool children, and 51.1 percent of mothers with infants under age 1 were in the labor force. The number of working mothers has increased by nearly half since 1975. (U.S. Congress, Committee on Children, Youth, and Families 1988, 4)

Although conflicting views exist, the committee concluded that the supply of child care lags far behind the demand. Too often families place their children in child care settings of poor quality because those are the only arrangements available to them (U.S. Congress, Committee on Children, Youth, and Families 1988, 17).

A Census Bureau report released in the summer of 1990 indicated that more families are utilizing child care arrangements and paying more for the services (Barringer 1990, A10). According to the report, 29 million children are in child care arrangements. There has been a 9 percent rise in the number of children under age 15 using child care since a 1987 report. The use of child care for children under the age of 5 has risen by approximately 11 percent, reaching a total of 9.1 million. In 1990, 55 percent of mothers of preschoolers worked outside of the home, as opposed to 35 percent in 1987. Of those preschool children in child care arrangements, 25 percent are in some type of group care. This figure represents an increased trend in the utilization of group arrangements as opposed to home-based care by relatives or others. In a ten year period the use of group care for preschoolers has risen from 13 percent to 24.4 percent (Barringer 1990, A10).

The cost of care has risen with demand. A family with an average income uses 7 percent of its income to obtain child care services. A family at or near poverty level expends more than 20 percent of its income for child care expenses (Barringer 1990, A10).

The degree to which there is an actual shortage in the supply of child care services is debated by economists and has been a pervasive point of contention throughout the discussions on child care policies (Barringer 1990; CRS 1989a, 5; Galinsky 1989; CCAC 1988; Hofferth cited in U.S. Congress, Committee on Education and Labor 1989; Rose-Ackerman 1986; Haskins 1988; Brown and Haskins 1989). The collection of accurate data on the number of available spaces in child care facilities is difficult to amass due to inaccurate reporting of utilization and widespread use of unregulated centers and family day care homes. The National Association for the Education of Young Children (NAEYC) estimated that 40,000 licensed centers had the capacity to serve 2.1 million children in 1986 (CRS 1989a, 5). The Children's Defense Fund and the Child Welfare League of America have reported widespread gaps in services across the country (CWLA 1988, H.R. 3660; CDF 1990h; CDF 1990k).

Those that do not recognize a crisis in the supply of child care claim that the market is operating in equilibrium. Nevertheless, even these market economists acknowledge gaps in the availability of care for specific geographic areas, certain populations, and certain types of care, such as infant, school age, the sick, and handicapped (CRS 1989a, 5, 7; Galinsky 1989, 2–3; CCAC 1988, 30–33). The Child Care Action Campaign (CCAC) noted in its policy report, *The Bottom Line* (1988), that even if the market could be considered in equilibrium there is a twofold problem. First, not every potential consumer of child care services can find available services. Second, the available care is often of poor quality. Therefore, economists do not define the market as being out of equilibrium, which is what "shortage" implies. Instead, these economists view the problem to be a lack of available funds to subsidize high quality care. Thus, consumers have the choice of dropping out of the labor force, which lowers the demand, or utilizing poor quality care, which too often is unlicensed (CCAC 1988, 30–31).[1]

While recognizing the policy implications due to ongoing economic debate and the everpresent need to collect data on the supply and demand for child care services, this book, nevertheless, acknowledges both a furor and panic across the nation in private households, public forums, and all facets of the media over securing child care arrangements. There is an expressed need for nontraditional care of children and great public concern over the issue of child care that, in addition to the Select Committee's Report, is evident in the published research of the National Research Council, *Who Cares for America's Children?* (NRC 1990) and the *Family Survey II: Child Care*, conducted for the Philip Morris Companies Inc. by Louis Harris and Associates (1989).

The purpose of this book is to analyze policy options for the sponsorship of institutional arrangements for the care of preschool children. *Preschool children* refers to the population of children younger than a state's compulsory age for entering the public educational system, which is customarily age 5 or 6. *Child care* is defined as the nonparental care of children during an extended period of time, but less than twenty-four hours, while their parents work or are unavailable for other reasons. Problems in the delivery of child care often are defined according to age range, in spite of the fact that the issues of all age groups are interconnected. The population of analysis for this book are 3, 4, and 5 year olds. The particular concerns of that population are addressed while recognizing the implications for the wide age range of children needing child care arrangements. Although the focus of this discussion is the 3–5–year-old population, the narrower focus does not imply that the problems of caring for 6 year olds and above, and infants and toddlers are not equally problematic.

Infant-toddler care, which spans the ages of birth through 30 to 36 months, is reviewed in relation to the 3–5-year-old age range. The multiple needs of infants and toddlers demand very special considerations that go beyond the scope of this study. The specific focus for this analysis provides a clearer conceptualization of the overall problem of designing child care services that adequately serve the developmental needs of children. Center based care arrangements for 3–5-year-old children has been more well received and supported throughout the nation, than the group care of infants and toddlers. A policy analysis of the 3–5-year-old population suggests policy directions for the infant-toddler period and school-age children.

This inquiry is premised on two important points. First, the debate over whether the expansion of child care services was "psychologically" appropriate peaked, and then resolved itself, in the mid-1980s. The women's movement of the 1960s and 1970s, together with the changing economic demands on families due to increases in the cost of living, provided the impetus for the influx of mothers from all social classes into the labor force. The actual need for child care services has always existed for families belonging to the lower socio-economic classes and for single parent families. The problem of availability of child care services has drawn more attention in recent years than in the past because the need has reached into the ranks of middle and upper class families.

From the late 1960s until the middle of the 1980s, media and academic attention centered on the question of the *appropriateness* of "institutional care" as compared with "maternal" care. The attention of both scholars and the public eventually turned away from a preoccupation with appropriateness and focused instead on a concern over the *availability* of care. The public recognized the overwhelming practical need for care regardless of any theoretical debates. Cognizant of this expressed need for child care, scholars began examining the variables that determine the "quality" of care, realizing that the issue of "appropriateness" was supplanted by the demand for care outside of the home.[2] Mothers could no longer be presumed to be the sole caregivers.

The research for this book began after the issue of appropriateness paled, and a new debate over which formal institution should provide the needed child care services surfaced. This debate forms the second premise of the book. Outside of the theoretical discussions on the significance of maternal care, a debate has been raging for the past twenty years over the issue of sponsorship. The issue of control over a system of child care services in the United States has been controversial ever since legislation was proposed that provided for federal involvement in the provision of such services in the late 1960s. The question of *who* shall provide and administer child care programs has divided the public, as well as child care advocates, for many years.

The issue of sponsorship prolonged the debate over the provision of needed services. In 1975, Jule Sugarman, the former director of the National Head Start Program, noted:

If you were to read what must now be close to three thousand pages of public testimony about the Comprehensive Child Development Bill, the Head Start program, and day care, I would be surprised if you found more than 50 pages that were devoted to the substance of the programs. You'll find 2,950 pages that are devoted to the question of who should run the program and who should have the power in it. (Sugarman cited in Sugarman, Martin, and Taylor 1975, 107)

Sponsorship continues to be one of the most critical issues for resolution before measures can be implemented to meet the need for more child care facilities. The former assistant executive director of the Child Welfare League of America, William Pierce, testified in 1978 on the obstacles preventing the expansion of child care services:

Parents are afraid for their children. Religious organizations fear incursion of secular values into their young. Businesses fear the loss of a profitable industry. Community organizers fear the loss of a powerful organizing tool. Operators of day-care services fear the loss of programs and, thus, their jobs or their power or their profits or their income. Workers in day-care programs fear the loss of their jobs to some other more professionalized or less professionalized group, or some other union. Taxpayers fear the costs of day-care added to the already high taxes for schools. And local, county and state elected officials fear the combined reaction from all of the above. (Pierce cited in U.S. Congress, Committee on Human Resources 1978, 691)

The divisiveness of the issue of sponsorship hindered the formulation of a national policy on child care.

This book presents the position that conflict over who will deliver child care services has existed among the following five sectors of society for at least two decades: the social service system of public and private nonprofit agencies, religious organizations, corporations, for-profit enterprises, and the public schools. Furthermore, the role of the public schools in the delivery of child care services has always been of particular concern, and until the late 1980s, the unnamed nemesis in the whole debate. The unmatched weight of the schools in the arguments over sponsorship of child care has finally been recognized at the onset of the last decade of the twentieth century. In fact, the issue of who should sponsor child care services can be more succinctly broached by asking point blank whether the public schools should form the basis for an American system of child care services.

The American approach to child care is commonly referred to as a *patchwork system*, a term and concept attributed to Margaret O'Brien Steinfels (1973) who adeptly described the happenstance manner in which child care services developed in this country. This patchwork system is composed of the aforementioned sectors, each of which has a vested interest in maintaining or expanding its claim to controlling child care services. However, the problem of child care has grown in such magnitude that issues in delivery which have been festering no longer can be denied or discounted.

Each of the five sponsors of child care performs a unique role in society at large, and concomitantly provides the service with particular goals in mind, whether these goals are manifest or latent. Policy makers and taxpayers have to decide how to invest limited public resources, and choices need to be made over which sponsors to support and which to reject. The analysis that follows is intended to contribute to this policy decision and place the current federal resolution, as manifested in the Child Care and Development Block Grant of the Omnibus Reconciliation Act of 1990 (OBRA 1990) into a historical context.

The issue of sponsorship merits extensive examination because historically it has been so controversial and obstructive. A broad perspective was taken for research purposes, which included all of the sectors for analysis, to survey the entire array of child care providers and ideally contribute to a more complete picture of the debate. During the preparation of this book, Alfred Kahn and Sheila Kamerman published their important work, *Child Care: Facing the Hard Choices* (1987), which dovetails the analysis provided herein. Kahn and Kamerman recognized the same issues and provided definitive empirical information on several of the key sponsors. Additionally, as this book was being prepared for press, the National Research Council of the National Academy of Sciences released the formidable work on current child care policies, *Who Cares for America's Children?* (1990), edited by Cheryl D. Hayes, John L. Palmer and Martha J. Zaslow.

The present analysis departs from Kahn and Kamerman in several ways, and seeks to take up the debate where they left off. First, this study is historical in nature and uses sociological theory as a framework for arriving at a policy decision. Second, Kahn and Kamerman did not directly include the special role of the church as sponsor, a role that becomes central in this analysis. Instead, they devote considerable attention to the topic of family child care services, which is not included in the present discussion, except in the context of the other five sponsors. Most important, the research for this book suggests that the role of the public schools must be compared against all other sponsors. Kahn and Kamerman's discussion supports this direction. In their conclusion, the two authors argue in favor of more school involvement in the delivery of child care. Sharon L. Kagan and Edward F. Zigler in *Early Schooling* (1987a) also suggest reframing the issues of child care delivery to engage the question of the appropriateness of the schools as prime sponsors.

Although it is encouraging that the question of whether the schools should offer universal child care services has finally come to the pinnacle of the controversy over expansion of child care services, the power of the schools has been consistently present and overshadowing throughout the last twenty years. Child care advocates faced decisions regarding the role that the schools should perform on the federal level and will face the same crossroads on the state level. The tortuous federal debate over child care services was resolved, without special deference given to the public schools, in favor of maintaining a multiple provider delivery system.

In 1987, Kahn and Kamerman demanded that *hard choices* be confronted as to how the nation would move forward in providing the care necessitated by the new social arrangements. The contents of this book document some of the choices that have been made since 1987 and the lengthy debate over choices during the past twenty years. The discussion that follows seeks to delineate the values in conflict and the implications of policy decisions. Although policy decisions on the federal level downplayed the role of the public schools, the history of the present debate and the history of the past debate over the sponsorship of kindergartens during the Progressive Era suggest that the potential of the public schools in delivering child care services cannot be dismissed, diminished, or negated. Schools will continue to be contenders in the delivery of early childhood programs and merit particular attention.

To arrive at a policy position regarding the appropriate relationship of the public schools and child care services, two methodological decisions were implemented. Expanding on the content and methodology of Grubb and Lazerson's works (1977; 1982), the historical significance of the previous debate over sponsorship of kindergartens during the Progressive Period was researched. Research into social movements of the past offers the opportunity to see the present from a new perspective. Historical research places current perceptions and philosophies in a more objective, analytic framework by the juxtaposition of the contemporary period with a time past, in which similar concerns were addressed within a markedly different context. By analogizing to a parallel movement, barriers or obstacles that emerge and reemerge in the American policy making process can be highlighted and analyzed.[3]

The American kindergarten is considered the first year of public schooling, although private programs also are offered for young children. Kindergarten is now recognized as a formal institution of one year duration for 5- and 6-year-old children. Our understanding of kindergarten as this one year institution is assumed as a given; yet, kindergarten as we know it today developed only after an entire period of movement and debate. Kindergartens, like today's child care centers, were implemented in piecemeal fashion under various sponsors. Analysis of current positions with respect to sponsorship of child care can be seen in a new perspective by studying this past movement. In addition to the significance of the origin of the contemporary kindergarten in the debate over the direction of current child care policy, it is equally significant that the kindergarten of today itself is at a historical juncture. School district administrators, parents, and educational professionals are debating the advantages and disadvantages of extending the kindergarten day without openly acknowledging that a primary force behind the all day kindergarten movement is the demographic need for child care arrangements (Olsen and Zigler 1989). The delivery and expansion of all day kindergarten has not emerged from a research base on the merits of all day programming because findings on all day programming are mixed (Olsen and Zigler 1989). Given this current kindergarten trend, the history of the kindergarten and child care are merging. Although the historical significance and impact of this merger is discussed later, it is important to note that a common crossroads is being faced by both services and their respective traditions.

A form of functional analysis has been adapted from sociological theories in conjunction with the methodological approach of looking to the past for insight into the present. A functional framework is applied because of its heuristic value in clarifying the consequences of the different policy options. Although the arguments are presented within a functionalist perspective, conflict theory underlies the discourse.

Conflict theory (Dahrendorf 1959; 1962; 1968; Eitzen 1986; Horton and Hunt 1984; Turner 1982) examines ideological value systems held by different interest groups and recognizes the incompatibility of certain institutional claims in society. The many divisions in society by class, race, gender, organizational hierarchies, and occupation promote differing ideologies, which are at odds. Conflict theorists acknowledge that the values of the most powerful groups in society predominate over other value systems and ideologies and form mass rationalizations. The value systems and ideologies of the most influential social members define and dictate policies.

Conflict theory and functionalism are built on different premises (Turner 1982; Eitzen 1986; Horton and Hunt 1984). Functionalists assume that society is in a state of equilibrium with designated members and institutions contributing to the maintenance of the stable condition by performing particular functions. An emphasis is placed on forming consensus among factions of society. Functionalists focus on the maintenance of the status quo or the desired state of equilibrium and view change as dysfunctional, functional, or nonfunctional to the operation of society (Horton and Hunt 1984).

Conflict theory places emphasis on an underlying power struggle among interest groups and classes, rather than on a functional need for harmony. Conflict theorists view change as the outgrowth of negotiations and accommodations among interest groups (Horton and Hunt 1984). Ongoing tension is seen as the given structure of social relations. Social problems and work-related problems are resolved through a cyclical process of conflict and temporary resolutions.

This book is written from a perspective that acknowledges child care as a multifunctional service dependent upon the institution that sponsors it. The questions posed are based in the foundation of conflict theory because the fabric of the status quo is brought into question. Moving beyond the functionalist description of normative functions, conflict theorists probe the consequences of structure-function relations (Horton and Hunt 1984, 17). This analysis of the manner in which our society deals with the problem of caring for its youngest members specifically asks the following questions: To whom is the service of child care functional? What function does child care perform under various auspices? How does the institution's function in society affect the function of child care? What are the ramifications of different policy directions regarding sponsorship of child care services? The discussion proceeds from the conflict theory perspective on the assumption that myriad interest groups have battled unremittingly over turf in the quest for delivering, and thereby, controlling child care services.

A historical analysis shows that child care has functioned in the interests of certain groups, as did the kindergarten of the past. The questions of this analysis build from a conflict perspective because the conflict between interest groups is pronounced and will become evident in the discussion. To arrive at answers, Robert Merton's (1968; 1976; 1978) functional framework has been adapted. Merton's framework in conjunction with the social policy theorist Yelaja's (1978) have been selected after a close study of the literature on child care. The issues in need of resolution call forth the aforementioned questions, which naturally fall into the functional framework. The question of sponsorship suggests multiple options with diverse consequences. The functional framework teases out the advantages and disadvantages of specific policies.

In his review of functionalism, Jonathan H. Turner (1982, 100–102) acknowledges four different forms of the theory. Turner describes Robert Merton's version as "net functional balance" functionalism (p. 101). Merton broke away from Talcott Parsons's grand theorizing and concentrated on theories of a middle range. He was particularly interested in the relation of parts of a system to the whole system and each other.

To develop theory and test functional concepts, Merton advocated examining an empirical system. By examining the empirical, alternative possibilities regarding the items under analysis become more visible. Merton introduced the concepts functional and dysfunctional and identified manifest and latent functions:

First, items may be not only positively functional for a system or another system item, but also dysfunctional for either particular items or the systemic whole. Second, some consequences, whether functional or dysfunctional, are intended and recognized by system incumbents and are thus *manifest*, whereas other consequences are not intended or recognized and are therefore *latent*. (Turner 1982, 73)

As with most modes of inquiry, functionalism has been subjected to much criticism. However, the theory has been applied in the field of social policy development in a pragmatic way (Yelaja 1978, 16). In the essay "What Is Social Policy? Its Assumptions, Definitions and Uses," Shankar A. Yelaja emphasizes the importance of Merton's functional analysis for social policy development. Yelaja distills three important questions from functionalism for use in social policy analysis: "What structures are involved?" "What functions have resulted?" "What functions take place in terms of given structures?" Furthermore, he clarifies the terms *function* and *structure*: "The term 'function' is any condition, any state of affairs, resultant from the operation of a structure, and the term 'structure' is a pattern, i.e., an observable uniformity in terms of which action takes place" (Yelaja 1978, 16–17).

For the purposes of this book, the goals or intended outcomes as well as the actual outcomes of child care will be viewed as the "functions." The "structure" is seen as an empirical, or existing, institution through which the functions are pursued: the social service system composed of public and private nonprofit agencies; the public school system; industry; for-profit organizations; and religious organizations.

The literature on child care has recognized the multifunctional aspect of the service; and, it is exactly this multifunctional aspect that ignites the controversy surrounding sponsorship. Writers in the field of child care policy have categorized the functions of child care in diverse, but similar ways. Several theorists have discussed child care in terms of three functions expressed as the social service, the economic, and the educational (Mahoney 1985; Gray 1980; Steinfels 1973; Murray 1985). Gray (1980) and Steinfels (1973) have provided a history to these functions by tracing the development of child care services in the United States. Gray built on Steinfels's earlier work and illustrated how different functions became tied to specific structures.

Other commentators have described child care with a dichotomous functional perspective (Almy 1982; Caldwell 1986; 1989b; Fishhaut and Pastor 1977; Greenman 1978; Grubb 1987, 23–33; Kagan 1987, 10–12; 1989a; 1989b; Morgan 1989; Shanker 1987).[4] This dual functional framework reflects the public's perception of the service and defines child care in relation to the education profession. These dichotomous views discuss child care services in two contexts. On the one hand, child care is viewed as performing a "custodial care" function that contrasts with an "educational" function. This custodial care function is attributed to the social work heritage of child care services and implies a service that acts as a mere time-filler for children while their parents are at work. When seen in this light, a stigma is attached to the service in contrast to the "educational" function that implies that children's cognitive needs are addressed.

In another context, the *custodial* emphasis is disregarded and the *care* aspect of the service is highlighted. *Care* is then equated with the favorable activity of meeting the socioemotional needs of children. This idealized view of child care services contrasts with an unfavorable image of the education function, which stresses cognitive development at the expense of affective development. The "caring" function rather than the "education" function has been linked with a "developmental" perspective or the teachings of child psychology; whereas, the education function has been linked to pedagogical thinking.

Kagan (1989b) purports that a shift in this dichotomous paradigm is underway. Caldwell (1989b) argues that the dual images of child care be discarded in favor of a unitary vision of the service as "educare." This book breaks away from the perspectives that define child care in terms of two or three functions by suggesting that the service performs at least nine functions. The discussion that immediately follows will define these functions and describe their history, significance, and interrelatedness.

In "The Social Work Profession and Day Care Services: Social Policy Issues, 1890 to 1990" (1980), Gray discusses functions in terms of goals or strategies. The first goal of child care, as seen by Gray, is a social service strategy. In this context child care is meeting residual needs in society and is tied to the social welfare profession and system. Child care is seen as a service for low-income families. It serves the function of enabling poor mothers to work and, thereby, reduces the welfare rolls. For the purposes of the discussion in this book, this first function will be referred to as the *welfare reform* function of child care. Senator Russell B. Long advocated this function by supporting the Child Care Services Act of 1971. As chairman of the Committee on Finance, Long argued that "adequate provision for the availability of child care is a key element of any attempt to reform the welfare system" (Long quoted in U.S. Congress, Committee on Finance 1971, 4). In contrast to Senator Long, Arlyce Currie, a member of an information and referral program for child care centers in California, commonly referred to as *Bananas*, testified in 1977 at the *Child Care and Child Development Programs* Hearings as follows:

It is all too clear that the job of child caring or that children per se are not what is valued or even why child care is subsidized at all; the political rationale of subsidizing child care seems to be that welfare costs society too much and by some mysterious means we will wipe out welfare by paying for the care of some of the children in the lowest economic - strata. (U.S. Congress, Committee on Human Resources 1977–78, 157)

This welfare reform function is associated with another function child care has served within the welfare system, which shall be referred to as the *social service* function. It meets the needs of the low income user by providing "welfare" or "relief" services. This function's history is tied to the professional-ization of social work and a focus on increasing the self-sufficiency of low-income people and preserving the family unit.

The social service function has a long history that ties child care to welfare sponsorship. The early development of child care centers in the United States dates back to the mid-1800s with proliferation beginning in the 1890s (Steinfels 1973; Gray 1980). These early child care centers were called *day nurseries* and modeled after the French creche (Steinfels 1973, 37).

Steinfels's description of the day nursery movement suggests three distinct periods. The earliest period involved the formation and establishment of the service. A second stage, during the Progressive Era, was marked by the social work profession's efforts to institutionalize and formalize the service, while social workers themselves strived for professionalization. Steinfels classifies a third modern period when the service is in demand by more families as a result of demographic changes and the women's movement. The decades in the second period, between 1930 and 1973, are significant for two reasons. First, the operation of the day nurseries remained stable by servicing a targeted population that was not prone to demographic fluctuation. Second, the "day nursery," later to be recognized as "day care" and then "child care,"[5] became stigmatized and classified as a "custodial" service, despite its social service function that focused on family needs. The custodial connotation reflected the link with the welfare system, which carried its own stigma in society, as a service system for those that could not manage on their own.

Steinfels's and Gray's reviews of child care's early history support the position that the service has served multiple functions and sponsors. "The two most important forces behind the expansion of child care during the turn of the century were leaders from the charity organization movement as well as the settlement house movement" (Gray 1980, 3). The charity organizations applied the new concept of scientific charity, by which the recipients of charity were investigated and scrutinized to see if they were worthy of receiving support. The goal of the movement was to encourage self-sufficiency (Gray 1980, 3).

This new scientific approach to giving charity, however, categorized people into the deserving and the undeserving. With regard to child care, mothers were screened to determine whether their need for the service was legitimate. Child care was allowing poor women to go to work by providing care for their children. The mothers entitled to use the service were those willing to work, many of whom were widowed or deserted by their spouses. The charity organizations did not provide charitable services to families in which the causal factor for their poverty was the husband's "poor conduct": that is, lack of employment or alcoholism (Gray 1980, 4). Poor women and their families sustained scrutiny to determine their worthiness as recipients for support, a procedure spared their better-off counterparts. A two-tiered sorting system originated that, as a consequence, helped define the social status of those who utilized day nurseries as "welfare recipients." This *social status* function will be explicated further later in the discussion.

Child care's social service and welfare reform functions in the Progressive Period consequently provided an alternative to the institutionalization of children, a social strategy practiced in the previous decade. Reformers during the 1800s had solved social problems by separating children from their parents by building institutions for their residential care or by placing poverty stricken urban children with foster families in rural areas (Gray 1980, 4; Steinfels 1973, 40, 50). The day nursery was perceived as a means of preserving the family unit, which was a social goal in resurgence during the period between 1919–1930.[6]

While charity organizations practiced scientific charity which focused on individual ability and character, settlement house workers of the Progressive Era adopted an environmental perspective. Within the ongoing nature-nurture debate, they emphasized the significance of environmental influence on individual and social problems. Settlement house workers acknowledged a normative need for two worker families in an era of increased industrialization, urbanization, and immigration (Gray 1980, 5).

Leaders of the settlement movement provided day nursery services without investigating the character of the mother and the family. Nevertheless, the traditional functions of the day nursery remained: (1) to enable a mother to work, and thereby assure her independence from "relief"; and (2) to preserve the family unit. These day nurseries also provided the "social service" function by offering additional services that included emergency night care; visiting nursing care; instruction in cooking, sewing, English, and child rearing; and after school care for older children (Steinfels 1973, 42). The day nursery became one service among many for this lower class population.

In addition to the social service function, the preservation of the family function, and the enabling of women to work function (which in essence is an *economic* and welfare reform function), the day nursery movement rebuffed criticisms that it merely provided custodial care by acknowledging two other purposes: "character building" and "prevention." Children were seen as being better off in the day nursery setting than in tenement houses, even if their mothers were present in the home. The day nursery advocates argued that day nursery experience prevented future relief problems (Steinfels 1973, 50–51). These last two purposes are echoed in today's literature on the social and economic benefits of early childhood education and give credence to the welfare reform function. The research on early childhood programs for the disadvantaged indicates that "early intervention" prevents or retards school-related problems, as well as juvenile delinquency and future welfare dependency (Berruta-Clement et al. 1984).

The child saving attitude that developed the early day nurseries changed with the professionalization of social work (Steinfels 1973, 59; Gray 1980, 8).

Day nurseries were scrutinized in a retrenching of the social work profession after the first World War. The function of the nurseries was questioned by those in the welfare field. Analysts debated the function in terms of the clientele and admission policies:

What standards of admission should the day nursery adopt? The answer depended, of course, on prior assumptions about what the day nursery was. If the day nursery was primarily a service for working mothers, then the standards of admission were clear: the day nursery accepted children whose mothers worked. If, on the other hand, the day nursery was a social welfare agency, then the standards of admission were somewhat more complicated. (Steinfels 1973, 60–61)

At the 1919 National Conference of Social Work, Grace Caldwell of the New England Center of Day Nurseries answered this debate over the function of day nurseries. Her speech set a specific course and image for child care that remains today. "Miss Caldwell's speech in 1919 marked the beginning of a long process of change in the day nursery, from a useful, broadly defined, simple child helping service to a marginal and limited agent of social welfare" (Steinfels 1973, 62–63). Caldwell's speech included much social work terminology: "maladjustment," "temporary expedients," "problem families," "correct social diagnosis," "social evil and the larger picture" (Steinfels 1973, 61).

Caldwell defined the day nursery in three ways. First, the day nursery served to adjust the maladjusted family. Second, the day nursery functioned only as an expedient; it served as a stopgap alternative to home care. The child's true place was in the home with a nonworking mother. Third, day nurseries were seen as functioning to undermine the wages of men and therefore posed an economic threat in certain communities. The nurseries were seen as an expedient means of solving a temporary problem and limited to a population that had particular troubles (Steinfels 1973, 61).

A pathological taint was placed on child care when it became a specific branch of the social welfare profession. Linking the sponsorship of the welfare system and the function of serving the needs of "maladjusted" families has had important ramifications in the overall development of the child care system in the United States. From this brief historical sketch, it is evident that structure and function have had a symbiotic relationship. The "welfare reform" function and the "social service" function traditionally have been tied to sponsorship by the welfare profession. In addition to these two manifest functions, day nurseries operated according to the ideology of the times as an alternative to institutionalization and a preserver of the family unit. Furthermore, as will be discussed later, the day nurseries functioned as a socializing institution.

The third manifest function that child care serves is *educational*. It is a service that when so designed, can meet the developing intellectual needs of children. This functional aspect of the service links child care to the education profession. A significant body of research indicates that the first five years of life are the formative period in human development, an antecedent to all later experiences, and provide the crucial foundation for future satisfaction in life. Given this body of knowledge, by servicing the under-six population, child care centers have an important role in meeting the developmental needs of their charges.

Government involvement in the early education of the young began in the 1960s with Project Head Start. Head Start is a prototype early intervention program aimed at the underprivileged population of 3 to 5 year olds. It functions as a compensatory educational program; research on the success of Head Start supports the importance of this early educational experience for disadvantaged youngsters (U.S. Department of Health and Human Services 1985; Schorr 1988, 184–200).[7] The positive results of Head Start, the general research on the importance of the early years, and the growing body of literature on high quality early childhood programs suggest that the child care experience should be as enriching as possible. This enrichment-educational approach contrasts with the custodial approach to child care that developed under the early sponsors of the day nurseries and the welfare system (Steinfels 1973).

The educational function of child care builds from a theory base that was not used by the charity and settlement house workers. Although some day nurseries did offer enriched educational programs, the primary concern of most nurseries was custodial (Steinfels 1973, 37, 52). The history of early educational programs is rooted in the kindergarten movement between 1860–1930 and the nursery school movement during the 1920s. Some day nurseries incorporated ideas from these movements (Steinfels 1973, 46–48). However, the kindergarten and nursery school movements grounded themselves in the education profession, not the social work profession.

The significance of the educational function of child care is that educators claim a sponsorship interest, and the service is seen as universal, rather than selective. Education is recognized as a service for the general public. It is not seen as a service for a "relief" population.

The historical debate over admissions policy surfaces again with the entree of the education profession. Rather than being debated solely within the welfare system as was true in 1919, the issue at this point is debated between systems. Is child care primarily a service for children of working mothers? How should welfare dependent mothers be served? Should child care be a universal service for all children because of its enriching potential? And, should child care function in the social welfare mold of being a custodial service, or should child care deliver high quality early childhood education? The answers to these questions will depend on the sponsoring institution and the amount of funding provided.[8]

The fourth function or role that child care has played is that of "*liberator*," from here on referred to as the *liberation-universalization* function. The 1960s gave rise to this vision of child care when feminists envisioned the service as a means of liberation for women (Gray 1980, 15). Through the use of child care services, mothers would be able to voluntarily take leave of their children to pursue other goals. Viewed in this light, child care should be readily available to anyone who desires to use the service. In essence, child care would function as a social utility, universally available to all women and families. When remarking on the celebrated passage of the Act for Better Child Care in the Senate on June 23, 1990, Senate Majority Leader George Mitchell eloquently articulated one interpretation of this function:

This is an important day for the Senate, for American families, for American children. But I think, most important, for American women.

This is titled "a child care bill," and indeed it is. But I believe a central issue, running through this legislation and this national concern is equal economic opportunity. The scarcity, in some areas the total absence of decent, affordable, safe child-care facilities has deprived millions of American women of their equal economic opportunity.

They have been forced to make a painful choice between the economic imperative of working to supplement their families income and the anxiety of concern for their children's health, safety and well-being. And until the day that our society makes child care readily available, readily affordable in safe and secure settings for all American women, we will not have achieved our ideal of equal opportunity for all Americans. (U.S. Congress, *Report on Act for Better Child Care* 1989, S 7478)

Feminists have been divided in their view of child care over the past twenty years. Radical feminists envision child care in a more utopian fashion than their liberal cohorts, who see child care in a more pragmatic and realistic light. Writing in an issue of *Social Policy,* Katherine Ellis and Rosalind Petchesky (1972–1973) attacked the alleged bourgeois functions of child care, and highlighted more revolutionary functions:

. . . Work equality for all women would be impossible without the provision of socialized child care facilities. Thus child care is a crucial plank in the strategy for women's liberation. Child care struggles are crucial, moreover, as a means of raising consciousness about the traditional family and its reinforcement of sex-role stereotypes; about the socializing functions of educational institutions at all levels of capitalist society; and about the possibility of freer, more social childrearing alternatives. (p. 19)

Ellis and Petchesky recognized that these idealized functions of child care cannot be achieved unless a movement supporting such functions develops. They wrote:

We envisage day care centers that (1) actively support the restructuring of men's work to allow their participation in child care struggles and programs; (2) attempt to establish cooperative, nonhierarchical relationships among staff (through, for example, abolishing ranks and pay scales); and (3) give priority to the socialization of children in terms of cooperative, nonauthoriatian, antiracist, and antisexist values. (Ellis and Petchesky 1972-3, 22)

Less radical feminists, as represented by the National Organization for Women (NOW), supported the expansion of child care services and viewed the service as a basic right for all citizens, rather than as a public welfare service. (NOW prepared statement cited in Committee on Labor and Public Welfare 1971, 754). Jan Calderon Yocum, the executive director of the Day Care Council of America in 1981, expressed the public utility function of child care most succinctly:

Child care should be part of our public utilities, the things that are necessary for people to be able to function—child care is not a "social service"—those are for deficit or pathological families or individuals. Day care is a need of normal, healthy families. . . . Americans must be educated to the fact that child care is something we must provide and pay for, like gas and lights. (Yocum cited in Davis 1981, 71)

These two voices within the women's movement remain disconnected in the movement for child care. This lack of unity within the feminist community, coupled with the social and economic stratification evident among today's women, places feminists in a vulnerable position for receiving criticism about their lack of mobilization on the issue of child care. A review of the literature on child care in both the popular and scholarly press indicates a lack of adequate interest and vociferousness over this major social problem by feminists. Child care is becoming a more prominent platform for women's groups only as more of the middle and upper classes are themselves affected by the unavailability of care and the problems of bridging work and family. Feminists have been preoccupied with the issues of abortion rights and the Equal Rights Amendment (Bowe 1986, 299).[9] Betty Friedan's book *The Second Stage* (1981) and Arlie Hochschild and Anne Machung's *The Second Shift: Working Parents and the*

Revolution at Home (1989) address some of the weaknesses in the feminist's past and present platforms regarding the problem of child care.

Returning to the two perspectives that prevail among those feminists who *have* addressed the plight of children and the crisis over balancing work and family, Spakes (1989) highlights an underlying contradiction. According to Spakes "liberal" feminists acknowledge the special maternal function of women; whereas, "radical" feminists only recognize the reproductive abilities as the line of demarcation between the sexes. From Spakes's viewpoint, current policy agendas that are referred to as *pro-family* seek to support the family, but simultaneously perpetuate a pronatalist philosophy that contradicts and undermines the equality of the sexes philosophy of radical feminists. Pronatalistic thinking ties women to traditional familial boundaries. Spakes would like to push the debate into a new territory by emphasizing the elements of a patriarchal society that prevent progress in equalizing the status and potential of the sexes.

Barbara Levy Simon (1988) links this patriarchal society with capitalism. Socialist feminists view "capitalism and patriarchy as interdependent and reciprocal systems that conjointly keep women in a secondary position" (p. 65). Socialist feminists seek an increase in the accessibility of services and a reduction of capitalism's damage, especially to countries and women in the Third World (Simon 1988, 65). Progressive thinking feminists strive to develop short- and long-term goals. Short-term goals address the immediate problems of women, such as the problems created by working and mothering. Long-term goals focus on changing the patriarchal system of female dependency and the irresponsibility of this patriarchy that permits women to assume the primary responsibility for child rearing (Spakes 1989).

The issues surrounding child care are very much intertwined with feminist theory because of traditionally held views about the mother-child bond, the glorification of the mother role, and the gender stratification of occupations. Child care is not only problematic from the consumer side, but is a grave concern from the perspective of child care workers and providers. The majority of child care workers are women and their work is grossly undervalued in economic and social status terms. Ninety-seven percent of child care workers are women according to a national survey of 227 centers in five metropolitan areas (Child Care Employee Project 1989, 8). The implicit and explicit relationship between caregivers and parents may be seen in some contexts as exploitive and fallacious. In her important article, "Women as Fathers: Motherhood and Child Care Under a Modified Patriarchy," Barbara Katz Rothman (1989) calls to task the assumptions on which contemporary child care arrangements are based:

We hire baby-sitters, day-care workers, nannies, housekeepers, to "watch" our children. The tasks are the traditional tasks of mothering—feeding, tending, caring, the whole bundle of social and psychological and physical tasks involved in the care of young children. When performed by mothers, we call them mothering. When performed by fathers, we have sometimes called it fathering, sometimes parenting, sometimes helping the mother. When performed by hired hands, we called it unskilled.

We devalue these nurturing tasks when we contract for them. When we do them ourselves because we want to do them, we see them as precious, as special, as treasured moments in life. That is the contradiction that allows us to value the children so highly, to value our special time with them, to speak lovingly of the child's trust, the joys of that small hand placed in ours—and hire someone to take that hand, at minimum wage. (Rothman 1989, 97)

Given this tacit social arrangement, child care performs a *social status* function, which was seen earlier in the era of the day nurseries when mothers were determined "deserving" or "undeserving." The social status function maintains a social strata among women. Contrary to its idealized function as an agent of liberation and social change, child care often upholds the status quo by enabling some workers to advance up the economic ladder at the expense of their coworkers' low pay. This should be a unifying issue for feminists and socialists. Upwardly mobile mothers have the power to utilize the service for their own advancement while paying the caregivers of their children low wages. This wage differential, however, does vary across the range of classes. Often the child care user is only slightly higher on the economic scale than the center child care worker. Upper class parents tend not to rely on child care centers to the same degree as middle and lower class parents, but employ private caregivers.[10]

This social status function maintains the social strata in most cases, but simultaneously advances the status of certain subgroups of women up the wage scale. In other words, child care has benefited some women at the expense of others on two levels. First, upper class and upper middle class women advance by suppressing the wages of their children's caregivers.[11] Second, access to employment varies by region and corporate employer. Some lower income and minority women have entered the job market because of the combined availability of child care services and employer need. This combination of factors in the market economy indicates that the social status function of child care is neutral, depending on the context of its use. Whether functioning as a sorter for social status or as a liberating service universally accessible, child care's multiple functions in society call forth feminist dilemmas.

In conjunction with the feminist interpretations of child care's social functions, which erupted in the 1960s, social activists of the times envisioned child care as a center for community action. Child care was to function as an instrument for *social reform* (Steiner 1976, Chap. 5). The child care center would be a common meeting place while also promoting local control, which was a popular issue in the 1960s and early 1970s (Wilks 1973, 17–20). William V. Shannon (1972) cites Mrs. Maurien McKinley's community action view in his article critiquing child care centers, "A Radical, Direct, Simple, Utopian Alternative to Day-Care Centers." At that time Mrs. McKinley was associate director of the Black Child Development Institute. She saw a definite function for child care, and spoke for a specific constituency:

We believe that child-development centers can be the catalyst for total community development. It is to the advantage of the entire nation to view the provision of day-care/child development services within the context of the need for a readjustment of societal power relationships. . . . As day-care centers are utilized to catalyze development in black and other communities, the enhanced political and economic power that results can provide effective leverage for the improvement of the over-all social and economic condition of the nation. (McKinley cited in Shannon 1972, 82)

The *economic* function of child care is manifold. On one level, the service meets a requisite of society as a whole in allowing the economy to function with a greater number of workers in the work-force. On another level, child care meets a familial need and enables parents to join the work force (Mahoney 1985, 338). Expanding on Mahoney, a third level exists that satisfies the needs of individual companies and corporations. Child care enables a particular work force population to compete and participate in the marketplace. A corporation's involvement in child care often benefits that corporation's bottom line. This issue will be discussed in depth in a later chapter.

Additional functions of child care are ideological and involve the social-ization of children. These functions are often latent. The practice of child care implies the group rearing of young children outside of the home. This form of collective child rearing clashes with the American familial method of rearing the young. Child care can be used explicitly or implicitly as a means of socialization, or as Merton suggests, the socialization can be latent or manifest.

The latent consequences of the *socialization* function are rarely raised in discussions over child care. Ruth Sidel highlighted the significance of the function in her review of a book describing a storefront child care experiment in Berlin, when she noted the connection between politics and child rearing: "every society is teaching its young a system of values of that society whether or not the values are explicitly spelled out" (Sidel 1974, 24). Sidel discusses how a society's choice in raising children to be competitive or cooperative contributes to the fabric and ethos of that society. Child care centers socialize the young in one direction or another. This function of child care has been slighted in the debates, but in fact is the most crucial function for further debate. The function is given most attention by those fearful of "sovietizing" American children in state run centers and those who support at-home rearing of children.[12]

The "socialization" function was manifest in the late 1800s and early 1900s. As mentioned earlier, the sponsors of the child nurseries acknowledged this function as an important part of their work. Since the early day nurseries serviced many immigrant families, the workers attempted to acculturate the children and mothers to American values and child rearing:

On a day-to-day level, the day nursery's primary concern was physical care of the children—feeding, bathing, and keeping them safe from the evils and danger of street and tenement. But most day nurseries expressed an equally strong concern for the moral care and proper upbringing of the child. (Steinfels 1973, 45)

Concomitant with this socialization function, child care performs a *religious* function. Child care can function as indoctrination to a particular set of religious values. Simultaneously, child care can meet the needs of the sponsoring religious institution by widening its outreach.

The nine aforementioned functions—(1) welfare reform; (2) social service; (3) education; (4)liberation-universalization; (5) social status; (6) social reform; (7) economic; (8) socialization; and (9) religious—will be analyzed in relation to the five contending sponsors for child care in the United States. Implicit in these nine conceptualizations of child care's function in society are the latent social policy issues of equity and accessibility. The debate over sponsorship of child care must deal with these issues. Equity and accessibility, as well as the issues of quality of the service (as determined by the standards of care) and cost of the care, vary by sponsor. These are some of the consequences that need to be examined according to Merton's functional paradigm.

Kathleen Murray's (1985) distillation of the contemporary debate over sponsorship recognizes the tension over functions and the underlying issues. She sees the debate on two levels:

First, one level of the debate asks whether child care should serve primarily as a support to parental employment or if it should be a means to promote the education and development of children. On a second, related level the debate queries whether child care is a service needed by—and appropriate for—lower income families or whether it is a service important at all economic levels. (p.271)

The history and significance of this debate as related to the issue of sponsorship will be developed in the following chapters.

Although functional analysis is employed for pragmatic purposes of policy development, the unraveling of the history of the present and past debates will substantiate conflict theorists' premises. This research framework suggests that policy can be informed through an interdisciplinary approach and need not rest solely on empirical research. The heuristic value of two disparate sociological theories can be harnessed for the purpose of guiding policy. The importance of history to the process of illuminating policy problems cannot be overemphasized. Whether one is a student of history, conflict theory, functionalism, or politics, the story of the enactment of child care legislation in America is testimony to the provocative nature and deep-seatedness of the "child caring" chord in the whole of American society.

NOTES

1.   For further information on the debate over the shortage issue on child care, see the discussion of Rachel Connelly's commissioned paper, "The Barriers to Increasing the Supply of Quality Affordable Child Care," published in the Child Care Action Campaign's 1988 publication *The Bottom Line*, pages 30–32. See also the separate testimonies by the Heritage Association and Deborah Phillips on June 28, 1988, on the Act for Better Child Care of 1987 (S. 1885) (Subcommittee on Children, Family, Drugs and Alcoholism of the Committee on Labor and Human Resources, 100th Congress, 2nd Session); Sandra Hofferth's testimony on February 9, 1989, provided in *Hearings on Child Care* (House, Committee on Education and Labor, 100th Congress, 1st Session). For additional references, see Zigler and Finn-Stevenson (1989); Kahn and Kamerman (1987); and Rose-Ackerman (1986).

2.   Theoretical debate over the appropriateness of child care continues to exist. However, the main concern of researchers regarding the "appropriateness" of care revolves around the infant-toddler period. Controversy exists over the appropriate age for entry into care and optimum period of time away from the primary caregiver. For a discussion on the effects of child care on child development, refer to Chapter 2 of *Who Cares for America's Children?* (Hayes, Palmer, and Zaslow 1990), published by the National Research Council of the American Academy of Sciences. Research on the 3–5-year-old population concentrates primarily on the quality of different care settings, as well as on the multivariate nature of caregiving. Current research centers on the interactive effects of home and caregiver environments. Thus, there have been three waves of research on the effects of child care on child development: (1) from the late

1970s through the early 1980s, which examined the differences between home-reared children and those enrolled in child care settings; (2) from the middle of the 1980s until the late 1980s, during which the variables that defined high quality child care were examined; and (3) the present focus at the turn of the decade on the link between family and caregiver environments.

3.   One cannot make direct or exact analogies, however. The examination of another time period only highlights those trends and variables peculiar to the context of an era in question.

4.   This dichotomous analytic framework informs the field and is not limited to the authors listed. The perspective was infused throughout the multitude of testimonies on child care, during the many years of debate.

5.   The term *day nursery* was eventually replaced by the term *day care*. During the 1980s the term *child care* replaced *day care* for two reasons. Professionals wanted to emphasize the fact that the *child*, not the day, was the subject of the care. Additionally, recreation programs for the aged were becoming popular and were referred to as *day care*.

6.   Family "preservation" currently is in resurgence as a social strategy with the influx of children born into dysfunctional families or poverty. As will be seen in later discussions, child care advocates have strived to elevate the role of child care to mainstream society. In so doing, the more residual functions of the service have waned. Child care has performed "therapeutic" and "prevention" functions when abused children or children at risk of abuse have been placed in the facility. For the purposes of this book, the therapeutic and prevention functions are included as part of the social service function. The use of child care for this population of children merits more attention in the contemporary debate. See the testimony of Thomas L. Birch, legislative counsel for the National Child Abuse Coalition, in *Child Care: The Emerging Crisis*; Hearings before the U.S. Congress, Select Committee on Children, Youth, and Families (House), 99th Congress, 1st Session, July 30, 1985, pp. 145–197. The testimony included material from the National Committee for Prevention of Child Abuse (NCPCA). The service of child care needs to be linked to the health system, the special education system, and the protective services system among others discussed in this book.

7.   For the history of Head Start, refer to *Project Head Start: A Legacy of the War on Poverty* (Zigler and Valentine 1979). See also the September 1990 issue of *Young Children*, which is devoted to the celebration of Head Start's twenty-fifth anniversary. For additional information, refer to the interview with Wade Horn, the commissioner of the Administration for Children, Youth and Families in the Department of Health and Human Services, in the October 1990 issue of *Child Care Exchange*, pp. 13–15.

8.   The latter question has driven the debate that juxtaposes care and education. In her timely article, "The Care and Education of America's Young Children: At the Brink of a Paradigm Shift," Sharon Lynn Kagan (1989b) proposes that the question currently is

being addressed and will result in a merger. This merger will address the concern over the split view expressed by Bettye Caldwell (1986; 1989b), Gwen Morgan (1977; 1989), and many others. The need for a paradigmatic shift in thinking has existed for at least twenty years.

9.   When child care was under consideration in the second session of the 101st Congress, many women's groups were preoccupied with the nomination of a new justice to the United States Supreme Court, with Justice Brennan's retirement in 1990. Feminists were very worried that a new justice selected by President Bush would overturn *Roe v. Wade*, which gave women specific rights to an abortion.

10.   This practice of employing private caregivers (i.e. nannies, governesses, and au pairs) creates yet another social class and connotes new social relationships rift with contradictory assumptions. Future analyses need to focus on the effect this privileged caregiver has on the mainstream caregiver, and the relations between the two groups, as well as between the privileged caregiver and her employer.

11.   For information on the status of child care workers, see Kathy Modigliani, "Twelve Reasons for the Low Wages in Child Care," *Young Children* (March 1988): 14–15; and, the Child Care Employee Project's *Who Cares? Child Care Teachers and the Quality of Care in America. Executive Summary National Child Care Staffing Study* (Oakland, Calif.: author, 1989).

12.   Researchers have examined the effects of child care on cognition, socioemotional growth, and social competence. The research indicates that children with child care experience tend to be more peer oriented than home reared children. This peer orientation has resulted in positive and negative correlates (Hayes, Palmer and Zaslow 1990, 61-65). For additional reviews, see Frederick Morrison's "Child Care for the 21st Century: An Overview and Commentary," *Canadian Psychology* 30, no.2 (1989): 148–151, and Sandra Scarr, Kathleen McCartney, and Deborah Phillips, "Dilemma of Child Care in the United States: Employed Mothers and Children at Risk," *Canadian Psychology* 30, no.2 (1989): 126–139.
      Although research is being conducted on the social and psychological effects of child care experiences, the overall discussions on child care do not seem to focus on its implicit consequences. The liberal-democratic ideology is assumed as a given, but deserves to be probed. The significance of the socialization function of child care could become more obvious in international studies that compare cultural differences in child care arrangements.
      Darla Miller addressed the question of socialization for infants and toddlers in *First Steps Toward Cultural Difference: Socialization in Infant/Toddler Day Care* (1989) published by the Child Welfare League of America.
      Danny Wilks addressed the implications of the socialization function in "'Save the Children': Implications of Day Care," *The Black Scholar* (May–June 1973): 14–20.
      The socialization function of child care is brought to the surface and becomes a central point of debate by conservative groups. Members of the moderate and extreme right are concerned about the potential effects of group care arrangements on the

socialization process and prefer the traditional familial means. These conservative groups still debate the "appropriateness" of child care, rather than the more specific issue of sponsorship.

2. Legislative Background

The legislative history of child care is long and tortuous. Each time child care has been introduced as major legislation in the political arena, it incited heated debate. Policy decisions on providing care for young children are extremely provocative because they call forth deep-seated sentiments about the corresponding roles of government and family. The overarching debate between the broad interests of government and more parochial familial interests encompasses other divisive issues such as collective versus private responsibility, and universal brother-sisterhood versus cultural and religious identity. At risk in this debate is the socialization of generations of children. Instead of children, the vested interests of public and private providers become the basis for long-term policy decisions. Gilbert Steiner provided the definitive analysis of this debate on Capitol Hill and the fare of children during the years 1968–1975 in *The Children's Cause* (1976). This chapter summarizes Steiner's conclusions and further traces the history from 1976–1990.

The year of publication for Margaret O' Brien Steinfels' book on the status of child care in America, *Who's Minding the Children?* (1973) was significant because the concern over child care had recently catapulted to the forefront of public thought in the late 1960s. Steinfels aptly described the tenor of the times and captured the popular interest in the topic. She recounted the history of the day nurseries that served the working poor and some lower middle class families from the turn of the century through the 1960s. The women's movement and increases in the cost of living brought more women from the middle and upper classes into the labor market at the end of the 1960s. With the influx of these working mothers and the residual interest in the disadvantaged class from the War-on-Poverty era of the middle 1960s, "day care" became an issue for congressional attention and action in the late 1960s and early 1970s.

Previous government interest and involvement in child care had coincided with the Works Program during the Depression in the 1930s and later with labor shortages during World War II. Government's ventures at both junctures supported the economic function of child care. Federal efforts to provide jobs for the unemployed during the Depression involved sponsoring nursery schools under the Works Progress Administration (WPA). Unemployed teachers were given jobs and the children of families in distress were provided care (Zigler and Goodman 1982, 342).

The Lanham Act of 1941 allocated federal funds to states for the provision of early childhood programs. These day care centers and nursery schools functioned on behalf of the war efforts by enabling women to enter the work force.[1] Although many women wanted to stay in the labor force after the war, federal funding was withdrawn in spite of protests. This retreat by the federal government from supporting child care is viewed with hindsight as a terrible mistake (Zigler and Goodman 1982, 342–343). The withdrawal of Lanham funds after World War II was the first of two policy decisions that failed to foresee the need for a national base for the development of a system of child care services throughout the country. The second opportunity appeared in 1971 during the onset of the women's movement.

Federal involvement in the direct provision of child care services was conspicuously absent for over twenty years after the Lanham Act. Norgren (1981, 131–132) identifies two federal initiatives on behalf of "day care" services during the 1960s, an era marked by the implementation of the Head Start Program. In 1962, funding was allocated for day care as part of the Public Welfare Amendments to the Social Security Act. The intent of the legislation was left ambiguous, but shaped by advocates from both the "social welfare, child-focused" constituency and the "workfare" for welfare recipients constituency. The latter envisioned child care as enabling welfare recipients to enter the work force or job training programs. Norgren highlights the modest amount expended through this legislation. Although $25 million was authorized for the first three years, only $8.8 million was appropriated by Congress from 1962 through 1965.[2]

The second federal initiative in the 1960s regarding child care involved another amendment to the Social Security Act. In 1967, child care funding was allocated at 75 percent of costs for parents participating in the Work Incentive Program (WIN) and for recipients of Aid for Dependent Children (AFDC). Norgren differentiates the 1967 amendment from the 1962 amendment by attributing a manifest intent in using child care for welfare reform purposes.[3] Poor mothers with young children were now specifically targeted for workfare or training programs; therefore, their children needed care. In analyzing the effects of this legislation, Norgren found that the supply of child care centers in New York City increased because the eligibility guidelines were liberal and funding was available. However, the increased enrollment was attributed to the working class and some middle class professionals. The welfare rolls were not significantly affected (Norgren 1981, 132).

Thus, the federal government had sporadic, narrow involvement in child care before 1971, with the economic and welfare reform functions taking precedence. The 92nd Congress (1971–1972) became pivotal in the contemporary history of child care services and the debate over federal involvement in such services. The social service and education functions finally were brought to the floor and openly discussed at this juncture.

On December 9, 1971, President Nixon prevented the development of a comprehensive federal policy toward child care by vetoing the 1971 Comprehensive Child Development Act, Title V of the Economic Opportunity Amendments of 1971 (S. 2007), which had been passed by Congress that fall (CQA 1972, 914). Two generations of children later, Congress and the president wrestled again with child care legislation, which became the heir to the vetoed Comprehensive Child Development Act. The years 1971 and 1990, and the 92nd and 101st Congresses, respectively, shared a common agenda: a flurry of legislative action on child care.

In the February 20, 1971, issue of the *Saturday Review*, Susan Boyer described the major bills before the Congress in an article entitled "The Day-Care Jungle." Erika Streuer (1973), wrote on the 1971 legislative proposals, in which she summarized ten key pieces of legislation that addressed child care. The "Washington Update" of *Young Children* marked the 100th Congress as an historic session because more bills concerning children were introduced than ever before ("Washington Update" 1988a, 56). The Congressional Research Service reported the introduction of more than 100 bills with child care provisions in the 100th and 101st Congresses (CRS 1988, 1; 1989a, 3; 1990a, 2).

Activity on child care legislation during the 101st Congress focused on two historic pieces of legislation passed by each congressional body: The Act for Better Child Care of 1989 (ABC or S. 5), which was approved by the Senate on June 23, 1989, and The Early Childhood Education and Development Act of 1990 (H.R. 3), which was passed by the House on March 29, 1990. The seeds of earlier legislation merit discussion before analyzing these contending child care proposals, which were the antecedents of the landmark Child Care Entitlement Grant and the Child Care and Development Block Grant, passed as Chapter VI, Sections 5081 and 5082, respectively, of the Omnibus Budget Reconciliation Act of 1990 (H.R. 5835, 101st Cong., 2d Sess., 136 Cong. Rec. 12491-96, October 26, 1990).

There were three milestone legislative initiatives during the 1970s under the Nixon, Ford, and Carter administrations: the Child Development Act of 1971, the Child and Family Services Act of 1975, and the Child Care Act of 1979, none of which became law. In "In Search of a National Child Care Policy," Jill Norgren (1981) acknowledges the Nixon-vetoed 1971 Child Development Act as the "benchmark of national comprehensive child care politics," but noted that congressional activity continued with hearings held in 1974, 1977, and 1978, and bills sent to committee in 1972, 1975 and 1979 (p. 134). After these aborted attempts to pass child care legislation during the 1970s, the Reagan administration instituted a policy of privatization, the limitations of which set the tone for policy debate in the 1980s, and fueled the rebuilding of the child care advocacy community by the end of the decade.

These legislative initiatives over the past two decades failed because of the controversial sponsorship question and other related issues. Thousands of pages of congressional testimony reveal persistent rifts in the child care community over who should deliver the service. The competing interest groups, inherent in a pluralistic society, were unable to resolve their differences and thus failed to reach any consensus on the issue of service delivery. Until 1990, the economy functioned without any major adjustment in federal involvement in the delivery of child care. Once the majority of the middle class became affected by the lack of adequate child care services, the limited supply of those services no longer could be considered functional to the overall structure of the economy or society at large.

In the most recent legislative initiatives during the Bush Administration, the problem of child care was perceived as no longer merely a problem of the poor and disenfranchised. By 1990, the sheer size of the number of families with child care needs had thrust the issue to the forefront of the public policy agenda, enabling the passage of historic child care legislation.

In *The Children's Cause*, Gilbert Steiner (1976) meticulously illustrated the political fight for passage of the Comprehensive Child Development Act of 1971. He described the intensity of the debate and the varying levels of conflict among child care advocates and between the Congress and the Executive Office. Steiner identified key points of controversy that were eventually resolved through the efforts of a unique child care coalition.

The ultimate failure of the Comprehensive Child Development Act to become law, because of President Nixon's veto and the Senate's failure to overturn the veto, set in motion a chain of events in ensuing years during which child care advocates argued among themselves over issues of power and control; that is, turf. Steiner argued that the next major piece of legislation, the Child and Family Services Act of 1975, received less unified support from the child care community. This lack of consensus among the former proponents of the defeated Comprehensive Child Development Act of 1971 caused a major blockage in the movement for a pro-active federal policy for children and families. Nevertheless, the Child and Family Services Act of 1975 (S. 626, H.R. 2966), which was a "scaled-down version" of the 1971 act, did pass both houses, only to be vetoed by President Ford (Zigler and Goodman 1982, 345; CQA 1975, 693).

Senator Alan Cranston sponsored the Child Care Act of 1979 (S. 4) (*Congressional Record* 1-15-79, S 180). This act involved many hearings, but failed to emerge from committee due to the lack of congressional and presidential support under the Carter administration. Carter's assistant secretary of HEW for Human Development Services, Arabella Martinez, delivered a stinging testimony at the Cranston hearings. Martinez argued (1) that American parents preferred home-based care; and (2) that the government supported increased standards for child care, but did not want to build a new fragmented system of services that relied on categorization and bureaucratization (Norgren 1981, 134; Zigler and Goodman 1982, 346–347).

Each of these pieces of legislation attempted to deal with the question of sponsorship. Although sponsorship is being raised in this text as a primary stumbling block in the development of legislation, the issues of regulation, state versus local responsibility, staffing, taxation, and state control versus familial control are all considered to be subsumed within the broader concept of control through the sponsoring institution. The remaining part of this chapter will delineate the key points of the landmark pieces of legislation in the history of child care as they relate to the issue of sponsorship.

The Comprehensive Child Development Act of 1971 (S. 2007) was passed after many hearings on the proposed Comprehensive Preschool Education and Child Day-Care Act of 1969 (H.R. 13520), which was sponsored by Representative John Brademas. Brademas and colleagues advocated an approach to child care delivery that promoted the education function. Proponents of H.R. 13520 did not target a particular population; instead, Brademas proposed a program of preschool education for all American children. Brademas's original approach held three key tenets that differentiated it from the bill (S. 2007) sponsored by Senators Walter Mondale and Gaylord Nelson. In addition to emphasizing the educational component of child care and its benefit for all children, the sponsoring representatives lobbied for larger government units as prime sponsors than Mondale's supporters and defended the idea of designating state agencies as grantees for federal funding (Steiner 1976, 102; 109). Brademas advocated a granting formula that would favor states with a large number of disadvantaged families, but also enabled families of the nonpoor to be recipients of child care services (Steiner 1976, 91; Streuer 1973, 53).

Steiner emphasized the significance of these issues in his discussion in *The Children's Cause*, "The Politics of Comprehensive Legislation" (pp. 90–117). Although there was a general consensus and movement to pass child care legislation on both sides of Congress at the end of the twentieth century's sixth decade, the differences in approaches were pronounced. Given the divisiveness within the ranks of the congressional leadership on key points of legislation, the eventual passage of the Comprehensive Child Development Act by the separate congressional bodies is viewed as a true victory in the history of child advocacy. However, the points of contention remained strong after Nixon's veto and loomed to the surface in subsequent years. Furthermore, Steiner theorized that Nixon could have vetoed the act by emphasizing pragmatic concerns over the construction of the legislation, rather than choosing to voice an ideological position on the primacy of the family over the state. In a message to the Senate, President Nixon stated his reasons for vetoing the Economic Opportunity Amendments of 1971 (S. 2007):

But the most deeply flawed provision of this legislation is Title V, Child Development Programs . . . the intent of Title V is overshadowed by the fiscal irresponsibility, administrative unworkability, and family-weakening implications of the system it envisions. We owe our children something more than good intentions.

We cannot and will not ignore the challenge to do more for America's children in their all-important early years. But our response to this challenge must be a measured, evolutionary, painstakingly considered one, consciously designed to cement the family in its rightful position as the keystone of our civilization . . .

. . . the child development envisioned in this legislation would be truly a long leap into the dark for the United States Government and the American people. I must share the view of those of its supporters who proclaim this to be the most radical piece of legislation to emerge from the Ninety-second Congress. (Nixon 1971, 1635)

Nixon described his view of the federal government's role as "one of assisting parents to purchase needed day care services in the private, open market, with Federal involvement in direct provision of such services kept to an absolute minimum" (Nixon 1971, 1635).

Before the presidential veto, the split between Mondale's approach, Brademas's approach, and that of the administration revolved around the function of child care and the appropriate size of a designated prime sponsor. Mondale, with the support of Marian Wright Edelman's growing child care coalition, sought the actualization of the social reform function of child care. Keeping in sync with the civil rights movement, proponents of the Senate's version hoped to capitalize on child care's potential for acting as an agent of community change. Supporters held fast to the viewpoint that reform was the outgrowth of grass-roots community action. Therefore, throughout the legislative drafting, they lobbied for local units as the preferred prime sponsors. The competing approaches were debated in each legislative branch, and then sent to a conference committee. As Steiner noted:

Whether or not comprehensive child development legislation was an appropriate subject for congressional action was not an issue in the Select Subcommittee on Education or in the full House Education and Labor Committee. The divisive issue was how to do it rather than whether to do it. Some members of the committee favored setting a prime-sponsor population limitation at 500,000; others wanted to go to zero. Brademas characterizes the prime-sponsor population limitation as "without question" the most difficult issue considered in committee deliberations on the bill. (Steiner 1976, 109)

The administration's Health, Education and Welfare secretary, Elliot Richardson, was not only in favor of a large population size for prime sponsorship, but also favored a state control approach for the delivery of child care services. Speaking for the Executive Office, Richardson held fast to the position that any legislation created for the specific purpose of delivering child care services should follow a federal to state funding and organization scheme. The administration did not want to establish a cumbersome, bureaucratic system. This federalist approach was in keeping with President Nixon's overall attitude toward "day care," which he envisioned functioning on behalf of his welfare reform goals.

The final version of legislation was the result of much compromise on the part of members from the House, Senate and Administration. The Comprehensive Child Development Act of 1971 (S. 2007) consisted of language that gave prime sponsorship to local units of governance or nonprofit agencies that met specific conditions and held that the minimum population size should be 5,000 (Steiner 1976, 113; Streuer 1973, 57; S. 2007 1971). In spite all of the effort and sentiment expended on drafting this milestone legislation, President Nixon vetoed the act because he viewed it as radical policy that could irrevocably change the course of American society. He further contended that legislation of such controversial content demanded much more fervent, encompassing national debate (Steiner, 108–109, 113).

Looking back on this legislative debate now, it is obvious that the ideological stance to which Nixon committed himself remains present today, though in varying degrees among diverse factions of society. Government involvement in child rearing and the role of women in the work force continue to be areas of controversy between conservatives and liberals. However, the plea for a great national debate on directing federal funds to child care has been positively dealt with as of 1990. A long awaited, much heralded federal initiative emerged from a consensus built of bipartisan support, a dynamic coalescence of diverse viewpoints that can be attributed to the significant demographic changes in the work force participation of mothers.

After the defeat of the 1971 act, Congress passed the Child and Family Services Act of 1975. This piece of legislation marks the turning point in the controversy over public school involvement in child care delivery. Although, Brademas's 1969 legislative initiative laid some groundwork by highlighting the worth of a public preschool system. It was at this crossroad in 1975 that the powerful voice of the American Federation of Teachers of the AFL-CIO made itself heard through its long-time leader, Albert Shanker. Shanker argued that the schools should be designated presumed prime sponsors of newly funded child care centers. Presumed prime sponsorship implied that the schools would be designated the lead agency for the delivery of child care, but would contract with other community agencies interested in providing the service should the school be unable or unwilling to provide child care. Shanker's position will be discussed more thoroughly in a later chapter. However, Jill Norgren's earlier summation is historically and analytically noteworthy on this development:

The demands of the AFL-CIO that responsibility for the future development of child care in the United States be given to the public schools have been particularly divisive. With the public schools as prime sponsors, longstanding questions of licensing, local versus federal standards, and community versus professional control would be resolved. (Norgren 1981, 134)

Although 1975 marked the formal entrance of the organized educational community into the debate on child care delivery, the actual language of the Child and Family Services Act did not designate the public schools as the prime sponsor of child care services. Rather, the bill was a "scaled down version" of earlier legislation (Zigler and Goodman 1982, 345) and resolved the prime sponsorship issue by allowing the federal government to authorize sponsors on either the state or local level, which in turn would delegate funds to grant applicants. Local councils would determine the prime sponsorship eligibility criteria and policies for the projects. These councils were required to have parent representatives as the majority of their members. Sponsors other than local or state designees could apply and receive funding, including educational agencies or institutions, if they met specific standards (CQA 1975, 693; H.R. 2966 1975; S. 626 1975).

When the schools stepped forth as major contenders for sponsorship, their competitors were forced to surface and articulate opposing views. As the pre-1970 history of child care in America indicated, an informal delivery system was created by sundry organizations and interest groups. Without the passage of legislation that would pro-actively plan further development of centers, children and families continued to be served through an informal, patchwork system. Therefore, by 1975 competing interests were well entrenched.

William Pierce, then the assistant executive director of the Child Welfare League of America, summarized the political scene in a telling article for the Social Legislation Information Service in the December 13, 1976, issue of the *Washington Social Legislation Bulletin*. In the article, "Prospects for National Day Care Legislation," Pierce laid out the various camps forming over the sponsorship issue, which he recognized to be a major "hurdle" for the new Carter-Mondale administration. The fact that the heralded leader of child care legislation, Walter Mondale, was vice president, but still could not effect the passage of major child care legislation speaks to the underlying controversy and power struggles throughout the child care community at the time. As Steiner (1976) surmised, and Zigler and Goodman (1982) confirmed, the child care community was embroiled in internal strife that would take over a decade to iron out before leading to the eventual compromises needed for the drafting of the historic 1987–1990 legislative initiatives for comprehensive child care services.

Pierce highlighted several developments in the child care arena. First, he credited the Democratic platform with changing the emphasis of child care from being seen primarily in its social service and welfare reform functions to being viewed for its education function. Although Brademas and his colleagues had taken this position earlier, Carter's statements brought this perspective to the public in a manifest fashion. The Democratic platform had given child care a high priority under its education agenda, rather than social services. Pierce noted this change in the link of structure and function as significant.

This shift in thinking highlighted the goal of providing a universal service of delivery, which was more in line with the public education system than the social service system. In spite of this new emphasis on education from an administrative perspective, another concurrent goal in the child care campaign remained. Carter supported the pluralism already inherent in the existing, unformalized child care delivery system (Pierce 1976, citing Carter's October 4, 1976 speech, to the National Conference of Catholic Charities, 186). While interest in the education function mounted and the schools vied for a more prominent position, the perennial American belief in freedom of choice prevailed, further complicated by the struggle of family versus state control of child rearing. Thus, the prime sponsorship question moved away from a local versus state control debate and began to involve specific institutions such as the schools, churches, social service agencies, and the burgeoning for-profit organizations.

Foreseeing the magnitude of the service delivery problem, as well as understanding the potential that the political period offered for moving forward to resolve child care problems, the *Washington Bulletin* conducted an opinion survey on major national groups which had a stake in legislation pertaining to young children (Pierce 1976, 186). Pierce reported the following findings from the 22 groups polled. The groups represented "national voluntary groups, education, organized labor, private for-profit providers, and day care advocates representing both a national perspective and community-control and minority ethnic interests" (Pierce 1976, 186).

The respondents were split as to whether there should be a prime sponsor at all. Of those that did want a prime sponsor, six were in favor of local education units, six wanted states and localities. Eight organizations responded negatively to the statement: "Local education agencies (public schools) should be the presumed prime sponsors." These negative respondents included community-control groups, unions, groups funded by HEW's Office of Child Development, and for-profit operators. The issue of profit making became more prominent in the middle-1970s as the school issue rose to importance. Pierce reported in the *Washington Bulletin* survey that eleven out of twenty-one groups responded negatively to the notion of for-profit involvement in child care.

Pierce also discussed the respondents' sentiments to the welfare reform function of child care. The majority of those that responded to this inquiry felt that the "jobs-related" function of child care was secondary to the educational. The incoming Democratic administration promised to move away from the Republican welfare reform orientation. Nevertheless, child care could still be seen as intricately tied to any appropriate welfare or employment related legislation (Pierce 1976, 186).

Unfortunately, neither the Ford nor Carter administrations championed the child care cause. A so-called smear campaign in 1975 had shattering effects on The Child and Family Services Act, which had been sponsored by Mondale and Brademas. The bill found itself to be the target of an aggressive conservative mail campaign that argued that American children would be "sovietized" as a result of the bill's enactment (Pierce 1976, 187; CQA 1975, 693). The Child and Family Services Act did not come to the floor again, and the public school question remained unanswered and, therefore, latent.[4]

The next major congressional initiative on behalf of child care services was sponsored by Senator Alan Cranston, but as Norgren (1981) noted this initiative never came out of committee. Cranston's bill did not advocate public schools as the prime sponsor; instead, it devoted considerable attention to the issue of parental choice and participation. The proposed Child Care Act of 1979 provided that each state should designate a state agency to oversee and administer a state plan. This state agency would be subject to a state advisory panel. On a national level, the secretary of Health, Education, and Welfare would designate a specific administrative unit and director for carrying out the provisions of the act. The Child Care Act would have allowed for a diverse range of providers, as long as they met quality standards and were licensed. Priority would be given to those providers that serviced families on the basis of need (*Congressional Record* 1-15-79, 180–190).

The Reagan years are signified by the enactment of the Economic Recovery Tax Act of 1981 (PL 97-34) and the Omnibus Budget Reconciliation Act of 1981 (PL 97-35). These two acts marked a major change in tax laws by providing individuals and businesses significant tax cuts and credits, while slashing social service spending. President Reagan consolidated federal categorical grants into block grants and resorted to a "new federalism" (CQA 1981, 91–92, 465). The effects of these acts on federal funding for social services in general and child care in particular have been well documented by Kahn and Kamerman (1987) and the Children's Defense Fund (Blank and Wilkins 1986; Blank, Savage and Wilkins, 1988). President Reagan advocated more corporate responsibility for child care services and ascribed to public-private partnerships. Initiatives favorable to child care during the Reagan administration centered on indirect benefits through the tax system, rather than the provision or support of direct services.

Middle and upper middle class families benefited from a 1981 increase in the dependent care tax credit, which was the largest federal program aimed at enabling families to purchase child care. Before OBRA 1990, Kahn and Kamerman (1987) wrote, "This tax credit benefits only those whose income is above the tax threshold established in the 1980s—not the poor or near poor" (p. 21). Based on income, families were able to deduct at least 20 percent of child care expenses up to a specified cap from their federal income taxes. The amount of the deduction was inversely related to income levels; thus, lower income families could take a greater percentage of child and dependent care expenses as a tax credit. Another federal tax initiative involved businesses. Employers could set aside money used for employees' child care expenditures that are not included in the employees taxable income (Kahn and Kamerman 1987, 21).

Reagan's tax initiatives helped the middle and upper classes, but other policies set in place by OBRA 1981 hurt the lower classes. There was a 14.5 percent decline in constant dollars from 1980 to 1986 in direct federal expenditures for child care. OBRA 1981 had cut back funding for direct social welfare services, and dismantled Title XX of the Social Security Act by creating a Social Services Block Grant that did not require the states to provide a 25 percent match to federal funds. In sum, OBRA 1981 instituted the following detrimental changes: appropriations were cut by one-fifth; the training program within Title XX was eliminated, as was the Comprehensive Employment Training Act (CETA) program that was a major source of child care staff; funding for the Child Care Food Program was substantially cut; funding for AFDC recipients was capped and eligibility requirements for allowable work expenses were tightened (Kahn and Kamerman 1987, 20). OBRA 1981 also saw to the final elimination of the already suspended Federal Interagency Day Care Regulations (Phillips and Zigler 1987, 21).

The Bush administration found itself struggling with the aftermath of Reagan's privatization policies. Because the Reagan initiatives did not substantially increase the supply of child care services, the child care community regathered its strength to push for the long-overdue federal funding of comprehensive child care programs with the Act for Better Child Care (S. 5) and the Early Childhood Education and Development Act (H. R. 3).

Looking back to the earlier fight for the Comprehensive Child Development Act of 1971, it is noteworthy that at both times lobbying efforts were lead by coalitions of child welfare oriented groups, early childhood professionals, labor unions, and other organizations. Marian Wright Edelman was at the forefront of each battle; the twenty year time spread between lobbying efforts was well utilized by Edelman, who turned the initial coalition's interests into the renowned Children's Defense Fund, of which she is the current president. The precursor of the Children's Defense Fund was Edelman's Washington Research Project Action Council (Steiner 1976, 99). In the more recent movement, the Children's Defense Fund joined other organizations to form the Alliance for Better Child Care in the push for enactment of the Act for Better Child Care (S.5).[5] The alliance officially began in January 1987, although the seeds for the idea began in the winter of 1986, with the express purpose of developing comprehensive child care legislation that would be introduced in the 100th Congress (personal communication with Oakes 1990; Phillips and Zigler 1987). The goals of the alliance included nine specific points:

1. Improve access to quality care for all families; 2. Aid low-and moderate-income parents in paying for such care; 3. Provide for sliding fee scales to help facilitate the socioeconomic mix of children within child care facilities; 4. Strengthen regulatory standards and improve their implementation; 5. Strengthen family day care as well as child care centers; 6. Support parental involvement in child care; 7. Support the development of training programs to ensure qualified staff in child care programs; 8. Encourage coordination among the various state and local agencies which affect young

children and their families; 9. Provide sufficient funds to serve more children, assure quality and improve the level of compensation for child care workers. (Phillips and Zigler 1987, 33)

As was true with the Comprehensive Child Development Act of 1971, conflict raged within both houses of Congress, within the child care community, and between Congress and the president during the legislative drafting of S. 5 and H.R. 3. The push for S. 5, the Act for Better Child Care, began in 1987 when Democratic Senator Christopher Dodd introduced the bill as S. 1885 in the Senate on November 19, 1987. Republican Senator John Chafee cosponsored the bill with more than twenty additional senators. In his opening remarks, Senator Dodd highlighted the support the bill enjoyed from the recently instituted Alliance for Better Child Care. Representatives Dale Kildee (D-MI) and Olympia Snowe (R-ME), Augustus F. Hawkins (D-CA), and others introduced the House child care vehicle, H. R. 3660 (*Congressional Record* 11-19-87).

The Act for Better Child Care (S. 1885) was drafted to meet the three critical issues in the delivery of child care: availability, affordability, and quality of services. The legislative intent was to design and implement a new, federally funded infrastructure for child care delivery across the country. The bill did not support a prime sponsor for the delivery of services, but maintained a multiple-sponsor system by funnelling in federal funds under the auspices of a new umbrella agency. Under the act public and private nonprofit agencies, as well as local educational agencies and family child care providers, were eligible for funds from the state block grant. For-profit providers were excluded from participating in the grant program. Federal funds would be distributed to the states on an 80 to 85 percent basis, depending on how the state complied with minimum federal delivery standards. The distribution of funds would vary according to the distribution of state populations by age of children and income levels. States were required to designate lead agencies and develop long-range state plans as to the distribution of funds to eligible providers (Section 7). S. 1885 authorized $2.5 billion for fiscal year 1989 and such sums as necessary for fiscal years 1990–1993 (*Congressional Record* 11-19-87; CRS 1988, 15–18).

The uniqueness of the act involved the use of a certificates program, as defined in (Section 3 (2)). In addition to the dispersion of the block grant through grants to or contracts with child care facilities, states were required to provide eligible parents with a certificate that could be used at a center of their choice as long as that center complied with local and state standards in accord with the guidelines set forth in the federal act. The act specifically set forth requirements that states set standards that comply with minimum standards set by a National Advisory Committee on Child Care Standards, which was required to arrive at an understanding of "median standards for all States as of the date of enactment of this Act" (Section 18).

The proposal for the implementation of federally defined standards was to prove controversial, as were Sections 19 and 20, which prohibited the expenditure of funds for certain purposes and mandated nondiscrimination in hiring and admissions practices. These two sections provoked much discord among supporters of church sponsorship and will be discussed in detail in Chapter 4. As originally written and introduced in November 1987, the Act for Better Child Care specifically prohibited the expenditure of federal money to programs with sectarian content. Institutions sponsoring child care programs with sectarian components were also prohibited from receiving capital improvement funds otherwise available under the act.

The restrictions contained in Title VI of the Civil Rights Act of 1964, 42 U.S.C. 2000d; Title IX of the Education Amendments of 1972, 20 U.S.C. 1681, et seq.; the Rehabilitation Act of 1973, 29 U.S.C. 794; and Title VII of the Civil Rights Act of 1964, 42 U.S.C. 2000e, et seq., notwithstanding the exemption in section 703 of Title VII, were specifically set forth in ABC (S.5). Thus, although Title VII permits religious institutions to discriminate in hiring and admissions under its section 703 exemption, ABC required religious institutions receiving federal financial assistance to waive these Title VII exemption rights.

Drafting continued on both the House and Senate versions of ABC for the next eighteen months. Hearings were held on S.1885 by the Senate Subcommittee on Children, Family, Drugs, and Alcoholism on June 11, 1987; March 15, 1988; and on June 28, 1988. Testimony covered the critical issues of cost, standards, and coverage. All issues were related to sponsorship and the three identified problems of availability, affordability, and quality. The following aspects of the act became central to the debate: (1) the appropriateness of federal standards; (2) the proper role of religious providers; and (3) the appropriateness of a block grant approach as compared to an alternative tax-based approach.

On July 27, 1988, the Act for Better Child Care was reported out of the Labor and Human Resources Committee by unanimous voice vote. The new bill, S. 5, was introduced on January 25, 1989, by Democratic Senators Christopher Dodd, Ted Kennedy, and Barbara Mikulski, and Republican Orrin Hatch (*Senate Report* 100-484; 101-17; *Congressional Record* 1-25-89, S 189). The involvement of Senator Hatch was indicative of broadened bipartisan support because of his previous stance against child care legislation and the constituency he represented (Hatch 1982; see Dodd in *Congressional Record* 6-23-89, S 7477; CQW 6-24-89, 1544). His active leadership proved critical to the outcome of the debate. Democratic Representative Dale Kildee and Republican Representative Olympia Snowe concurrently reintroduced H.R. 30, the house vehicle for

ABC (S. 5). The revised ABC bill incorporated the following component parts, among others: eligible families were defined as those whose income did not exceed 100 percent of the state median income; children were deemed eligible up to age 15; priority was given to low income families; the establishment of a National Advisory Committee that set minimum health and safety standards in key areas for those centers and family child care providers receiving funds; 10 percent of funds were required to extend Head Start programs; and the establishment of a five year state plan (*Senate Report* 100-484).

Pertinent to this discussion, the revised language incorporated for-profit providers among those eligible to receive grant money. Additionally, amended language was introduced by Senator Dodd on June 8, 1988, for Sections 19 and 20 of the bill. Religious organizations still were restricted to the provision of programs that had no religious content, but the amended language enabled religious schools to receive money for before and after school child care programs. The new language revoked the prohibition against religious discrimination in hiring (*Senate Report* 100-484, 77-80).

While hearings were being held and S. 5 and H.R. 30 were marked up in their respective committees, child care became a key topic during the presidential election campaign during the summer of 1988. Both the Democrats and the Republicans addressed the need for increased child care funding and services. The Democratic platform supported ABC's approach, whereas then Republican presidential candidate George Bush proposed a four point plan that would have appropriated $2.2 billion toward the solution of the child care problem by (1) creating a new refundable children's tax capped at $1,000 per child for children under age 4 for families with incomes under $10,000; (2) making the existing tax credit refundable; (3) allocating $50 million for the encouragement of employer sponsorship, with the federal government to serve as a model employer; and (4) maintaining choice and diversity through the dissemination of information. Bush also supported the expansion of Head Start services through phase-in funding that would enable all eligible 4 year olds to attend ("Washington Update" 1988b, 59; Euben 1988, 7-8).

Bush's proposal reflected the Republican platform that was based on the following key priorities (CCAC 1988, 7-8). First, single earner families who elect to have one parent stay at home, rather than join the paid labor force, need to be protected from discrimination in the tax code. Second, limited public money for child care were to be targeted to those most in need of government support. Federal strategies were to assure (1) a diverse range of providers, including home based-care; (2) encouragement of employer involvement; (3) support for child care services for teen parents; and (4) the facilitation of the provision of care by family members.

Conservatives preferred to solve the child care crisis through the tax system without creating a new social program. Wishing to avoid a new bureaucracy and excessive expenditures, the Republican party developed strategies that at once targeted the poor for federal help and promoted the potential of the free market system. President Reagan's former emphasis on public-private partnerships was not abandoned, but new emphasis was placed on revamping the tax system to better address the needs of lower and middle income families. Throughout the legislative battles, President Bush opposed the Democratic block grant approach (CQW 3-31-90, 1000).

At the onset of the first session of the 101st Congress, when Representatives Kildee and Snowe proposed the new House version of ABC (H.R. 30) and S. 5 was introduced in the Senate, the chair of the House Education and Labor committee, Representative Gus Hawkins (D-CA) sponsored a competing bill, the Early Childhood Education and Development Act (H.R. 3). This bill, which was introduced on January 3, 1989, highlighted the controversial nature of the sponsorship issue in the ongoing debate over how to deliver child care services. The Early Childhood Education and Development Act quite pointedly raised a crucial point of divide and elevated the issue to the center of the debate: the role of the public schools. Any special weight the public schools might possess was conspicuously absent in the Senate bill.

Hawkins's House bill (H.R. 3) and Dodd's Senate bill (S. 5) approached the issue of sponsorship in fundamentally different manners. The respective sponsors of the bills answered the basic inquiry of this book in two disparate ways. Under H.R. 3 special consideration was bestowed on the public schools, as well as the Head Start Program. Such deference was not exhibited in the language of S. 5, the Act for Better Child Care.

The House Committee on Education and Labor held hearings on February 9, 1989; March 6, 1989; and April 5, 1989. The bill enjoyed broad and bipartisan support with 115 congressional members joining Representative Hawkins as cosponsors and the endorsement of many key organizations (*H.R. Report* 101-190, Part I, 30–31). As originally drafted, H.R. 3 contained the following five titles (*H.R. Report* 101-190, Part I). Title I expanded the Head Start program from its current status as a program that served children according to the school calendar year and for only part of the day, to serve children for the full calendar year and the full working day. This expansion included the provision to widen the eligibility range to include children of families above the poverty level, but below 150 percent of the Lower Living Standard Income Level (LLS) on a sliding fee scale.

Title II, entitled Early Childhood Development and School-Related Child Care, amended the Elementary and Secondary Education Act of 1965. The

Secretary of Education would grant money to the states "to assist in the expansion, establishment, or operation of early childhood programs and/or before- and after-school programs or both" (H.R. Rept. 101-190, 36). Children below the poverty line whose families work or are enrolled in education or training programs would qualify for services at no charge. States were to establish sliding fee scales for low income families.

The local education agencies had the option of whether to serve 3 year olds. LEAs were permitted to contract with other public entities and eligible private nonprofit community based organizations to provide services. However, priority was to be given to programs which would be offered in school buildings.

Title III, which was modeled after the ABC block grant, targeted funding for infants, toddlers, and young children. Children eligible for full day programs included those that were below the compulsory age of school attendance. Children under age 13 were eligible for before and after school care, thereby establishing a lower age limit than ABC, which designated age 15 as the eligibility limit. States were to designate lead agencies to administer the programs and carry out coordinating activities that were defined in Title IV; the title that required the establishment of Local Child Development Councils. The full range of providers were eligible to receive Title III funds, including for-profit organizations.

Title IV mandated a state plan for the implementation of resource and referral programs, staff training, the improvement of enforcement procedures, and the upgrading of caregiver salaries. A fifth title authorized $25 million for fiscal years 1990 through 1993 for the Secretary of Health and Human Services to administer, on a competitive basis, to businesses committed to the start up or expansion of on-site or off-site child care centers. The federal government would match one dollar for every three dollars expended by a grant recipient. These recipients must implement strategies that would assure the participation of low and moderate income employees. Furthermore, businesses with fewer than 100 employees would be shown preference. The title specifically provides for a wide range of potential employer recipients; that is, public employers, private businesses, and consortia of businesses.

H.R. 3 addressed the issue of quality assurance through standards by establishing a National Advisory Committee on Model Standards. States would be required to establish basic health and safety standards, but unlike ABC the federal government would provide only suggested standards, rather than minimum requirements. Eligible providers were then required to meet state licensing or regulatory requirements.

As to the issue of discrimination, the House bill ascribed to the language of the Head Start Act (Section 654(a)),[6] which prohibits discrimination by race, creed, color, national origin, sex, political affiliation, or beliefs. H.R. 3 also adopted specific language that prohibited the expenditure of funds for child care programs with sectarian content.

The general provisions of the bill authorized $1.75 billion for fiscal year 1990, contingent on Head Start and Chapter 1 funding. Appropriations were to be authorized for three succeeding years as necessary. Each title was designated a specific percentage of the funds: Title I (25 percent); Title II (25 percent); Title III (35 percent); and Title IV (15 percent). Title V received the specific $25 million annual authorization for three years. The state plan was required to be flexible, but limited to grants and contracts.

Both the House and Senate bills built in strong parent involvement components, including the right to unlimited access to their child's center. The state plans were to encourage consumer education services and the establishment of resource and referral agencies. The two legislative initiatives shared the same intent of widening parental choice. Respective parts of the bills addressed the problem of remuneration of child care providers.

While H.R. 3 and S. 5 were debated and moved through committees, other members of congress and the president formulated tax credit approaches.[7] Democratic Senator Al Gore (D-TN) and Representative Tom Downey (D-NY) introduced the Employment Incentives Act (S.364/H.R.882) on February 7, 1989, which would expand the Earned Income Tax Credit (EITC) and make the Dependent Care Tax Credit refundable up to $30,000. The legislation also would have increased the funding for the Social Services Block Grant (CQW 2-18-89, 326–328; "Child Care/Early Education Focus" 1989, 38). Downey and Gore hoped to redress the 1986 changes to the tax code that had eliminated approximately 6 million working poor families from the federal tax rolls. The refundable credit would permit those without taxable income to receive a return in cash for the expressed purpose of offsetting child care expenses. Senators Moynihan (D-NY) and Packwood (R-OR) of the Senate Finance Committee, along with five colleagues, introduced similar legislation on February 9, 1989. Moving beyond the Moynihan-Packwood bill in reach, the Downey-Gore bill would increase the amount of the earned-income tax credit and expand it for family size. Both bills would allocate more funding for child care through the Social Services Block Grant program (CQW 2-18-89, 326–328).

On March 15, 1989, Republican Senator Robert Dole introduced S. 601 and Representative Stenholm introduced H.R. 4294, the Republican vehicles for President Bush's plan for child care (CRS 7-16-90). President Bush's plan, referred to as The Working Family Child Care Assistance Act of 1989 was built on the aforementioned Republican platform. Specifically, President Bush and his Republican colleagues proposed yet another tax based approach that would make the dependent care tax credit refundable. Under the Bush plan, families with incomes below $13,000 would have to choose between an expanded dependent care credit or a new credit capped at $1,000 for each child under the age of 4 and based on 14 percent of earnings (CQW 3-18-89, 586; E. Dole cited in U.S. Congress, Subcommittee on Human Resources 1989, 230).

The new credit was proposed as a strategy to assure equitable treatment of dual-earner and single-earner families. Consistent with his campaign promise, President Bush sought to support the constituency of low and moderate income families where the mother opted to stay at home with the children. During hearings before the Senate Subcommittee on Human Resources, Secretary of Labor Elizabeth H. Dole put forth the administration's plan and offered the following reasoning: "Our tax credit just may provide that marginal assistance to enable the low income mother, who would prefer to care for her children, but feels she has to work to help make ends meet, just might help her be able to make the choice to stay at home" (E. Dole cited in U.S. Congress, Subcommittee on Human Resources 1989, 229).

In addition to the tax pieces, Bush proposed amendments to the Head Start Act. He would have increased Head Start by $250 million, which would have enrolled 95,000 more 4-year-old children (CQW 3-18-89, 586; E. Dole cited in U.S. Congress, Subcommittee on Human Resources 1989, 230). The president's plan included the implementation of a national "liability study" to determine the existence of barriers to employer attainment of liability insurance for the coverage of on- or near-site child care centers (E. Dole cited in U.S. Congress, Subcommittee on Human Resources 1989, 231).

While the Early Childhood Education and Development Act (H.R. 3), and the Act for Better Child Care (S.5) ultimately became the vehicles for child care legislation during the 101st Congress, it is important to note that other child care related bills were introduced between 1988–1990. In *Child Care: An Analysis of Major Issues and Policy Options Considered by the 100th Congress* (CRS 1989a), the Congressional Research Service identified nine provisions present throughout this legislative activity in various combinations: tax credits; voucher programs to states; employer tax incentives; subsidized child care for welfare recipients; liability insurance programs for child care providers; the expansion of existing federal programs that already included child care provisions; capital improvement loans to family day care providers; school-based child care initiatives; and mandated studies on both the barriers of providing employer-sponsored programs and the general availability or lack of availability of child care arrangements throughout the country (CRS 1989a, 4).[8]

On March 15, 1989, after a final set of testimonies were heard on January 24, 1989, Senator Kennedy held an executive session of the Senate Committee on Labor and Human Resources for a final mark-up of the Act for Better Child Care (S. 5). The committee adopted S. 5 in the nature of a substitute amendment with a roll call vote of 11–5 (*Senate Report* 101-17). The amended bill retained the basic structure of the bill introduced in January 1989, but had the following additions and modifications. As an advocate for child care legislation, but an opponent of federal standards, Senator Hatch insisted on reworking the language defining the role and responsibilities of the National Advisory Commission on Child Care Standards (*Senate Report* 101-17; CQW 3-18-89, 585, 587).

A $100 million liability insurance pool that would enable child care providers to obtain affordable insurance also was included. The language of the amended version clarified the guidelines on care provided by relatives. The amended language specifically allowed relatives to participate in the grant program so long as the provider met any existing state regulations regarding relative care and is at least 18 years old. Further modifications involved the percentage distribution of funds (*Senate Report* 101-17; CQW 3-18-89, 585, 587).

The committee unanimously voted to accept an amendment by Senator Dodd to Section 20(b) of the bill, which would enable discrimination on the basis of religion, both in employment and admissions practices, *if* the child care provider does not receive more than 80 percent of its funds from public sources. The language in Section 19(a) on the prohibition of sectarian practices under the act was retained. The Senate report expressed the majority view that the intent of the act was to sanction programs "completely nonsectarian . . . in nature and in content." The members added, "The Committee expresses no view concerning whether the restriction in Section 19(a) is constitutionally required by the Establishment Clause" (*Senate Report* 101-17, 49). A severability clause was added to the text to separate the church and state issues from the rest of the act should they be invalidated through court challenges. Committee members remained deeply divided over religious questions and issues surrounding national standards (*Senate Report* 101-17; CQW 3-18-89, 585, 587).

Approximately two weeks of debate ensued on the floor of the Senate before the eventual passage of S. 5 on June 23, 1989. Senator Robert Dole's administration-backed substitute failed by a vote of 44–56. After the defeat of Dole's bill, the Senate passed a version of S. 5 that had become known as the *Mitchell substitute* after Senate Majority Leader George Mitchell, who had surmounted the arduous challenge of assembling the final bill among competing amendments and riled colleagues. The final Act for Better Child Care consisted of both a block grant and tax credit component (*Congressional Record* 6-23-89; CQW 6-24-89, 1543–1546).

The House had considerably more difficulty passing child care legislation. The intensity of the debate delayed passage until the second session of the 101st Congress, almost a year after the Senate completed its work. In addition to differences between the Senate and House approaches, as indicated in H.R. 3 and S. 5, the House became embroiled in conflict between two versions of H.R. 3 passed by two different committees. The House Education and Labor Committee, chaired by Representative Hawkins, reported H.R. 3 out of committee on June 27, 1989. The bill, which was in the version described earlier, was sent to the House Ways and Means Committee, which then substituted language for the Education and Labor's Title III language (*House Report* 101-190, Part II; CQW 7-22-89, 1862–1863). Thus, the House Ways and Means Committee, chaired by Representative Dan Rostenkowski, supported legislation that was in direct competition with H.R. 3, as drafted by the House Education and Labor Committee, and the Senate bill, S. 5. The differences between the two House versions will be explicated in the following chapter.

The Ways and Means amendment of Title III was constructed primarily by Representatives Tom Downey, the Human Resources Subcommittee chair, and George Miller, chair of the Select Committee on Children, Youth, and Families. It subsequently became known as the *Downey Ways and Means Alternative* (CDF 1990a; 1990b). This alternative measure assumed the thrust of Representative Downey's earlier proposed bill that advocated a tax-based approach to child care, in conjunction with the expansion of funding through the Social Services Block Grant, which is under the jurisdiction of the Ways and Means Committee.

The Committee on Ways and Means reported H.R. 3 with amendments on September 7, 1989. The fall of 1989 proved a quagmire for child care legislation. With an impending budget reconciliation bill, House members hoped to resolve differences between committee versions. Decisions regarding child care legislation's place in the reconciliation measure and budgetary process were forthcoming (CQW 9-23-89, 2465). Meanwhile, the Senate debated the propriety of appropriating funds for child care when S. 5 had not passed the whole congressional body. Funding for child care was eventually included in the appropriations bill (H.R. 2990) for the Departments of Labor, Health, and Human Services (CQW 9-23-89, 2470).

The child advocacy community pressed for passage of child care legislation before Congress adjourned in 1989, as evidenced in the outpouring of telephone calls, telegrams, and letters from the NAEYC October conference in Atlanta and the rallying efforts of CDF and its alliance members. In November, the two House proposals were packaged into the budget reconciliation bill (H.R. 3299). Negotiators for the Senate and the House Education and Labor Committee laboriously arrived at a much celebrated compromise agreement on November

9, 1989, commonly known as the *Dodd-Hatch-Hawkins Agreement* (CQW 11-11-90, 3070; CQW 11-18-89, 3162; CDF 1990a; 1990b).

The House agreed to adopt much of the Senate language with the assumption that the deep differences over church-state language would be fought out on the floor through the amendment process. Nevertheless, this milestone agreement did not assuage the differences between respective proponents of the block grant and Ways and Means Committee approaches. On the insistence of Senate Finance Committee members, the conferees eventually removed the child care package from reconciliation consideration. The Senate members refused to negotiate the controversial approaches to child care within the context of the reconciliation bill (CQW 11-11-90, 3070; CQW 11-18-89, 3162; CQW 12-2-89, 3303).

In spite of the progress made between the Senate Labor and Human Resources Committee and the House Education and Labor Committee, the tax provisions could not be settled between the two chambers in time for either reconciliation or the passage of free standing legislation. The first session of the 101st Congress adjourned without the passage of child care legislation. Instead, bitter sentiments remained as a vestige of the futile and distasteful battle. Ways and Means Committee members Downey and Miller became the targets of criticism levied by Marian Wright Edelman, the discouraged leader of the alliance. More optimistic House and Senate leaders vowed to give child care a high priority in the new year (CQW 11-11-90, 3070; CQW 11-18-89, 3162; CQW 12-1-89, 3303).

At the onset of the new session, Representatives Downey and Miller of the House Ways and Means Committee steadfastly refused to yield, although much pressure was placed on them to make a "Children's Compromise" (CDF 1990a; 1990b). Finally, the much awaited House compromise was reached in March 1990 by merging the two competing measures. The Ways and Means Committee approach formed Title III.[9] H.R. 3 passed the House of Representatives on March 29, 1990, by a count of 265–145. An administration backed substitute by Representatives Stenholm and Shaw was defeated by 195–225. An earlier version of this Stenholm-Shaw bill had failed in the fall of 1989 (CQW 10-7-89, 2639–2640; CQW 3-31-90, 998–1001).

The House sent H.R. 3 to conference on May 9, 1990 (CQW 5-12-90, 1479). A June 1990 report, "Highlights of Labor Committee Conference Agreements on Child Care," released by the Senate Labor and Human Resources Subcommittee on Children, Family, Drugs and Alcoholism indicated agreement on a compromise act that would be divided into at least four titles according to the following components: Head Start, Early Childhood Education, a Child Care Block Grant, and a Public-Private Partnership funding provision.

Under Title I, Head Start would be expanded to provide full workday and full calendar year service. Title II granted sponsorship to state education agencies through the Chapter I funding formula to be distributed to local educational agencies that, in turn, would be responsible for the coordination of other programs in the service area. Title III provided funds for states to distribute through grants, contracts, or certificates. Families with children under age 13 with an income less than 75 percent of the state median income would be eligible for funding or service. Families below the poverty line would be provided free services. Eligible sponsors included public and private agencies, for-profit and nonprofit operators, schools, family day care homes, and churches. A separate title authorized $25 million for "public-private partnership activities."

During the conferencing process between the House and Senate, the already complicated negotiations on child care became more mired. The Senate Finance Committee members proposed that Title III of the June agreement that granted funds to states to increase the supply of child care be operated through Title IV of the Social Security Act, rather than through those mechanisms already passed by each body. The Senate version had adapted the new grant program approach and the House, after much negotiation, had approved dispersion of funds through Title XX of the Social Security Act, which is the Social Services Block Grant (CQW, 9-8-90, 2837; CQW 11-3-90, 3701, 3721–3722; CQW 10-27-90, 3605–3606).

During the quagmire presented in the House-Senate negotiations, the Senate and the White House came to their own accord on child care in mid-October (CDF 1990n; "Senate, White House Agree on Child Care" 1990). Negotiations on child care were only one of many politically volatile issues being undertaken at the time. All matters took second seat to the overriding negotiations on the budget deficit and the looming presence of the unsettled Persian Gulf crisis. Domestic issues such as child care were tabled with these two grave and threatening problems. Civil rights, a related policy issue, was being considered concurrently with the child care legislation. The proposed Civil Rights Act (S. 2104, H.R. 4000), was eventually vetoed by President Bush and sustained by the Senate with a 66–34 vote on October 24, 1990. Many liberal backers of child care were caught up in the civil rights debate and concerned about the civil rights implications of the proposed child care language.

Child care legislation was dependent on the outcome of the stalled Omnibus Budget Reconciliation Act. Congress, in unprecedented fashion, toiled around the clock to resolve the budget deficit with bipartisan consensus. Incumbent candidates in the November elections prevailed in Washington to complete the budget package before Congress could adjourn. The weeks of September 30, 1990, through October 27, 1990, were unrivaled in American history for both the chaos experienced and the stalemate confronting members. This enveloping tension over issues of broad economic concern affected the outcome of child care legislation, as the political atmosphere necessitated more than the usual number of compromises. Given the context of the debate in the final days of the fight for child care, the eventual structure of the Child Care and Development Block Grant Act becomes at once more understandable and more historically significant.

Gathered in the Rose Garden, on the afternoon of September 30, 1990, President Bush and congressional leaders announced that they had reached accord on a budget deficit reduction package. Later that same day, both the House and the Senate passed a stopgap spending bill to keep the government running until October 5 in the absence of a 1991 budget; and President Bush signed the extension the following day. In the next few days, the president and Senate Majority Leader George Mitchell appealed to the American people for support of the budget compromise. On the day that the stopgap measure expired, the House voted against the budget compromise in a 254 to 179 vote. Later, the House and Senate passed another stopgap measure; this time the measure would keep the government running until October 12, 1990. President Bush vetoed the second stopgap measure on October 6, the same day that the first stopgap measure expired; thus, the government was officially shut down. The House failed to override the President's veto by 6 votes (Apple 1990b, A11).

Literally working around the clock, the House passed a Democratic-proposed budget resolution on October 8, 1990, by a 250 to 164 vote. The resolution was similar to the earlier resolution that had been rejected, but it did not include the package of necessary tax increases and spending cuts. Instead, the resolution offered a broad outline for deficit reduction that needed further work by congressional committees to define the specifics. On October 9, Congress passed yet another stopgap measure enabling the government to operate through October 19, 1990; and President Bush signed this measure on October 9 (Apple 1990b, A11).

On the same day that he signed House Joint Resolution 666, President Bush announced at a news conference that he would be willing to compromise on the budget in favor of income tax rate increases, if Congress would reduce the capital gains tax rates. Later in the afternoon, the president reversed himself, which caused major political unrest for both parties (Apple 1990b, A11). Throughout all of these twists and turns in budget negotiations, child care advocates and conference committee members had to propose financial plans for the grant and tax components of the tabled child care legislation. The political feasibility and fiscal possibility of child care legislation hinged on resolution of the budget impasse. Three more House Joint Resolutions were needed as stopgap measures before the Omnibus Budget Reconciliation Act became law.[10]

While the Senate and House continued to negotiate the approach to financing and other undisclosed issues, the Senate and White House arrived at an agreement on child care legislation in mid-October 1990. The Senate-White House compromise authorized $750 million for fiscal year 1991, $825 million for 1992, $925 million for 1993, and such sums as would be necessary for the next two fiscal years. States would receive money based on number of children and school lunch recipients. Twenty-five percent of the allotment would be reserved for (1) quality improvement, and (2) early childhood–latchkey services, with a minimum level of allotment of at least 10 percent for each of the two categories. The remainder of the block grant could be used at the state's discretion. The sponsor would be the lead agency designated by the state. State plans would delineate approaches to coordination among agencies and funding streams that would supplement and not supplant existing programs; local consultation with respect to the use of funds; targeting children with low income and special needs; fee scales; use of funds; use of quality reserves; and provider payment-reimbursement procedures. Standards would be set by the states, but must cover designated health and safety issues. The compromise language maximized parental choice within a system composed of a wide range of providers (CDF 1990n).

With a Senate–White House compromise, the House was left in a weakened position for negotiations, especially as the 101st Congressional Session was coming to a close and the child care advocacy coalition was lobbying relentlessly. The final Child Care and Development Block Grant agreement between the House, the Senate, and the White House was reached on October 20, 1990. The agreement did not deviate greatly from the Senate–White House compromise, but was a major departure from the Labor Committee Conference agreement announced in June 1990.

The final version of child care legislation, known as the Child Care and Development Block Grant Act of 1990 (PL 101-508) amended Chapter 8 of subtitle A of Title IV of the Omnibus Budget Reconciliation Act of 1981 (PL 97-35). Congress resolved the debate over child care funding by earmarking $732 million for fiscal year 1991, with slightly larger appropriations scheduled for the following years. The new act defined eligible children to include children of working parents below age 13, whose family income does not exceed 75 percent of the state median income for a family of that size (Section 658P (4)). The final act provided that funds are to be distributed according to a slightly different split than the Senate-White House compromise proposed; however, the total appropriated amount of funds remained the same. Seventy-five percent of the total funds are reserved for providing child care services and increasing the avail-ability and quality of care through the use of grants, contracts, or certificates for any licensed provider within a maximum range of providers (Sections 658E(c)(3)(B), 658P(2), and 658P(5)). Twenty-five percent of the total funds are reserved for early childhood development services and latchkey programs and quality improvement (Section 658E(c)(3)(e)). Of the early childhood–latchkey reserve, at least 75 percent must be reserved for early childhood development and latchkey programs through the provision of contracts or grants (Section 658H(a)). Priority in awarding grants or contracts for development and latchkey programs will be given to geographic areas eligible for Chapter I grants pursuant to the Elementary and Secondary Education Act of 1965. At least 20 percent of the early development and latchkey reserve must be directed toward quality improvement in one or more of the following areas: resource and referral programs; grants or loans to child care providers to assist in meeting state and local child care standards; compliance monitoring, training, and staff com-pensation (Section 658G(1)–(5)).

Conspicuously missing from the Child Care and Development Block Grant is an increased role for the public schools. House efforts led by Representative Gus Hawkins to ensure a strong, school-based component were eliminated in the compromise bill. Seventy-five percent of the 25 percent reserved for latchkey and early childhood education may be targeted for school sponsorship, but it is not mandated by the statute. The agency designated by the state plan as the lead agency, in turn, may delegate authority to the schools for this portion of the grant. The option of designating a state's department of education, for example, is suggested by the statement of those that conferenced and constructed the final version of the act:

A state may assign responsibility for the administration of early childhood development and latchkey programs to an agency other than the lead agency, such as an agency that has experience in the administration of existing education or preschool programs. (*Congressional Record* 10-26-90, "Statement of Managers," H12691)

Equally relevant to the debate over sponsorship of child care is the inclusion of controversial language in the block grant that authorizes the use of certificates for sectarian child care programs. Each state must design a plan for the distribution of funding between the contracts or grants to providers of child care services and certificates to consumers of child care services. The state plan must include provisions for the use of child care certificates. The use of certificates is optional for eligible parents (Section 658 E(c)(2)(A)).

With agreement on child care as set forth in the Child Care and Development Block Grant, Congress finally passed, and the president signed into law, the Omnibus Budget Reconciliation Act of 1990 on October 27, 1990, and November 5, 1990, respectively. Included in OBRA 1990 is a landmark tax component for child care that benefited low income families in three ways that combined the president's proposed changes with those introduced by Senate and House members. The Earned Income Tax Credit (EITC) was expanded to include larger credits for working families; families with two or more children will receive a larger basic credit amount. This expansion of the child care tax credit is estimated to cost $12.4 billion in revenue loss over the next five years. In addition to this expansion, a young child supplement, commonly referred to as the *wee tot* credit was added to the EITC. Families have the option of claiming the wee tot credit for children under age 1 if they do not claim that child under the dependent care credit. The young child supplement is projected to cost $700 million over a five year period. A health insurance supplement was also instituted at a cost of $5.2 billion over five years. Low income families may claim this health insurance credit to offset costs of private health insurance coverage (*Congressional Record* 10-26-90, H 12711-14; National Women's Law Center 1990; CDF 1990f; Pear 1990, 14).

The measure, acclaimed as the largest federal deficit reduction in American history, was welcomed by many liberals as representative of a long-awaited shift in social policy:

The deficit-reduction bill passed today by Congress will touch almost everyone in the United States, from young children to frail elderly people, as well as farmers, bankers, college students, war veterans and foreign tourists visiting this country.

The bill has been promoted as a way to help save nearly $500 billion over five years, but it is also a grand statement of social policy and political priorities.

The measure, which includes higher taxes and spending cuts is notable for its relative generosity to poor children, who will benefit from $18 billion in new tax credits for low-income families over the next five years and from an expansion in health and insurance coverage for such families under Medicaid. (Pear 1990, 1)

The responses of various interest groups to this legislative milestone for children and families reflected their reasons for both celebration and concern, their political gains and losses. The October 29, 1990 press release by CDF, headed "Children's Defense Fund Hails New Child Care Law as Historic Step: Children Get off on Right Foot in the New Decade," read:

The new child care law President Bush is expected to sign as part of the Omnibus Reconciliation Act, is one of the most significant pro-family, antipoverty legislative initiatives ever enacted. . . . "With the enactment of this legislation, the needs of hard-working, struggling American families finally have climbed towards the top of the political agenda," said Marian Wright Edelman, President of the Children's Defense Fund. "It contains all the essentials on which to build a strong family support system that works for parents and nurtures children.". . . "Enactment of this legislation is a historic political win for families," Edelman said. "Washington lawmakers now have the opportunity to make the 1990s a decade of progress for American Children." (CDF 1990e)

The National Association for the Education of Young Children reported a summation of the act in the "Washington Update" section of the November 1990 issue of *Young Children* under the heading, "Child Care Legislation: Success at Last!"

Flash! For the first time in twenty years, comprehensive federal child care legislation has been successfully passed by the Congress and signed by the President. The agreement includes a new direct Child Care and Development Block Grant. It will give states money to provide families assistance with child care costs and to improve the quality and availability of services. . . . Significantly, many aspects of the earlier conference agreement between the Education and Labor and Labor and Human Resources committees have been retained. All funds will go directly to the states, rather than a percentage of funds allocated directly to Head Start programs and public schools to expand their child care services. Head Start and public schools would be eligible providers along with all other providers. (NAEYC 1990, 61)

With a vastly different voice, the education community (which has not been traditionally linked with the early childhood education community) focused on the Senate-White House compromise that formed the foundation of the final measure. In *Education Week*, Deborah Cohen reported:

While hailed by child-advocacy groups as a significant step in ensuring a federal role in improving child-care services, the agreement evoked disappointment from education groups that have sought a greater role for schools in the provision of early-childhood-education and "latchkey" programs.

To overcome White House resistance, Senate leaders watered down components of their chamber's bills that would have set aside funds for school-based programs and for an expansion of Head Start to offer full-day, full year programs. (D. L. Cohen 1990f, 1, 24)

The *Education Week* article proceeded to quote various proponents of the lost school based and Head Start components of H.R. 3. Representative Hawkins released the following thoughts about the Senate–White House agreement to the press:

I am disappointed with the compromise reached by the Senate and the White House on a child care bill. I believe that the compromise pales in comparison to the agreement reached by the Education and Labor and Labor and Human Resources subconference on H.R. 3. . . . Under the White House compromise, there is no expansion of Head Start for full-day care. . . . The public schools are part of the solution to the enormous latchkey problem. The schools are a logical partner to provide before- and after-school care as well as early childhood programs. Under the agreement there is no meaningful role for the schools. (Hawkins 1990)

The *Education Week* article (Cohen 1990f) also reported the views of the National Parent and Teacher Association and the National Association of School Boards of Education. Maribeth Oakes, a government relations specialist with the National PTA, expressed disappointment that the schools were not singled out for special funding measures. Instead, schools would have to compete with religious institutions and for-profit and nonprofit providers for funds. Oakes questioned the congruity of the Senate–White House agreement with the previously stated goal of the President and the governors that all children begin school ready to learn. From the viewpoint of the National PTA, the Senate–White House accord negated the importance of the education function of child care and the role of the public schools in addressing early childhood and child care concerns. Dorothy Clarke, a legislative analyst with the National Schools Boards Association, lamented the lost potential of the role of the schools that had been an important component of H.R. 3, but traded in the Senate–White House agreement. The *Education Week* article concluded by highlighting the dissension that remained over the inclusion of vouchers and permissive church-state language.

Various legislative measures underwent much debate and change before final passage of the Child Care and Development Block Grant Act of 1990. This act represents the first federal program specifically targeted for the delivery of child care services, other than the war related Lanham Act of 1941. Throughout the twenty-one years of debate over the approach to funding child care, the sponsorship issue remained divisive and controversial; and this pattern continued in the fight to enact the Child Care and Development Block Grant Act. The subsequent chapters of this book will examine the conflictive positions held by the various sponsors and their respective interest groups during the long legislative battle surrounding the CCDBG. The analysis also will illustrate the historical basis for these respective positions and reveal the functional gains and losses accomplished by the many compromises along the way. With the care of young children at stake, the remarkably long duration of the debate, the investment of so many participants, the compromise, and the process by which it was achieved, merit close scrutiny. The precedent for this struggle, which can be found in similar efforts in the past, requires examination. This legislation sets the nation forward on the path to building a delivery system for child care and, therefore, is of significance for future policy formation. A brief synopsis of the contenders' claims to sponsorship indicates the discord that will be examined subsequently in more depth.

The most troublesome issue among the sponsors and supporters of ABC and H.R. 3. has been the constitutional issue of church and state separation. The use of public funds in church sponsored child care is complicated, open to interpretation, and emotionally charged. In fact, the language in the finalized legislation will be subject to constitutional challenges in the courts.

There also has been debate as to the extent to which employers should be given tax incentives and tax breaks if they already are the beneficiaries of child care centers. Proponents of corporate sponsorship argue for the maximum employer sponsorship, with the a corresponding amount of government financial support or incentives. The different versions of legislation allocated different amounts for the development of employer sponsorship.

The issue of nonprofit involvement has been openly debated in relation to the controversy over the proposed expansion of Title XX, or the development of a newly designed infrastructure for child care services. The intensity of the split over funding approaches among so-called liberal Democrats is rooted in ideological perspectives and views about the function of child care and the structure of the social service system.

It appears that the for-profit sponsors did not need to lobby as hard as in the past. However, as in the case of church sponsorship, each bill had to contend with the issue of whether federal funds should go toward the support of proprietary centers. This debate has taken place in other social service fields, in particular nursing homes. For-profit firms are eligible participants in the final version of the act, although both the Senate and House bills originally had been structured to prohibit the proprietary sector's involvement. Throughout the debate, the private sector vested much energy in the negotiations over standards and the maintenance of the multiple sponsor system of delivering child care services, which had developed informally over the preceding twenty years.

The public school question drew significant attention because the Hawkins approach purposefully built on the public school system; in contrast, the ABC bill did not. Legislators guardedly drafted bills that delegated a certain limited amount of power and jurisdiction to the schools. Interestingly, some of the strongest school based approaches developed over the years were viewed in the historical context as merely complimentary to the major pieces of legislation or failed to emerge with enough political clout to compete with H.R. 3 and S. 5. Up until the final stages of negotiation, the degree to which the schools should be given special consideration (or power) in the delivery system proved conflictual. Negotiations between the Senate and the House during the summer of 1990 wrestled with the issue. Yet, after an agreement that included the House title for school based care was finally reached, the Senate conferred with the administration and backed down on the inclusion of a school based title.

In the end, the schools lost their case for concentrated power to organize and deliver child care. The predominant ideological beliefs in parental choice and religious child rearing obtained dominance over the American belief in public schooling. As of this historic juncture, the under-6 population is viewed as a population that should remain detached from the public school system. The political process on the federal level failed to promote the education function of child care over the religious function. The multiple functions of child care and the structure-function connections dominated the debates and will continue to affect the delivery of the service on the state level for years to come. Given the many points of controversy in drafting such wide-reaching and precedent-setting child care legislation near the end of the twentieth century, the remaining portions of the book are directed toward providing historical insight into this development and highlighting the significant implications for future policy development.

NOTES

1. According to the information available to senators during the recent debates over child care, the last time that Congress appropriated funds for child care before the celebrated 1990 act was in 1943 (*Congressional Record* 6-23-89, S 7395 S 7470). Most writers refer to the Lanham Act of 1941. On June 23, 1989, Senator Dodd made the following comment on the Senate floor:

[F]or the first time in forty-six years, we may have a major child-care effort.

I took note the other evening that the last time that a major child-care bill was enacted into law and was signed by the President was in June 1943.

It was a child-care bill that was sponsored by Senator Thomas of Utah. It was passed on the floor of the Senate on June 30, 1943 in the middle of World War II. The Senate allocated $20 million in the middle of the war effort for child care for American citizens. It passed on a voice vote. It was not even a recorded vote, Mr. President.

That was how strongly that legislation was supported. . . . (Dodd quoted in *Congressional Record* 6-23-89, S 7395)

Senator Riegle referred to the same action, but referenced it as June 29, 1943:

World War II marked the beginning of the greatest economic expansion in the history of the world; World War II also marked the last time this country, the site of that expansion, had a national child-care policy. On June 29, 1943, this body passed by voice vote a $20 million child-care bill. It was passed because mothers were needed to aid in the war production effort and the Nation recognized that the children of those mothers needed quality care. (Riegle quoted in *Congressional Record* 6-23-89, S 7470)

On researching the history of the Lanham Act in *Acts of Congress* (p.1129), the act was initiated on October 14, 1940 with the intent to provide public war housing. Amendments were added to the act in subsequent years from April 29, 1942 through August 22, 1974. The 1943 date of the two senators is consistent with the legislative history provided in *Senate Report* 100-484 (p. 54) and *Senate Report* 101-17 (p. 26).

2.   *See* footnote 13 in Norgren (1981, 131).

3.   Norgren cites Gilbert Y. Steiner in "Day Care Centers: Hype or Hope?" *Transaction* 8(July–August 1971): 51.

4.   The year following the failure of the Child and Family Services Act revolved around the implementation of federal staffing requirements for federally funded child care centers. On September 7, 1976, President Ford signed legislation (H.R. 12455–PL 94-401) which authorized $240 million of federal money for child care centers established for low income children. Ford had vetoed an earlier version of the bill that would have required states to meet federal standards (see CQA 1977, 620–628). After the 1976 statute, a second extension of time was provided in a 1977 statute that also continued the funding of the centers (CQA 1977, 489). The years between 1977 and 1990 continued to involve debate over the appropriateness of federal standards and the definition of standards. For detailed history of the debate over regulations, see the following two sources: John R. Nelson, Jr., "The Politics of Federal Day Care Regulations," in Edward F. Zigler and Edmund W. Gordon, eds., *Day Care: Scientific and Social Policy Issues* (Boston: Auburn House Publishing Co., 1982), pp. 267–306; and, Deborah Phillips and Edward Zigler, "The Checkered History of Federal Child Care Regulation," in Ernest Z. Rothkopt ed., *Review of Research in Education,* vol. 14, (Washington, D.C.: American Educational Research Association, 1987), pp. 3–41.

5.   For a complete listing of lobbying organizations at various points in time, see Steiner (1976, 99–102) and Appendixes A–E. Steiner discusses how Edelman pushed for the Mondale bill in 1971. Since that time she developed the nonprofit children's lobby group, the Children's Defense Fund. For a detailed biographical sketch of Edelman, see

Calvin Tomkins' article, "A Sense of Urgency," *The New Yorker* (March 27, 1989), pp. 48–74.

6.   Sections 654 of the Head Start Act is codified in 42 U.S.C 9849.

7.   H.R. 3 eventually became the house vehicle for child care legislation, rather than H.R. 30.

8.   For further information on legislative initiatives, see Sharon Stephan, Karen Spar, Anne Stewart, and Marie E. Morris, *Child Day Care: Summaries of Selected Major Bills in the 100th Congress*, published by the Congressional Research Service (CRS 1988); Anne C. Stewart's *Child Care: An Analysis of Major Issues and Policy Options Considered by the 100th Congress* (CRS 1989a); and, Anne C. Stewart's *Child Day Care* (CRS 1990a). See also Barbara Willer's comparative analyses of legislation, published by the National Association for the Education of Young Children on the following dates: March 3, 1988, January 31, 1989; March 31, 1989; July 29, 1989. For an analysis of the legislative activity in 1989, see Willer's, "Federal Comprehensive Child Care Legislation: Much Success in 1989 but More Work Ahead in 1990" in the January 1990 issue of *Young Children*. The Congressional Research Service (CRS 1990b) published an analysis of H.R. 3 and S. 5 on May 8, 1990, revised on May 23, 1990, *Summary Comparison of H.R. 3, as Passed by the House and as Passed by the Senate: Child Care and Other Provisions*, by Anne Stewart, Marie Morris, and David Ackerman.

9.   For a summary of the provisions, see CQW 4-7-90, 1097–1099.

10.   The six House Joint Resolutions (HJ Res) were signed during the eventful month of October 1990: HJ Res 655 (10-1-90 through 10-4-90); HJ Res 660, which was vetoed by the President (10-5-90 through 10-12-90); HJ Res 666 (10-9-90 through 10-19-90); HJ Res 677 (10-19-90 through 10-24-90); HJ Res 681 (10-25-90 through 10-27-90); and HJ Res 687 (10-28-90 through 11-5-90).

3. The Public-Nonprofit Sponsorship Position in the Contemporary Debate over Child Care Services

As stated in the first chapter, the public welfare system and the voluntary system of nonprofit organizations have been the traditional sponsors of child care in the United States. The welfare system has the longest tie to the service stemming from the sponsorship of the day nurseries. This welfare–social service system, as presently constructed, entails a myriad of child care related programs.

Until the passage of the Child Care and Development Block Grant and the Child Care Entitlement Grant, the most significant federal funding of direct services for child care was through Title XX of the Social Security Act (SSA). Title XX is a social services block grant amendment to the SSA enacted in 1975. At the time of its enactment, Title XX provided an innovative approach in the provision of social services because of the flexibility it provided states and its broad coverage of social service programs that did not rely on the standard categorical funding system (Nelson 1982, 282–284). When instituted, states matched the 75 percent grant from the federal government with 25 percent in matching funds. However, the 1981 Omnibus Budget Reconciliation Act did away with the state match, which decreased the amount of funds available for social programs (Kahn and Kamerman 1987, 20). Each state was responsible for allocating the funding among competing social services of which child care is one such service.

Title XX is limited to the low income population with eligibility requirements set by each state. Child care providers contract with state agencies or local delegates for funding. Recipients of Title XX funding must meet state and local standards; there are no federal standards. This lack of federal standards creates a delivery of services that is uneven and substandard in quality

(Kamerman and Kahn 1987; Blank and Wilkins 1986; Blank, Savage and Wilkins 1988; CDF 1990h; 1990i).[1] Providers can be from the for-profit or nonprofit sector. The 1981 reforms cut Title XX funding by 20 percent. According to the most recent Children's Defense Fund survey of state patterns in child care funding, the demand for services has risen, but funding has remained inadequate in spite of minor boosts since the 1981 cuts:

The Title XX pie suffered a one-fifth reduction in FY 1982, and since then has received only two modest increases, not enough to offset the impact of either that cut or of years of inflation. After adjusting for inflation, the federal Title XX appropriation for FY 1988 is less than half of that for FY 1977. . . . Even before the deep cuts, Title XX-funded child care programs in FY 1977 served only 12 percent of the 3.3 million poor children younger than age six . . . virtually the same amount of [inflation-adjusted] federal and state dollars were available in 1988 that were available in 1981 to serve families needing child care assistance. (Blank, Savage and Wilkins 1988, 5)

The other major federal direct service to preschool children is Project Head Start. Head Start is not, however, a child care program. Allocation decisions for Head Start have centered on whether to increase the number of children served by half-day programs versus meeting a smaller percentage of children for full-day care. Full-day services have been provided and utilized by a segment of the Head Start population since 1982 (U.S. Department of Health and Human Services 1989). The projected 1989 enrollment in Head Start programs was 452,314 children with a budget of $1,235 million. The average projected cost per child was estimated at $2,664 (U.S. Department of Health and Human Services 1989). The Children's Defense Fund reported in 1990 that only one in six eligible children were served by Head Start funding (CDF 1990i, 35).

The expansion of Head Start to serve children for the full workday was planned as part of Representative Hawkins's Early Childhood and Development Act (H.R. 3), but was not included in the final child care legislation. Instead, Head Start received an infusion of funds through the Augustus F. Hawkins Human Services Reauthorization Act of 1990, which was signed into law on November 3, 1990 (P.L. 101-501). The act provides annual authorizations that increase to over $7 billion by fiscal year 1994 (*House Report* 101-816; PL 101-501). A landmark component of the Reauthorization Act was the authorization of funding to provide Head Start services to all eligible 3 to 5 year olds by 1994. The act provided funds for the training and development of staff, quality improvement, increasing staff compensation, transportation, parent-child centers to serve infants and toddlers, research, and the establishment of a demonstration Head Start transition project. The success of Head Start is well recognized, but the program fails to meet the all-day care needs of many Head Start children and families. The failure to include a direct provision for extending the Head Start day in either the Human Services Reauthorization Act of 1990 or the Child Care and Development Block Grant of 1990 necessitates the development of wrap-around programs through the coordinated use of funds available from Title XX, the CCDBG, and the Child Care Entitlement Grant.

Another direct service provided by the federal government is the Child Care Food Program (CCFP). The program is administered by the U.S. Department of Agriculture and directs funding to state agencies with the purpose of supplying wholesome meals to child care centers. Federal regulations cover CCFP and establish eligibility. State agencies contract with local centers, Head Start programs, and sponsors of family day care home systems (Murray 1985, 297–298).

CCFP is a cumbersome program to administer and implement. It involves extensive paperwork as providers must be accountable for numbers served, kind of food, and amount of funds used. State and local laws and regulations govern participation in addition to the federal stipulations (Murray 1985).

The budget cuts of 1981 also affected this program. In a four year period from 1981 through 1985, $130 million a year was cut from the CCFP budget. The reductions caused some centers to close and others to raise their fees (CDF 1986, 184–185). In 1980, $239 million was expended on the Child Care Food Program. In 1986, $501 million was expended (Kahn and Kamerman 1987, 19).

Many other federal programs include child care services as part of their mission, but the breadth of such programs is minimal, often reaching very restricted populations. The Congressional Research Service reported a range of twenty-eight to thirty-eight federally funded child care related programs, depending on how child care and the assistance itself is defined (CRS 1989a, 2). For example, Community Development Block Grants (CDBG), administered by the Department of Housing and Urban Development, allows funding for public services of which child care is a component. However, only 10 percent of the overall assistance from the CCDBG can be used for public services. The Job Training Partnership Act of 1981 also includes child care in reference to the sup-portive services eligible candidates are entitled to receive. The Vocational Education Act of 1923 allots funding for the improvement of vocational education, and child care is a specified service for funding under this (Murray 1985, 298–300).

In addition to these direct services for child care provided by the federal government are indirect services that fall into two categories: (1) consumer tax deductions, discussed in Chapter 2; and (2) employer sponsored programs, discussed in the chapter on corporate involvement.

Special consideration is given to the population served by Aid to Families with Dependent Children (AFDC) under federal income tax laws, recently adjusted by OBRA 1990. AFDC allows recipients to deduct child care expenses under an income disregard provision in computing AFDC benefits. The Children's Defense Fund (1986) found three important flaws in the program before OBRA 1990 and the landmark welfare reform legislation of 1988. First, the maximum disregard of $160 per month per child was unrealistic in many communities where decent care exceeded that amount in cost. Second, no standards of quality were established for the care parents may select. Third, the after-the-fact reimbursement stipulation prohibited many families from entering the plan simply because they did not have the necessary out-of-pocket money to purchase care (CDF 1986, 46).

The Family Support Act (FSA), enacted October 13 1988, redefined the terms of the earned income disregard credit for families on AFDC by increasing the disregard of child care costs in the amount of $175 per child per month over the age of 2, and $200 per month for children younger than 2 (42 U.S.C. 602). It also provided for income disregard of advance payment or refund of federal income taxes relating to the earned income tax credit. Additional modifications increasing the amount of the earned income tax credit were addressed through OBRA 1990. The Child Care Entitlement Grant of OBRA 1990 extended the intent of FSA by targeting a total of $300 million per year to states for the provision of child care to families who need the care to work and otherwise would be at risk of becoming dependent on AFDC (*Congressional Record* 10-26-90, H 12491).

The Family Support Act of 1988 is a watershed in welfare reform legislation with particular ramifications for child care:

The Family Support Act's child care mandate, lowered age, and transitional care provisions should dramatically increase the demand for child care services in the states. The FSA provides an unlimited federal match (tied to the state's Medicaid matching rate which ranges from 50–79 percent) for child care expenditures by the state. Thus, the FSA now becomes one of the most significant sources of federal child care funds. (CLASP 1989, 4)

The FSA required all states to set in place a Jobs Opportunities and Basic Skills Training Program (JOBS Program) for AFDC recipients and mandated that parents with young children participate in the program. The age of the child, together with the age and educational experience of the parent, determines the extent of the parent's training requirements. Parents of children 3 and older are required to participate in the training program. Parents of 1- and 2-year-old children will be subject to their state's regulations, but the states could mandate participation in the program for up to twenty hours a week (Blank, Savage and Wilkins 1988, 17; Family Support Act of 1988, PL 100-485).

The Family Support Act includes a child care "guarantee" for parents in the JOBS Program. This guarantee was designed in response to the ongoing problems of welfare recipients caught in a catch 22 system. AFDC parents have had the persistent problem of being unable to seek or maintain employment because of the lack of available or affordable child care arrangements. Many welfare recipients become dependent on the welfare system because of the low wages provided by the jobs open to them and difficulty in obtaining adequate child care. Thus, the Family Support Act specifically seeks to address this pervasive problem of cyclical dependency. Within this statutory framework, child care functions as welfare reform; without the guaranteed provision of child care services the goal of reducing welfare dependency is unattainable.

The realization of welfare reform, however, is dependent on the availability of a sufficient supply of child care facilities, a condition not guaranteed under the Family Support Act. FSA was enacted in anticipation of the passage of the Act for Better Child Care, or a child care legislative vehicle. When Congress failed to act on child care in 1988 or 1989, the intent of the Family Support Act was diminished. The Child Care Act of 1990 closed some of the gaps left open by FSA.

In October 1989, federal regulations were issued for the Family Support Act that concurrently excused from participation those parents of young children who could not secure child care arrangements and sanctioned the use of informal care arrangements (Johnson 1989; *Federal Register* 10-13-89, 42263–42267). The shortcomings in FSA and the regulations jeopardize the intent of the law and place some children and families at greater risk than others. Teen-age mothers and single women constitute a large percentage of the AFDC population; without government support these women are particularly vulnerable to the aforementioned cycle of poverty. It is common knowledge that a contributing factor to the child care supply problem is the inaccessibility of the traditional back-up support for child care arrangements: grandmothers and other relatives. Grandparents and other mature relatives are no longer assumed to be available to provide care for their grandchildren for two reasons: they often are employed themselves or live in a different city from the target population. Economic pressures and the success of the women's movement have contributed to the high employment rate of women across all ages and social classes.

Poor teen-age mothers often are the daughters of young women in their prime who themselves are employed or in training and, therefore, unavailable to look after their new grandchildren (Johnson 1989, 12). An intent of FSA was to enable teen-age mothers to complete high school. Yet, without the adequate provision of child care facilities, this intent cannot be actualized. Low income teen-age mothers are left to compete in the sparse child care market without buying power, often without the education or maturity necessary to make informed decisions about quality of care or without the clout to insist on reasoned choices. Piecing together child care arrangements is a monumental task for many single parents and married couples; teen parents have the additional burdens of coping with school and adolescence. When child care is viewed as only a welfare reform measure, and as such lacks the necessary pieces of complementary legislation to assure the adequate supply of high quality centers, targeted families lose; and the class system of society that mistreats children of the poor is perpetuated.

The federal government's investment in welfare reform through the Family Support Act was limited in practice (CLASP 1989; Cooper 1989c), until the passage of the Child Care Entitlement Program and the Child Care and Development Block Grant in 1990. FSA not only failed to address the supply side of the child care problem, it also lacked a provision for monitoring and regulating the child care selected by participants. The American work ethic was pushed for welfare mothers, yet their children were directed to an arbitrary child care setting. Insufficient attention and concern had been given to the needs of the welfare mother's children. Child care was included in the FSA in its purest welfare reform function.

Child care serves as a means to the end of dependency on welfare, but this end appears unreachable in a system that shuttles parents away from their young without a clearly conceived plan for the children's well-being. The Family Support Act could not function adequately on its own without a companion bill that envisioned child care in its social service and education functions. The limited view of child care as welfare reform places the population of children most at risk at even greater risk. In "Child Care Shortage Clouds Future of Welfare Program," Julie Johnson (1989), a reporter for *The New York Times*, quoted Representative George Miller's critique of the Bush administration's fiscal conservatism, which was acutely demonstrated in the FSA's failure to provide the necessary support structure to make its own goals attainable:

I think that they are conflicted between their ideological desire or belief that women should be at work and their unwillingness to pay for services that are necessary to enable low-income women to work. (Miller cited in Johnson 1989, 2)

The implementation problems of FSA will have negative consequences for children and families unless high quality child care programs are available. Those parents that fail to find adequate child care arrangements will be in the position of selecting between a setting of substandard quality for their offspring or not participating in the educational or vocational opportunities available to them (if that is an option in their state given the age of their children).

Securing high quality child care is a critical concern of all families and a laborious, frustrating task for all in today's child care market. The federal regulations for FSA stipulated that (1) centers must meet basic state and local standards in the areas of safety and health; (2) centers develop guidelines for family care programs (*Federal Register* 10-13-90, 42266). Some children are at greater risk than their peers of being placed in substandard settings, and the FSA did not adequately protect these overlapping groups: infants, toddlers, and children of teen-age parents. The Health and Human Services regulations for the FSA had been criticized for encouraging the utilization of the informal, unpaid child care provider market (Blank and Ebb 1989, 7). The criticism leveled against the proposed regulations regarding the reliance on the informal, unregulated child care market was not acted on in the final regulations.[2]

Once again, a patchwork approach to policy making was adapted in drafting FSA, which further complicated the child care scene, set stumbling blocks for the realization of the program's own goals, and failed to address the supply problem in child care. The eventual passage of the Child Care Entitlement Program and Child Care and Development Block Grant and the tax reforms of OBRA 1990 rectified residual problems in the welfare system.

The enactment of FSA and its relation to the delivery of child care represent a common trend in welfare reform legislation. When child care functions as welfare reform, children's needs are only an afterthought. Developmental concerns do not supersede the goal of reducing welfare dependency, a goal more closely tied to the objective of assuring cost efficiency and effectiveness in government spending (Phillips and Zigler 1987, 7–10). Linking child care's welfare reform function with the public welfare system continuously restricts the development of a comprehensive approach to child care that could capitalize on all of the functions child care performs. Furthermore, "the checkered history of federal child care regulation" as described by Phillips and Zigler (1987) in their article of the same title cramped the development of FSA. All of the debates over federal regulations for child care inhibited quality assurances in the newly designed FSA.

Regardless of the problems inherent in any welfare reform legislation, there are many positive attributes of the FSA. As noted earlier, in addition to guaranteeing child care provisions and requiring participation in the JOBS Program for AFDC participants, the Family Support Act raised the amount of the income disregard provision for employed parents receiving AFDC and authorized federal funding for child care subsidies for those families that moved out of the AFDC eligibility bracket. Such parents would be able to receive subsidization for child care on a sliding-fee scale for a twelve month period of time; a component of FSA referred to as the Transitional Child Care Program (TCC). The TCC Program received strong support during the debates over the Family Support Act (Ebb et al. 1990, i). Child welfare advocates succeeded in instituting a number of important safeguards into the legislation. Importantly, the transitional child care services are required to meet the same regulations set for JOBS participants. A center that has an exemption from specific standards must meet basic health and safety standards of the state. Federal grants were offered for fiscal years 1990 and 1991 to upgrade standards and the monitoring capabilities of states. States were expected to match the grant by 10 percent (*Federal Register* 10-13-90, 42267; Blank, Savage and Wilkins 1988, 19).

The implementation of the TCC Program has been problematic for a number of reasons. One of the most significant obstacles has been defining the parameters of eligibility (CLASP 1990; Ebb et al. 1990). After defining who is eligible for services, states need to face the problem of matching the supply of available centers to the number of eligible families. Meeting the demand for slots is further compounded by the issue of quality. As is always the case in the provision of child care services, the consumer is subject to a wide variation in the quality of care available. In the case of TCC under FSA, the state has an expressed and implied mandate to guarantee care that meets minimum standards. Aside from the statute, policy makers must wrestle with a common social welfare problem of delivering the highest available quality of care to a population that is required to accept the services provided to them. Although parental rights to visit centers were guaranteed, the TCC recipients do not have much choice in the care available to them given their income restrictions. Choice regarding infant and toddler care is further complicated by the complexity of both delivering and utilizing the services provided for children of this age group. High quality infant-toddler care is even more expensive than preschool care, and the arrangement of part-time or full-time care poses developmental risk for the children regarding separation (CLASP 1989, 8-10).

Given all of these difficulties in the implementation of TCC and JOBS, the problem remains of continuity of care after the twelve month extension period. In *Transitional Child Care: State Experiences and Emerging Policies Under the Family Support Act* (Ebb et al. 1990), the authors recommend that specific policies be put into place to accommodate this next step in the lives of former welfare recipients. In particular, states should assess their Title XX target populations and designate the TCC families as preferred clients.

The Child Care Entitlement of OBRA 1990 specifically sought to rectify the residual problems of FSA. The entitlement program is projected to cost $1.5

billion over five years. The funding is through Title IV of the Social Security Act (*Congressional Record* 10-26-90, H12491–12492). This grant program falls under the jurisdiction of the House Ways and Means and the Senate Finance Committees. The intention of the entitlement is to prevent at-risk families from becoming dependent on the welfare system.

The previous discussion broadly describes the recently redefined federal role in child care and the diverse number of programs under federal sponsorship. On closer scrutiny, it is clear that the only major source of funding available for direct child care services fell under the Title XX funding stream until the passage of the Child Care and Development Block Grant Act and Child Care Entitlement Grant. The Child Care Food Program is a direct service, but it provides food to established centers; it does not provide child care per se. The other child care related programs are either add-ons to other social services, such as AFDC and Head Start, or indirect services through the tax system. Having described these federal programs, further discussion will analyze the position of nonprofit sponsors. The functions child care serves under Title XX sponsorship are important to understand, because the CCDBG mandates coordination, rather than supplementation of existing programs. An analysis of Title XX and the nonprofit sponsors' positions clarifies the antecedents of the fragmentation of the system that is slowly undergoing coordination and integration.

Logically, established child care providers seek to maintain their position in the child care marketplace. The encroachment of other providers, in particular the public schools, as well as competitors from other sectors, pose real threats to those already delivering child care services. Child care providers within the welfare system, which include voluntary, nonprofit organizations, assert several claims in an effort to maintain their key sponsorship role. First, they have a history and tradition of providing the service that holds them in good stead for further expansion and development. Second, they are reaching the segment of the population most in need and have the capacity to provide the needed family and child development services. The administrative structure is in existence and can administer programs according to licensing standards. Third, nonprofit auspices eliminate the profit motive, thus expending more resources for quality improvement. It has been argued in the past that public money should not be given to for-profit institutions. In keeping with this thinking, the original ABC and H.R. 3 bills did not include for-profit providers as recipients of federal grants.

The Child Welfare League, a large nonprofit organization dedicated to promoting the well-being of children, took a strong stand against for-profit sponsorship of child care during hearings on bills proposed during the 1970s. The Child Welfare League of America is a 70-year-old federation of 570 voluntary and government agencies serving over 2 million children in North America (CWLA 10-3-89). The league recognizes the power of the state to establish and monitor services for children. The organization takes a protective attitude toward children and strives to provide high quality programs that assure the healthy development of the children served. Thus, CWLA sees a need for comprehensive services for children and families. Within this context, the social service function of child care is advocated and promoted. In fact, CWLA has taken positions against the welfare reform function of child care.

Testifying on behalf of the Child Welfare League of America at the Child and Family Service Act hearings in 1975, Joseph H. Reid and Jeanne H. Ellis took the position that the bill should not presume a prime sponsor, and in particular, for-profit organizations should not be eligible for prime sponsorship. They cited the following examples of specific areas of the human services entered into by for-profit sponsors, in which patterns of low quality and questionable care have been distinguishing features: child care, blood banking, methadone clinics, nursing homes, hospitals, correspondence schools, child care institutions, and group homes (U.S. Congress, Committee on Labor and Public Welfare 1975, 190–191). "Enough is known about the poor performance of most for-profit children's services to recommend that no public moneys be provided to for-profit organizations through child services legislation" (Reid and Ellis cited in U.S. Congress, Committee on Labor and Public Welfare 1975, 191).

During the 1978 hearings, the Child Welfare League, represented by the executive director William L. Pierce, reiterated its concern for quality. Pierce stressed the league's concern for setting appropriate standards and voiced apprehension over cutting costs at the expense of children's welfare. The league acknowledged the harmfulness of an underground market in child care that is not licensed or monitored. Pierce summarized the six major concerns of the organization: government should set standards; services should be comprehensive to meet individual and familial needs, thus fulfilling the social service function; more funding and monitoring is needed, not more information and referral agencies; local control should be supported in the interest of the social reform function; there should be no presumed prime sponsor; child care should be seen as a "child benefit" program rather than "employment related"; and cost effectiveness should be viewed over a lifetime of children to ensure future social well-being (U.S. Congress, Committee on Human Resources 1977–78, 696-698). The league advocated a position in favor of the social service and social reform functions, but spoke out against the economic and welfare reform functions.

Although defending the setting of standards, Pierce implicitly acknowledged the nature of the relationship between the state and the family. The state can act as "protector or ultimate guardian in matters affecting the welfare of children"

(U.S. Congress, Committee on Human Resources 1977–78, 715). The government has the right to establish and maintain standards by exercising the benevolent police powers of the individual states and exercising the doctrine of *parens patriae*. These standards of quality reflect functional differences. In the functions of welfare reform and economic interests, the quality of the care of children is not primary; whereas, the functions of social service, education, socialization, and social reform inherently address the quality of the care provided the children and their families. The objectives of welfare reform and the economic function are satisfied by simply providing care under minimum standards.

In hearings on Senator Long's bill in 1971, the Child Welfare League disagreed with the requirement for welfare mothers to work: "Even if a welfare mother's employment could remove her from welfare rolls it would be society's loss not its gain if, in the process, her children were endangered or their development impaired" (U.S. Congress, Committee on Finance 1971, 485). The league argued that welfare reform legislation could include a provision for child care, but that child care should be seen as a separate matter for legislation in its own right. Child care should not be viewed as a "manpower device," and it should not be under the auspices of the Department of Labor, but under the Department of Health, Education and Welfare (U.S. Congress, Committee on Finance 1971, 487).

During the congressional hearings on the Comprehensive Preschool Act of 1969, Ned Goldberg, testifying on behalf of the National Federation of Settlements and Neighborhood Centers, communicated a strong position in favor of the bill, as well as in favor of continued sponsorship of child care services by voluntary agencies: "Each of us, as we testify, has his own special interest. Mine is that early childhood and day care programs continue as a paramount concern and program of voluntary agencies, particularly neighborhood centers and settlements" (U.S. Congress, Committee on Education and Labor 1969–70, 223). Goldberg emphasized the special role of the social service system, and the related needs of child care:

Whatever the setting or agency auspices, it should be made clear that day care services as differentiated from kindergarten and nursery, are a part of child welfare services. Day care must include all services fundamental to child growth and development, including education, health and welfare services, and parent participation. (U.S. Congress, Committee on Education and Labor 1969–70, 223)

Goldberg asserted that social agencies are "uniquely equipped to operate day care services" (p. 224). Their uniqueness derives from their ability to offer multiple

services and to protect the interests of the child. By separating child care from
nursery and kindergarten education, Goldberg articulated the viewpoint that envisioned the educational function as part of, or incidental to, the comprehensive
social service function.

In so differentiating child care from the other early childhood programs,
Goldberg built on the traditional social work orientation, where child care is seen
as providing supplemental care of children. He recognized an overlap between
the two orientations, but acknowledged a substantial difference. His orientation
perpetuates the common association of child care with the social work profession
and the custodial connotation:

We believe it important to differentiate between day care, on the one hand, and nursery
or kindergarten, on the other. While both have common elements of education, health
and welfare, day care's primary role is supplementation of the mother's child care role.
(U.S. Congress, Committee on Education and Labor 1969–70, 224)

In "An Update on Social Work in Day Care," Sheila L. Dobbin and
Andrew J. McCormick (1980) expand on Goldberg's earlier view. Social
workers have changed their ideas about child care and recognize that the service
is needed by a wider segment of the population. Nevertheless, the social service
profession continues to envision child care as a service suited for sponsorship by
social agencies.

When the article was published, Dobbin and McCormick were members of
the Associated Day Care Services (ADCS) organization located in Boston.
ADCS was funded by the United Way to plan, operate, and consolidate child
care services in the metropolitan Boston area. In 1980, seven child care centers
served 400 children under the auspices of ADCS. The authors had assessed the
goals of the social services provided by ADCS. They concluded that child care
services functioned in a preventive manner and reasoned that the agency provided
an integrative approach in delivering the service:

The social service program offers an integrated preventive service to meet the needs of
the children and their families. Day care provides an ideal setting for preventive social
service. Daily contact between parents and staff and the constant awareness of the
individual child's development provide ongoing opportunity to evaluate child and family
functioning, and access for early intervention in problem situations. (Dobbin and
McCormick 1980, 99)

It is clear from this discussion that members of the social welfare
community have acknowledged functional differences when social agencies
sponsor child care services as compared to for-profit firms, education institu-

tions, or employment related sponsorship. This conceptualization of the social welfare profession's role has at once built from its past history and expanded in keeping with contemporary issues and attitudes. The sponsorship of child care services by the social welfare profession under public and voluntary auspices suggests a continuation of its multifunctional approach within the overall goal of offering comprehensive services to children and families.

The social service function of child care is naturally linked to social welfare sponsorship and serves as a primary function of child care under such sponsorship. In the ideal, the social work profession targets its services at the family unit and aims to prevent future problems while offering developmentally sound programs in a community context. Accordingly, the function of social reform would also be furthered. Yet, because the social work profession is dependent on government funding for social services, the population served often remains within the traditional domain of social welfare services in the United States, the low income population.

Targeting those most in need for federal funding is based on two types of thinking. First, political pragmatists would contend that real or perceived fiscal constraints necessitate decisions regarding the allocation of resources according to degree of need. Second, ideological thinking presumes that minimal expenditure on the part of the government is adequate to provide the floor from which individuals and family units can then mobilize and compete. These two underlying assumptions guided the development of a two-tiered system of child care up to the ABC debate and then continued throughout the debate resulting in a block grant targeted at the low income population. The fact that such funding came through is commendable, but the fact that the multiple delivery system and the separate targeting of low income people is maintained leaves open the question of how well the supply of care will be increased and whether a more socioeconomically mixed system of care will develop. The new policy remains within the past mode of thinking as will be seen in the following discussion of Title XX.

Title XX offered a mechanism for the expansion of child care services. Being a social services block grant program, Title XX could either fulfill the welfare reform function of child care or the social service function or both. Morgan (1977) noted the wide-reaching potential of the block grant legislative approach. Title XX was not initiated as welfare related legislation. The block grant mechanism provides the potential for universal accessibility to the service; thus, moving the service out of the welfare model. By providing funding through a grant, it also would be possible to move away from a provider orientation to a consumer orientation that gives to the ultimate users more power and choice (Morgan 1977, 5). The regulations governing dispersion of funds under the act are extremely flexible. In the abstract, a wide range of people could be served under this funding stream. "Because the law governing Title XX expenditures is so flexible, Title XX funded child care can be used to meet the needs of infants through school-age children" (Blank and Wilkins 1986, 40).

Title XX was the most unified stream of funding available for child care from the federal government before the Child Care and Development Block Grant Act. It is a program with potential, but besieged with problems. The role of Title XX was extremely controversial in the drafting of the Act For Better Child Care, as was noted in the previous chapter. In spite of Title XX's potential to be the cornerstone for all government involvement in providing child care services, the program fails to meet existing needs. The major problems in the program are lack of adequate funding; eligibility rules that are exclusionary, inconsistent, and shortsighted even in meeting the goals of welfare reform; and variability in funding by states to complement federal funding.

Title XX, like the Head Start program, had never reached the majority of children in need of child care before the 1982 budget cuts; and, as noted earlier, the number of children served after the cuts was an even lower percentage because of the combined effects of reduced funding, inflation, and increased need. The Children's Defense Fund's periodic state surveys indicated variation among the states in the allocation of resources for child care before 1990, but concluded that the need for increased funding was substantial (Blank and Wilkins 1986, 33; Blank, Savage and Wilkins 1988, 4–9; Kahn and Kamerman 1987, 18–22; CDF 1990h, 50).

The cuts to Title XX resulted in severe administrative consequences, varying in degree across the states. Those states that tried not to reduce the number of children served compensated for loss of revenue by reducing other services to families in poverty or reducing reimbursements to the providers of child care. In compensating for the budget cuts, states made choices that hurt the quality of care provided. Reduction in training funds, lowering standards, and lower reimbursement fees to providers caused more staff turnover and difficulties in recruiting trained caregivers (CDF 1986, 290–291).

Although the potential for building a universally accessible system of child care seemed to exist within Title XX's block grant structure, the program in reality serviced only a limited portion of the low income population. The welfare reform function of child care operated through the Title XX program because the limited available resources were targeted to the lowest income population for the two reasons mentioned earlier.

Eligibility for receipt of Title XX services is set by each state. Many states have a "notch" effect in their regulations; parents benefiting from the child care service often are penalized when their wages increase because they no longer qualify for eligibility. Eligibility rules also defeat Title XX's purpose because they are too restrictive. Some states disqualify parents in training programs or school. Others limit involvement to a certain time period (Morgan 1977, 6; CDF 1986, 290; Blank and Wilkins 1986, 42–43). Such policies prevent families from entering the system of child care and cause others to drop out. Parents are punished for attempting to advance themselves, and children are offered sporadic, inconsistent care. Often times, parents were provided care while in training, but lost such care when the training ended, thus precluding the acceptance of a job. The inconsistency and inefficiency of the system prevents the welfare reform function to be fully satisfied.

Title XX depends on state funding to supplement federal dollars. The ability and willingness of the states to match the federal grant varies, and thereby an uneven delivery system throughout the country has been created. The overall economy of a state dictates its ability to build a viable child care system (Blank and Wilkins 1986, 5). Aside from the economic situation, states attribute different priorities to child care, and the percentage of Title XX funding targeted for child care varies by state (CDF 1986, 288).

In "The Trouble with Title XX," Gwen Morgan (1977) listed twenty-three problems associated with the program. Adapting Morgan's work to this analytic framework, very real difficulties in fulfilling the functions of child care under Title XX came to the surface. Morgan claimed that the common alignment of Title XX with state departments of social service restricted child care to the function of welfare reform and a narrow view of the social service function. The social service function was delivered within the old "pathological" framework, dating back to the early days of the social work profession. Families served by Title XX have been seen as "problematic" in the tradition of the day nursery that temporarily served families with "problems" to solve:

Since the United States has a commitment to the private sector, policymakers avoid government intrusion into the family. Our agencies are therefore all geared to respond to some problem, not to support the healthy, garden variety family. It would be difficult for existing agencies to offer support for families without identifying problems. An exception is the Education agency, but here there is a tendency to supplant the family for a narrowly defined purpose: learning. This agency looks at the child, too often, out of the family context. (Morgan 1977, 7)

The social reform function of child care has also been stifled under Title XX due to the relationship of federal and state funding. The state control of funds tends to reduce community planning on the local level for the coordination of needs and services with states varying in the ratio of state to local monies committed. Morgan recognized the advantages of state money, but cautioned against the lack of local financial participation:

Local financial participation produces a local involvement and commitment to stability which is desirable for certain kinds of services, such as services to the elderly, and child daycare. Local financing may be difficult to establish, but programs without it are more easily eliminated with shifts in policy trends. (Morgan 1977, 15)

The mandate for state plans and coordination in the CCDBG together with FSA address problems found in the implementation of Title XX.

The potential of creating a universally accessible system of child care through Title XX has not been met in part because states set different fee schedules. Title XX allows for the arrangement of a sliding fee scale, but the states determine upper and lower limits, and the actual amount of the fee to be paid. Title XX's fee schedules and eligibility restrictions perpetuate an income segregated system of child care (Morgan 1977; (Blank and Wilkins 1986; Blank, Savage and Wilkins 1988; Kahn and Kamerman 1987; CDF 1990h):

Our country tends to develop a dual social service in every field, with the middle class using different services than those used by the poor. The services to the poor then have low status, both for the children and the professionals who work in them, but they serve the function of salving our consciences while protecting us from contact with the poor. (Morgan 1977, 10)

As Morgan (1977) and others have repeatedly emphasized, child care services need not follow this dual system pattern of delivery because elements in its history, and in modern times, suggest that it could readily become a universal service. Contemporary society has undergone such a revolution in the work patterns of women across economic strata that child care should be a support service for all income groups. In another system of delivery that breaks away from the dual income level approach, child care could function as social reform and social utility under the liberation-universalization function.

In sum, Title XX limits the full potential of child care and is a difficult program to administer and regulate. There are cash flow problems due to the delayed payment method of financing. Child care under Title XX also suffers from uneven monitoring and licensing. The lack of federal standards too frequently allows for state standards considered minimal by child development experts. Additional problems have included the lack of personnel for monitoring and training. The requirement that the funding flow through one agency has exacerbated coordinating Title XX services with other child care programs. It is hoped that the Child Care Act of 1990 will alleviate some of these problems in delivery.

Morgan also found fault with what she calls the provider orientation of Title XX. The system of "contracting, eligibility determination, and referral is tending more and more to emphasize provider issues and to force parents into feelings of dependency on the system" (Morgan 1977, 11). Morgan's 1977 work foretold the philosophy behind the advocacy movement in the ensuing years. This sentiment against a "provider orientation," coupled with a belief in empowering the poor with the benefits perceived to be enjoyed by the middle class, roused ABC advocates to insist on legislation that guaranteed parental choice. Overall, the drafters of the 1990 legislation elected to increase consumer purchasing power, rather than to increase the supply of centers.

Perhaps the most significant administrative consequences of Title XX are that an income segregated system of child care prevails; the low income population in need of the service is not fully served; and the quality of services varies widely without a guaranteed minimum standard of care nationwide. The quality of the child care provided is questionable and at best uneven, due in large measure to the inconsistency of regulations that vary by state, with many states not in compliance with professionally recognized standards of care.

Having analyzed the Title XX funding mechanism and the social welfare system for its strengths and weaknesses, the function of child care under the social welfare system's auspices becomes clearer. Federal legislation has promoted the welfare reform function of child care through the public welfare and nonprofit delivery system. Although the effects of FSA and the Child Care Act of 1990 cannot be analyzed, the mainstay of the welfare system until 1988 was Title XX, which has been shown to have failed in meeting the goals of welfare reform or the child care needs of the targeted population, let alone the needs of the ever-expanding number of working families in need of child care who do not qualify for federal subsidies.

The social service function also is dominant in the nonprofit sector. This function is met through the work of the sponsoring social agency receiving Title XX funding. However, the social service function's effectiveness is restricted to the narrow population eligible for funding. An inherent conflict exists between the social service and welfare reform functions. Welfare reform is addressed to a subpopulation, but the social service function has a universal potential. Not all families are at risk of becoming dependent on the welfare system or are striving to move out of its dependency. Most working families, however, are in need of the social service function, which in this analytic framework represents a developmental orientation to individual children and family units.

The Title XX linkage casts the social service function in the residual framework that views child care utilization in a pathological light. Until recent years, child care within this context has been seen primarily as "custodial." Yet the social service function is much broader than this stereotypic image. Instead, the social service function meets the affective needs of children and the multiple needs of families by offering additional support services, such as medical care, nutritional care, counseling, and referral information for other social services.

Research indicates that many nonprofit child care centers are offering high quality programs that include the education function (CCEP 1989; Kagan and Newton 1989). Thus, the automatic association of "custodial" care with welfare sponsorship is not justified. The nonprofit delivery system has moved far beyond the scope of the early day nurseries, but still has a long route to travel given the variance in state standards and the availability of qualified staff members.

The level of public funding and the mixture of public and private dollars under CCDBG will need to be studied closely to ascertain how well the three problems of availability, affordability, and quality are being addressed. Limited research suggests that the level at which resources are available and the mix of public and private funding makes a significant difference to the scope and quality of services offered (Kagan and Newton 1989). The fact that the nonprofit sector is composed of two subsystems, public and voluntary, is of critical importance. More research is needed on the quality of programs delivered when measured against these two different types of nonprofit sponsors to clarify the variance of public-private partnerships and their impact on quality control.

Delving further into an examination of the structure-function relationship in this nonprofit sector, it seems on first glance that social reform has functional potential in the sense that local control and community involvement are possible on an agency level. On another level, social reform is not realistic when the sponsoring structure is the welfare system, because this system maintains the economic order to support the status quo.

The social status function is highlighted under welfare sponsorship, because the status of the low income population is at issue. The provision of child care services mediates the recipients' mobility on the social and economic ladder. The social status function is at play not only by maintaining a social structure, but by differentiating welfare mothers as a class unto themselves with special needs.

Social welfare sponsorship promotes the religious function when churches and synagogues contract with Title XX and serve low income families. Child care as a social utility, a consequence of child care's liberation-universalization function, is possible only when the service is open and accessible to all strata of society. The social welfare system, and Title XX in particular, target the lower classes, whereby the economic function operates incidental to welfare reform in those instances when the provision of child care allows welfare recipients to break out of the cycle of dependency.

The significance of the nonprofit claim to the delivery of child care services and the multidimensional functions that child care performs became most apparent in the clash over the House Ways and Means Committee's alternative approach to S. 5 and H.R. 3, which occurred in the winter of 1989–1990. The conflict over funding approaches was one of two primary obstacles in passing a House version of ABC, the other was the dispute over the funding of religiously affiliated centers (Rasky 1989; Eaton 1990a; 1990b; Holmes 1990a; 1990b; Johnston 1989a; 1989b; Willer 1990a).

Downey and Miller's proposal was based on the premise that the funding for child care should be funneled through an existing funding stream (Title XX), which would at once avoid duplication and the problems of an appropriations process (*House Report* 101-190 Parts 1 and 2). Proponents of the Downey Ways and Means Alternative contended that Title XX, as an entitlement program, ensured that funding would always remain available and accessible, rather than subject to the discretion of Congress, as in the appropriations process set forth in ABC. According to the representatives thinking, child care would be further guaranteed through earmarking the entitlement grant's funds. Representative Miller hoped to avoid "overpromising" and "underdelivering," an observable trend in government spending (CQW 7-22-89, 1863).

Supporters of the Dodd-Hawkins-Hatch agreement professed that the earmarking of the Social Services Block Grant would pit the needs of children against the needs of the aged and other deserving groups served by Title XX. In their minds, Title XX's entitlement status was negated by the cap placed on it. In a capped entitlement, funds are distributed to states based on population up to a designated total amount of funds. In 1989, the cap was $2.7 billion, although the reconciliation provisions set $3.3 billion as the cap for fiscal year 1993 (CQW 7-22-89, 1862). Alliance members criticized the Downey-Miller Alternative for three essential reasons: (1) the funds would be "grossly inadequate," thus enabling 400,000 fewer children to be served than the House Leadership Package; (2) it jeopardized quality improvement provisions by placing the program under Ways and Means with its poor record on assuring high quality for child care service, rather than under the Education and Labor Committee; and (3) its primary reliance on the Earned Income Tax Credit (EITC) failed to meet the tripartite demands of affordability, quality, and availability (CDF 1990b, 4–5).

The diverse approaches to funding child care incited much dissension among liberal democrats. Representatives Miller and Downey found themselves on the defensive in a hard hitting lobbying effort by Marian Wright Edelman:

In a blistering three-page memorandum to the lawmakers, Mrs. Edelman, the president of the Children's Defense Fund, blamed them for the Congressional delay, which she called "the latest in a series of efforts you have engaged in to sabotage groundbreaking child care legislation all year for petty jurisdictional and power reasons.

Mr. Downey, who called Mrs. Edelman's memorandum "immature and inaccurate" said the postponement of further work on the bill followed the realization that the many significant disagreements over the bill could not be resolved before adjournment. "We have a number of major issues that did not lend themselves to overnight negotiations," he said. (Johnston 1989, 10)

Members of Edelman's coalition accused the Ways and Means Committee of sacrificing the welfare of children for jurisdictional power. Edelman, determined to push forward with ABC, denounced Miller and Downey of unnecessarily obstructing the passage of the bill out of self-serving interests to maintain control of Title XX child care services, which is under the jurisdiction of the Ways and Means Committee. In "Turf, Not Toddlers, the Issue," Edelman accused the Ways and Means Committee of causing the delay in House action:

Despite the years of work that went into the child care proposal, a few in Congress led by Rep. Tom Downey, D-N.Y., wanted to gut the direct child-care assistance portion of the agreement, cut out 80 percent of its money and replace it with a mere $200 million for the existing Title XX social services block grant program, a program over which Rep. Downey's Ways and Means subcommittee has sole control. Moreover, he rejected compromise offers again and again, and the House already has rejected proposals similar to his.

While it is turf, not toddlers, at issue, the bottom line for families is that hundreds of thousands fewer children would receive child-care assistance and quality assurances for parents would be jeopardized. (Edelman 1989, 7-B)

In an adjoining article on the same page of the Cleveland *Plain Dealer*, Representative Don J. Pease of Oberlin, Ohio, a member of the House Ways and Means Committee, rebutted Edelman in "No, Funding the Bottom Line":

But the money ABC promises is contingent on the annual appropriations process, which imposes its own program priorities. In short, ABC may not be able to deliver what it promises.

The ABC approach is not inherently bad. It is just impractical in a time of severe budgetary pressure. If this were the 1960s, the ABC-style investment in child care with close federal supervision would be in keeping with the trend toward expansive government. Today, however, the public attitude toward government has a strongly consumerist cast. People still recognize when a federal role is appropriate, but they expect their tax dollars to go—as directly as possible—where they will be used most efficiently and effectively. (Pease 1989, 7-B)

Pease contended that the Ways and Means approach was more pragmatic and better targeted those most in need through the expansion of the earned income tax credit portion of the bill.

The confrontation between Edelman and Representatives Downey and Miller received much media coverage and caused a major rift in the communication system between lobbyists and key congressional members (CQW 11-18-90, 3162; Lewis 1990). When approached for his perspective after this clash, Representative Miller rebutted Edelman and her colleagues with a letter to the author in which he addressed his opposition's contentions regarding the content of his proposed legislation, the alleged delay, and the alleged loss of funds for fiscal year 1990. In the letter, he acknowledged the widespread media impact of Edelman's actions, "News reports of jurisdictional disputes and failed compromises have been frequent and harsh, and on more than one occasion, misinformation about the differing proposals have been widely circulated." Miller claimed that the alleged loss of funding set aside for child care was not the case for two reasons. First, funding deadlines already had been missed; and second, nearly all of the "reserved" money for child care already had been committed to antidrug efforts (personal communication with Miller 1990).

The schism between Edelman and the proponents of the Ways and Means bill not only represented disparate views on child care funding, they also reflected differences in ideologies and political strategies (Pease 1990; Lewis 1990). In "Lobbyist's Bitter Attack on Congressmen Reverberates from the 60's to the 90's," Neil A. Lewis described the debate over child care as a collision of old and new liberalism. The resolution of differences in the delivery of child care services as contained in the Child Care and Development Block Grant Act of 1990 is illustrative of the struggle for dominance in contemporary liberal politics. Child care, as a component of the Omnibus Budget Reconciliation Act of 1990, finally emerged as a result of the backlash of social problems resulting from years of neglect under the Reagan administration, and as an example of a resurgence in the "old liberalism" approach to packaging legislation:

Of all the new initiatives, the child care program bears the closest resemblance to legislation molded the old-fashioned way. Financed partially by grants to the states and expansion of an existing tax credit, it was the centerpiece of both Democratic and Republican agendas this year despite a price tag of more than $20 billion over the next five years. The great majority of benefits would go to low-income families through the tax credit. (Rasky 1990b, 4–1)

The actual victors in the old versus new liberalism approach to funding is ambiguous. The jurisdictional disputes over which congressional committees would control the new programs resulted in a compromise that may be construed as a mixed victory for all players. The resultant legislation gave control of the tax credit provisions and the Child Care Entitlement Grant to the House Ways and Means Committee and the Senate Finance Committee. The Child Care and Development Block Grant, which closely follows the intent of the original ABC, was granted to the House Education and Labor Committee and the Senate Labor and Human Resources Committee (DSG 1990c, 2). At each turn in the long process of developing comprehensive child care legislation, compromises were devised on issues of substance regarding amount of funding, scope of funding, target population, program content, and institutional and governmental jurisdictional authority. During the conference committee meetings on S. 5 and H.R. 3 in the second session of the 101st Congress, conferees in the Senate Finance Committee and the House Ways and Means Committee remained at odds. House conferees steadfastly insisted on Title XX as the funding mechanism even though the Senate had rejected that idea a year earlier; and throughout the conference negotiations, the president resisted the idea of a grant program until the bitter end. President Bush would have preferred legislation that relied solely on the tax system (CQW 10-6-90, 3235; CQW 11-3-90, 3722; Cooper 1990b, 6; 1990c, 4).

The public and private nonprofit welfare system's involvement in the delivery of child care provides the foundation for other institutional claims and the background against which further analysis of the child care sponsorship problem must be viewed. The flow of funds from the federal government to the states places the states in the position of allocating the grants among competing providers. With major emphasis placed on the primacy of parental choice, parents are placed in a position of selecting among a range of diverse sponsors. The choice of parents, if in fact there is an adequate supply in a particular market from which to choose, and the allocation decisions of state planners will have ramifications on the functions of child care and the viability of the different sponsors. The consequences of these decisions are circumscribed by the conflict among interest groups and claims vested long before the passage of the Child Care and Development Block Grant of 1990 and the Child Care Entitlement Grant of 1990.

The three problems inciting the passage of the 1990 child care act remain: availability, accessibility, and quality. These three related problems can be attributed to the dysfunctional nature of the multiple sponsor system that relied on Title XX funding before 1990. It is debatable how far the new legislation will move the country forward in achieving the three stated goals, because it is predicated on another block grant approach targeted at a population at 75 percent of a state's median income or below and maintains the multiple sponsor approach to delivery. Although the passage of the legislation is considered to be historically monumental, it is by no means the "radical" legislation President Nixon feared.

The adjustments to the tax system on behalf of low and moderate income families should prove pivotal to the successes of the 1990 child care initiative. The new committee jurisdiction of the block grant and the state plan mandating the coordination of funding streams that relate to early childhood and child care programs are structural changes that should have an impact on the function of child care. The exact nature of the changes will depend on the state plans. If programs are developed that draw consumers together from a wide pool of socioeconomic classes, it is likely that the welfare reform function will be deemphasized and the multiple functional aspect of the service will be maintained.

NOTES

1.   The role of the federal government in setting standards for child care programs has a long history in and of itself. The issue of federal sponsorship has and continues to be quite controversial. As part of OBRA 1981, federal standards for Title XX funded centers were dismantled. For a discussion of the effects of child care regulations, see Susan Rose-Ackerman, "Unintended Consequences: Regulating the Quality of Subsidized Day Care," *Journal of Policy Analysis and Management* 3, no. 1 (1983): 14–30. For a discussion of the characteristics of the nonprofit child care market, see Anne E. Preston, "The Effects of Property Rights on Labor Costs of Nonprofit Firms: An Application to the Day Care Industry," *Journal of Industrial Economics* (March 1988): 337–350.

2.   For detailed information on the criticism of the Family Support Act and the final rules and regulations, refer to (1) 45 CFR Chapter 11 (10-15-89 Edition), Office of Family Assistance, Family Support Administration, Department of Health and Human

Services, pp. 200–207; and, (2) *Federal Register* 54, No. 197, Rules and Regulations (October 13, 1989): 42146–42149, 42215–42242.

4. Church Sponsorship
and the
Religious Function

The church has provided child care for a long time and is considered the single largest provider of the service in the country (Lindner, Mattis, and Rogers, 1983; Phillips, 1987). The National Council of Churches (NCC) conducted a major nationwide survey on church sponsored child care, *When Churches Mind the Children: A Study of Day Care in Local Parishes* (1983) by Eileen W. Lindner, Mary C. Mattis, and June R. Rogers.[1] The National Council of Churches is a coalition of thirty-two denominations or communions founded in 1950. It consists of "mainline Protestant" denominations and Anglican and Orthodox churches. The NCC reaches 41 million American christians. The organization does not include the Roman Catholic Church, or the Southern Baptist Convention (Lindner et al. 1983, 4–5).

SURVEY FINDINGS OF THE NCC
CHILD DAY CARE PROJECT

The survey was undertaken by the Child Day Care Project of the National Council of Churches. The project was initiated in 1980 as a part of the Child Advocacy Office of the NCC, which had identified child care as a pressing problem in need of further study. The Child Advocacy Working Group recognized the lack of statistical data on church involvement in child care and took the initiative to collect data that would provide information on existing programs and point to directions for future child care policy.

The survey was conducted in February of 1982 utilizing fifteen of the National Council of Churches member denominations or communions. A brief questionnaire was mailed to 87,562 parishes in February. A follow-up survey was then sent to the parishes with centers. The initial survey found that about one-third (8,767) of the parishes offered some type of child care program; many housed more than one type. The total number of programs offered was 14,589.

The Children's Advocacy Committee (CAC) of the Episcopal Church conducted its first child care survey in March 1989. Because the Episcopal Church is one of the largest denominations within the National Council of Churches organization, the data on the 985 Episcopal congregations that participated in the study updated the 1983 NCC study. Two-thirds of the respondents had a child care center on the premises. The majority of these church centers are in metropolitan areas and are state certified and professionally accredited. Most of the programs under church sponsorship do not impart a sectarian program, and the majority are open to families outside of the congregational flock (CAC n.d.).

The original NCC study in 1983 cannot be generalized beyond the fifteen denominations represented, and of these there was only a 29 percent response rate. Furthermore, the study sample "disproportionately represents churches located in suburbs and small cities or towns of the Midwest—churches serving mainly white, middle-class congregations" (p. 12). However, the survey did contribute much needed information to the National Council of Churches that facilitated policy development. The purpose of the survey was

to identify the general types of programs available, if any; the relationships of programs to congregations; the types of communities in which parishes were located; and, most important for the continuing work of the Project, the names of child day care program directors. (Lindner et al. 1983, 11)

Having compiled the data from the survey, Lindner, Mattis, and Rogers concluded that the issues surrounding church involvement in child care differ on the local and national levels. The local involvement indicates that "the Church is a major *direct* provider of child care in the United States" (p. 15). The church is also a major *indirect* provider. The church serves as a landlord for centers, often free of charge or for minimum charge to the provider. Of the respondents to the initial questionnaire, 53 percent of all programs were operated by the parish, with 47 percent operating independently on church premises (pp. 14–15).

The survey germinated because of the lack of a formalized system of addressing the child care problem on the national level. Prior to the Child Day

Care Project there had been no national network for the many programs out in the parishes. There was a "total absence of guidelines and recommendations for child care provision emanating from church hierarchies" (p. 15). Since the initiation of the project and the completion of the survey, the National Council of Churches developed a policy statement in 1984 (NCC 1984) and a newsletter, *Ecumenical Child Care Newsletter*, for church providers of child care.

The development of church sponsorship has been a grass-roots phenomenon (Lindner et al., 1983). Child care centers sprung up in individual parishes in response to particular community needs. "The church as an institution did not consciously decide to become a provider of child care" (p. 22). The survey was undertaken to answer and measure this haphazard growth in church provision of child care, which mirrors the overall development of the American child care system.

The programs within the sponsorship of the church span a wide continuum. There are mothers' support groups, infant programs, toddler programs, preschool programs of full-day duration and half-day duration, and after-school programs for school-age children. These programs are either church operated or church housed. *Church housed* connotes that the church contracts with another party to operate the program; whereas, *church operated* means that the church itself operates the program.

According to the authors of the survey, churches are both desirable locations for child care centers and receptive to the community's needs and wants. Churches have several attributes that make them desirable to house child care. They are in prime locations in communities; they often have available space; and they have a tax exempt status. The buildings have adequate space because they have classrooms used for religious school on the weekend, which are not used during the week (Lindner et al. 1983, 21). There are many reasons for church involvement in the provision of child care, but the available, unused space in church buildings is a key attraction. Lindner, Mattis, and Rogers note:

It can safely be asserted that the Church is one of the most significant property owners in the country. Its buildings dot the skylines of virtually every town. Church architecture has expressed itself in a variety of ways from the spacious and dominant to the modest and circumspect, from Gothic cathedrals to urban settlement houses. During the post-World-War-II era, when America was preoccupied with education, economic prosperity, and the baby boom, many churches undertook programs of building expansion. Much of this activity was channeled into the erection of "educational wings" or classroom facilities built adjacent to the sanctuaries of parishes. When new church construction took place in the suburbs during the 1960s, original building plans called for the inclusion of classrooms, parish halls, all-purpose rooms, and fellowship halls. These buildings were added to the churches' already substantial property holdings in community buildings, settlement houses, and urban mission centers built in earlier years. With their vast property holdings and historical patterns of construction, many parishes are well equipped to provide facilities for child care. (Lindner et al. 1983, 17)

Church location is also conducive to child care because it is usually situated in the center of a community. Virtually every town has churches, and most of these are easily accessible to the parent commuting to work. Another asset of the church is its tax exempt status:

First, child care programs can simply be operated under the churches' nonprofit articles of incorporation, eliminating the need to establish a new corporation. Second, costs are lower because no taxes are paid, yet churches receive city services: fire and police protection, garbage disposal, and so forth. (Lindner et al. 1983, 19)

Although these three features—space, location, and tax exemption—make the church an attractive candidate for providing child care to outside providers, the religious mission of the church provokes action from within the church itself. Lindner, Mattis, and Rogers were able to categorize six different "ideas of ministry" that inspire church involvement in child care. These different ministries suggest different functions that child care plays under church sponsorship and also indicate that the populations served can differ by the type of ministry followed.

Translating their paradigm into the present form of analysis, child care under the church fulfills multiple functions. The religious function involves "Christian education," "pastoral care," and "evangelism." Each of these variations on the religious function involves different populations. Pastoral care implies the care of a church's membership; whereas, evangelism involves a particular church reaching out for more congregants. Christian education can involve those utilizing a church child care program even if they are not members of the sponsoring church (Lindner et al. 1983, 20).

Many churches involve themselves in "community service," which is the idea that the church has "some general responsibility to meet the needs of others" (p. 20). In this context, child care functions as social service. Here, the child care center would be open to non-church members. It is also "this view of ministry that often leads churches to respond positively to requests from child care directors to take up residence within the church building" (p. 20).

Social reform is a function of church child care programs when the sponsoring church strives to promote "social justice." Through this function particular populations of children and families are served, such as low income families, disabled children, racial-ethnic minorities, or single parents (p. 21).

The welfare reform function is addressed when church centers contract for Title XX funds or receive the recently initiated federal grant money under CCDBG or the Child Care Entitlement Grant (CCEG). The economic function of child care is realized under church sponsorship on the familial level by providing care that enables parents to work. The economic function is also evident in the for-profit church centers when the providers rely on the operation of the center for income. Naturally, child care functions under the church will vary by the composition of the congregation. Often several functions will work in conjunction with each other; on other occasions, functions will compete with each other, often causing strife and confusion within a parish (p. 21).

As stated earlier, the programs offered by the churches span a wide range. However, the modal type is child care for preschoolers, children aged 3–5 years. It is important to note that although sponsorship is by the church, 99 percent of the programs surveyed were open to the community at large. "The vast majority of church-housed child day care programs can be viewed as programs for the community, whether operated by a church or only based in church property" (Lindner et al. 1983, 26). The 1989 Episcopal Church survey supported the earlier finding on the broader population. Approximately 90 percent of the Episcopal Church centers that responded said that they provided the center as a service to the community. A significant majority of the centers served less than 20 percent parish children (CAC n.d.).

The NCC researchers followed up the original 1983 survey, by dividing the sample into subsamples to discover possible differences among them. Three subsamples were defined, the first two being of interest to this book. The first subdivision of the entire sample was between church operated and independently operated centers. The second division was between for-profit operations and nonprofit operations. The third division divided the programs between full-time and part-time programs. Some important similarities and differences among these subsamples are worth noting.

Regarding the population served, independently operated centers "are more likely to serve families who receive public assistance and are somewhat more likely to enroll black children" (Lindner et al. 1983, 40). The difference is probably attributable to the fact that church operated programs are more often in large, heavily populated areas and build programs in response to their congregation's needs (p. 40). In comparing the populations served by for-profit versus nonprofit church-based centers, "non-profit centers are more likely to serve families who receive public assistance, who belong to minority groups, and who live in larger, more densely populated communities" (p. 41). The authors of the study suggest that the first two differences can be explained on economic grounds. The third difference is a result of market forces, because smaller communities are less able to develop large, competitive nonprofit operations (p. 41).

When comparing differences among centers by function, the following data was found. Church operated centers indicated more concern with "providing love and warmth and an increasing concern with spiritual development" than did independently operated centers (p. 49). Therefore, as expected, church operated centers promote the religious function.

The independent centers "exhibited more concern with normal cognitive development through the toddler period, shifting to concern with preparation for school along with the promotion of self-reliance and independence during the preschool years" (Lindner et al. 1983, 49). These centers stressed the educational function as well as the socialization function. The independent centers also were more likely to list the relief of parents for work and other activities as a goal, thereby acknowledging the economic function and the liberation-universalization function (p. 49).

The survey did not have a substantial number of for-profit programs in the infant, toddler, and school-age categories, so these findings cannot be generalized. However, the preschool findings are more straightforward. The for-profit centers were found to emphasize obedience, manners, discipline, and school preparation. In other words, child care under their sponsorship had an educative function and a socializing function. The nonprofit centers were more concerned with spiritual development, providing love and warmth, and relieving parents for work and other activities (p. 49). The nonprofit centers included a religious function, did not stress the educational function, and had a socialization function that stressed different values than those stressed by the for-profits.

When examined for differences in administrative approach affecting delivery, differences among types of centers were not great when compared for hiring practices (pp. 51–53). There were no differences between church operated and independently operated centers with respect to educational background of staff. Nor did the for-profit and nonprofit centers differ with regard to educational level of the staff:

On the whole, directors of church-housed programs are quite well educated. Fully 87 percent have college degrees, and 25 percent of these have post-graduate degrees of some sort. Teachers in church-housed programs are also generally well educated: 74 percent have college degrees; 8 percent of these have post-graduate degrees. These levels of educational qualifications seem substantially higher than is characteristic of child day care directors and teachers nationally. (Lindner et al. 1983, 50)

Some differences were found in regard to religious beliefs. The majority of church operated centers (78 percent) gave consideration to religious beliefs when hiring staff compared to 39 percent of independently operated centers (p. 52). Nonprofits (64 percent) were more likely to hire according to religious beliefs than for-profits (44 percent) (p. 53). This finding is not surprising as most nonprofit centers are church operated.

The quality of church housed child care was measured according to the National Day Care Study (Ruopp 1979) criteria. The NDCS study set forth three key variables to measure quality from a macro perspective: staff qualification; adult-child ratio; and group size. The church survey found "that a majority of infant and preschool programs comply with NDCS recommendations for staff/child ratio but that a majority of toddler programs do not" (p. 55). When examining for education or training in early childhood education, the follow-up survey showed that 91 percent of centers had at least one teacher meeting the qualifications and 87 percent of program directors met the qualifications (p. 55). The criteria for group size were generally in keeping with NDCS findings and recommendations (p. 56).

When looking across subsamples on measures of quality, the following differences were found. Independently operated centers had slightly more teachers trained or educated in early childhood education than church operated ones, 94 percent versus 91 percent; among aides, 75 percent to 66 percent (p. 58). The independent centers had more favorable staff-child ratios at the infant and preschool level, "66 percent of independently operated centers, but only 53 percent of church operated centers, have ratios more favorable than 1 to 9" (p. 59). No difference was found between church operated and independently operated centers on group size.

In comparing for-profit centers with nonprofit centers, one difference was found among the indicators of quality. The for-profit centers had smaller groups in infant programs than the nonprofits (p. 59). It is difficult, however, to generalize from this sample because the number of for-profit centers in the sample is very small and not representative of for-profits in general (p. 59). Out of the entire sample, only 10 percent of the centers were categorized as for-profits (p. 35). This is an unbalanced comparative sample. In contrast, 56 percent of centers were classified as church operated and 44 percent as independently operated (p. 34).

The 1983 NCC survey concluded that churches are a major provider of child care in the United States, a fact that remains true. As with any sponsor, there are negative and positive elements to church based child care. The authors listed the following features as strengths of church sponsorship:

A diversity of program types serving a multiplicity of needs; A broad base of funding and in-kind support that makes it economically more robust than child care provisions in general; Grassroots sensitivity to changing family needs for child care services; Adaptability and flexibility in meeting these changing needs; Experienced and able staff; Generally sufficient structure and organization to provide reliable and stable community-based child care. (Lindner et al. 1983, 101–102)

Although not explored in *When Churches Mind the Children* (1983), there are problem areas in church housed child care. Difficulties arise over the sharing of space, maintenance, the relationship of the center to pastor and congregation, control over the budget, and teacher salaries and benefits (*Ecumenical Child Care Newsletter* Winter 1985, 6).

The NCC study concluded by outlining six areas-issues for the Child Day Care Project to pursue: developing a statement of policy and purpose; developing a network for the centers; building and working with child care coalitions; continuing to study the centers and new programs; providing technical assistance; and providing program resources for specific needs (Lindner et al. 1983, 103–105). The authors summarized the development of church housed child care by acknowledging that centers evolved from a confluence of local needs, historical coincidence, and religious conviction. They credit the resulting diversity with reflecting the pluralism of religious and secular life in the United States (Lindner et al. 1983, 73). Although addressing the strength of church housed child care, the report ends with a cautionary observation "that the strengths born of its entrepreneurial and grassroots nature must be carefully guarded from the potentially negative effects of over-enthusiastic institutionalization" (Lindner et al. 1983, 105).

THE CATHOLIC PERSPECTIVE

During the course of legislative hearings on child care over the years, representatives of the Church have taken different positions on issues pertaining to religious sponsorship and the question of proprietary sponsorship, which involves a subset of church housed programs. The National Conference of Catholic Charities (NCCC) has spoken out against profit making in child care because of evidence of poor quality in other human service programs (Monsignor Thomas J. Reese cited in U.S. Congress, Committee on Labor and Public Welfare 1975, 674; National Conference of Catholic Charities cited in U.S. Congress, Committee on Labor and Human Resources 1979, 460).

The Catholic Church also has opposed prime sponsorship of child care going to the public schools. In a letter to Representative Brademas in 1975, the United States Catholic Conference opposed public school sponsorship (U.S. Congress, Committee on Labor and Public Welfare 1975, 1253). The conference argued that the restriction to public schools seemed "senseless," as child care and early childhood programs traditionally have been private and nonprofit. In his testimony on behalf of the National Conference of Catholic Charities, Monsignor Thomas J. Reese spoke in favor of a flexible arrangement that would allow for public *and* parochial school systems to sponsor child care (U.S. Congress, Committee on Labor and Public Welfare 1975, 674).

During the drafting of ABC, Representative Kildee, an original sponsor of the bill, worked closely with the Catholic lobby and supported the lobby's interests (Conn 1988). The Catholic Charities USA and the United States Catholic Conference actively supported the ABC bill passed by the Senate and lobbied for a similar version in the House. USCC spoke out against Title II of the Early Childhood Education and Development Act (H.R. 3) in a letter addressed to conferees:

The USCC has opposed the inclusion of Title II in new child care legislation since its introduction in the House in early 1989. It is important to note that this title authorizes *both* a new public school based pre-school program as well as a new extended day program for school aged "latchkey" children of working parents. We particularly object to the creation of a new federally financed pre-school program. This is bad policy which duplicates Head Start and will drain scarce federal funds away from that proven and valued program. We support the new Head Start provisions in the House bill which allows the program to be more responsive to the needs of working parents. (USCC 1990)

Catholic organizations sought a legislative package that would meet six criteria: (1) effective assistance to families; (2) targeting those in greatest need; (3) support of a pluralistic system; (4) participation of religious and community groups in new programs; (5) improving availability, affordability, and quality; and (6) realistic and workable regulations focused on children's health and safety. Given these criteria, the Catholic lobby sought legislation that would include three key components: tax credits for low income parents, direct aid to parents in the form of vouchers, and aid to providers. During the last stages of negotiations between the House Ways and Means Committee and the House Education and Labor Committee, Reverend Thomas J. Harvey, executive director of the Catholic Charities USA, pushed for increased funding authorization of Head Start and the creation of a new infant-toddler program under the Title XX Social Services Block Grant (USCC 1989, 2; Harvey 1990a).

As members of the Independent Sector, an umbrella organization for nonprofit agencies, the Catholic constituency also advocated for the protection of the charitable tax deduction from the reconciliation budget cuts of 1990 (Harvey 1990b). The charitable tax deduction sustained a reduction in the final federal deficit reduction accord, but not to the extent feared by Catholic Charities

USA. Congress included a 3 percent floor on itemized deductions, including charitable deductions, rather than the 8 percent proposed by the administration. The lobbying efforts of nonprofit organizations also succeeded in blocking the implementation of a cap on itemized deductions. A sunset provision of five years was implemented on the 3 percent floor (Independent Sector 1990).

Donald V. Fandetti (1976) provided insightful research on the role of the Catholic Church in the delivery of child care in ethnic neighborhoods. He undertook his research at a time when social services tended to serve a socioeconomic mix of clients. Fandetti wanted to shed light on the preferred choice of child care services within ethnic communities before policy standards were established that would affect these preferences. Fandetti looked at the socialization function of child care from the point of view of the consumer-parent. He conducted a survey in the Highlandtown area of east Baltimore, an area populated by Germans, Greeks, Italians, and Poles. His study concentrated on the Polish and Italian citizens.

Fandetti's research methodology was a survey questionnaire. His goal was to discover the type of child care arrangements preferred by the selected population and "to determine whether traditional structures of assistance, such as the extended family and the church, were important as sources of child care outside of the home" (p. 620). The findings indicated that the first choice for child care were informal arrangements with senior relatives. Grandparents were seen as the primary source of care (p. 620).

If such an informal arrangement were not possible, respondents were asked to rank the following institutions as an alternative choice: state, welfare department, public school, Catholic Church, local ethnic organization, or proprietary organization. The majority of both the Italian and Polish respondents favored the Catholic Church. Fandetti wrote:

The popularity of the Catholic Church as an institutional sponsor for day care centers reflects a perception of the church as a place where discipline and respectful attitudes toward adults are likely to be stressed, and a belief that children are more likely to get individual attention in Catholic institutions. Finally, respect for religious training and a general sense of trust in the Catholic Church also account for acceptance of the Church as a resource for day care. (p. 621)

Fandetti's findings suggest that the church is the choice of many in Italian and Polish neighborhoods for the sponsorship of child care if the family members cannot provide the service. The church is looked to as the primary support of family life and child rearing outside of the family itself. Child care under its auspices has three functions: to provide a religious education, to socialize the young into the Catholic culture (as well as into the culture at large), and to support family life with social services. The educational function is secondary, and varies by program. Fandetti concluded that residents of European ethnic neighborhoods do not want a monopoly in child care by public organizations. He argued that organized child care would be accepted more readily, as would other social services, if the service were provided under religious auspices (p. 624). Thus, Fandetti's findings support the case for a pluralistic policy of child care delivery, rather than a unitary system such as the public schools.

Turning again to the position of the National Council of Churches, it followed up the 1982 survey study with a policy statement in the winter of 1984 (NCC 1984). The statement recognized the state of disarray in child care and the lack of directive policy coming from either the national government or the church itself, even though it was the largest single provider of care in the country. The NCC position statement attempted to remedy the absence of clear directions by the church pertaining to child care policy.

The 1984 statement identified the church's perception of the function of child care and the role of the church as a sponsoring institution. The church saw child care as a "family strengthening service," not as a replacement for the family (NCC 1984, 2). The statement began with the assumption that the delivery of care should further the cause of social equity. The vision of the church was that child care services be

available to all families on an equitable basis, draw resources from all sectors of the society, support the development of the child and the stability of the family, and be regulated in such a manner that encourages the development of a variety of program types of high quality in which health and safety are assured. (NCC 1984, 2)

The church sees the provision of child care as part of its ministry: "The ministry of child care is yet one more way in which the Christian community is called to extend both the nurturing ministry of the church and the prophetic proclamation of justice to all children, families, parishes and the society" (NCC 1984, 3). In essence, the church recognized its role in perpetuating the social service and social reform functions of child care. The 1984 statement is ambiguous, however, as to the church view of the liberation-universalization function. On one hand, it failed to uphold the view that child care should be a social utility because the primacy of the family in child rearing is held as sacred. On the other hand, the church clearly stated its strong belief in the availability of child care to all children on an equitable basis. Earlier reference to the liberation function by some church providers in the NCC survey suggests that the service is presently used to enable parents to pursue activities other than employment.

The NCC policy statement recognizes the various types of ministry delineated in *When Churches Mind the Children* (1983). The NCC reasons that regardless of the type of ministry or program, the governing body of the sponsoring congregation should be conscientious about the delivery of the program. High quality and parental knowledge of the role of religion in the program should be assured.

The NCC policy statement acknowledges the church's role as advocate for high quality child care and a comprehensive national policy that would assure equity in services. The 1984 statement listed several basic areas for advocacy and prepared a foundation for lobbying efforts during the debates on ABC and H.R. 3. The NCC platform upheld a strong position on the right to parental choice and the need for quality assurance standards. The council did not want standards set that would interfere with cultural differences and preferences. The statement sought to assure equity in the quality of the programs provided, urging that all programs should meet certain standards regardless of the funding or source of payment. Standards for programs should be independent of the form of financing. The 1984 position statement also endorsed the establishment of information and referral centers, which are necessary in a pluralistic delivery system. It advocated adequate remuneration and provision of benefits for providers and their employees. Wages should be consonant with the caregiver's experience and education (NCC 1984, 4–5).

THE JEWISH PERSPECTIVE

The National Council of Jewish Women (NCJW) has also assumed a leadership role in promoting high quality child care. The council had conducted a landmark study on the quality and supply of child care centers in the early 1970s, which is still considered to be a baseline study. In the late 1980s, the NCJW launched nationwide studies on the interrelationship of work and family life. The council currently is promoting the development of sound family child care networks and the development of intergenerational programs (NCJW 1990a; 1990b). The National Council of Jewish Women was one of the organizations on the original steering committee of ABC and an active lobbyist; however, NCJW withdrew its support of the final child care bill after the inclusion of vouchers for the utilization of sectarian programs (Lyss cited in U.S. Congress, Committee on Labor and Human Resources 1988, 189–195; see Appendixes A–C). Several other Jewish groups were members of the Alliance for Better Child Care; for example, American Jewish Congress, American Jewish Committee, B'nai B'rith Women, Council of Jewish Federations, and Union of American Hebrew Congregations (see Appendixes A–E).

The Orthodox Jewish groups are new players in the child care debate. Although not an active voice in the twenty year debate, the Orthodox Jews emerged as key participants in the debate over the Child Care and Development Block Grant Act of 1990. Their role in the development of the recently passed legislation will be evident in the next section of this chapter.

THE BAPTIST AND FUNDAMENTALIST PERSPECTIVE

Baptist and fundamentalist religious groups also were earnestly involved in the most recent federal debate. During the debate, many Baptist groups were represented by the organization Americans United for the Separation of Church and State, which took a leadership role in articulating the opposition's views to church-state language contained in the Act for Better Child Care and the Early Childhood and Development Act. Other Baptist and fundamentalist groups aligned themselves with the Catholic constituency and Orthodox Jewish constituency in support of the final version of the CCDBG. The emphasis placed on the religious function of child care by Baptist and fundamentalist groups has contributed to the development of complicated administrative and legal issues in child care delivery, which will be discussed later.

CHURCH AND STATE ISSUES

Congress shall make no law respecting an establishment of religion, or prohibiting the free exercise thereof. . . .
—United States Constitution, First Amendment

The structure-function dichotomy becomes very apparent in discussions on church involvement in child care services. Church involvement in child care programs raises controversial issues involving constitutional law under the First Amendment's Establishment Clause and Free Exercise Clause and their underlying doctrines of voluntarism and the separation of church and state.[2] The First Amendment's religion clauses complicate the debate over church sponsorship of child care because the two clauses, though at times congruent, often are at cross purposes.[3] One clause prohibits the government's establishment of religion and generally is interpreted to prohibit public funding of activities involving the inculcation of religious ideas, and the other guarantees individuals the freedom to practice religion without government interference. The tensions between the two clauses are evident in the struggle to craft child care legislation as efforts to provide government assistance in the provision of child care services inevitably encounter the perplexing questions of religious involvement in the delivery of those crucial services.

Child care concerns are closely tied to deep-seated religious beliefs, to fundamental tenets of child rearing that disdain government intrusion and to general perceptions of child care's function in relation to the family and the state. The link of the church to the provision of such a basic and needed service in contemporary society as child care has provoked many organized religious interest groups to mobilize lobbying efforts. The major issues no longer are latent consequences of church sponsorship; rather, they have also ignited the involvement of proprietary providers, state administrators, organized labor, public interest organizations, and other child advocacy groups and attracted the attention of the press and the legal community. At the same time, the manifestation of these issues hindered the drafting process and eventual passage of the Act for Better Child Care of 1989 (S. 5) and the Early Childhood Education and Development Act of 1990 (H.R. 3).[4]

State Licensing Exemptions

Church exemption from licensing standards is one issue that has plagued state legislatures and federal courts throughout the country. Regulating child care centers, as noted earlier, has been problematic whenever legislation has been considered during the last twenty years. The approach taken in Title XX of the Social Security Act placed the onus on the states to create and monitor standards of care for child care centers. The Association of State Governors successfully lobbied against the imposition of federal standards for child care (Kean cited in U.S. Congress, Committee on Labor and Human Resources 1988, 222; Craft cited in U.S. Congress, Committee on Education and Labor 1989, 430; Phillips cited in U.S. Congress, Committee on Labor and Human Resources 1988, 331). The 1990 legislation requires certain state standards for those child care centers that receive federal funding under the CCDBG, but does not impose federal standards. Under the new act, centers must comply with standards in the areas of health and safety. These standards must include rules on the regulation of immunization shots, expectations for staff training on issues in health and safety control, and procedures to ensure the prevention and control of infectious diseases. To be eligible to participate in the new legislation's funding programs, child care providers must be licensed, regulated, or registered (OBRA 1990, 921–924).

In many states, however, churches are granted exemption from certain licensing standards. In other states, church groups continue to lobby for exemption status. According to a September 1990 report by the Children's

Defense Fund, one-third of all child care programs are operated by religious organizations and thirteen states fully or partially exempt these programs from licensing ("Laws on Child Care Centers Rapped" 1990; CDF 1990d). Yet, child advocates repeatedly argue that children in any setting, in any state, deserve a minimum standard of care, one that has been validated by empirical research and a professional child development knowledge base. Thus, the involvement of the church compounds this already thorny problem of regulation.

In a publication of the Child Care Law Center, law professor Carol Sanger provides a legal analysis of the exemption issue (Sanger 1983). Most of the groups lobbying for religious exemptions are fundamentalist Christian churches. They object to the state interfering with their religious programs in any manner. Opposition to exemption status comes from child advocacy groups as well as other religious organizations. The majority of church run centers advocate for the uniform application of licensing requirements. Among the organizations that support licensing are the National Lutheran Council, the Salvation Army, the National Conference of Catholic Charities, and the National Council of Churches of Christ (NCC) (Sanger 1983, 2). The NCC 1984 policy statement supports licensing procedures and does not seek or promote church exemption from such standards. The policy position is that the setting of regulations "is the appropriate responsibility of the state and this need not interfere with the free exercise of religion" (NCC 1984, 9). Yet, the statement stipulates that a boundary should be set in the drawing of regulations so that standards do not interfere with "cultural choices." The NCC maintains that "public policy should be confined to regulations concerning enforceable health and safety standards and the requirement of screening to determine the emotional and mental competence of all potential staff persons" (NCC 1984, 8).

The two sides in the exemption debate differ in their interpretation of the mandates of the First Amendment's two religion clauses. Those in favor of exemption argue that the state's licensing of centers violates their freedom of religion. They contend that child care is part of the church's ministry and that licensing is in effect licensing the church. At the very least, it interferes with their religious practices.

Proponents of uniform regulation of child care centers argue that standards are established in the interests of children's welfare and as "a form of consumer protection for children and their parents" (NCC 1984, 8). When defending the existence of uniform regulation of centers, advocates point out that the licensing requirements from which the centers are being exempted do not in any way encroach on religious freedom. Rather, the standards establish a floor for the delivery of programs that promote children's welfare.

Sanger's analysis breaks the debate over religious exemptions into several component issues. First, she points out three different factual settings for litigation. One setting involves states that have enacted religious exemptions. In that setting the nonexempt centers sue the state for violating the First Amendment's Establishment Clause. A second factual setting encompasses those states that require uniform standards for licensing. In those states, some fundamentalist centers refuse to obtain or renew a license, which provokes enforcement litigation against them by the state regulatory agency. The centers then defend their actions on the basis of the First Amendment's guarantee of free exercise of religion. The most common factual setting takes place in states that do not exempt religious centers. The fundamentalists in these states lobby for exemption laws by arguing that the Constitution guarantees religious freedom (Sanger 1983, 2–4). These different fact patterns involve an array of interest groups at odds over the church's role in delivering child care in light of the applicable provisions of the United States Constitution:

There is a diverse cast of characters now involved in the dispute over exempting church-run day care centers from licensing requirements. Owners of day care centers, church leadership, parents, day care center workers, state officials, educational organizations, lawyers, and legislators are lining up on both sides of the issue. There is, of course, one more group whose voice is rarely heard but whose interests should remain primary—the children in day care centers. They are affected most directly by the licensing or lack of licensing, and by compliance or non-compliance with the standards for the center where they spend their days. (Sanger 1983, 5)

Sanger points out three consequences that result from religious sponsorship of child care centers when those centers are not in compliance with licensing standards: (1) some children spend their time in facilities thought to be substandard by the legislature; (2) if an open enrollment policy actually exists, the exemption applies even though some children attend who do not practice the religion that was the basis for the exemption being granted; and (3) the exempt facility operates at a lower cost, causing unfair competition in the market and possibly discouraging the obtainment or renewal of licenses by nonexempt centers, a situation that "sets bad public policy" by creating an "economic disincentive to comply with the law" (Sanger 1983, 12–13).[5]

States differ in their approach to both the setting of standards and exemption from those standards. Child care licensing regulations include both operating standards and inspection standards. Exemptions from licensing standards vary, from broad, complete exemption to limited exemption from selected standards. The cases that have challenged religious exemptions or argue for them reflect the various approaches to these licensing exemptions (Sanger 1983, 34–37).

After examining court decisions in which the majority of cases upheld the right of legislatures and regulatory bodies to set and enforce standards, Sanger reasons that the continuing efforts to establish or maintain exemptions, based on the argument that licensing church run child care centers violates the First Amendment, "may be made in good faith, but are largely unsupported by case law" (Sanger 1983, 38). The case authorities establish three precedential principles: (1) "operating a day care center is not a religious activity protected under the First Amendment"; (2) "'preschool ministries' are not free from regulation because of the states' compelling interest in protecting the safety and health of children in child care"; and (3) "licensing statutes neither prohibit nor discourage religious practices; thus there is no conflict between licensing and the religious activities" (Sanger 1983, 38). In light of this analysis of the licensing issue, Sanger concludes in favor of uniform regulation of all centers.

In addition to the new legislation in 1990, new case law has been decided since the Child Care Law Center published Sanger's analysis.[6] Although these decisions affect the legislation in particular states, the controversy continues over state exemption. The impact the new federal statute will have on the practice of exemption also remains to be seen. The courts undoubtedly will continue to wrestle with the issue.

Federal Funding of Child Care Sponsored by Religious Institutions

The question of exempting centers sponsored by religious institutions from licensing standards is just one of two points of contention in the disputes over the delivery of child care services by religious organizations. The other major issue is whether federal funds should be granted to religious organizations and, if so, under what stipulated conditions. Whereas the exemption issue was subsumed within the dispute over federal versus state authority in setting child care delivery standards, the second major question was more central to concerns in the drafting of federal legislation and the ongoing debate in the formulation of the Act for Better Child Care (S. 5) and the Early Childhood Education and Development Act (H.R. 3).

The church-state separation issue was extremely factious in the development of the Act for Better Child Care of 1989 and the Early Childhood Education and Development Act of 1990. Opponents of federal funding of church sponsored child care programs cut across political and religious groups resulting in strange bedfellows and deeply wounded traditional allegiances. Members of the original Alliance for Better Child Care were so divided on this issue that founding members broke away from the coalition and withdrew their support of pending legislation.[7] Long-time children's advocates found themselves forced to choose between sincerely held beliefs: that the separation of church and state is a fundamental constitutional principle, that the state has a responsibility in meeting the need for high quality care, and that religious institutions have become legitimate providers of care and need state support to continue the service. Drafting legislation that would assist church sponsored child care centers without destroying the wall separating church and state presented a formidable challenge.

When first introduced in November 1987 during the first session of the 100th Congress, the Act for Better Child Care, the ABC act (S. 1885), provided for church sponsorship of child care, but prohibited funding programs of sectarian content. The block grant approach was designed to enable states to purchase child care from providers through the use of three funding mechanisms: grants, contracts, and certificates. The use of certificates, commonly referred to as vouchers, would enable low income parents to purchase the child care of their choice. Whereas the overall intent of the legislation was to provide affordable, accessible high quality child care, the intent behind the use of several funding patterns was to maintain the diversity in the existing delivery system and emphasize parental choice.

In its original version, ABC prohibited church sponsored centers from teaching children about religion or otherwise promoting religion and required the removal or covering of any religious symbols. Providers also were originally prohibited from discriminating in favor of the religion of the sponsoring institution in admission or hiring policies. ABC's nondiscrimination provisions referenced the language in Title VI and VII of the Civil Rights Act of 1964, Title IX of the Education Amendments of 1972, and the Rehabilitation Act of 1973 (*Congressional Record* 11-19-87).

The original ABC bill represented a moderate position in the debate that ensued. Members of the Alliance for Better Child Care helped draft this original language. At the time, the alliance included the Children's Defense Fund and other child advocacy groups, education groups, and the "mainline" religious organizations, which represented the vast majority of religious sponsors of child care (Social Justice and Peacemaking Office 1989).[8] This more moderate voice condoned federal funding to child care facilities housed under religious institutions' auspices *as long as the program content is not sectarian*. The moderate position was clearly articulated by the Social Justice and Peacemaking Office of the Presbyterian Church (USA), on behalf of a coalition of organizations, in a letter sent to members of the House:[9]

Specifically sectarian programs should be supported by those who share the same beliefs expressed and not by government funds gathered from all taxpayers. This is the core idea in the separation of church and state. The best guideline for the proper formation of church and state partnerships is whether or not the partnership serves a public purpose rather than serving to advance specifically religious purposes. (Social Justice and Peacemaking Office 1989) (emphasis in original)

The most influential education groups, the National Parent-Teacher Association (PTA), the National Education Association (NEA), and the American Federation of Teachers Association of the AFL-CIO (AFT) shared the moderate perspective that religious providers of nonsectarian programs should receive government funding (Waterman [PTA] cited in U.S. Congress, Committee on Education and Labor 1989, 318–321; Melley [NEA] cited in U.S. Congress, Committee on Education and Labor 1989, 294, 300, 301; Shanker [AFT] 1989). However, some members of the public education constituency opposed the use of certificates to provide that assistance.[10] Several education organizations, led by the NEA and the PTA, claimed that the use of certificates, whether with sectarian or nonsectarian programs, would negatively affect the public school system. They feared that these vouchers would open the door to the use of public funds for religious education in elementary and secondary schools and for private education in general:

By channeling potentially large sums of federal funds to private institutions through a certificate/voucher mechanism, the ABC bill moves the structure of federal education and social service programs into uncharted waters. While the right of parents to select an appropriate child care facility for their children is unarguable, the use of a certificate/voucher to accomplish this raises several questions and possible problems. (National PTA 1988b, 3)

Throughout the drafting process, the education groups emphasized the education function of child care. During the ensuing disputes over church-state language other groups emphasized child care's religious and social service functions. These definitional questions played a major role in the church-state debate and undoubtedly will be the focus of much attention in future litigation.

In addition to the education constituency's special interests, and antivoucher platform, major challenges to the original ABC bill came from diametrically opposed interest groups. On one side, groups such as the American Civil Liberties Union and Americans United for Separation of Church and State argued that child care programs affiliated with religious institutions should not receive *any* federal assistance. The ACLU emphasized the need to maintain a clear separation between church and state as mandated by the First Amendment and longstanding Supreme Court precedents. Americans United asserted that "as a practical matter, it is absolutely impossible for government to determine whether a church-affiliated day care program is too religious to receive federal funds" and that "government involvement and intrusion in church affairs, the ultimate effect of this legislation" is just as "intolerable" (Americans United for Separation of Church and State, "The Act for Better Child Care," 1).[11] Other religious organizations that opposed any federal support to child care centers sponsored by religious institutions included the Baptist Joint Committee on Public Affairs, the Southern Baptist Convention, and the General Conference of Seventh-Day Adventists ("Day Care Bill Advances Despite Church-State Disagreement," 1988). Although these groups constituted the majority of groups taking this position, it is not exhaustive. A few Protestant and Jewish groups also objected to any form of entanglement.[12]

The position on the opposite extreme was taken by religious groups interested in obtaining assistance for their child care programs regardless of whether they had a religious component. The United States Catholic Conference, the public policy agency of the Catholic bishops of America, and Agudath Israel, which represented Orthodox Jewish groups and the National Society for Hebrew Day Schools, were the two most prominent lobbyists for support of sectarian child care. These groups rejected an absolutist approach to the First Amendment; throughout the legislative process they maintained that the Establishment Clause does not prohibit all forms of federal assistance to sectarian institutions. They argued that the church-state issue should not be resolved by excluding providers of sectarian programs, but rather that the participation of their religious programs was constitutionally permissible. Moreover, these sectarian sponsors maintained that they should not be required to completely secularize their child care programs to be eligible to participate.

During the drafting of ABC, the various interest groups chiseled away at the "moderate" language of the original bill, gradually deferring to the interests of the sectarian providers. The first sections to undergo change were Sections 19 and 20. Section 19(a) was the provision in the original ABC bill that specifically prohibited the expenditure of funds for "sectarian purposes or activities," which were defined to cover all religious instruction or activities, including any services performed by teachers in the sectarian schools, and the display of religious symbols. Section 19(b) prohibited the use of federal funds for physical improvements to religious property; and 19(c) prohibited funds being expended for school-age students during the regular school day or any services for which school-age students receive academic credit. Section 20 contained the nondiscrimination provisions for the hiring of staff and admission of children (*Congressional Record* 11-19-87).

Viewed as safeguards against the establishment of religion by government, the two sections of the bill were criticized, by both the strict separationists and those committed to the involvement of religious institutions in the delivery of child care, for encouraging *entanglement* of the church and state. The provisions would have necessitated monitoring religious institutions as to compliance with the statute ("Church, State and Child Care Policy" 1988; Conn 1988).

The sections also were challenged by sectarian providers for several other reasons. The stipulations set forth in these provisions were too prohibitive for many of the existing providers to be considered in compliance. For example, nuns teaching in Catholic schools would not be available for employment as child care workers on the premises, nor would any other teachers or teachers' aides otherwise employed to perform educational services on the premises of a pervasively sectarian institution. Furthermore, the children already attending the parochial elementary school would not be able to receive child care services before or after school on the premises unless all of the religious symbols were removed. As another example, many church affiliated centers would need to upgrade their facilities to comply with proposed new health and safety standards and would be ineligible for the capital improvement funds needed to do so.

Section 20(c)'s nondiscrimination provision was criticized by sectarian groups as going beyond the employment discrimination prohibitions in Title VII of the Civil Rights Act of 1964 and other federal laws. The original language had prohibited "any discrimination prohibited by title VII of the Civil Rights Act of 1964 . . ., notwithstanding the exemption in section 703," which allows religiously affiliated educational institutions to use religious preferences for members of their particular religion in their employment policies. Agudath Israel took issue with how that language "would have *explicitly* overridden" the Section 703 exemption and "imposed unprecedented additional anti-discrimination requirements upon religiously affiliated child care providers" (Agudath Israel 1988, 10). In addition to Title VII, Agudath Israel cited "Title IX of the Education Amendments of 1972, which allows religious schools to make distinctions on the basis of sex, if such practice is consistent with the religious tenets of the school" as precedent for allowing religious institutions to use "religiously motivated policies that would otherwise constitute illegal discrimination" (Agudath Israel 1989g, 3). Agudath Israel's position was premised on the idea that lawful discrimination (in hiring and admissions) was necessary to maintain "the very character of religiously affiliated child care institutions," that such discrimination is not "morally offensive," but "merely . . . maintain[s] an environment best suited to promote the religious principles for which [the child care providers] exist" (p. 3).

Pressure to change the two sections mounted early in the legislative drafting process from pro-parochial groups such as the Catholic League for Religious and Civil Rights, the United States Catholic Conference, Agudath Israel, The National Association of Evangelicals and other groups from the "Religious

Right" (Boston 1988, 4–5). These sectarian groups viewed the original bill as unnecessarily singling out child care programs with sectarian content. They contended that the provisions requiring the complete secularization of all aspects of child care services were impractical and, in any event, not required by the Constitution. Their desired changes were steadfastly opposed by, among others, the National Education Association (NEA) and the National Parents Teachers Association, both of which insisted on retaining the language in Sections 19 and 20 of the original bill that prohibited the use of government funds for religious purposes and prohibited discrimination on the basis of religion (Conn 1988; National PTA 1988a; personal communication with Oakes 1990).

The Children's Defense Fund took the lead in bringing the criticisms to the legislative process in a pragmatic effort to find more general church-state language that would maximize religious sponsorship without threatening the momentum behind the proposed legislation. Marian Wright Edelman and her colleagues at CDF determined that the need for child care legislation was so pressing that the legislation simply could not be delayed by disagreement over specific provisions that could be left to the regulatory process and the courts to resolve. On February 12, 1988, Edelman sent a memorandum to alliance members stating the group's position on Sections 19 and 20. Importantly, the memorandum offered new language on the two sections pertaining to the prohibition on the expenditure of funds for certain purposes and nondiscrimination. The new language at once gave more flexibility to religious interests by allowing greater participation of church based programs, but retained the prohibition against the delivery of programs with sectarian content. Specifically, Edelman set forth three purposes behind the new language. It mandated that the "funds expended under the Act be used only for secular purposes and activities" and prohibited the use of funds "for tuition for regular school instruction." The proposed language subjected "providers who receive grants, contracts, or child care certificates to the strictures of the civil rights acts" (Edelman 1988a).

The memorandum by Edelman clearly voiced her unwavering belief that the need for child care among low income families was grave and urgent. She suggested the new language to expedite a painstakingly slow initiative for child care that had begun twenty years earlier. Appealing to the alliance membership, she wrote:

I hope we will not let issues which do not need to be resolved in the statute itself slow down the positive momentum to enact ABC. There are later forums for all concerned to pursue church-state concerns *after* the bill is enacted. While the bill should have a general prohibition against spending federal funds for religious activities, going into detail on what is and is not prohibited in the statute is unprecedented and creates unnecessary political problems. It is no accident that virtually every federal social service statute is silent on church-state issues or contains merely a general prohibition. (Edelman 1988a) (emphasis in original)

Under Edelman's leadership the majority of mainline religious groups that otherwise most likely would have supported a more stringent application of the doctrine of separation of church and state joined the Catholic and Orthodox Jewish constituency in seeking changes in the original wording of ABC. The groups were motivated by their desire to ensure the expedient participation of the many church- and synagogue-based nonsectarian programs that would be unduly hampered in their ability to provide services under the original language (Cooper 1988).

A long-time advocate for Catholic concerns, Congressman Kildee took on the cause of those interest groups seeking changes to Sections 19 and 20 by proposing an amendment to his colleagues in the House on May 19, 1988 (Conn 1988, 5; CQA 1988, 367). Senator Dodd who had worked closely with Edelman and her colleagues in the original drafting offered amended language for the Senate bill on June 8, 1988 (*Senate Report* 100-484, 65). The amended language in both the House and Senate versions of ABC (Sections 19 and 20 had become Sections 18 and 19 in the House version) adapted the proposed CDF revisions. Thus, the new language permitted religious symbols to be displayed and allowed discrimination in the admission of children and employment. The *Senate Report* emphasized the committee's intent to allow admission preferences for "before and after school child care to children who are enrolled in the regular instructional programs of the schools" and to allow "religiously affiliated schools to participate without revoking any religious preference for the admission of children to unsubsidized slots" (*Senate Report* 100-484, 79; *House Report* 100-985, Part 1, 24).

As for employment discrimination, the new language did not specifically refer to Title VII. By dropping this reference to Title VII and the clause "notwithstanding the exemption in section 703," the committee effectively reinstated the exemption, thus permitting the sectarian providers to discriminate on the basis of religion in their employment policies (*Senate Report* 100-484, 79). The *Senate Report* explained only what the committee did not intend by striking the original bill's prohibition against religious discrimination:

This omission should not be interpreted as an indication that the Committee endorses employment discrimination on the basis of religion, or to confer an exemption not otherwise conferred by Title VII of the Civil Rights Act of 1964 or from any other statute which applies to child care providers who receive funds under this Act. (*Senate Report* 100-484, 79)

The Dodd and Kildee amendments were adopted by the Senate Committee on Labor and Human Resources and the House Committee on Education and Labor. The Senate committee, generally more inclined toward religious participation and preoccupied with disputes over funding and the use of tax credits (the thrust of the Republicans' child care plans), accepted the amendments much more readily than the House, where significant dissent was voiced as committee members battled over the changes to the new church-state language. The new language, as emphasized by Senate committee members in the *Senate Report*, was still intended to promote *secular* child care programs (*Senate Report* 100-484, 78). The report of the House committee, however, reflects its members' persistent concerns about entanglement and the abdication of rights guaranteed under the First Amendment. The House committee members had concluded: "The church-state separation problem is intrinsic to this bill's approach to the child care issue and protracted litigation will undoubtedly result if the bill is enacted" (*House Report* 100-985, 33).

The changes in Sections 19 and 20 particularly disquieted Representative James Jeffords who offered two defeated amendments that would have ensured that no child or potential employee would be discriminated against on the basis of religion (*House Report* 100-985, Part 1, 40–41). Jeffords and his colleague Paul B. Henry raised new concerns over the failure of committee members to take into consideration the implications of the newly passed Civil Rights Restoration Act (PL 100-259) that extended Title IX and Section 504 nondiscrimination requirements to "the entire plant or other comparable, geographically separate facility to which federal assistance is extended" (*House Report* 100-985, Part 1, 42). Henry asked what the impact of that provision would be on churches and private schools that rent space to child care providers that receive ABC funds (*House Report* 100-985, Part 1, 42).

Representative Pat Williams highlighted the controversy over child care's functional differences. The complex nature of the service had legal ramifications for the use of public funds for religiously affiliated programs. Williams framed the question that addressed the long-standing tension over how to define child care. She questioned whether federal funds could be allocated to child care when it is defined by its education function, given the legal precedents prohibiting federal assistance to parochial education. Williams wrote:

Child care is education. It is shocking that this Committee, the House Education Committee, declares that child care is simply custodial care. The reality is that education will take place in both the pre-school and after-school care. Education will and should be provided to children in child care settings. There has been a long constitutional history prohibiting federal funds being sent to religious institutions to provide childhood education. It is naive to believe that a child care program in a religious setting controlled by a religious group is not going to intentionally or inadvertently instill specific religious values in our children. (*House Report* 100-985, 43)

Representative Williams pressed for a nonsectarian operating board for child care programs that are "physically located in churches or otherwise associated with churches" (*House Report* 100-985, 43).

Although these dissenting views were voiced in the committee, full and open debate on the complicated and controversial issues of church and state had been inhibited by the political expediency concerns of the proponents of the revised church-state language. Heavy lobbying during the summer of 1988 by interest groups supporting the amendments impelled representatives conferring on the bill in mark-up to proceed without holding hearings on the religious issues (CQA 1988, 368). As one journalist reported:

A staff member of the Senate Subcommittee on Children, Family, Drugs and Alcoholism candidly told Americans United government liaison Kim Yelton that the bill's proponents do not want to air such controversial constitutional issues in a public forum. It might endanger passage of the bill. (Conn 1988, 5)

Despite ABC proponents' efforts to quell concerns over church and state issues, some former supporters and original alliance members retracted their support once the amended language was adopted (CQA 1988, 367). Those who had opposed amending the nondiscrimination provision in Section 20 feared that its strict prohibitions were necessary to safeguard the constitutional separation of church and state, and that the license to discriminate violated civil rights principles. Furthermore, opponents argued that, as the bill did not endorse sectarian program content, there was no reason to encourage this type of discrimination. The permission to discriminate in hiring could result in the unintended consequence of employing a staff with members from only one religion, which in turn could lead to the inculcation of religious beliefs (Cooper 1988). The NEA criticized the amended language as promoting a system of child care that sanctions discrimination (CQA 1988, 367). The American Jewish Congress withdrew its support for ABC, claiming that the effect of the new provisions would be to create "a segregated child-care system based on religion" (CQA 1988, 367). In the eyes of some, the Children's Defense Fund's alliance with pro-parochial groups compromised efforts previously made by alliance members to ensure the separation of church and state. In the summer of 1988, Joseph L. Conn of *Church and State*, a monthly publication of Americans United, wrote:

In the meantime, instead of improving the ABC Bill, lobbyists and congressional sponsors seem intent on making it worse. Religious groups that want to receive a no-strings-attached share of the public funds have persuaded the ABC Bill coalition to agree to loosen its church-state restrictions. (Conn 1988, 5)

Although mainline religious members of the alliance remained divided on the issue of religious discrimination in hiring, the prohibition against sectarian activity was not a problem for the National Council of Churches because the majority of its members' programs already were nonsectarian in nature (Cooper 1988; CQA 1988, 367; Boston 1988, 6). The mainline religious institutions saw their child care programs as serving a "community service" or social service function and "not as an opportunity to inculcate religious views" (Boston 1988, 6). The research findings of the 1982 NCC survey (Lindner et al. 1983) contributed to policy development and position statements at this turn in the legislative drafting of child care legislation because the survey had found that the majority of the non-Catholic and non-Baptist church-based child care centers were *not* operating sectarian programs; therefore, strict church-state language would not affect the participation of these providers. From the NCC perspective, legislative language should enable the existing church provided child care delivery system to comply with health and safety standards, but not encourage discrimination or sectarian practices (Cooper 1988).

Some members of the alliance (including a number of the education groups and the National Organization of Women) that had accepted the idea of religious institutions participating in the block grant program not only adamantly opposed the amended language in Sections 19 and 20, but also remained opposed to the voucher concept. Foreseeing the problematic nature of vouchers even before Congress confounded the issue by sanctioning their use for sectarian purposes, the National PTA had offered alternative funding patterns to the voucher plan in a 1988 paper entitled "Alternatives to Vouchers" (National PTA 1988b). In its 1988 proposal, the PTA reiterated its fundamental concern that the voucher plan would undermine the public educational system in favor of private and parochial education,[13] and identified additional consequences of a voucher component. If implemented, the child care act would be the first social service or education voucher program ever tested on a "billion dollar scale" and thus presented new questions regarding effective administration and quality control. Moreover, the voucher mechanism could encourage the flow of federal money to the promotion of particular religions via the institutional support of sectarian child care programs, provoking court challenges as to its constitutionality and complicating the problem of monitoring compliance (p. 3).

The PTA paper presented several alternative models for federal funding of child care that incorporated the concept of parental choice and referenced other federal programs that provide aid to or services through private institutions and agencies. Eight organizations sent a letter to Representative Kildee on June 6, 1988, opposing the voucher concept and suggesting alternatives:

There are alternative models of financing quality child care programs besides vouchers. Such vehicles as contracting out, using community based and existing public school facilities, or reimbursing qualified care providers are all possibilities. The divisiveness and interruption of service that years of litigation would cause would indeed undermine the extensive efforts that you have already committed in finding the best means of child care services.

The letter was signed by the following groups: National Education Association, National PTA, National Association of Elementary School Principals, American Association of School Administrators, National School Boards Association, Council for Great City Schools, National Organization for Women, and the National Association of State Boards of Education. At this 1988 juncture, the AFT did not join with its fellow education groups because it was willing to compromise on the use of vouchers as long as the vouchers were not going to be used for sectarian programs (personal communication with Humphrey 1990). The failure to enact legislation in 1975 and the conflicts it had in the past with CDF contributed to AFT's decision to meet CDF and its supporters half way.[14] As the opponents of the voucher concept lobbied against the provision, voucher proponents capitalized on the voucher concept as a mechanism by which the provision of sectarian programs could be enabled.

The divisiveness among alliance members is reminiscent of the constitutional controversy surrounding the Elementary and Secondary Education Act of 1965 (ESEA), which was contested in court for twenty years (Boston 1988, 6). Under Title I of the act, now referred to as Chapter I, government aid was provided to religious schools for the benefit of "educationally disadvantaged" children. Chapter I of ESEA allowed public school teachers to provide remedial instruction in parochial schools. Much like the provisions in the original ABC bill, religious instruction by the public school teachers and religious symbols in the classrooms used by the teachers were prohibited. Periodic inspections were required to monitor compliance.

Many advocates and legal scholars were divided on the constitutionality of using federal funds for children in religious schools at that time. Proponents of the permissive language in the act contended that children were the beneficiaries, not the schools. Groups that traditionally promoted the separation of church and state supported the provision of aid to parochial schools on the premise that poor children were being assisted; a "child benefit" theory was adopted (Boston 1988, 6). ESEA's opponents, such as Americans United for Separation of Church and State, argued that "the difference between aiding schools and pupils was fictional: the end result was unconstitutional government aid to religious schools" (Boston 1988, 6). In 1985, after years of litigation and the expenditure of millions of dollars, the provision of the act that condoned the use of government funds at religious institutions was held unconstitutional by the United States Supreme Court in *Aguilar v. Felton*, 473 U. S. 402 (1985) (Boston 1988, 6). The "child benefit" thinking of this earlier era resurfaced in the deliberations over ABC in the late 1980s. This child benefit rationale prevailed in 1988 and motivated the pivotal actions of Marian Wright Edelman.

1989 REVISIONS TO THE ABC BILL
(S. 5/H.R. 30) AND THE NEW HOUSE BILL (H.R. 3)

At the onset of the 101st Congress in January 1989, Representative Hawkins introduced a new child care bill, the Early Childhood and Development Act (H.R. 3), as an alternative to the House and Senate ABC bills (formerly H.R. 3660 and S. 1885), which were introduced respectively as H.R. 30 and S. 5 in the new Congress. Hawkins's bill offered alternative church-state language and a five title approach that included a school-based component. The original version of H.R. 3 prohibited federal funding of programs with sectarian purposes and activities by referencing language in Head Start (*House Report* 101-190 Part 1, 53).

Continued Action on ABC

While Hawkins and some other members of the House were moving forward with H.R. 3 as an alternative measure to ABC, pro-sectarian groups continued to lobby for more latitude in the delivery of sectarian programs in the ABC bill. In the spring of 1989 the U.S. Catholic Conference, Agudath Israel, and some fundamentalist groups of the religious Right wedged further into the crack in the church-state wall, which Edelman's coalition had allowed to open in 1988. The Catholic constituency and the Orthodox Jews, in keeping with their ongoing battle for federal subsidization of parochial education, pushed for language that would assure the right to receive funds and practice religious education in the child care setting ("Day Care Bill" 1988; "Church, State and Child Care Policy" 1988; Conn 1988; United States Catholic Conference 1989; Agudath Israel 1989a; Agudath Israel 1989b; personal communication with

Cohen 1990). Mary Anderson Cooper of NCC reported that this political maneuvering incensed many of the interest groups because it came "despite weeks of negotiations between Catholic, Protestant, Jewish and education groups and the bill's chief sponsors which yielded a constitutionally acceptable church-state compromise" (Cooper 1989, 6).

Legislatively active from the onset of the debate, Agudath Israel and the United States Catholic Conference were leaders in the efforts to maximize participation of sectarian providers; that is, religiously affiliated institutions providing child care programs with sectarian content. Agudath Israel had circulated a memorandum in 1988 to the members of the Senate Committee on Labor and Human Resources and the House Committee on Education and Labor proposing amendments that would permit providers of sectarian child care to receive federal assistance (Agudath Israel 1988).[15] Agudath Israel proposed changing the language in Section 18(a) (formerly Section 19), which stipulated that "no financial assistance provided under this Act shall be expended for *any* sectarian purpose or activity, including sectarian worship and instruction" (emphasis added), to read as follows: "No financial assistance provided under *section 8(a)(1)(A) or section 8(a)(1)(B)* of this Act shall be expended for any *predominantly* sectarian purpose or activity, including sectarian worship and instruction" (Agudath Israel 1988, 9) (emphasis in original). In other words, Agudath Israel sought to apply the restrictive language "only to funds distributed directly from government to child care providers, not to child certificates distributed to parents"; the restriction would not apply at all to the certificate program (p. 9). Moreover, this restriction was intended to disqualify only sectarian programs whose sectarian purpose was predominant, rather than incidental (p. 9).

According to the legal reasoning of Agudath Israel, its proposed revisions were constitutionally permissible. The memoranda it circulated on the Hill in 1988 and 1989 cited key Supreme Court decisions as authority for its positions.[16] Relying on *Lynch v. Donnelly*, 465 U.S. 668, 673 (1984), the Orthodox Jewish group contended that the Establishment Clause of the First Amendment "neither mandates nor desires impregnable barriers between religion and state" (Agudath Israel 1989b, 3). *Lynch* also raised the issue as to whether a program's purpose is incidental or predominant. Agudath rejected an absolutist approach to Establishment Clause doctrine and claimed that the bill expressed "hostility toward religion" by restricting the ability of sectarian providers to receive federal benefits (Agudath Israel 1988, 4; 1989b, 4).

One of Agudath's main arguments was that child care was "essentially a form of social service" under ABC, rather than an educational service, and Supreme Court precedent permitted federal funding for social services under religious auspices (Agudath Israel 1989, 6)[17]. Agudath Israel cited the Court's 1988 decision in *Bowen v. Kendrick*, 108 S. Ct. 2562, which upheld as constitutional the Adolescent Family Life Act, "a federal law authorizing grants to religious organizations (among others) for providing counseling and other services with respect to adolescent sexuality and pregnancy" (Agudath Israel 1989b, 6; 1988, 5).

Another major contention for Agudath Israel throughout the legislative process was the parental right to choose sectarian child care through the use of a voucher system. Regardless of the restrictions the First Amendment placed on direct government funding, those restrictions, according to Agudath Israel, did not prevent grants to individuals to use as they deemed appropriate (Agudath Israel 1988, 7; 1989b, 4). The indirect subsidization of sectarian child care through certificates or vouchers used by an individual independent agent, rather than a direct federal grant to an institution, is considered to be within the parameters of the Constitution. On this point, Agudath Israel cited *Witters v. Washington Department of Services for the Blind*, 474 U.S. 481 (1986), which sustained the use of a vocational rehabilitation grant by a blind person to enroll in a religious college and train for the ministry. Acknowledging the difference between the use of vouchers for the most impressionable young, rather than during the higher education years, Agudath also referred to *Mueller v. Allen*, 463 U.S. 388 (1983), a decision in which the Supreme Court upheld "against establishment clause attack a Minnesota law conferring tax benefits upon parents who incur expenses for the *elementary or secondary* education of their children" (Agudath Israel 1988, 7–8) (emphasis in original).[18]

The United States Catholic Conference made many of the same arguments in its lobbying efforts for sectarian care. The USCC also emphasized the constitutionality and wisdom of a voucher system that would maximize parental choice, including the right to select religious child care. In 1989, the organization's associate general counsel, John Leikweg, contended that the First Amendment did not require the complete secularization of all child care activities (Liekweg 1989, 1).[19] Noting many of the same Supreme Court decisions relied upon by Agudath Israel, Liekweg wrote that the First Amendment "does not prohibit all forms of government financial assistance, direct or indirect, that may benefit religious institutions, even though some of them may be what the Supreme Court has described as 'pervasively sectarian'" (Liekweg 1989, 2). He further suggested that "the Establishment Clause does not require that legislation must include an express statutory secular use restriction. Thus a possible pragmatic political solution would be to simply not include a church-state provision in the statute itself" (Liekweg 1989, 2). In short, because religious providers represent substantial providers of the nation's child care, the USCC insisted that any legislation include their participation (p. 1).

Whereas Agudath Israel and USCC pushed for more sectarian involvement, other interest groups, such as the American Civil Liberties Union and Americans United for Separation of Church and State, persevered with their position against any religious sponsorship. Barry Lynn, the American Civil Liberties Union's legislative counsel, testified at House child care hearings on April 5, 1989. Robert Maddox, executive director of Americans United for Separation of Church and State, submitted testimony to the House committee on April 21, 1989. The ACLU's Lynn spoke out against the church-state language in H.R. 30, the House vehicle for ABC, both in oral and written testimony, and sought to clarify the language of H.R. 3 so that there would be no ambiguity. Lynn questioned the constitutionality of a proposed voucher system and argued against the incorporation of one into H.R. 3.

Lynn's argument rested on the Supreme Court's seminal decision in *Lemon v. Kurtzman*, 403 U.S. 602 (1971), which provided a three-pronged test for evaluating the constitutional validity of legislation under the First Amendment's Establishment Clause: "First, the action must have a valid secular purpose. Second, it must not have as a primary effect the advancement or inhibition of religion. Third, it must not foster 'excessive entanglement' between government and religion" (U.S. Congress, Committee on Education and Labor 1989, 396). Lynn reasoned that the legislation satisfied the first prong of the Lemon test because the bills were clearly intended to provide secular care. However, the intent regarding the second prong was questionable. He cited Supreme Court decisions that invalidated public assistance to religious schools that originally had been granted for the following diverse reasons: maintenance and repair grants, nontextbook instructional materials and equipment, issuance of revenue bonds, bus transportation for field trips, provision of part-time instructors for "enrichment" courses in private schools, and the use of Chapter 1 funds in the aforementioned case *Aguilar v. Felton* 473 U.S. 402 (1985) (U.S. Congress, Committee on Education and Labor 1989, 397). Lynn acknowledged cases upheld by the Supreme Court that allowed for free bus transportation to and from school, loans for state approved textbooks, and the provision of state-prepared achievement tests (U.S, Congress, Committee on Education and Labor 1989, 397–398).[20]

According to Lynn, one distinction between the cases that were upheld as involving a constitutional use of public funds and those that were not was whether there "is any flexibility in the intended use of the state-supported item" (p. 398). Practices were forbidden when they involved items whose uses were under the control of the school's teachers or administrators because these adults could be motivated by religious concerns. In keeping with this reasoning, child care programs under H.R. 30 would be highly discretionary because they have the potential of advancing religion (p. 398).

Lynn interpreted *Bowen v. Kendrick*, the case upholding the Adolescent Family Life Act and relied upon by Agudath Israel and the USCC in their analyses, as supporting his position against the inclusion of a voucher program. In that ruling, Justice Rehnquist upheld grants to religious organizations that were not believed to be "pervasively sectarian" (p. 399). Lynn emphasized that the proposed child care legislation permits the participation of "pervasively sectarian" religious organizations through either direct grants or vouchers (p. 399). The ACLU took the position that any child care program in a religious setting, intentionally or inadvertently, could inculcate the children through the physical surroundings or through the presence of religiously garbed church members present at the site (p. 399).

When examining the child care legislation according to the third prong of the *Lemon* test, the ACLU concluded unwaveringly that the effect of the legislation would be excessive entanglement between government and religious institutions. The Establishment Clause clearly prohibits the excessive monitoring that would be necessary under the legislation to ensure that there was no sectarian content (p. 402).

At the conclusion of his testimony, Lynn reiterated ACLU's position on the nondiscrimination provisions in the legislation that the organization considered "shockingly inadequate" (p. 403). The incongruity of the nondiscrimination provisions was highlighted. In the ACLU's view, if there was to be no sectarian content to the child care program, there is no rationale for any employment "decision[s] to be made on the basis of participation, membership or beliefs in a specific religious body" (p. 404). Furthermore, the restriction of child care slots based on religious affiliation also undercut the overall intent of the legislation to open up the child care market by making care more available and accessible (p. 404).

Americans United for Separation of Church and State adhered to the ACLU's reasoning, but added a few other points through Maddox's written testimony. Maddox provided insight into the motivation behind "church run" child care: "Religious education is a crucial component of church-run child care. Evangelization through this educational component is nearly always the primary reason why churches operate child care centers. As a pastor of the Southern Baptist Convention, I understand that fact" (U.S. Congress, Committee on Education and Labor 1989, 498). Maddox claimed that the Supreme Court has repeatedly acknowledged that "the parochial school is an integral part of the religious mission of the church" (p. 499). Child care offered at the same site as the parochial schools similarly falls within the domain of the church's mission (p. 499).

Maddox carried his argument further by indicating that Americans United for Separation of Church and State would likely contest through the courts the constitutionality of any child care program that violates the principle of separation of church and state. He warned that such litigation would be costly to the children whose care most likely would be eliminated in the same fashion as were the Chapter 1 funds in *Aguilar v. Felton* and in a companion case, *Grand Rapids v. Ball*, 473 U. S. 373 (1985) (p. 499). Not only would the result of litigation prove contrary to the interests of children and the intent of the legislation, but during the interim period of litigation an infrastructure of child care would develop only to be held unconstitutional. Americans United for Separation of Church and State hoped Congress could avoid such lengthy litigation and the waste of time and resources by crafting constitutionally sound legislation (pp. 499–500).

In his written testimony, Maddox also addressed the problems with the nondiscrimination provisions and the different titles in H.R. 3.[21] Maddox claimed that the new discrimination language resulted in a bill that was even more unconstitutional than before. Because one of the nondiscrimination provisions allowed religious organizations that received less than 80 percent of their funding from the government to discriminate on the basis of religious criteria in the hiring of staff and admission of children for nonfunded slots, Maddox wrote:

The threshold of 80 percent is absurd. Whether it receives one dollar or 80 percent of its funding from government, a church-run child care center should not be permitted to discriminate in any way. If that center receives as much as 80 percent of its funding from tax dollars, it is essentially a government agency. (U.S. Congress, Committee on Education and Labor 1989, 496)

He continued his criticism of the nondiscrimination language by claiming that it ran counter to the new Civil Rights Restoration Act, which specifically condemned discrimination in a facility that received a portion of its funding from the government (p. 497).

The basic theme underlying the position of Americans United for Separation of Church and State was that excessive entanglement occurs through federal funding of religious programs and that the First Amendment is violated through the funding of programs affiliated with religious institutions, regardless of the age of the children involved:

There seems to be an assumption by some that because only children up to age three would be included under Title III that the care is merely custodial and that there is no educational aspect to the program for these children.

In fact, many church-operated child care programs utilize even the pre-three year old aspect of their program to teach religion, to evangelize and to funnel children into the church school educational programs. (U.S. Congress, Committee on Education and Labor 1989, 503)

The ACLU's Lynn and Americans United for Separation of Church and State's general counsel, Lee Boothby,[22] took issue with the legal reasoning of Harvard University's legal scholar, Laurence Tribe, who had written a letter to Senator Edward Kennedy on July 13, 1988, in which he claimed that the Act for Better Child Care was constitutional in the proposed use of federal funds for religious institutions' sponsorship of child care programs.[23] At that time, Tribe concluded that the bill was within the constitutional guidelines because *child care served a custodial function, not an educational function; child care was a "social welfare" program, not an "education" program* (emphasis added):

The Establishment Clause analysis is very different with respect to the ABC bill, which stresses simple child *care* rather than child *education*. Here the precedents condemning the direct aid to parochial schools have little application. This is a general social welfare program designed to protect children from the dangers of poor child care; it has little to do with education and hence does not present any obvious danger of religious indoctrination. (Americans United for Separation of Church and State, citing Tribe, in "Additional Comments" n.d., 2) (emphasis in original)

Tribe's argument, one which was of major significance to the drafters of ABC, rested on an interpretation of child care's *function*. Thus, a pivotal issue in the development of major child care legislation revolved around two different interpretations of child care's function and the resulting consequences of the link with a religious institutional structure. The ACLU's Lynn challenged Tribe's perception:

One threshold matter is whether child care as supported by this bill is an educational program. Notwithstanding efforts by some supporters of the legislation to downplay this aspect of child care, child care cannot be viewed as non-educational or as a mere custodial act. Indeed, the hearing record of this Committee is replete with testimony chronicling the belief of proponents that adequate child care is essential to preparation of students for elementary school. This preparation is nothing short of academic and social education. (U.S. Congress, Committee on Education and Labor 1989, 395)

Lynn further argued that "the Constitution requires more than that specific federal grant or voucher dollars not be traceable to sectarian activities. . . . [It] requires that Federal funds not be made available for generally enhancing the educational efforts of these 'pervasively sectarian' institutions" (U.S. Congress, Committee on Education and Labor 1989, 394).

Boothby also responded to Tribe. "Our disagreement with Professor Tribe's analysis is more a disagreement as to an initial and decisive factual question than a dispute on the law" (Americans United for Separation of Church and State, "Additional Comments" n.d., 2). Boothby emphasized the different functional perceptions: "We believe Professor Tribe's factual understanding of the Bill's concept of providing child care is off the mark, and his concept of church-operated child care programs is unrealistic" (p. 2).

S. 5 eventually was passed, but only after the incorporation of two key amendments that satisfied the Catholic, Orthodox Jewish, and fundamentalist constituencies. Senators Wendell Ford (D KY) and David Durenberger (R-MN) introduced their "Parental Choice Amendment" based on Agudath Israel's proposal. This amendment permitted the use of certificates for the purchase of child care that includes daily worship and religious training. Senator Robert Coats (R-IN) introduced the other amendment, which broadened the discretion of religiously affiliated child care programs to discriminate in their employment policies. The Coats amendment added a provision permitting the sectarian providers to require that their child care workers "adhere to the religious tenets and teachings of such organization" and "adhere to rules forbidding the use of drugs and alcohol" (CQW 6-24-89, 1546).

The Ford-Durenberger amendment, which has proven to be extremely controversial and provides the basis for constitutional challenges, was negotiated into the ABC bill before the floor debate in June 1989. Senator Durenberger had voiced his dissent in *Senate Report* 101-17, which was issued on April 12, 1989. Senate Majority Leader George Mitchell negotiated a leadership package before ABC was brought to the full Senate in which he included the Ford-Durenberger language. In summarizing the debate over S. 5, Senator Mitchell made the following comments:

Mr. President, I want to say that this has been a vigorous, competitive, instructive, informative, and beneficial debate. It has been long—seven full days on the Senate floor. It has been tiring for all concerned, but I believe it demonstrates our process at its best because I believe that the legislation that we are about to enact is much better than the bill that we began debating seven legislative days ago, better still than the bill that emerged out of committee and better yet when the bill was first introduced. I think we can all agree that we still have work to do. We can still improve it. We learned during this week from its critics. Much of the criticism was constructive and positive. The bill was changed to accommodate that criticism, and that process will continue. (*Congressional Record* 6-23-89, S 7478)

During those days of floor debate, reference was continuously made to the "Ford-Durenberger" amendment that already had been folded into the bill between April and June 1989. For example, in addressing his fellow senators on June 23, 1989, Senator Jesse Helms declared:

Mr. President, I have been particularly intrigued by the provision referred to as the Ford-Durenberger amendment. This provision would supposedly make it possible for parents to use child-care certificates authorized under this bill to purchase religious day care if—and I repeat—if the courts do not strike it down.

Now here is the point, Mr. President: if this bill becomes law it will provide child-care assistance to fewer than 1 million out of the approximately 12 million children who would be eligible for assistance—just 1 child out of 12. Thus, in a sense, the bill creates a giant lottery for the available assistance. The question for the religious day cares in this country is whether or not the children they care for will be allowed to compete for these Federal funds. (*Congressional Record* 1-23-89, S 7440)

Senator Helms also proposed at that time the following amendment: "If any provision of this section or the application thereof to any individual or circumstance is held invalid, the invalidity shall cause the entirety of this Title to be invalid" (*Congressional Record* 6-23-89, S 7440). Helms opposed the existing severability clause that allowed for the severance of the specific provision held unconstitutional, for example, the certificate program, rather than invalidating the act in its entirety.

The National Council of the Churches of Christ had circulated a position statement (May 31, 1989) among its members, encouraging lobbying efforts to defeat the amendments. The council feared that the amendments would have several far-reaching, negative consequences. First, if a final version of the bill was passed that contained the amended language, it would be subject to judicial review and if ruled unconstitutional could result in the broad prohibition of church participation. This would leave low and moderate income families who depended on the sponsorship of churches without child care. Second, if the Ford-Durenberger amendments weakened the chance of the ABC bill's passage, it would have the effect of strengthening the position of certain members of the Senate who favored a tax based, grant free approach to solving the child care crisis. Finally, the council was worried that the amendments would only obstruct consensus building in the House of Representatives:

Beyond the obvious constitutional problem posed by this amendment, the proposed change further jeopardizes the bill by playing into the hands of those in the House who oppose all involvement by the religious community in the provision of government-funded care. The church-state concerns are so great in the House that a Senate-passed bill with an unconstitutional provision to fund worship and religious instruction would most likely remain trapped in Committee, never reaching a vote. (National Council of Churches 1989b)

In one of the more interesting passages in this legislation's long and tortuous history, Tribe submitted another letter to Senator Kennedy, dated May 5, 1989, prior to the vote adopting the Ford-Durenberger language, in which he questioned the constitutionality of the proposed amendment exempting the certificates from the prohibition in Section 19(a) against the expenditure of federal funds "'for any sectarian purpose or activity, including sectarian worship or instruction'" (*Congressional Record* 6-23-89, S 7443-44). In his letter, Tribe evaluated the constitutionality of the proposed change under the three-part *Lemon* test. Although Tribe did not think that adoption of the amendment would "violate the secular purpose requirement" of the first *Lemon* test, he believed the bill's prospects under the latter two *Lemon* criteria would be far more problematic (*Congressional Record* 6-23-89, S 7443). Tribe explained:

It is true that the "form" of federal assistance— the fact that ABC funds would flow to sectarian programs as a result of individual parents' decisions regarding where to use their child care certificates, rather than an explicit statutory directive—will undoubtedly weigh favorably in the Court's deliberations. There is nevertheless a significant possibility that the measure would be held unconstitutional, because the child care certificates differ substantially from the forms of government aid to religious institutions previously upheld by the Court. (*Congressional Record* 6-23-89, S 7444)

Moreover, the amendment's adoption would place the government in the position of having to monitor the sectarian institutions' compliance with the statute's requirements, thereby presenting a serious question of excessive entanglement. Indeed, Tribe points to the situation in *Aguilar v. Felton*, 473 U.S. 402 (1985), in which the Supreme Court struck down New York City's Title I program on entanglement grounds, as precedent for his conclusion that monitoring compliance with ABC would require a pervasive state presence in the sectarian schools receiving funds (*Congressional Record* 6-23-89, S 7444).

According to Tribe's analysis, the amendment was likely to "create a significant likelihood that the ABC bill would be held to have the primary effect of advancing religion" under the second test, and was likely "to create an unacceptable entanglement of government with religion" under the third test

(*Congressional Record* 6-23-89, S 7444).   Thus, Tribe believed the Ford-Durenberger amendment "pose[d] a substantial threat to the constitutionality of the ABC bill" (*Congressional Record* 6-23-89, S 7444).

The adoption of these two amendments not only had a wide-ranging impact on the final outcome of child care legislation, but also laid the foundation for future constitutional challenges to the CCDBG.   The acceptance of these amendments by a majority of alliance members shattered the alliance's unity. Many already had been disgruntled by the earlier revisions to Sections 19 and 20 pertaining to staff hiring and admissions of children.   In addition to the dramatic transformation of the bill by the Ford-Durenberger amendments, the Coats amendment was also problematic because it jeopardized the civil rights of child care workers, who could be hired and fired on the basis of their views regarding abortion and birth control, among other controversial issues of belief (Holmes 1990a, A-13).

Action on the New House Bill (H.R. 3)

Having lost the battle on S. 5/H.R. 30, many of the moderates switched their focus to the new House bill (H.R. 3) introduced by Representative Hawkins, which did not allow for the funding of sectarian programs.   In 1989, before the long march toward passage of the House leadership bill, Mary Anderson Cooper, the Washington-based NCC legislative analyst, wrote:

H.R. 3 handles the church-state issue in a way that satisfies most mainline religious groups.   The bill includes language by Rep. Jontz (D-IN) stating that no religious indoctrination or worship is permissible in programs funded by the bill.   H.R. 3 also invokes language from the Head Start law prohibiting discrimination, including that based on beliefs, in both hiring and admissions.   Since Title III funds are not available through vouchers, H.R. 3 avoids ABC's constitutional deficiency of letting federally-funded certificates pay for care in church-housed programs with religious activities.   (Cooper 1989b, 2)

The same problematic areas of church and state existed in the House as in the Senate, but the added problem of the two conflicting committee proposals defused the amount of attention that could be given to church-state concerns.   As with the Senate, partisan fighting prevailed over the advantages and disadvantages of tax credit or block grant approaches.   While the Senate was voting in favor of S. 5 in June 1989, the House was far from a compromise on many issues. Party loyalties were so strong that most Republicans boycotted a June 22 Education and Labor Committee meeting that was to serve as a mark-up and used other tactics to delay the bill's progress (CQW 6-24-89, 1543, 1546). Hawkins finally rescheduled the mark-up for June 27, 1989 (CQW 6-24-89, 1543). The House Education and Labor Report 101-190, Part 1 was filed on July 27, 1989, and the House Ways and Means Report 101-190, Part 2, was filed on September 12, 1989.

The House Education and Labor Committee resolved church-state concerns by including the participation of religious organizations, as long as their program content was nonsectarian. The committee referenced the Head Start language that strictly prohibits sectarian worship or instruction in any program receiving federal assistance (*House Report* 101-190, Part 1, 17). The Education and Labor Committee also restricted the mechanism by which providers would receive funds to grants or contracts. Committee members did not include a certificate program as an optional means of funding child care (*House Report* 101-190, Part 1, 14). By contrast, the Ways and Means Committee chose to remain silent on the church-state issues.

The House spent the second half of 1989 deliberating over the merits of the Title XX approach versus the ABC approach and increasing the EITC or the tax credit. Representative Mickey Edwards (R-OK) offered a substitute that promoted an expansion of the EITC. Although backed by the administration because it favored the tax credit approach, Edwards's bill was defeated 140-285 (CQW 10-7-89, 2639-2640). Representatives Charles Stenholm (TX) and Clay Shaw (FL) offered a bipartisan bill that had some support from the White House. The Stenholm-Shaw alternative combined increased funding for Title XX and Head Start with an increase in EITC (CQW 10-7-89, 2639–2640). During debates on the substitutes, it was clear that the House was far from reaching a consensus on church-state issues. The representatives remained divided over the funding of sectarian programs, as well as over the appropriateness of funding churches at all (CQW 10-7-89, 2640).

By November 1989, the House conferees "agreed to disagree over the most difficult issue dividing them—whether to permit ABC funds to be funneled into child-care centers owned or sponsored by churches and other religious groups" (CQW 11-11-89, 3070). The House leadership agreed to incorporate the Senate church-state language when they arrived at the Dodd-Hawkins-Hatch agreement in November 1989 (CQW 11-11-89, 3070; CDF 1990a). Representative Gephardt came forward with a written and public commitment during the conference negotiations to move the House toward adopting the Senate language (Monahan 1990a, 1). Gephardt agreed to offer an amendment on the floor of the House that would include most of the Senate language (CQW 11-11-89, 3070). Not subject to this Senate-House agreement, the Ways and Means alternative bill remained silent on the issue of church-state (*House Report* 101-190, Part 2; Monahan 1990a, 2).

In spite of the Senate-House agreement, Congress adjourned in 1989 without passing child care legislation. At one point the Dodd-Hawkins-Hatch language was packaged into the 1989 budget reconciliation bill, but was eventually deleted when Senate and House negotiators could not reach an agreement on the tax portions of child care legislation in time for congressional action, either as part of reconciliation or as a free standing bill (CQW 11-11-89, 3070; 11-18-89, 3162).

1990: CHILD CARE AT LAST

In March 1990, the House finally agreed to a leadership bill that represented a compromise between the Education and Labor Committee and the Ways and Means Committee (DSG 1990a, 1–2; Monahan 1990a, 2; *Congressional Record* 3-29-90). This package incorporated the Senate's church-state language as was agreed on in November 1989 by members of the Education and Labor Committee. It was not known, however, until the week before the final House vote on March 29, 1990, that both House committees had agreed upon that language. House Speaker Thomas Foley announced the compromise between Education and Labor and Ways and Means over the funding mechanism for child care in the middle of March. It then took over a week of tense negotiations between the two committees to iron out differences on the use of certificates for sectarian programs. Representative Downey of Ways and Means had steadfastly argued for a bill that remained silent on church-state (Monahan 1990a, 1–2). Yet, he finally conceded to incorporate the Senate language under pressure from interest groups and Democratic party members. The United States Catholic Conference, for one, had threatened to withdraw its support of H.R. 3 in favor of a Stenholm-Shaw alternative bill if the leadership failed to include the Senate language as was agreed upon in November by the Senate-House conferees (Monahan 1990a, 2). Agudath Israel also pressed fervently for the inclusion of sectarian programs and mandatory certificates (Agudath Israel 1990c; 1990d).

Because there had been some uncertainty until a week before the House vote on the leadership package as to the exact nature of the church-state language, members of the National Coalition for Public Education sent a letter to all representatives on March 2, 1990, protesting the inclusion of any language that would incorporate the Senate certificate program for the purchase of sectarian care.[24] Members of the Coalition had hoped to retain the original intent of H.R. 3 which rejected both the use of vouchers and the inclusion of sectarian programs into the block grant approach (*House Report* 101-190, Part 1, 14).

The Stenholm-Shaw substitute provided parents with funds for the purchase of sectarian care and permitted the hiring of employees according to religious tenets, but it also would have substantially reduced funding and quality improvements for child care facilities. Unlike H.R. 3, the Republican measure did not provide for school based care. A similar measure by Representatives Stenholm and Shaw had been defeated the previous year, despite intense petitioning by groups such as Agudath Israel (CQW 3-17-90, 840; 3-31-90, 1000; DSG 1990a; 1990b; BNA 1990a, A-13; Holmes 1990a; 1990b; CDF 1990g; Cooper 1990a, 1–3; 1990d, 2; Agudath Israel 1989e).

The leadership package (H.R. 3) succeeded with a 265 to 145 vote on the House floor (*Congressional Record* 3-29-90, H 1338). In part because the leadership package included the Dodd-Hawkins-Hatch agreed-upon Senate language, the Stenholm-Shaw substitute was defeated by a 195 to 225 vote (*Congressional Record* 3-29-90, H 1336).

Those who had lobbied relentlessly for the moderate position on church-state separation were extremely disappointed when the House defeated amendments proposed on the floor by Representatives Edwards and Price on March 29, 1990. The Price amendment would have allowed states the option of implementing the voucher program (BNA 1990a, A-14; DSG 1990a, 21–24). The Edwards amendment would have prohibited federal assistance in any manner to sectarian programs while permitting the expenditure of federal funds to religious organizations that sponsor nonsectarian child care services (BNA 1990a, A-14; DSG 1990a, 21–24). The Edwards amendment also would have eliminated the provision of the bill that permitted discrimination on the basis of religion in hiring staff and filling nonfunded slots. Edwards had disapproved of the leadership's agreement with the Senate to include language that permitted the preferential hiring of staff and admission of children based on religious criteria. The final version of the House bill also followed the Senate's lead by permitting adherence to religious tenets to be a requirement of employment. Although this general provision was contested by the Edwards amendment, the amended language offered would not have applied to employees already employed, even if a religious preference had been used when they were hired. Furthermore, the proposed amendment did not eliminate the language allowing a "sectarian organization [to] require that their child care workers adhere to rules forbidding the use of alcohol or drugs" (*Congressional Record* 3-29-90, H 1313).

Additionally, the amendment would have ensured that state constitutions and state laws that prohibited the use of public funds for sectarian purposes, or by sectarian institutions, would not be superseded or modified by the bill (*Congressional Record* 3-29-90, H 1313; DSG 1990a, 21).

As expected, the Edwards amendment provoked a very divided response. Among those opposing the amendment were the United States Catholic Conference (Monahan 1990a, 3), Agudath Israel (Agudath Israel 1990c), the National Association of Evangelicals, the Eagle Forum, and the Family Research Council (DSG 1990b, 3). Among others, the ACLU, Americans United for Separation of Church and State, and some key members of the alliance, such as the NCC, NAEYC, and several labor groups, expressed their support of the amendment. The Children's Defense Fund supported the leadership bill as presented. CDF did not indicate any support for the Edwards amendment.[25] Some proponents of the Edwards amendment threatened to withdraw their support of the bill *if* the amendment were *defeated*: the Americans United for Separation of Church and State, the American Jewish Committee, the National Education Association, the American Federation of Teachers, the National Parent Teacher Association, the National School Boards Association, the American Civil Liberties Union, and the Americans for Democratic Action (DSG 1990b, 3).

The NCC and other centrist religious groups voiced their support of the Edwards amendment, but did not threaten to withdraw support of the bill should it fail to pass. Those groups that threatened to oppose the bill if the Edwards amendment failed to pass lamented the implementation of a voucher system, which they feared would weaken the foundation of the public educational system and provoke constitutional challenges in the courts on church-state separation grounds. Once again, organizations were forced to choose among competing values of self-interest, political expediency, and the constitutional safeguards of the First Amendment.[26]

During the debate over the Edwards and Price amendments, the mainline church groups were in a politically vulnerable position, as they were providing a significant portion of the available child care. That the majority of these programs were nonsectarian in nature confounded the constitutional questions. From the perspective of the religious providers, the existing delivery service they provided did not overstep the accepted boundaries separating church and state. As long as the religious providers restricted program delivery to those that were nonsectarian in nature, their programs were less likely to be jeopardized by any future constitutional challenges, especially if the severability clause remained in the final version of the bill.

Nevertheless, to many mainline religious groups, the inclusion of sectarian programs under the bill posed a difficult dilemma. In addition to the political position that funding sectarian programs with taxpayer dollars violated the highly valued constitutional principle of church-state separation, the problem also presented a practical quandary. Mainline religious providers worried that the bill would not pass if it did not include provisions allowing sectarian programs to participate in the certificate plan. Yet, they also feared that if it passed with provisions that permitted sectarian participation, but without a severability clause, the entire act would be at risk of invalidation in the courts. Should the entire act be declared unconstitutional, the delivery of child care to many needy children and their families would be jeopardized. The stakes, therefore, were defined differently for the majority of mainline religious groups than for either their pro-sectarian counterparts or the proponents of the public schools.

Although it was true at the time that the majority of churches sponsored nonsectarian progams (Lindner et al. 1983), the possibility existed that the trend in delivering nonsectarian programs would be altered under legislation that permitted sectarian program content. If funds would become available under the new legislation, nothing would prohibit churches from reshaping their programs to include sectarian components. Religious sponsors operating nonsectarian programs with Title XX funds, however, would be unlikely to sacrifice that funding by becoming sectarian.[27] In any event, these mainline groups had much less to lose and more to gain by aligning themselves with the orthodox religious groups than did those organizations belonging to the National Coalition for Public Education.

After much heated debate on the floor of the House on March 29, 1990, the Edwards amendments were defeated en bloc by a vote of 297–125 (*Congressional Record* 3-29-90, H 1322), and the Price amendment was defeated by 243–182 (*Congressional Record* 3-29-90, H 1312).[28] The March debate culminated the years of deliberation over child care legislation and the question of religious institutional sponsorship, but it also signaled the uphill battle for a Senate-House compromise measure that the president would not veto. In the end, the final versions of both ABC and H.R. 3 contained the language of the final act that permitted federal funding of sectarian programs through the use of vouchers.

Albert Shanker, president of the American Federation of Teachers, wrote an editorial in *The New York Times* on June 25, 1989, imploring the restoration of the original ABC bill:

The new ABC bill will defeat the idea of child-care programs that are hospitable to kids of all races and religions. . . . The new ABC bill will also set a dangerous precedent, opening the back door to federal and other public funding of religious training in elementary and secondary education. After all, many will say, if it's okay to pay for religious instruction for 3-year-olds, why not for 8-year-olds or 16-year-olds? We could even find ourselves in the position of using federal funds for extremist religious groups. (Shanker 1989)

Shanker sought to hold those willing to compromise on church-state issues for political reasons accountable for the drafting of tenuous legislation that would most likely be subjected to court challenge. As Shanker commented, "It's bad business to pass bad legislation and then expect the courts to straighten out your mess for you."

Because both the House and Senate had adopted similar language regarding the role of religiously affiliated providers of child care, the church-state issue was not problematic during the conference committee meetings in the summer of 1990, especially as the approach taken by both chambers was in line with the president's position. The House leadership already had buckled under to the strong Catholic and Orthodox Jewish lobby groups during the House Education and Labor Committee's conference with the Senate in November 1989, and again in March when the Edwards and Price amendments were defeated. The adopted language was a major victory for Agudath Israel, the United States Catholic Conference, and some members of the religious Right, after having expended two years of concentrated lobbying efforts for the purpose of securing the inclusion of a sectarian child care option for parents and providers.

At the time of the conference committee meetings on S. 5 and H.R. 3, leaders from key organizations met in a rallying effort in Washington D.C. on July 12, 1990, to demonstrate support of the bills.[29] During the final push in the 101st Congress to pass child care legislation, CDF and NAEYC led a month-long lobbying campaign in September 1990. Mass mailings went out to the thousands of members of the two organizations to encourage concerned members participation in the advocacy process. Included among these mailings was a calendar outlining advocacy steps that specified the key congressional leaders who needed to be contacted on a weekly basis and reminded that child care was a high priority item among all pending legislation. Advocates feared that any delay of action on the part of Congress would prevent passage of child care legislation for years, as the momentum and interest gained over the past three years could not be maintained. At this point in the fight, little mention was made about the church-state dilemmas. The attention and energy of the alliance were channeled toward passing a child care bill. The gravity of the church-state issues no longer was viewed as a subject for congressional consideration. Rather, the battles remaining to be fought in the fall of 1990 were over fiscal and jurisdictional issues, as well as the designated role of the public schools.

The need for political expediency had pressured many within the liberal religious community, and the liberal community in general, to compromise on church-state issues. The Children's Defense Fund appears to have taken the position throughout the compromises over ABC that the social good of increasing the availability and affordability of child care programs; and maintaining the existing child care system's infrastructure, where church based care forms the backbone, was paramount. Marian Wright Edelman and her colleagues were concerned with expediting the process of enacting comprehensive child care legislation that would reach the most children, with the limited, available resources particularly targeted at those most disadvantaged. From the viewpoint of Edelman, a retraction from church sponsorship would dismantle the largest provider of child care in the country; the result would be the displacement of thousands of children already being served. When the provisions allowing sectarian participation were included in the House bill March 1990, Mary Anderson Cooper observed:

Unfortunately, the Leadership caved in on the church-state issue, incorporating from the Senate-passed bill language which the NCC and much of its constituency regards as unconstitutional. . . . Church-state concerns have plagued this legislation from the start. The courts have repeatedly held that federal funds may not be used for sectarian religious purposes, especially with impressionable young children. (Cooper 1990d, 1)

Proponents of the comprehensive child care legislation recognized that the statutory basis for federal funding of child care would be challenged in court regardless of the final version of the act. Therefore, the legislation was crafted in such a way that its provisions were severable, and the balance of the act could remain intact should a particular provision be held unconstitutional. Senator Helms had hoped to prevent the inclusion of a severability clause. He had argued that the act in its entirety should stand or fall on the basis of the provision of sectarian programs.

Strict separationists had backed the defeated Edwards amendment to block federal funding of any program with a sectarian component because of philosophical and practical concerns over church and state entanglement. The Americans United for the Separation of Church and State, the American Civil Liberties Union, and various fundamentalist groups did not support funding *in any manner* for child care centers under religious auspices. They asserted that even if funding were allowed for church housed programs that were nonsectarian, the enforcement and monitoring of programs for their religious content would be impractical and unconstitutionally entangling. Catholics, Orthodox Jews, and other fundamentalist religious groups, however, *would never have supported* legislation that did *not* permit the use of vouchers for sectarian programs. The education groups adamantly opposed the voucher and discrimination provisions under consideration. The conflict among diametrically opposed interest groups prompted the mainline groups to promote legislation that they felt was the most politically feasible. The highly charged political climate, the desire to avoid undue delay for the sake of the children, and the fear that the opportunity to enact comprehensive child care legislation might not present itself again in the near future, compelled the majority of alliance members to back the bills. These reasons, together with the realization that any further expenditure of time on the language during the drafting process would be futile because of inevitable court litigation, motivated the many middle of the road groups to cast their votes with the sectarian proponents.

Questions of church and state entanglement over the issue of licensure of child care centers clearly bring the service of child care in its religious function to center stage. Conflict has arisen because fundamentalist church groups claim that this religious function is being superseded by the role of the state, whereas other church groups want federal funds to support their free exercise of religion and freedom of choice.

The second major controversial issue in church sponsorship of child care arises because of the interconnection of the religious function with the education function of child care. The drafting of the Act for Better Child Care of 1989 and the Early Childhood Education and Development Act of 1990 invoked heated discussion over whether federal funds should be granted to child care centers sponsored by religious organizations. The fact that child care's education function has gained recognition only recently has become a double-edged sword for child care advocates who support federal subsidization of church centers. After having fought the battle to have child care's multifunctional nature legitimized, proponents of federally supported church centers clash with those contesting federal outlays for sectarian educational programs. When seen as an education service, old arguments about the constitutionality of federal expenditures for parochial schools, whether in the form of grants or vouchers, permeate the debate. Those who contend that child care is a social service with a "custodial" connotation, and not an educational service, ignore the historical merger of early childhood education and child care and the reality that children are learning throughout the course of the day in an incidental, experiential manner.

The multifunctional nature of child care services compounds the problems surrounding church sponsorship. Implicit in the religious function is the idea that children are being "reared" with home values. This child rearing, or socialization function, is not the same as the education or cognitive stimulation function of child care now recognized as an essential component of a high quality early childhood program. Throughout the drafting of S. 5 and H.R. 3, decisions had to be made as to the statutory language dealing with program content, hiring, and admission policies of child care centers under religious agencies' sponsorship.

All of these decisions will affect the market value of child care and the range of choices from which parents will be able to choose a service.

Although the funding of religiously affiliated centers attempts to ensure the maintenance of the existing delivery system and the number of children already being served, the statute's provisions pertaining to federal funds for sectarian programs and the provision legitimizing religious discrimination in admissions and hiring have far-reaching, latent consequences. On the consumer level, parents' choices could very well be restrained by religious factors, rather than expanded. For example, families could find themselves in a situation where the only available high quality child care programs are sectarian, but they would prefer either a nonreligious program or a sectarian program of another faith. Young children, too, will be vulnerable to discriminatory admission practices.

State plans will have to take into consideration the "range" of providers in any one locale, safeguarding the interests of all parents. Federal regulations and state plans must prevent situations in which parents are left with the choice of enrolling their children in a sectarian program or no program at all and the complementary situations in which children are excluded from care because they do not meet the religious criteria of the only available centers.

On the staff level, federal safeguards against employment discrimination based on religion have been diluted in the final version of the statute. The nondiscrimination provisions in Section 658N are problematic. In construing the provisions of Section 658N, subsection (a) references other federal laws relating to religious discrimination in (a)(1)(A) and provides an "exception" in (a)(1)(B) that expressly permits a sectarian provider to consider its employees' adherence to religious tenets and teachings in its employment policies. In subsection (a)(3)(A), however, the statute prohibits religious discrimination against employees whose "primary responsibility is or will be working directly with children in the provision of child care services." It is not clear from the language or logic of Section 658N just how the exception is to be reconciled with the specific prohibition language regarding those working directly with children.[30] Moreover, subsection (a)(3)(B) permits child care providers to employ prospective employees who already are participating members of the organization when two or more prospective employees are qualified. The implementation of this subsection, not to mention its potential abuse, also opens the door to discriminatory practices. These provisions likely will be addressed by the regulatory processs and the courts. In any event, many child care workers will be vulnerable to close scrutiny of their personal beliefs. Although it is yet to be determined precisely what discriminatory practices will be permissible, it appears that, at least for individuals not working directly with children, beliefs on such matters as abortion, contraception, evolution, and homosexuality, among other issues, could serve as the basis for hiring, promotion, discipline, or even discharge.

Ambiguity about church-state issues is also present in the provisions regarding "Construction of Facilities" in Section 658F, which deals with "limitations on state allotments" under the block grant program. Subsection (b)(1) prohibits the use of any funds obtained through the block grant on any building construction or improvement "other than minor remodeling." Section (b)(2) provides an exception to (b)(1) by allowing a sectarian child care provider to expend block grant funds "to the extent that renovation or repair is necessary to bring the facility . . . into compliance with the health and safety requirements." It is unclear whether the sectarian groups' "renovation or repair" encompasses more or less than the "minor remodeling" permitted of the nonsectarian groups. Those who supported the legislation, and who do not want to see it invalidated, will contend that the "renovation or repair" allowed by the exception was intended to be less than that provided by the general provision limiting construction to minor repairs. Proponents of the legislation, and especially the sectarian providers, also will claim that the government's interests in ensuring that health and safety standards are met in this program are compelling. They will point to the fact that the funds allocated for repairs under these two subsections are relatively insubstantial and argue that minimal financial assistance for minor building repairs is not exactly support for sectarian activities. That distinction, however, will not likely dissuade the pro-separation groups from challenging the subsection as explicitly permitting direct federal assistance to sectarian programs in violation of the First Amendment.

It remains to be seen how compliance with these provisions regarding building repairs will be monitored. The same is true for the nondiscrimination provisions. The language in both of these sections is open to different interpretations. The final version of the statute reflects the years of compromises, concessions, amendments, mark-ups, and revisions; it is the product of the various interest groups and their alliances, their conflicts and common ground. Thus, the years of debate resulted in legislation being enacted, but did not fully resolve many of the perplexing church-state issues.

At present there is still a lack of consensus on the appropriateness of using federal funds for child care centers under religious auspices. That child care is not just an educational service or solely a religious service complicates issues imbued with the doctrine of separation of church and state. For example, Head Start has been tied to church sponsorship for a long time, but the Head Start model does not have a religious component or mission. In drafting S. 5 and H.R. 3., House leaders originally looked to the Head Start program as a precedent for funding social services housed in religious institutions. However, the nondiscrimination and nonsectarian language in the Head Start statute were not adopted in the final child care act.

The controversy over the consequences of federal funding of child care centers funded by religious organizations encompasses age-old concerns over parental choice and parental rights, but is exacerbated by the vulnerability of the population in question for ideological inculcation and socialization. Thus, not only is religious freedom at issue, but the ever-present tension between family and state is played out on a battleground of impressionable young children. On the one side, interested parties contend that child care is educational and that the American legal tradition does not endorse the state's financing of sectarian education. Those on the other side stress child care's socialization and religious functions, and the right of familial choice in child rearing matters. They argue that parents should not be denied the right to raise their children in keeping with their cultural and religious values.

The line demarcating the appropriate age at which state intervention in the "rearing" and "schooling" of children begins has shifted downward. The major institutions of society, which include the family, the church, and the state, including the courts, are not ready to deal with all of the ramifications of this shift. As conflict theorists would conjecture, the strength of lobbying forces tilted the pendulum in favor of the more dominant set of beliefs on the divisive issue of separation of church and state. The political fight for child care is the classic example of means justifying ends. Most members of the Alliance for Better Child Care were moderates on church-state issues, but they banded together in the interest of political expediency at the risk of compromising long-held constitutional principles. They sought to appease the orthodox religious constituency while assuming that the courts ultimately would rule on the church-state issues regarding the specific service of child care.

The more powerful voices succeeded in securing the permissive language in the Child Care and Child Development Block Grant Act of 1990 in support of church sponsored sectarian programs, a decision that undoubtedly will be subject to constitutional challenge in the courts. Significantly, an alliance of many prominent organizations from diverse sectors of society maintained a steady voice for church sponsorship throughout the fight for comprehensive child care legislation. The unification of powerful interest groups over a common goal to increase federal involvement in the child care system enabled many compromises and some risk taking over points of contention among alliance members. At the same time, key members of the original coalition disavowed their support of the legislation because of language drafted in each of the two bills. From their perspective, the language in the final act violates the constitutional guarantee that church and state will remain separate. Those opposing the final language contend that civil rights will be violated as a consequence of the non-discrimination provisions in the act.

Conflict theory would suggest that the struggles and shifting allegiances over these controversial issues were resolved on the basis of power. The beliefs supported by the most powerful interest groups, those that represented the most dominant beliefs, governed the outcome of the debates. The sides were drawn between those willing to compromise on church-state issues for the sake of obtaining historical child care legislation and those who were not. The rallying together of at least 100 organizations to form the Alliance for Better Child Care congregated power. Although conflict over church-state language chipped away at this power base, causing a splintering of the organizations that had allied themselves in 1987 in the interest of passing an "act for better child care," the aggregate power of the remaining alliance members succeeded in achieving the enactment of long-awaited child care legislation.

Legislators have wrestled with the issue of federal funding for social services housed in church settings before, but the functions of those services were not as intricately tied up in the intersecting domains of education, religion, and socialization as those of child care services. The issue of church sponsorship has direct and significant ramifications for the institution traditionally responsible for education, the public school system. The pervasive role of religious organizations in the delivery of child care services poses a real challenge to those whose interests are vested in the school system and seek to strengthen the schools' role.

NOTES

1.   Although the study was published in 1983 and has not been updated, the data seems to remain an accurate reflection of church involvement in child care services to date, based on demographic extrapolations and incoming data from ongoing, and informal, denominational internal studies; that is, Children's Advocacy Committee of the Episcopal Church's 1989 survey (CAC 1989). The 1982 study, which was published in 1983, is still referred to by child care advocates as the baseline demographic report on church provided child care.

2.   For a useful general analysis of the First Amendment's religion clauses, see Laurence H. Tribe, *American Constitutional Law* (1988), pp. 1154–1301. According to Tribe, "voluntarism" and "separatism" are the two major principles emanating from the core of the First Amendment's religion clauses (p. 1160). Tribe refers to the Free

Exercise Clause as "a mandate of religious voluntarism" (p. 1160). Freedom of conscience is guaranteed; no coercion, direct or indirect, with respect to one's religious beliefs is tolerated by the Free Exercise Clause. The Establishment Clause also can be understood in terms of voluntarism as it "assures that the advancement of a church comes only from the voluntary support of its followers and not from the political support of the state" (p. 1160). Separatism often is referred to as "the 'noninvolvement' or 'nonentanglement' principle" and embodies the view of James Madison "that both religion and government function best if each remains independent of the other" (p. 1161).

Noting the ambiguity of the historical record and the futility of attempting to determine the framers' intent, Tribe describes the influence of Roger Williams, Thomas Jefferson, and James Madison on the doctrines underlying the two religion clauses (p. 1158). Williams is associated with the "evangelical view" that saw "separation largely as a vehicle for protecting churches against the state" and "imposing on the state the burden of fastening a climate conducive to religion" (pp. 1158–1159). In contrast, Jefferson viewed "separation as a means of protecting the state from the church . . . [and believed] that only the complete separation of religion from politics would eliminate the formal influence of religious institutions and provide for a free choice among political views; he therefore urged a 'wall of separation between Church and State'" (Tribe 1988, 1158–1159, citing *Everson v. Board of Education*, 330 U.S. 1, 16 [1947]). The Madisonian view posited that the interests of both religion and government "would be advanced best by diffusing and decentralizing power so as to assure competition among sects rather than dominance by any one" (p. 1159). Madison believed that the best safeguard against any religion's dominance was to prohibit all government interference, except as needed to preserve public order or protect each sect against infringement of its legal rights by others (Tribe 1988, 1159, citing *The Writings of James Madison*, Vol. IX, 487 [G. Hunt ed. 1910]). In its reflections on constitutional history, the Supreme Court has considered "the ideas of Jefferson and Madison as the direct antecedents of the first amendment and as particularly relevant to its interpretation" (Tribe 1988, 1160).

3.   The inevitable tension between the two religion clauses are a theme reflected throughout Tribe's discussion of "The Rights of Religious Autonomy" in Chapter 14 of his treatise. Tribe explains how "the religion clauses, which for the framers represented relatively clear statements of highly compatible goals, have taken on new and varied meanings that frequently appear to conflict" (Tribe 1988, 1154). Tribe points out that the two clauses can be understood as overlapping or reinforcing one another also (p. 1157).

4.   The consequences of church sponsorship were and are of such significance that a national symposium, Acting For Better Child Care: A National Symposium on Church/State Issues was convened on December 7 and 8, 1989, in New York City, under the organizational leadership of the Child Advocacy Office of the National Council of Churches.

5. For a thorough discussion of the constitutional issues related to licensing exemptions, see Sanger (1983).

6. See, e.g., *Forest Hills Early Learning Center v. Grace Baptist Church*, 846 F.2d 837 (4th Cir. 1989) *cert. denied*, 109 S.Ct. 837 (1989). See also Child Care Law Center July 9, 1990 draft update of *Day Care Licensing and Religious Exemptions*.

7. See Appendixes A–G for listings of the alliance membership at various junctures. Some member groups have remained silent on the issue of church and state, but cast their vote for the passage of ABC and H.R. 3.

8. Mary Anderson Cooper reports on the status of legislation in the National Council of Churches' newsletter, *Mark-Up*. She refers to her constituency as "mainline" members of the religious community.

9. The organizations that signed the letter under the auspices of the Social Justice and Peacemaking Office of the Presbyterian Church protesting the inclusion of a provision to enable sectarian content in child care programs included the following: American Ethical Union; Lutheran Office for Governmental Affairs, Evangelical Lutheran Church in America; Issue Development and Advocacy Union, General Board of Church and Society, the United Methodist Church; Unitarian Universalist Service Committee; Presbyterian Church (U.S.A.) Washington Office; Church of the Brethren, Washington Office; National Council of the Churches of Christ in the USA; Office for Church in Society, United Church of Christ; Union of American Hebrew Congregations; Church Women United.

10. Letter to Representative Kildee dated June 6, 1988 signed by the following organizations: NEA, PTA, National Association of Elementary School Principals, American Association of School Administrators, National School Boards Association, Council for Great City Schools, National Organization for Women, and the National Association of State Boards of Education.

11. For a complete analysis of the Americans United for Separation of Church and State's position on the church-state issue, see two papers published by the organization: "The Act for Better Child Care Services: Summary of a Church-State Analysis" and "Additional Comments on the Proposed Act for Better Child Care Services." See also the article by Americans United's general counsel, Lee Boothby, "The Establishment And Free Exercise Clauses Of The First Amendment And Their Impact On National Child Care Legislation," *Harvard Journal on Legislation*, Summer 1989, Vol. 26, No. 2, pp. 549–563; and testimony submitted on behalf of Americans United for the Separation of Church and State by Dr. Robert L. Maddox, executive director, on H.R. 3, The Child Development and Education Act of 1989 and other Child Care Legislation on April 21, 1989, to the House Committee on Education and Labor, contained in *Hearings on Child Care* (U.S. Congress, Committee on Education and Labor 1989, 495–505).

12. A letter with a list of sign-on names was sent to Representative Kildee on September 23, 1988. The letter set forth the position of religious members opposing the ABC bill.

13. In recent years, several lawsuits have been initiated under state statutory and constitutional law to allow parental choice of elementary and secondary school education through the use of a voucher mechanism. These litigation efforts substantiate some of the concerns that motivate those in the education constituency to lobby against the use of vouchers (Wells 1990).

14. See Chapter 2 for a discussion on the conflict between the two organizations (AFT and CDF) in the 1970s.

15. This original proposal for sectarian sponsorship was referred to as the "Zwiebel Amendment" after Agudath Israel's general counsel David Zwiebel (personal communication with Cohen 1990).

16. The memorandum of July 20, 1988, was prepared by David Zwiebel, director of government affairs and general counsel, and Morton Avigdor, executive director and associate general counsel. Another memorandum, prepared by Zwiebel and Abba Cohen, director of the Washington office of Agudath Israel, was delivered to House and Senate conferees on June 2, 1989. Various memoranda and letters were sent by Agudath Israel's legal counsel to members of Congress throughout the long months of negotiations over the child care legislation.

17. Interestingly, Agudath Israel argued with respect to the Establishment Clause concerns that child care's function under the ABC act was not educational, but essentially one of "social service." Presumably this distinction makes a difference in the constitutional analysis. Yet, regarding the ABC bill's nondiscrimination provisions, Agudath Israel emphasized that lawful discrimination (in hiring and admissions) was necessary to maintain "the very character of religiously affiliated child care institutions, . . . [and] maintain an environment best suited to promote the religious principles for which [the child care providers] exist" (Agudath Israel 1989g, 3). These positions may be at odds to the extent that the Establishment Clause proscribes government assistance that advances religion. The concern with aid to parochial education is tied to the potential inculcation of religion. Whether the statute seems to define child care by its social service or educational function, Agudath Israel's purpose, as it admits, is to provide an environment that best promotes child care's religious function. This purpose does not exactly support Agudath Israel's First Amendment position.

18. Agudath Israel's interpretations of the law with respect to the proposed certificate program were largely supported in a legal analysis submitted to the Senate by the Congressional Research Service's American Law Division (*Congressional Record*, Senate, June 22, 1989). That analysis was prepared by David Ackerman for the Congressional Research Service, Library of Congress, May 9, 1989.

19.   When approached by the author for its positions on the proposed legislation, Pat Cannan of the United States Catholic Conference provided the following article by John Liekweg, "The Establishment Clause Does Not Prohibit the Participation of Religious Providers in Federal Child Care Legislation: Unrestricted Vouchers Are a Constitutional Alternative That Deserves Serious Consideration by Congress," which was an earlier version of an article to be published in the *Harvard Journal on Legislation*. See also Liekweg, John A. "Participation of Religious Providers in Federal Child Care Legislation: Unrestricted Vouchers Are A Constitutional Alternative," *Harvard Journal on Legislation*, (Summer 1989): 26, no. 2, 565–572. The earlier version and the journal article both contain disclaimers that the views presented are the author's and not those of his employer, USCC.

20.   See *Committee for Public Education v. Nyquist*, 413 U.S. 756 (1973); *Meek v. Pittenger*, 421 U.S. 349 (1975); *Hunt v. McNair*, 413 U.S. 734 (1973); *Wolman v. Walter*, 433 U.S. 230 (1977); *Grand Rapids School District v. Ball*, 473 U.S. 373 (1985); *Aguilar v. Felton*, 473 U.S. 402 (1985); *Everson v. Board of Education*, 330 U.S. 1 (1947); *Board of Education v. Allen*, 392 U.S. 236 (1968); and *Committee for Public Education v. Regan*, 444 U.S. 646 (1980) (U.S. Congress, Committee on Education and Labor 1989, 397–398).

21.   Maddox also questioned the language of H.R. 3, that provided new funding for Head Start.   Americans United for Separation of Church and State has had ongoing conflict over Head Start language and sought to rectify ambiguous language at this point in the drafting process (pp. 500–501). See the testimony for Maddox's arguments about the constitutional problems with Titles II and III of H.R. 3 (pp. 502–505).

22.   See Americans United for Separation of Church and State, "Additional Comments on the Proposed Act for Better Child Care Services" n.d.

23.   Tribe wrote another letter to Senator Kennedy dated May 5, 1989, which will be discussed later in this chapter.

24.   See appendixes for a list of organizations that compose the National Coalition for Public Education and a list of the organizations that signed the letter to members of the House on March 2, 1990.

25.   The Democratic Study Group (DSG) undertook a poll before the final vote on H.R. 3 and the proposed amendments.   The lists compiled by DSG as an aid to Democratic representatives should not be construed to be exhaustive on any of the expressed positions.   DSG published a supplemental fact sheet on group positions one day later, "Child Care" No. 101-26 (1990a); DSG Supplement Fact Sheet No. 101-26, "Child Group Positions" (1990b).

26. After the defeat of the Edwards amendment, some organizations circulated a flier urging congressional members to vote against the bill as the Edwards amendment had been defeated (see Appendix I). See Appendix G for a list of organizations that made up the National Coalition for Public Education and Appendix H for a list of the organizations that signed the letter to members of the House on March 2, 1990.

27. Many states allow Title XX funding to be used for church sponsored programs, and some states permit the funds to be used for the support of sectarian programs (CDF 1990a).

28. Several issues in the debate over sponsorship are clarified by a summary review of the arguments for and against the amendment, prepared by the Democratic Study Group of the House of Representatives a few days before the final House vote (DSG 1990a, 22–24). Legal advocates for and against the amendment, each interpreted differently *Witters v. Washington Department of Services for the Blind*, 474 U.S. 481 (1986) and *Mueller v. Allen*, 463 U.S. 388 (1983) and ultimately left constitutional issues over federal expenditure to sectarian sponsorship of child care through a certificate system for the courts to resolve.

Those in favor of the Edwards amendment had several key arguments. First, the provision of aid to nonsecular institutions was not questioned as long as the program content of the services was nonsectarian in nature. Financial assistance to sectarian child care centers was analogized to the unconstitutional act of providing such aid directly to elementary and secondary education sponsored by religious institutions. Second, proponents of the amendment did not accept the certificate program as a constitutionally safeguarded means of providing support to programs with religious content. Whether or not a parent is the conduit of the federal money, the money originates with the federal government and is used for religious purposes. Third, the act permits the exercise of preference in hiring staff and admitting students. The final version of the act was written to preclude any religious sponsor from discriminating on the basis of religion if it received 80 percent of its funds from the block grant. Proponents of the Edwards amendment claimed that few institutions would reach that 80 percent ceiling on federal assistance; instead, the majority of providers, who would be receiving less than 80 percent, would be "free to discriminate on the basis of religion." Such overt discrimination should not be sanctioned by the federal government, they said (DSG 1990a, 22–23).

Those against the amendment countered with the following arguments. First, the certificate system supports parental choice and thereby does not violate the First Amendment's mandate of the separation of church and state. The certificate mechanism does differentiate between direct government and parental support of child care centers with sectarian auspices and program content. Second, the reality of the child care delivery system necessitates an accommodation to the fact that one-third of all care is provided by religious institutions. The opponents of the Edwards amendment stressed the importance of recognizing this reality. Third, the opponents of the amendment stressed that the certificate program assures the existence of choice for all parents and the maintenance of a multiple delivery system. Finally, the discrimination provisions of the act were defended on the basis of the indirect system of the certificate program, and on First Amendment grounds that providers have the right to exercise their religious beliefs (DSG 1990a, 23–24).

The DSG did not include in its summary the more radical position that religious providers should be prohibited from federal aid of any kind.

29.   The following organizations were represented by their respective leaders at the June 12, 1990, press conference for the passage of child care legislation: the Child Welfare League of America, the Children's Defense Fund, the National League of Cities, the National Council of Churches, the Association of Junior Leagues, the U.S. Catholic Conference, the National Women's Political Caucus, the National Association for the Education of Young Children, the Child Care Action Campaign, and the National Women's Law Center (CWLA 1990, 2).   Noticeably, the three powerful education groups— the National Education Association, the American Federation of Teachers, and the National Parent-Teacher Association— did not participate in the rally.   These groups had split with the alliance over the church-state language early in the drafting.   Yet, other labor organizations remained in the alliance, setting up a test of institutional power within the political process, and dividing the labor movement.

30.   The various House and Senate committee reports and the conference report do not explain this ambiguity.

5. For-Profit Sponsorship
and the
Economic Function

One of the factors complicating an attempt to decipher the profile of church involvement in child care is the overlap between church sponsorship and for-profit sponsorship. For-profit child care centers comprise a wide spectrum of different types of which church housed for-profit enterprises are one segment. In keeping with the American concept of private enterprise, the private sector holds a considerable share of the child care market and vigorously urges that the service should be a part of the free market system.

At the onset of the last decade of the twentieth century, the child care market is dominated by proprietary providers. This for-profit majority reflects a considerable change in the child care industry brought on after the Reagan initiatives of the early 1980s, which succeeded in causing significant shifts in the field of child care delivery (Kahn and Kamerman 1987; Neugebauer 1989; 1990a; 1990b). In 1977, six out of ten centers were operated on a nonprofit basis according to the National Day Care Study (Neugebauer 1990b, 21). Today the nonprofit sector finds itself in direct competition with the for-profit sector (Neugebauer 1990b). Testifying during hearings on child care in 1989, on behalf of the proprietary lobby, the National Child Care Association (NCCA), Nick Craft, operator of three centers in Georgia, estimated that the proprietary sector represents one-half of all child care in the United States. The child care industry is allegedly contributing $15 billion to the gross national product with an expected growth rate of 21 percent through 1995, when it will be producing $48 billion a year (U.S. Committee on Education and Labor 1989, 409, 412).

The for-profit sector expanded at an annual rate of 10 to 12 percent during the 1980s; whereas, the nonprofit sector expanded at less than half of that rate

(Neugebauer 1990a, 31; 1990b, 21). However, the following factors in the current economic market will inhibit growth in the for-market sector: the price sensitivity of the service, the shrinking labor supply, threatened increases in licensing requirements, the increased difficulty and cost of developing new sites, the oversupply of centers in specific locales due to competition, an aging infrastructure with repair and reorganization needs, and the leveling off of demand (Neugebauer 1990a, 31).

Roger Neugebauer, editor of *Child Care Exchange*, reported in February 1990 that the for-profit market of approximately 35,000 centers was composed primarily of single or dual operator providers. Chains operate 10 percent of for-profit centers. The largest ten chains operate less than 9 percent of the for-profit market. Neugebauer (1990a) classified the chains into three subcategories based on the number of centers they operate.[1] The three large chains that operate more than 400 centers include Kinder-Care Centers (1260 centers), La Petite Academy (722 centers), and Children's World Learning Centers (474 centers). Mid-size chains, operating between 40 and 120 centers, include the following: Children's Discovery Centers (118 centers), Gerber Children's Centers, (117 centers), Rocking Horse Child Care Centers of America (100 centers), Creative World Schools (45 centers), New Horizons Child Care (40 centers), and Magic Years Child Care and Learning Centers (40 centers). The remaining forty-two centers on Neugebauer's list of the top fifty large for-profit organizations are considered "small" chains (Neugebauer 1990a, 32–33). The three large chains, plus Gerber and Children's Discovery Centers, are national operations (Neugebauer 1989, 19). According to Neugebauer, the fastest growth has occurred in the regional and mid-size chains (Neugebauer 1989; 1990a).

The three largest chains had a combined annual expansion of only 3 percent in 1989, but were projected to do better in 1990. Their difficulties were more internal than market related. Between 1980 and 1985, the three chains expanded at an average of 26 percent per year. In 1986 to 1988, they expanded at a rate of 12 percent per year. In 1989, mid-size chains expanded by 20 percent, and small chains expanded by 13 percent (Neugebauer 1990a, 32). The *Child Care Exchange* surveyed the major for-profit providers and found that they intended to focus their attention on increasing enrollments, rather than on constructing new centers in 1990 (Neugebauer 1990a, 32).

Because chain operations present a unique perspective on the delivery of child care, any discussion of for-profit child care must consider that there is a range of types and that the chains do not reflect or always represent the small, independent operators' interests. Regardless of type, however, for-profit centers sponsor child care for the provider's economic gain. The degree of profit varies by center, but all for-profits share the primacy of the economic function. Under private sponsorship the center operates to provide income to the provider through the profit margin. The degree of margin distinguishes large business operations from single center providers who are attempting to sustain moderate gains.

HISTORY OF FOR-PROFIT PROVIDERS

Proprietary sponsorship of child care began to proliferate in 1969 at the time of marked legislative activity in favor of increased federal funding to centers. Child care was a ripe market for several reasons. First, the increase in the number of working mothers was more dramatic and better known to the public. Second, a gap existed in the need for services and the number of available spaces. Third, Congress and President Nixon were grappling with proposed increases in federal subsidies for child care centers.

Articles began to appear in popular periodicals and business magazines that described the sudden interest in child care on the part of business. Titles of such articles are indicative of the times: "Day Care: The Boom Begins" (*Newsweek* 12-17-70); "Nursery Schools Will Be Opened by Chicken Chain" (Morton in *The National Observer* 2-17-69); "The Day-Care Business: Which Comes First the Child or the Dollar?" (Lake 1970); "The Day Care Problem: Kentucky Fried Children" (Featherstone 1970). These articles underscored the connection between federal attention to the long-time problem of child care and the entrepreneurial reaction to a perceived profitmaking opportunity: "Sniffing possible federal largesse, some fifty firms have rushed into the business of franchising or packaging day care centers. Some are embarrassingly promotional. Others are very serious entrants, such as Singer, General Learning and Gerber" ("Corporate Baby Sitting" 1971, 20). Another article provides:

All these bills, but particularly the Nixon Administration's possible extension of day care, have attracted the attention of a number of new businesses that are springing up to cultivate what many believe to be a national market for various kinds of child services. A few are fired by the vision of federal largesse for services to welfare mothers. Some are more interested in the possibility of an expanding middle-class market. In fact, most actual, working centers cater to parents well above the poverty line. The level of investment in research and tentative promotion is bigger than the level of actual operations: most of the businesses remain fairly small, local operations. (Featherstone 1970, 15)

The American Federation of Teacher's 1976 position paper on child care sponsorship noted that, "New companies were created overnight and some offered securities on the stock market" (AFT 1976, 95). Citing a 1971 article in *Barron's* magazine, the AFT stated that over twenty-five child care operations were reported to offer stocks to investors in the two year period 1969-1971 (p. 95).

In 1970, Alice Lake reported, "Already forty corporations are splashing around millions of dollars to create a profitable industry. Children will be its products" (p. 61). A dozen of the biggest companies were already operating 100 centers in twenty-one states by 1970. Six of the companies expected to serve 50,000 children by the end of 1971. "It's a popular notion that day care is for the poor, but the businessman who has surveyed the potential market knows better" (Lake 1970, 61).

Successful entrepreneurs from other fields entered the child care market and brought with them the popular business technique for expansion: franchising. George Nadoff, formerly president of International Food Service and a franchiser of Kentucky Fried Chicken in the New England area, started Living and Learning child care centers. Gerald Spresser, a hotel restaurateur of twenty-five years, founded Mary Moppets. Perry Mendel, a southern real estate developer founded Kinder-Care centers. The giant corporations, Singer and Gerber, started franchise operations. The franchising conglomerate, CenCor, established La Petite Academies and American United Inns, owner of the Ramada Inns, began Amerikid centers (Goldman 1975, 81). The goal of these investors and entrepreneurs was to deliver child care on the lines of other franchise operations that performed a high volume business with low cost. They wanted to market child care as one would market a McDonald's burger. The franchise model, which was successfully delivering fast food, car repair, miniature golf, and nursing homes, was the model for providing child care (Goldman 1975, 81). John Jay Hooker of Performance Systems, Inc., formerly Minnie Pearl's Chicken System, Inc., a founder of Child Care Centers, commented: "What we are doing is selling a system of running a small business. We have centralized accounting, we have various techniques, we have a method of reducing it to a system" (Morton 1969, 20).

Unfortunately for many of these companies, the anticipated federal legislation that would have provided subsidies to centers was not passed. This factor, in addition to the higher than anticipated cost of starting child care centers, caused many of the new ventures to fail. However, those companies able to weather the downside grew to form a multimillion dollar industry (Goldman 1975, 81). Many of the big business ventures began as franchise operations, but eventually switched to company owned and operated businesses because they afforded better administrative control (Goldman 1975, 82). The financial backers found that the local franchiser was often too inexperienced to handle a child care center successfully. As of 1975, only Mary Moppets,

Amerikid and Alphabetland continued as franchises (Goldman 1975, 82). Perry Mendel, the founder of Kinder-Care, abandoned the franchise notion after seven months (Bellm 1987, 36). By 1983, only Mary Moppets operated as a franchise (Fenn 1983, 108). And as of 1986, Mary Moppets either owned or franchised centers ("A New Builder Amenity: Day Care Centers" 1986, 158). According to Lynn White, the director of the National Child Care Association, franchising has entered a period of resurgence. Currently two primary franchise players are based in Georgia; Primrose Country Day Schools and Kids Are Kids (personal communication with White 1990).

An upsurge in interest and expansion of the chains first seen in the period 1969–1972 was observed again in the early 1980s under the Reagan administration. This movement has continued into the 1990s. At the end of the 1980s, the child care industry began to consolidate with many small contractors of child care services wanting to sell out or seeking capital infusion. The investment banking firm, Le Percq de Neuflize & Co., is an example of the new trend in buyouts of corporate child care providers. Le Perq invested in American Family Service Corporation, a start-up company entering the child care field with an interest in targeting the "upscale working professional families" (Parker 1988). This trend, set in place during the late part of the 1980s, suggests that the field is ripe for continued development by large investors: "Many small independent operators are eager to sell, fed up by increasingly burdensome licensing regulations, escalating insurance and real estate costs, difficulties in securing expansion financing and heavy competitive and marketing pressures" (Parker 1988, 52).

The Economic Recovery Tax Act of 1981 also bolstered the child care business. The chains and other proprietary centers benefited from two new federal policies. The tax breaks for child care costs encouraged parents to utilize centers, and tax breaks for employers encouraged employer subsidization of employees use of centers (Fenn 1983, 104; Kahn and Kamerman 1987).

The Economic Recovery Tax Act also implemented the wage-benefit package for employers by facilitating industry's support of child care with tax incentives that had the unintended consequence of encouraging new relations between the child care chains and corporations. The chains began developing vendor programs with industry. Individual companies could either contract with a chain to manage an on-site facility or contract with the chain to subsidize its employees' use of the chain's off-site center ("Child Care Grows as a Benefit" 1981, 94). Kinder-Care marketed a program known as *Kindustry* (Fenn 1983, 106).

During the late 1980s, and the beginning of the 1990s, a new trend emerged between corporate America and child care entrepreneurs. Management consulting firms were organized to contract with businesses on child care and family related issues. Some of the new consulting groups have been established on a not-for-profit basis, others on a for-profit basis. The firms vary in their approaches with some restricting their practices to the development or management of nonprofit centers or both. The common thread among these organizations is their consulting activities with companies over child and family concerns, commonly known as *work-family* or *dependent care* issues. Although a subspecialty of these management consulting firms deal with the direct service of child care by developing and managing centers, others aim their consultation at indirect services, such as benefit packages and time-management policies. The first compilation of these consultation groups was published in the February 1990 issue of *Child Care Exchange*. The Association of Child Care Consultants International (ACCCI) was incorporated in 1988. *The Associate*, the ACCCI newsletter, noted that within a period of fifteen months the association grew from 2 founding members to over 250 (Nye 1990a, 1).

Taking heed of this trend, major corporations are getting in on the act by offering their services or products to the consultants. Manufacturers of educational material such as Lakeshore Learning Materials, Childcraft and Integral Environments market their wares by providing child care management with promotional material and special financial arrangements (personal communication with Kurtz 1990). National Cooperative Bank and its affiliate, NCB Development Corporation solicit child care consultants and offer financing packages. The Development Corporation offers term, interim, line of credit financing, and "Business Planning Advances," which provide funding for feasibility studies (National Cooperative Bank 1990). The Marriott Corporation has entered the field of child care as an avenue for expanding its food and janitorial services by forming a partnership with Corporate Child Care (Oliver 1990; Boyle 1990).

In spite of the new players in the field, particular economic advantages have propelled the growth of child care chains, in addition to the aforementioned tax incentives to both employees and employers. These incentives include growth in the size of the chains' middle class target population, those "whose incomes are too high for federally subsidized day care and too low for private alternatives" (Goldman 1975, 82); the benefit of buying supplies in bulk quantity, an advantage unavailable to the small proprietor; and, the financial support of a parent company that facilitates fee setting at a competitive rate (Fenn 1983, 104). A major competitive edge of chains and other for-profit operations had been their lack of reliance and dependency on federal subsidies, which left them in a better position than nonprofits that traditionally have been vulnerable to federal cutbacks ("A Boom Ahead for Kid-Care Companies" 1984; Kahn and Kamerman

1987; Neugebauer 1990b). In 1983, less than 2 percent of the children using the chains received some type of federal subsidy (Fenn 1983, 104). The new child care legislation will affect the way that chains and other for-profit operations compete in the marketplace.

The utilization rate of chain centers by low income clientele continues to remain low and contributes to the segregation by income seen across the child care industry. Yet, the Reagan privatization initiatives positively affected the expenditure of subsidies by low income families at proprietary centers, including the large chains. Kahn and Kamerman found that Reagan's policies, which advocated demand subsidies rather than the subsidization of supply, increased the choices for some recipients of public funds. Some heads of proprietary chains reported that the tax credit bolstered their business by encouraging those receiving subsidies to utilize their centers (Kahn and Kamerman 1987, 99). Nevertheless, Kahn and Kamerman also noted that the majority of for-profit centers, and the chains in particular, do not select child care sites in the inner city. Their middle class target precludes utilization by the poor and near poor who inhabit urban and rural regions. This deliberate marketing of suburban, middle class centers on the part of the providers, combined with the restrictions placed on eligibility criteria for recipients of public subsidization, confines the for-profit sector to servicing the middle class and excluding the low income population from their services (Kahn and Kamerman 1987, 105–106).

RESEARCH FINDINGS ON FOR-PROFIT STATUS

The National Child Care Staffing Study (NCCSS) was coordinated by the Child Care Employee Project (1989) with the specific purpose of gathering information on (1) the utilization of centers in the United States; (2) the quality of the centers' environments for children and staff; and (3) the status of child care providers. This study contributed landmark findings pertinent to the issue of for-profit sponsorship. Centers were classified as either independent for-profit, chain for-profit, nonprofit, or church sponsored. The research team examined the utilization of centers by the socioeconomic status of children and auspice. The data revealed that children from low income families were predominantly in nonprofit centers. High income families primarily utilized nonprofit centers and to a lesser extent independent for-profit centers. The middle-income families were found disproportionately represented in for-profit centers. Church-sponsored centers served low and middle income families (CCEP 1989, 16).

Sharon Lynn Kagan and James W. Newton (1989) conducted a statewide analysis of differences between for-profit centers and nonprofit centers, which was published close to the publication date of the National Child Care Staffing Study. Kagan and Newton's comparison study of a sample of Connecticut facilities indicated that income and ethnic stratification is a very real phenomenon in the child care system as presently constructed. Government subsidized nonprofit centers served 40 percent black or Hispanic children compared to the 6 percent served in privately supported nonprofit centers, and the 4 percent served in for-profit centers (Kagan and Newton 1989, 7).

Kagan and Newton's study was undertaken in the spirit of deflating ideological debates over the for-profit status in child care in favor of empirical evidence for or against such sponsorship. The researchers undertook the project with the purpose of contributing to a resolution of the "raging debate" over the quality of care provided by for-profit providers, because the main issue of controversy over proprietary child care is whether making a profit is compatible with the delivery of high quality child care. Inherent in the dilemma are both realistic and ethical concerns. Critics question the morality of profiteering off children. Others point to the logistical impossibility of making a profit and providing high quality care, stating that the two are mutually exclusive due to the labor intensive work and the nature of the service.

The pivotal question has been whether the profit motive undermines the quality of care. Critics contend that one reason that quality is sacrificed in for-profit settings is because profits are made by underpaying the staff. The low wages set in cycle a deterrence to the delivery of high quality programs. Low wages encourage hiring untrained workers and high turnover rates, which together ultimately cause harm to young children who need consistent care to develop. Fewer staff members are hired, which raises the ratio of children to teacher above the ratios suggested by the professional standards set by the old Federal Interagency Day Care Requirements (FIDCR) and NAEYC.

The for-profit centers cut their costs on a number of key variables that are essential for maintaining and delivering high quality programs. The National Day Care Study (NDCS) (Ruopp 1979) in a four year study found the following variables to be critical measures of quality in child care programs: child to staff ratio; group size; and teacher qualifications. Many for-profit centers fail to meet standards established around these three variables as suggested by the study. The NDCS found group size to be most significant. The smaller the group size the greater is the potential for delivering high quality care. Large group sizes were found to be detrimental to young children just learning to cope with group life.

The child to staff ratio was found to be less important than group size except in the delivery of infant and toddler care (Ruopp and Travers 1982, 82). Nevertheless, suggested ratios were given for 3, 4, and 5 year olds. The study suggested that for cost saving purposes the standard staff to child ratio need not be more stringent than 1:7. The study "offered three different policy options ranging from 8:1 to 10:1 for enrollment, and 7:1 to 9:1 for attendance" (Nelson 1982, 299). The trade-off was between cost reduction and quality.

The National Day Care Study further found that teacher experience was a significant factor in determining the quality of care provided. Specialized training in early childhood education and child development made a difference in the interaction between the staff and the children (Ruopp and Travers 1982, 82). The level of education was less significant, however, than the type of education and experience.

The variables selected by the NDCS were selected as important because they are indicators that can be controlled. The group size, teacher-child ratio, and teacher educational experience were found to be substantive program policies where for-profit centers fell below accepted professional standards to maintain profitability. The proprietary sector has fought certain regulations in these areas. For-profits have received support in their efforts from administrators who did not want their already strained budgets and personnel utilized to provide the necessary monitoring and enforcement (Phillips and Zigler 1987, 20). In 1980, a strong coalition of thirty child care groups fought to have a long-debated set of standards, known as the Federal Interagency Day Care Requirements (FIDCR), adopted, but were unsuccessful. The proprietary lobby, National Association of Child Care Management (NACCM), opposed setting standards, especially group size and child to staff ratios (Fenn 1983). Opposition to federal standards remains strong among proprietary groups (Craft cited in U.S. Congress, Committee on Education and Labor 1989, 410–411; "The Impact of the Federal Regulations" 1988; Dermott 1989, 9; Muscari 1988).

The National Child Care Staffing Study (CCEP 1989) found that for-profits, both chains and independents, spent less of their budgets on teaching staff than did nonprofits. Upon examining the percentage of expenditures for salaries and benefits, it was discovered that chains allocated 41 percent and independents allocated 49 percent; whereas, nonprofit and church-run centers allocated 62 percent and 63 percent, respectively. The National Child Care Staffing Study (NCCSS) concluded that "auspice," here referred to as *sponsor*, was the strongest predictor of quality. The findings clearly indicate that quality is sacrificed in for-profit settings through the low wages of the employees. The low wages have a negative spiraling effect on employee morale, rate of staff turnover, and hiring practices (CCEP 1989). One of the most significant policy recommendations of the Child Care Employee Project is the grave need to upgrade compensation for child care providers. The entire industry suffers from abysmally inadequate compensation, with the proprietary segment representing the lowest level of remuneration for caregivers.

A main reason for the proliferation of for-profit enterprises in the child care market is that children and child care workers are particularly vulnerable to economic exploitation. In 1983, Fenn found that chains spent 30 percent less per child than nonprofit providers (p. 104). Kagan and Glennon (1982) found that for-profit centers that did not receive any federal funding expended the least amount of money per child compared to nonprofit, non-federally funded centers and for-profit federally funded centers that spent similar amounts. In analyzing the consequences of the child care policies of the 1980s, Kahn and Kamerman (1987) concluded:

Clearly, the private sector programs are being operated at lower cost than the public programs were; the quality is lower, too, however. In general, privatizing the delivery of child care centers, in particular, increasing the proportion of proprietary centers, may have led to lower costs per child but at a "price" in quality that many would question: lower staff-child ratios, larger groups, larger centers, less equipment, lower caregiver salaries. Even the best of the for-profit chains will not locate in states with high minimum standards because of the costs imposed. They cannot meet the competition with regard to fees. Also, even the best of the proprietary chains define as a minimum size for a facility (100 to 150 children) one that many view as too large for an environment for the very young. A smaller facility is not viewed as economically feasible; yet 50 to 75 children is often cited by others as a desirable standard. (Kahn and Kamerman 1987, 111)

Kagan and Newton's 1989 findings on quality differences by the form of provider are not reported in total dollar costs per child. However, their report did indicate that government supported nonprofits ranked higher on each of the following key variables, followed by private nonprofits, which ranked slightly higher than for-profits:

ratios of children to paid staff; ratios of children to all caregivers (including volunteers); and services offered to children, including screening and referrals for vision, hearing, social work, and psychological care, as well as field trips and library contacts. Similar differences were found in services to parents, including counseling on family matters and assistance in obtaining community or personal services, and frequency of communication with outside agencies such as human resources, education, health and fire prevention. (Kagan and Newton 1989, 7)

Although there were many similarities among all three provider types on program goals and six out of the ten Child Development Associate (CDA) checklist indicators, significant differences were found between for-profit centers and nonprofit centers on two CDA criteria. Both nonprofit types rated significantly higher on the environment and creativity components of the CDA checklist. Caregivers of nonprofits also rated higher on caregiving behavior measures. Only one type of nonprofit auspice ranked higher than for-profits on self-concept and group management measures (Kagan and Newton 1989, 6–7). The researchers also found that centers differed by sponsor type in the degree to which the parents were involved in the program. The type of parent interaction varied across all sponsor types, but formal involvement in policy decisions was highest among government subsidized nonprofit centers (86 percent), and only 5 percent of for-profits; 52 percent of private nonprofits reported parent involvement in formal policy decisions. Private nonprofit directors reported the highest amount of volunteerism by parents (p. 8).

Kagan and Newton discussed the implications of their findings and concluded that government subsidized centers were held to the highest standards, but that for-profit status did not automatically condemn a program to poor quality. On the three key policy indicators identified by the NDCS, for-profits were significantly lower only on the ratio of children to caregiver. No significant differences were found among all three types when compared for degree of child related training or when compared on the measure of group size. Kagan and Newton found overall that government subsidized nonprofit centers were held to the highest standards in the industry. They concluded that regulation, monitoring, parent involvement, and link with community resources and services seem to correlate with high quality delivery and merit further investigation (pp. 8–9).

The two major, definitive empirical research studies on differences among child care centers based on type of auspice discussed here, Kagan and Newton (1989) and NCCSS (CCEP 1989), provide justification for the unrest that has surrounded the role of the private sector in child care delivery. At the same time, the reports raise questions for future research and press policy makers, providers, and consumers to pay closer attention to the impact of structure on function. The research indicates that the sponsor does have important conse-quences for the delivery of high quality child care programs. Kagan and Newton's work highlights how the type of provider affects child care's social service function. Government supported nonprofit programs offer social services, but the for-profits do not. The goals of child care vary according to the providers' organizational structure and the degree of government subsidiza-tion. The varying results of these different structures are most evident in the quality of programs, the population served, the status and compensation of the child care workers, the range of services, and the degree of parent involvement.

KINDER-CARE: A CASE EXAMPLE

Although the quality measures and provider goals mentioned earlier engender controversy, further analysis of the positions for and against for-profit sponsorship should await close examination of an actual for-profit provider. An example of American entrepreneurship set within the child care industry is Kinder-Care, Inc. Because Kinder- Care is the largest commercial child care chain and has such a large share of the for-profit sector, it is of heuristic and historical significance.

Kinder-Care filled a gap in child care left unfilled by the public sector twenty years ago. As indicated in this book, it is not speculative to suggest that had legislation supporting an expanded public role in the delivery of child care services passed when first proposed twenty years ago, the proprietary sector, which now offers considerable competition to the nonproprietary sector, would not be so potent a factor today. Given the growth in the for-profit sector over the intervening years, proprietary providers are now deeply vested in protecting and securing their position in the child care market.

Kinder-Care is the "brainchild" of Perry Mendel, a former real estate developer in Montgomery, Alabama. Mendel conceived the idea of commercial child care in 1968 after noticing a friend whose wife operated two nursery schools and brought in enough income to support a comfortable life-style. Mendel opened the first Kinder-Care in Montgomery in 1969 with a logo that has become synonymous with Kinder-Care, the orange and red-roofed bell tower (Englade 1988, 45). All of the Kinder-Care facilities follow a prototype (Kinder-Care 1989a). The physical plant and the program itself follow a standard set by the company. "Atop each Kinder-Care is a red roof and steeple with a black bell subliminally suggesting to parents their children are 'enrolled' in day care" (Lynn 1978, 19). The majority of centers serve 100 to 150 children. The architecture consists of a wide open space subdivided by partitions that allow for much background noise. Infants do not share this wide open space, but are placed in a separate room (Lewin 1989, 89).

Kinder-Care originally was based on the idea of leasing. An investor or developer builds a Kinder-Care center on a half-acre site and then leases the building to Kinder-Care on a long-term basis, usually twenty years. Or, Kinder-Care buys the site, and uses long-term financing for the center's construction after negotiating with a contractor (Lynn 1978, 18). In 1981, after the prime interest rate soared upward, Kinder-Care turned to convertible debentures. At that point in its history, Kinder-Care moved away from lease arrangements to buying its land and buildings (Magnet 1983, 153).

In 1989, Kinder-Care employed 17,000 workers in forty states and Canada. It had quarterly operating revenues of nearly $75 million, and net profits of $6.25 million (Lewin 1989, 30). The company operates 1,200 centers; one franchisee located in a small southern area operates twenty centers (Kinder-Care 1989a).

Kinder-Care has evolved into a wide-ranging operation. The company went public in 1972 when there were thirty-four centers and 250 employees. By 1975 there were six regional areas in seventeen states (Kinder-Care 1989c). Two years later, Kinder-Care undertook its first acquisition of fifteen Playcare centers. In the same year, the company's stock had its first split and paid its first cash dividend. One year later the company began a major new expansion effort by creating and promoting Kinder Life Insurance Co. (Kinder-Care 1989c).

Kinder-Care's venture into business relations with other corporations began in 1979 when it opened a center directly across the street from the Ralston Purina headquarters in St. Louis. This venture set the stage for the Kinder-Care at Work program. By 1979 Kinder-Care employed 3,000 people and operated 436 centers (Kinder-Care 1989c). "Kindustry," a component of Kinder-Care at Work, was developed in 1981 to address the problem corporations were experiencing in retaining key personnel and to serve latchkey children. Kindustry offered a combined escort and educational-recreational service. A Kinder-Care employee transported children to and from Kinder-Care centers, both before and after school. The school-age children were coined *klubmates* and given special areas and activities at the centers. Products were developed and sold for "klubmates," including T-shirts and educational tapes ("Kinder-Care Makes Employers into 'Uncles'" 1982, 52, 54).

The company's newsletter, *Centerline*, reported on the status of Kinder-Care at Work in its February 1990 issue. The program offers a corporation the following options: on-site or near-site care; a management contract to operate an existing or new center; Kindustry that involves a minimum contribution of 10 percent by the employer to the employee's participation in the service; and consulting services. As of 1990, the company had twenty on-site operations, three of which were under construction.

The controversial, company tailored curriculum, known as the GOAL program, was initiated in 1980 (Kinder-Care 1989c). This curriculum is divided into themes by months and weeks. Calendars suggesting various themes and activities for different age groups are sent out monthly to each center. Teachers are told to use them as guides; thereby, the teacher's experience or lack of experience will influence to what extent suggested lessons are used. They are expected to follow the basic requirements of the calendar, however (Englade 1988, 47; Lewin 1989, 89). The quality of the programs delivered as a result of this mix between teacher experience, company expectations, and company suggested guidelines is open for evaluative research. The undisputable facts are that a standardized curriculum does exist and Kinder-Care employs many inexperienced teachers and directors:

Kay Albrecht, who visits day care centers across the country as a representative of the National Association for the Education of Young Children (NAEYC), says, "I've been in excellent Kinder-Care centers and awful ones." But Albrecht, who is NAEYC's most experienced associate, adds that she has also been in excellent and awful nonprofit and corporate-sponsored day-care centers.

Albrecht believes that the key to quality is each center's director, his or her training and experience. About Kinder-Care directors, she says, "They're usually young. They're less often experienced, and experience is a great teacher in this business." (Englade 1988, 48)

Kinder-Care continued to expand its product line by targeting its own parent-consumer group. The Kinder Life insurance venture merged in 1985 with another company Perry Mendel acquired, the Pioneer Western Corporation of Clearwater, Florida. By the time of the merger, Kinder Life had sold more than $300 million worth of life insurance policies, benefiting 60,400 children. Mendel then ventured forward to sell mutual funds, stocks, bonds, and tax sheltered products through Pioneer Western. Soon thereafter, Mendel bought Centerbanc, a savings and loan association headquartered in St. Petersburg. He acquired Centerbanc to assist in financing Kinder-Care's growth (Englade 1988, 51).

The company's management viewed these expansions as an "evolutionary step." The current consumers of the company's direct services represented a captive and logical market for financial planning. Young middle class families with children were struggling with major financial hurdles and needed loans for homes and cars. Filled with aspirations for their children's well-being, these young families would readily invest in saving plans and insurance policies (Bellm 1987, 36; "Day-Care Network Takes on Unusual Charge" 1987; Engardio 1986, 34; Englade 1988, 51).

At the same time, Kinder-Care continued its growth beyond the child care market, by acquiring the Sylvan Learning Corporation in 1985, a chain of 160 learning centers. With this move, Kinder-Care moved into the tutoring business (Kinder-Care 1989c; Engardio 1986, 35; Bellm 1987, 36). Capitalizing further on its growing clientele, Kinder-Care initiated a mail order business of clothing, tote bags, and books. The Kinder-Care name was licensed to manufacturers (Bellm 1987, 36).

Along the way, in 1985, Kinder-Care joined hands with Jerry Lewis's promotion of the Muscular Dystrophy Association (MDA). Kinder-Care became a national corporate sponsor of the MDA, after having participated in MDA fund drives since 1978. Mendel articulated a desire to instill a "charitable" disposition in the children (Kinder-Care 1989b; 1989c). The same year Kinder-Care responded to a rise in concern over child abuse by introducing the "Listen to Dolly" program. The program's logo is a Doberman pinscher with a bonnet and granny glasses that says, "I never let my puppies go with strangers!" (Kinder-Care 1989c; Bellm 1987, 36). The company also implemented its Quality Focus program in 1987, which serves as its internal monitoring and credentialing system (Kinder-Care 1989c; personal communication with Muscari 1990).

On July 3, 1987, Kinder-Care stock garnered favorable publicity as an appropriate target for the wise business investor. "Kinder-Care stock is attractive. It is ranked to outperform the market averages in the coming year" (*Value Line Investment Survey* 1987, 354). At the time, *Value Line*, a magazine for investors, saw child care as part of the service industry which was doing well in the market. There were 6,200 stockholders, with insiders owning 8.2 percent of the common stock (*Value Line Investment Survey* 1987, 354). The company and its executives prospered; in 1986, Kinder-Care had earnings of $33.3 million. Perry Mendel, a principal owner and originator of Kinder-Care, earned more than $1 million. The company's president, Richard J. Grassgreen made over $800,000 (Bellm 1987, 35).

In the years following, Kinder-Care has faced various financial problems that resulted in a significant restructuring of the company. These difficulties may have been due to the large growth in Kinder-Care run child care centers, together with the link of Kinder-Care Learning Centers to the slower growth of Kinder-Care, Inc.'s financial services and retail operations. The later acquisitions had drained capital from the primary business and weakened its value. The company's 1988 pretax earnings were $48.7 million. The child care and educational subsidiaries accounted for $22.4 million. The financial services generated $12.6 million, and retail stores accounted for $4.5 million. Revenues were $936 million in 1988 (McGill 1989, D-9).

During 1988, Kinder-Care developed and opened eighty-six child care centers, as compared with sixty-three in 1987 (Standard and Poor's Corporation 1990). An initial public stock offering in August 1988 resulted in Kinder-Care retaining an 87 percent interest in the learning centers division.

In May 1989, the company finally moved to separate its financial services and retail business from its learning centers and child care operations; that is, Kinder-Care Inc. and Kinder-Care Learning Centers Inc., respectively. The company needed to bolster its relations with customers and investors. The restructuring was anticipated as a means of providing more efficient management, while emphasizing the importance of child care as central to the company's operations. The restructuring placed Grassgreen as chairman and chief executive of Kinder-Care, Inc. Perry Mendel became chief executive of Kinder-Care Learning Centers, Inc. (McGill 1989). The spin off of Kinder-Care Learning Centers by Kinder Care, Inc., now known as Enstar Group, Inc., to its shareholders was completed in November 1989.

In 1988, Kinder-Care Learning Centers, Inc., was reported to have had operating revenues of $300.1 million. For the thirty-nine weeks prior to September 30, 1989, operating revenues showed a 15 percent annual increase since 1987. Despite this increase, profitability was reduced in 1989 due to higher interest rates on debt, increased debt to construct new centers, and a one time charge to pretax earnings due to investment liquidations (Standard and Poor's Corporation 1990).

POSITIONS IN FAVOR OF FOR-PROFIT SPONSORSHIP

Kinder-Care's dominating presence has been a major factor in the development of the proprietary lobby. The influence of Kinder-Care has permeated the internal and external relations of the proprietary providers. The background on Kinder-Care provides insight as to the workings of one chain, as well as a description of those attributes that define the business of delivering child care through a standardized mechanism. The wealth and power of Kinder-Care highlights the plight of the small, independent provider who finds himself or herself navigating a problematic service in a highly competitive field.

Fenn (1983) attributed the continued growth in chain child care to their acquired political clout. The for-profit providers of child care providers began lobbying in 1973 under the name, National Association for Child Development and Education (Fenn 1983). The lobby eventually reorganized. During the 1980s providers organized under the name National Association for Child Care Management (NACCM) (NACCM 1984a; 1984b). Eventually, NACCM was dissolved. The present lobby, organized in 1988, is known as the National Child Care Association (NCCA). It represents statewide organizations of small, independent proprietors (Neugebauer 1989, 19; Craft cited in U.S. Congress, Committee on Education and Labor 1989, 409):

Membership in NCCA is offered to persons, firms and corporations which are licensed and organized principally to provide child care and services to the public. Suppliers, manufacturers and supporters of the child care profession also are eligible for membership in NCCA. (NCCA 1990e)

NCCA did not encourage the participation of chain providers. In fact, the previous attempts at organizing proprietary providers had been problematic due to the inequitable influence of the chains (Fenn 1983; Neugebauer 1989). In 1988, NCCA actively sought the defeat of the Act for Better Child Care by hiring a D.C.-based lobbyist to work on behalf of the proprietary sectors interests (Neugebauer 1989, 19). During the debates on ABC, the three major chains—Kinder-Care Learning, La Petite Academy, and Gerber Children's Center—formed their own lobby known as the Child Care Coalition (Child Care Coalition n.d.).

In 1981, NACCM joined forces with other interest groups to lobby in favor of increasing the tax credit for child care costs. The association worked with the Day Care Council of America, the Children's Defense Fund, and the National Campaign for Child Daycare for Working Families. The Economic Recovery Tax Act of 1981 put the tax credit on a sliding scale, which pleased the constituency. However, it did not make the credit refundable, which was another goal of the lobby (Fenn 1983, 104).

The National Association of Child Care Management lobby also worked within a coalition to fight against cuts in the Child Care Food Program. Their efforts, however, were concentrated on making the for-profits eligible for federal funds. They had a partial victory in 1981 when the "senate amendment altered eligibility to include for-profit centers where 25 percent of the enrolled children are supported at least partially by Social Services Block grant funds" (Fenn 1983, 106). The NACCM's goal was to have the money follow the child, not the center; a goal that continued to exist for NCCA and the Child Care Coalition during the drafting of the 1990 legislation.

Private providers see child care under for-profit sponsorship as consistent with the American way of life and thought. The "mom and pop" operators of individual child care centers rely on their centers for their livelihood. Speaking for black concerns in 1975, Evelyn Moore, executive director of the National Black Child Development Institute, differentiated the small provider and the entrepreneur. She did not advocate federal money going to the "big guys," but did not want to set into motion the demise of "mom and pop" operations: "I think we ought to be able to put together some language to be able to maintain some of those small centers that are really not making a big profit but are the heartbeat in the Black communities across the country" (Moore 1975, 174–175).

Moore was referring to language in legislation that would clarify the federal government's financial arrangement with for-profit centers. During the past twenty years, the appropriateness of subsidizing proprietary child care centers with public money has provoked controversy. Moore's concern for the small for-profit black provider that serviced the black community, in which the need for care has been consistently high, foreshadowed the subsequent debates over the church-state language in the Act for Better Child Care and the Early Childhood Education and Development Act. As discussed in Chapter 4, those within the liberal coalition that compromised on language to allow federal funding for sectarian programs had the interests of both the black providers and the black community at heart, because an infrastructure of service delivery is well developed within the auspices of churches in inner cities.

The contemporary debate over church-state language has focused on the consequences of church sponsorship. In 1975, however, Moore was bent on eliciting support for the interests of independent black providers when the issue at stake was not one of separation of church and state, but rather the use of public money for private enterprise. Subsidization of proprietary centers was a heated issue in the 1970s, but was resolved after language granting federal funds to such centers was included in Title XX, the Social Services Block Grant. With such statutory language were planted the seeds for the current debate over subsidization of for-profit, church-based centers, and all other proprietary centers.

In general, the private sector views itself as providing a needed service at a reasonable cost. For-profits argue that through private enterprise parents are assured diversity and choice. Furthermore, private providers contend that they help close the gap between available services and need for child care. They argue that they bring efficiency to the job of delivering child care.

The Private Nursery School Association of California suggested looking at a vendor-voucher system during 1977 hearings on the child care problem before the Senate Subcommittee on Child and Human Development (U.S. Congress, Committee on Human Resources 1977–78, 334–342). The association asserted that 75 percent of the child care in California was provided by the private sector and listed several advantages to private sponsorship: parents are given a choice of program and location; a socioeconomic mix of children can occur; market factors fix the cost; quality is assured through competition; diversity is assured; no money from the government is needed; existing resources are utilized; local needs are met; and costs are lower than in public centers (p. 335). The private sector strives to deliver child care as a social utility, with economic benefits gained by the providers as well as the parents.

Richard Ney, then vice-president of the Management Committee of Universal Educational Corporation, testified on behalf of private enterprise during hearings on the Comprehensive Preschool Act in 1969. He argued that this country had a historic tradition of achieving some of its finest accomplishments when federal programs were carried out by private corporations under contract with the government (U.S. Congress, Committee on Education and Labor 1969–70, 239). He urged the federal government "to take advantage of the very considerable resources of talent, managerial skill and experience of private industry" (p. 330). Ney also argued that the private sector can be held accountable.

Members of the medical community echoed Ney's argument. Dr. Amos Johnson, then trustee of the Family Health Foundation of America and of the University of North Carolina, cited the efficiency of private hospitals over public hospitals as an example of the direction child care could move under private sponsorship (U.S. Congress, Committee on Education and Labor 1969–70, 612). In 1975, the American Academy of Pediatrics came forward with support for proprietary involvement during testimony on the Child and Family Services Act (U.S. Congress, Committee on Labor and Public Welfare 1975, 174). Dr. Richard Lourie, speaking on behalf of the Joint Committee on Mental Health, analogized child rearing to an industry and envisioned children as the commodity:

Child-rearing is a major industry in this country. It involves by far the most people and the most money, and unfortunately it is one of our most inefficient industries. This country, which prides itself on its efficiency in industry, should have the conscience which this bill begins to address itself to, to apply its best know-how in terms of efficiency in the rearing of the most precious commodity that we could be producing, our children. (U.S. Congress, Committee on Education and Labor 1969–70, 596)

Dr. Milton Akers, president of the National Association for the Education of Young Children, in 1969, expressed concern and hesitation over the role of the private sector in delivering child care, but supported the opportunity for their involvement as "a chance to find out with people of real integrity and with the money to give it a fair test" (U.S. Congress, Committee on Education and Labor 1969–70, 20). Also testifying in 1969, Mayor Koch of New York City did not come out in favor of expending federal money on for-profits, but did suggest that there was room in the field for the private sector's involvement. He believed that private industry was anxious to be involved and serve the social good (U.S. Congress, Committee on Education and Labor 1969–70, 297–298).

Akers willingness to "test" the private sector's commitment to early childhood programming and delivery skills set a course followed by NAEYC for years to come. Now, twenty years later, with a field composed of a majority of private providers, spokespeople for the NAEYC and many distinguished members remain open to the potential of the private sector. Ellen Galinsky, former president of NAEYC, has stated that she is not categorically against a proprietary interest in child care delivery; rather, she prefers to examine centers on a more individual basis and would encourage parents to be more educated consumers (Lewin 1989, 90; Galinsky 1990, 2). Sharon Lynn Kagan of the Bush Center in Child Development and Social Policy remains open to private sector involvement in early childhood program delivery (Kagan and Newton 1989; Kagan 1987, 21).

Writing in 1983, Donna Fenn took the position that private enterprise benefited parents by providing them with a "growing industry that's lobbying to make child care more affordable and available" (p. 106). She noted that 99 percent of the income to private providers comes from tuition, and therefore, parents interests are protected because the provider must strive to keep the consumer happy (p. 108). Consumer contentment is a driving force within the policies of the for-profits. One issue of critical importance to parents is affordability.

In 1989, a Kinder-Care representative, Maureen Dermott, testified before the Senate Committee on Finance, which was considering the ABC bill, that "affordability" should be the federal government's main concern, rather than quality or availability. For-profit operators stress several basic points. First, they cite data that supports the contention that the "gap" in child care is related to specific populations and regions. They do not accept the notion that there is a crisis in coverage throughout the nation (Dermott 1989).

Second, they challenge the need for federal regulations on several counts that are critical to their argument. Upgrading child care standards would inflate the cost of delivery, which, in turn, would be borne by parents. Families presently in licensed centers would be forced by increased costs to utilize unlicensed centers that were more within their price range. According to a survey conducted by *Child Care Review* ("The Impact of the Federal Regulations in the ABC Bill" 1988), the proposed ABC bill would have resulted in a closure of 20 percent of all licensed centers unable to meet federal standards and prompt a projected displacement of 786,400 children. Ten southern states would absorb nearly four-fifths of the total cost increase, center closings, and child displacements. The projected cost increase nationwide to parents would be approximately $1.2 billion a year ("The Impact of Federal Regulations in the ABC Bill" 1988, 5).

Coincidentally, the ten states most affected by proposed regulations in 1988 had high staff-child ratios and more licensed child care centers. A vicious cycle has developed as a consequence of low standards for child care centers. For-profit providers entered states with low standards simply because the standards were low. The private operators now dominate the market in these states and fight any effort to raise the standards (Travis cited in U.S. Congress, Committee on Education and Labor 1989, 145).

The third major objection to the ABC/H.R. 3 bills made by representatives of the private sector was that a new federal bureaucracy would be built as a result of their passage. Old arguments about government inefficiency surfaced. The fourth objection to the bills was that states' rights would be violated. Opponents of federal standards assert that states could assess and regulate their needs better than the federal government.

Members of the proprietary sector proposed alternative routes for federal involvement. The language of any such legislation preferably would include (1) a refundable tax credit with a phase-out provision; (2) a block grant program targeted at low income families administered through existing state agencies by means of a voucher system; and (3) state developed standards with increased resources for monitoring (Craft [NCCA] cited in U.S. Congress, Committee on Education and Labor 1989; Rosenberg [NCCA] 1988; Muscari [Kinder-Care] 1988; Dermott [Kinder-Care] 1989; Child Care Coalition n.d.).[2]

The resultant legislation for the most part satisfied the proprietary providers because the majority of their objectives were included in the final act. The Omnibus Budget Reconciliation Act of 1990 failed to meet the following three objectives of the proprietary providers, however. First, the amount of the dependent care tax credit did not increase. Second, the dependent care tax credit was not made refundable. Finally, a phase-out provision that would have worked to eliminate the tax credit for taxpayers above a specific income level was not included in the act.

The chains also had expressed interest in promoting tax incentives for businesses. The Child Care Coalition had developed a platform of fourteen recommendations for federal legislation and several of these recommendations targeted family providers. It would be in the chains' interests to upgrade the standards of family providers to a level that would make their compliance prohibitively expensive. The coalition took a stand during the ABC debate for legislation that would incorporate liability insurance, parental involvement, consumer education, and coordination with other federal programs, such as those involved in welfare reform (Child Care Coalition n.d.).

POSITIONS AGAINST FOR-PROFIT SPONSORSHIP OF CHILD CARE

The primary reason for opposing for-profit sponsorship, as noted earlier, is based on the issue of quality. Opponents of such sponsorship contend that the economic function overrides all other functions. Children's needs necessarily are sacrificed to turn a profit for the provider. Some child advocates argue that the delivery of high quality child care programs is incompatible with profitability (Featherstone 1970; Meisels and Sternberg 1989). The American Federation of Teachers' 1976 position paper highlighted six areas in which the proprietary center jeopardizes quality: staff-child ratio; salaries and wages; size of center; space per child; special services staff; and parent involvement (AFT Task Force on Educational Issues 1976, 98–99).

In the early stages of the development of proprietary child care, critics compared the centers' development to that of private nursing homes. Private industry stepped in to the nursing home gap about ten years before public interest in child care developed. Although the chain owned homes usually were clean and efficient, the general opinion was that the homes were less than ideal. They were criticized for being understaffed and short on programs (Lake 1970, 96). Featherstone (1970) elaborated on this analogy between nursing homes and child care. In discussing the problems of monitoring child care centers and establishing standards, Featherstone wrote:

The situation on the local level reminds many people of battles some time ago in state legislatures to establish some sort of standards for nursing homes. These battles in most places were lost to nursing home interests, which then went on to make fortunes out of federal medicare and medicaid windfalls, without any improvement in their abysmal services. In many respects the analogy is intriguing: young children and old people suffer worst of any groups from the existence of age ghettos in our society. (Featherstone 1970, 16)

Featherstone continued the analogy by noting how relatives of both groups do not always know, or wish to know, the criteria of a good program. The complaints of both the old and the young often are not heard, nor heeded. Yet, Featherstone acknowledged that the analogy breaks down in the respect that "there may never be as much money in child care as in supplying medical services, nursing care and drugs to captive old people" (1970, 16). The lobbying efforts on behalf of children by the Children's Defense Fund in particular and their coalition in general have succeeded in generating change for children as evidenced by the child care components of the Omnibus Budget Reconciliation Act of 1990. Yet, Featherstone's picture of the aged and the young of our society vying for a piece of federal resources is very telling. In fact, the debate over using Title XX as a key funding mechanism is linked directly to this problem of distributing limited funds across target populations.

The already difficult task of allocating funds for human services is exacerbated when the profit motive is involved. As Featherstone observed, "A great deal of profit can be made from a rotten program, whereas the bare essentials of a decent program soon run you into or very close to the red" (1970, 14). Delivering a high quality program is very expensive and a challenge in and of itself without trying to squeeze out a profit. Research efforts over the last twenty years have strived to determine whether there are significant differences in the delivery of quality services for the aged by the sponsor's status (Harris 1987). In a review of the literature, Harris concluded that the findings were mixed as to the correlation between profitability and quality.

In 1972, Mary Keyserling of the National Council for Jewish Women conducted a benchmark study in the literature on child care services, *Windows on Day Care*. Keyserling looked at the following variables across for-profit and nonprofit centers: staff educational level, salaries, teacher-child ratio, group size, educational programs, equipment, and facilities. The study concluded that 50 percent of the proprietary centers rated poor compared to 11.4 percent of the nonprofits (Keyserling 1972; Fenn 1983, 104).

To date, the private sector still is subject to scrutiny, as previously indicated in the findings of the two recent empirical studies that address the debate over the quality of for-profit child care services. Both the National Child Care Staffing Study (CCEP 1989) and Kagan and Newton's (1989) study of Connecticut centers found government subsidized nonprofit centers receiving overall higher ratings than for-profits. The Kagan and Newton research indicated, however, that for-profits did rate high in a number of key areas. More evaluative work needs to be conducted using the NAEYC accreditation program as a measure of quality.

No clear body of data presently is available on the number of chain centers that have applied for or received NAEYC accreditation. Chains vary in their policies toward accreditation. For example, Children's World Learning Centers has implemented a company goal of meeting NAEYC accreditation criteria. Kinder-Care, on the other hand, has opted for an internal monitoring process referred to as "Quality Focus." The company's accountability system, combined with consumer satisfaction and state licensing standards, is deemed an appropriate means of assuring quality. Kinder-Care does not recognize a need to invest additional dollars in the NAEYC accreditation process that necessitates a fee per center.[3]

In keeping with their stance against federal regulations and higher state standards during the 1980s, the NACCM also was against a nationwide standard for the licensing of child care workers. A wide range of hiring practices exist in the child care field. A special certification route has been developed, called the Child Development Associate (CDA), which is modeled on the concepts of competency based training and in-service experience. The NACCM did not endorse this route as a mandated requirement, but saw it as an alternative (Fenn 1983, 106).

At present there are no federal regulations concerning the training of staff. Rather, each state sets its own requirements for the hiring of child care workers. The National Child Care Staffing Study found that nonprofits hired teachers with higher levels of education and experience than for-profits (CCEP 1989, 14). Kagan and Newton did not find such a disparity; rather, their study indicated that for-profit centers and private nonprofit centers hired more college graduates than government subsidized nonprofit centers. Private nonprofits hired more staff with master's level education than the other two types of centers. Kagan and Newton found that government supported nonprofit centers hired more minorities (Kagan and Newton 1989, 7).

Responding to criticism of the for-profit's lack of policy in certain areas, the National Child Care Association instituted three new initiatives in the summer of 1990. The July 1990 issue of NCCA's newsletter, *National Focus*, announced the beginning of a National Teacher Credential Program. This program would provide its successful participants with the Certified Childcare Professional (CCP) credential. At the time of this announcement, the program called for thirty weeks of course work and in-center projects. NCCA began a nationwide project of establishing certification schools and institutes that would apply an approved set of criteria. The association intended to create partnerships with other accredited institutions, including colleges and vocational training institutions (NCCA 1990a, 1; 1990d).

The standards of the new accreditation system established by NCCA are not known at this time. The need for a special accreditation program within the private sector leaves the outside observer with many questions as to the reason for such an additional system, particularly after all the thought and concerted effort that went into development of the NAEYC accreditation program initiated in 1981. Furthermore, the NCCA program represents an unnecessary duplication of a valid, preexisting accreditation system by an industry long opposed to federal standards for child care. The NAEYC accreditation system is based on standards that define quality in ten programmatic areas:

The Criteria were developed over a three-year period from a review of existing standards, a review of the research literature on the effects on children of various aspects of a group program, and from the expertise of thousands of early childhood professionals who reviewed the proposed standards. . . . The accreditation process involves three steps: a self-study by the directors, teachers, and parents; an on-site validation by specially trained validators; and the accreditation decision by a commission of nationally recognized early childhood professionals. (NAEYC 1989, 2)

At the time its accreditation program was launched, NCCA also initiated a professional teacher recognition program based on a remunerative, competitive model. Hardee's Food System offered to present cash awards of $1,000 to nine runners-up, and $10,000 to the "nation's top child care professional" (NCCA 1990d; "NCCA Launches New Initiatives" 1990, 11; NCCA 1990b, 1). NCCA also moved forward with formulating three other policy related ventures: the Foundation for Child Care Research and Education, for developing an accurate data base on the child care industry; the American Association of Early Childhood Educators (AAECE), a professional organization for child care workers that would offer insurance benefits to members; and the National Childcare Parents Association (NCPA) for representing the interests of parents utilizing proprietary centers, benefit packages were to be offered to members ("NCCA Launches New Initiatives" 1990, 11; NCCA 1990c, 2).

Perhaps the area in which the for-profit sector is most vulnerable to criticism is personnel practices. The entire child care field suffers from underpaid personnel, but the private providers are notorious for underpaying their employees. Underpaying child care workers not only devalues their work, but leads to high turnover rates and low morale. The high rate of turnover in child care personnel is detrimental to children who need consistency and stability.

Kinder-Care also has been involved in legal battles over its personnel policies and has been accused of improper union busting tactics. The company's profits have been linked to suspect employment practices:

The company's executives are management experts who know how to cut costs and corners—often in violation of poorly enforced state regulations. Mendel has parlayed real-estate savvy into profits and has bought and created spin-off businesses to capitalize on what he calls his "captive market" of parents and children. But, above all, Kinder-Care's success depends on thousands of underpaid, unorganized, female child-care workers. To keep them from organizing, Kinder-Care has lately broken the law. (Bellm 1987, 34)

Some of the questionable personnel policies include lay-off procedures; sick leave; weekly hours; and parent-teacher interaction (Bellm 1987, 35). Aside from the low hourly wage paid to workers, full-time workers are based on a twenty hour workweek, although some do work more hours. The hours are so variable that it is difficult for workers to get a second job to augment their income (Bellm 1987, 35). The implementation of part-time hiring practices contributes to the low wages of child care workers, lack of benefits, and the violation of licensing regulations that demand specific staff-child ratios (Lake

1970; Bellm 1987; Lewin 1989). Such management policies promote profits at the expense of child welfare and the workers' economic status.

A campaign to organize child care workers in Kinder-Care centers in northern California took place in December 1985. This drive was the first attempt to organize workers in child care chains in the United States, and it was also directed at La Petite Academy centers. In 1982, some Kinder-Care centers were organized in Toronto by the Ontario Public Employees Union. The northern California drive was led by Mary Ann Massenburg, from the United Auto Workers, District 65. The impetus for organizing came from the firing of a worker, Johnnie Bradford. Bradford was fired from Kinder-Care allegedly for joining the union while in a management position. Company managers later came to the center and presented their position against unionizing. In November 1986, the National Labor Relations Board in Oakland found Kinder-Care guilty of four labor law violations. Kinder-Care was ordered to stop threatening employees and discharging employees for union activity. The company no longer can offer wage and benefit incentives as a means of discouraging union involvement. The fired worker was reinstated with back pay (Bellm 1987).

Although Kinder-Care claims, through its public relations' materials and representatives, to be invested in upgrading the quality of care and the education of its employees, critics doubt its altruistic intent and claim that the profit motive overrides such concerns. Company profits come first. Bellm (1987) reported that a socially responsible money market fund known as "Working Assets" chose to divest from Kinder-Care in 1986 because of the complaints against the company by child care activists. Bellm argued that all child care workers are underpaid, but that Kinder-Care has the power to alleviate the situation and chooses not to do so. For example, in 1986 Massachusetts activists secured $5 million in the state budget allocated to upgrade child care wages. Kinder-Care turned down its portion reasoning that to upgrade wages in state funded centers and not other company owned centers was "inappropriate." Additionally, wage increases would encourage a rise in parent fees. Bellm quoted Kinder-Care representative, Ann Muscari:

We have to keep costs down for parents and we do the best we can for our employees. We shouldn't be held responsible for the whole child-care industry. We engage in free enterprise without apology; it's what made America great. We offer the best quality for the best price. We don't overcharge and we don't underpay. (Bellm 1987, 37)

In September 1986, Campbell Soup failed to renew a contract with Kinder-Care. They had been involved in the Kindustry program at their headquarters in Camden, New Jersey, but did not want to continue the program because of the problems presented due to the low pay policy of Kinder-Care. The teachers were leaving at a high rate, and Kinder-Care could not recruit qualified people. After Kinder-Care left, the teachers' wages at the Campbell center were altered from hourly rates to a salary, averaging $9–18 an hour instead of the Kinder-Care wage of $5 an hour. The director went from $17,000 annually, to within a range of $25,000–$30,000 (Bellm 1987, 38; Lewin 1989, 90).

Bellm (1987) and Lewin (1989) reported examples of Kinder-Care's noncompliance with licensing regulations. Violations were cited in staffing procedures; that is, understaffing and hiring unqualified staff members. Kinder-Care is not the only center that fails to comply with regulations, but it is indicative of the tendency of Kinder-Care in particular, and the proprietary sector in general, to cut corners on quality standards.

The National Academy of Early Childhood Programs, NAEYC's accreditation system, began accrediting centers in 1987 and provided a profile of their accredited centers in January 1989. This general profile revealed that the majority of accredited centers were funded by parent tuition and were nonprofit (33 percent). Parent tuition for-profit centers constituted 13 percent; public schools accounted for 6 percent; Head Starts 3 percent; and publicly funded with multiple sources accounted for 15 percent. The academy emphasized the point that the lower number of for-profit accredited centers did not reflect the sector's inability to meet the standards, but their lack of participation in the process. NAEYC takes the position that more aggressive marketing techniques are needed to encourage for-profits and parents to engage in the accreditation system (Recken 1989).

Kinder-Care is an admittedly unique case example of a for-profit sponsor of child care. The chains in general are in a category unto themselves. Yet, the problems raised regarding for-profit sponsorship are consistent across the different types within the private sector. The profit motif only exacerbates the serious social problem of delivering affordable, accessible, high quality child care. Parents and taxpayers must recognize that high quality child care programs cost more than programs of mediocre or poor quality, but are worthy investments for their children and society at large.

Parents not only need to become aware of NAEYC's accreditation process, but they must seek the opportunity and encouragement to become involved in their children's child care experience. Parent involvement is cited by child care experts as a key component in the delivery of high quality care, because young children need the active participation of their parents both on the direct and policy-making levels. Chains, with their standardized curriculum and centralized policies, are subject to criticism on this criteria.

This potential lack of parent empowerment within the private sector provided the impetus for Marian Wright Edelman to view proprietary care as a rival to her preferred model of community based care (U.S. Congress, Committee on Finance 1971, 497). The conflict between parents and professionals is not limited to the for-profit sector, but proprietary sponsorship complicates an already delicate relationship. The community control model that gained popularity in the 1960s placed primary value on the role of parents. This emphasis on parent involvement not only was intended to benefit the children's development and relations with their parents, but to serve as a means of mobilizing low income and disenfranchised families. Head Start exemplifies this ideal, with mandated parent participation on several levels. Edelman perceptively acknowledged that, in the proprietary sector, this potential is inhibited. The program serves the needs of the proprietor, rather than the needs of a community. The social reform function that includes community involvement is not served under proprietary sponsorship nor is the social service function.

The predominance of the economic function poses many complications to the operation of high quality child care programs. Policy issues, such as adequate remuneration for employees, developmentally based curriculum, and parent participation, which are problematic throughout the child care industry, are magnified when the profit element is a motivating force behind the services. The multifunctional aspect is jeopardized by the added necessity to sustain a profit. In accordance with functional analysis, diligent inquiry must constantly monitor allocation decisions to ascertain for whom they are truly functional.

ADMINISTRATIVE ISSUES AND COSTS
IN THE PRIVATE SECTOR

In 1985, child care providers were hit with a new problem: rising insurance costs and nonrenewable insurance policies.[4] Attaining liability insurance is particularly difficult for the private provider, especially the small, independent provider. The barrage by the insurance industry on child care institutions in the mid-1980s was precipitated by widely publicized accounts of child abuse in unlicensed settings, and a generally very high claim period for the insurance industry. The insurance industry recently had experienced difficult economic conditions; falling interest rates; and soaring sums awarded by juries as damages in lawsuits involving public entities (Bridgman 1985b, 14). In 1984, the industry suffered its worst year in its history since 1906 (Bridgman 1985a, 13).

There was no apparent correlation between the claims history of child care, and company's insurance policies. A 1985 nationwide survey of 1,000 providers of child care and 200 Head Starts found that 70 percent had experienced policy nonrenewals, cancellations, or skyrocketing increases in premiums. Some of the increases were as high as twenty times the previous year's rate (Bridgman 1985b, 1). Another survey of insurance commissioners in all fifty states found all commissioners stating that it was very difficult to determine who would be writing insurance coverage from day to day (Bridgman 1985b, 14).

The impact of this insurance crisis on the child care industry proved dramatic. In the 1980s many centers closed because they could not meet the premiums set by the insurance companies for coverage. Others raised their fees to cover costs, which in turn affected utilization rates. Providers were caught in a catch-22 situation because many states were mandating insurance coverage for licensure, but the providers could not attain the necessary insurance.

Child care advocates began to examine the problem and work with state legislatures to address the insurance issue in 1985. The severity of the problem provoked a set of congressional hearings on the "emerging insurance crisis" in child care before the Select Committee on Children, Youth, and Families on July 18 and July 30, 1985. Federal legislators began to grapple with an approach to rectifying the situation that was problematic for providers, insurers, and child care consumers.

Attention was given to the insurance dilemma in drafting ABC and H.R. 3 in the late 1980s. The Act for Better Child Care authorized $100 million to establish child care liability risk retention groups that would promote the availability and affordability of liability insurance to child care providers (Section 124). Neither the Early Childhood Education and Development Act nor the final Child Care and Development Block Grant, however, included a provision for liability risk retention groups.

Small for-profit operations also had difficulty complying with state regulations; whereas, large operations that could more readily meet stringent standards favored lenient regulations that provided greater leeway to increase greater profits. Generally, for-profits contended that state regulations often were "counterproductive" because they set unrealistic standards that prevented the development of child care facilities. These regulations could be archaic, and often hurt the family child care provider (Lehrman 1985, 25). The state regulations were written for an earlier time when larger institutional arrangements, such as "schools serving larger numbers of children, or hospitals and orphanages providing round-the-clock care" needed monitoring (Lehrman 1985, 25). Historic patterns of regulation were imposed on child care without making the necessary adjustments to modern needs.

Many government departments are involved in setting the standards, such as health, building, and fire. One area causing significant roadblocks in the expansion of child care is zoning. Zoning commissions have set up restrictive regulations that inhibit providers from starting centers. These regulations often have little to do with the care of children (Lehrman 1985). The problem affecting family child care providers is that "most zoning commissions consider day care to be a small business and prohibit operation in residential areas. This prohibition extends even to individuals wishing to care for a few neighborhood children" (Lehrman 1985, 25).

SUMMATION

Having presented the arguments for and against for-profit sponsorship it is obvious that the pivotal issue is the delivery of high quality care under such sponsorship. The predominant function of child care under proprietary sponsorship is economic. As is the case with all of the five sectors, some functions become primary, others secondary, and some suppressed altogether. The welfare reform, social service, and religious functions rarely are linked to the structure of the private sector. Welfare reform was a motivating factor for some of the first entrepreneurs in the early 1970s, when federal legislation for increasing subsidies to nonprofit and for-profit centers appeared imminent.

An interest in serving low income families may become a stronger force in the private sector with the enactment of the Child Care Entitlement Grant and the Child Care and Development Grant. Otherwise, the private sector does not have as its goal the reduction of welfare rolls or servicing the needs of families on welfare. During the debates over child care in the late 1980s and 1990, proprietary lobbyists supported federal initiatives that targeted low income families as long as they would be recipients of grant money. In spite of their support for money targeted to the poor, private providers have targeted their services to the middle class. The main thrust of their lobby was toward the attainment of tax reform, including refundable tax credits and a voucher system.

A manifest consequence of the sanctioned role of private providers is the perpetuation of socioeconomic stratification. Providers would protest, however, that the newly implemented system of federal funds will facilitate the promotion of a more socioeconomically integrated system of services. Although proprietary sponsors condone the expanded support of the lower economic strata of society through the certificate and grant approaches, they look with apprehension on the use of the new grant money by competitor sectors. Most significantly, increased public school involvement threatens the hold that the proprietary centers now have on the middle class. Furthermore, for-profits have resisted federal grants to states, because that would infuse money into the nonprofit market with which they presently compete in a favorable fashion. The nonprofit sector's stability and competitiveness have been more tenuous than its for-profit counterpart because of its reliance on federal funds, which are frequently subject to budget cuts. Consequently, for-profit centers increasingly have found themselves in competition with not-for-profit centers for middle class clientele when the latter provider no longer could service as many low income families due to a decrease in government subsidization.

The function of education too often is a secondary consideration for many private sector providers. Private providers argue that they can deliver the highest quality of care, while allowing for diversity and parental choice, in the most efficient manner. In reviewing the literature on the child care chains, it appears that some programs being delivered are inappropriate for young children. Such programs have been labeled *homogenized pap* (Goldman 1975, 82). Rather than achieving the diversity many proponents expected, the larger chains are providing mass programming as their education and socialization functions.

The emphasis on standardized curriculum and school readiness is at odds with the criteria for developmentally appropriate practices (DAP), established by the National Association for the Education of Young Children (Bredekamp 1987). One criterion of DAP is that a curriculum should fit the needs of individual children and the needs of a particular group of children. Curriculum planning from a central office in a national chain of operations hardly fits such a criterion. Even assuming that chains (1) vary in their curricular approach and (2) grant autonomy and creativity to directors and teachers, the prefabricated, standardized curriculum is in direct opposition to traditional early childhood educational theory.

Given the argument that curriculum suggestions are only as good as the teacher who uses and implements them, the research has shown that for-profit hiring and staffing patterns are suspect. The Kagan and Newton (1989) study does indicate that for-profit centers tend to hire college graduates as much as private nonprofits and more than government subsidized nonprofits. All three types of centers had similar percentages of staff with specialized training in early childhood education and development (p. 7).[5]

The findings of the NCCSS were much more critical of for-profit staffing patterns and program practices. The findings indicated a definite correlation between poor quality programs and for-profit status. The intervening profit variable was of significance. The NCCSS also discovered that higher quality programs were correlated with higher state standards, compliance with FIDCR standards, and NAEYC accreditation (CCEP 1989, 14–16). Not surprisingly, for-profit centers are concentrated in states with lower standards.

Due to lenient state regulations, child care is a wide open arena for entrepreneurs from all backgrounds. Certainly, the proprietary providers are not rallying around the cause of upgrading the economic status of child care workers.

Nevertheless, a new commitment to satisfying the demand for staff quality improvement appears evident in the movement among the private providers toward in-house training, as exemplified by Kinder-Care's Quality Focus program and NCCA's credentialing program.

In 1983, Fenn pointed out that earlier critics of proprietary operations were finding more high quality programs in the chains and that quality varied from chain to chain. Lewin (1989) and Englade (1988) implied that quality also varied by center when examining the smaller, independent centers, as well as centers within chains. Having criticized such centers in 1970, Lake concluded, "Intrinsically, there is nothing evil in making a profit from a day-care center. The litmus test is not who sponsors child care, but which comes first—the child or the dollar" (p. 97).

It does make a difference, however, who sponsors child care. The function of the service is linked to the sponsor. Under for-profit sponsorship, the economic function is primary. Education, socialization, and liberation-universalization are secondary functions. The socialization function not always is fulfilled overtly, but is a consequence whenever children are in a group situation, especially for an extended and controlled amount of time. Furthermore, the structured programs of the chains promote a pattern of socialization, whether it be intended or not.

In regard to the administrative issues, private sponsorship has very definite implications. Although many argue that the delivery of high quality care has more potential under the private sector, it has been shown that high quality care is threatened where the need to make a profit overrides the requirement of a quality program dependent on a trained and stable staff, small group sizes, low teacher-child ratios, ample classroom space, appropriate materials, and a developmentally based curriculum.

On the issue of cost to parents, for-profit care does make the service accessible for the middle class. This accessibility to the middle class prohibits a socioeconomically integrated system of care because the lower economic classes cannot afford the service without subsidization and the availability of private sector care varies by locale.

Large operations favor (1) those states with minimum regulations regarding staff-child ratios and teacher training, and (2) regional locations with a high concentration of fee paying middle class parents. Zoning regulations and the high cost of operating a center have precluded many small center and in-home providers from the marketplace. The current trend seems to indicate that chains eventually will dominate the private sector market.

One cannot ignore the far-reaching beneficial effect changes in the tax structure and implementation of a voucher system would have on the for-profit sector. Yet, socioeconomic integration is not a likely consequence of such changes because the large operations would continue to serve a suburban, middle class clientele, and the smaller for-profit minority providers would serve their immediate community. The NCCA and particular providers favored an indirect approach to child care delivery on the part of the federal government during the 1987–1990 federal debate.

Tax credits may increase the market of potential consumers, while keeping the market supply of available centers open for future development. It is in the proprietary sector's interest to maintain a low and informal public supply of child care centers. Without such a gap in services and weakness in delivering care, there is no strong financial incentive—no motive—for venturing forward with additional centers.

Large proprietary operators are threatened by the idea of an increase in child care services emanating from the public schools. Schools have the power to encroach on the for-profits' territorial claim to serving the middle class and the suburbs. Small "mom and pop" operators also are threatened by the ability of the local school to serve local consumers in an efficient manner. When analyzing Title II of H.R. 3, the title that provided for school involvement in preschool and before- and after-school programs, the NCCA spokesperson stated:

Title II of H.R. 3 will have an absolutely devastating effect on the private child care industry in America. If enacted, the result will be the virtual elimination of the private before and after school care, which is the second-fastest growing segment of our industry.

Additionally, the convenient placement of 4-year-olds in the public schools for child care purposes will destroy an industry already struggling with enormous insurance rates, regulatory compliance, unequal competition, the rapid expansion of 5-year-old kindergarten programs in the public schools and inappropriate and often inaccurate publicity that we suffer.

I might mention that the effect of these provisions will not be isolated just to the licensed child care and preschool industry. Many nonprofits, nursery schools and religiously sponsored centers will also be forced to close their doors. (Craft cited in U.S. Congress, Committee on Education and Labor 1989, 409)

The CCDBG satisfied the proprietary sector on several counts. First, the tax credit approach was a primary component of the act. Second, the certificate program was included and encourages parental choice, including for-profit providers. Third, for-profit providers could compete for grants or contracts provided that they meet the necessary stipulations. Fourth, minimum state standards were prescribed that will ensure the competitive edge with home-based centers, but low enough not to upset the current operational status. Fifth, the schools were not given a major role in providing care.

More empirical research like the National Child Care Staffing Study (CCEP 1989) and that undertaken by Kagan and Newton (1989) is needed on how quality of care varies between for-profit and nonprofit sponsors, with particular attention given to the variation in types of for-profit sponsors. However, the more implicit consequences of proprietary sponsorship should be openly debated. The NAEYC has adopted an acquiescent point of view with regard to profit making in the delivery of child care programs. This move toward accepting proprietary sponsorship in caring for children deserves close scrutiny and as much skepticism as that directed toward the public schools.

Although the chains represent only a small portion of the for-profit sector, they merit specific examination as to their impact on the socialization of America's children. The entire for-profit sector must be held accountable for its contribution, or lack thereof, to improving the poor pay and status of child care workers. The social status function operates in a dramatically negative manner under proprietary sponsorship.

Greater attention should be drawn to the experience of the women who are using one or both career tracks that have opened within the proprietary sector. For example, women have the opportunity to advance within the Kinder-Care structure itself (Lewin 1989). The traditional corporate management model is now open to a vast number of women involved in the management and promotion of the chain concept of child care. The advancement of the managers, in part, will be at the expense of the underpaid direct service employees. Research into the career development of management level personnel within the chains could shed light on the economic mobility of women within the chain structure. How do these chains, which utilize a large pool of women employees, compare to other corporate models? Is there a discernable trend or does each company stand on its own merit?

Additionally, the new venture by entrepreneurs into management consulting on work-family issues pulls many women away from direct service careers and employment in early childhood education. These women compete with other women trained in human resources skills. Because the new consultants will be in a position of leadership and authority, it will be of particular importance to the women's movement that the women who take on these new positions maintain a commitment to change customary practices in favor of family supportive initiatives.

If the chains continue to proliferate, labor organizers and feminists will have access to large pools of child care workers ripe for organizing. In this regard, the collective grouping of workers under the corporate structure offers more potential for the unionization of child care workers than an unconnected system of independent centers. The rate of expansion of the chain operations not only will affect the social status function of child care, but all of the potential functions of the service.

The CCDBG has signaled a new era for proprietary involvement in child care and sanctioned the private sector's hold on the market. The for-profit sector has obstacles to confront in its delivery of high quality child care programs, but it has a secure historical and legislative foundation from which to operate. The next decade undoubtedly will experience much expansion in the private sector, but within that sector two inherent conflicts remain. First, the industry must constantly contend with the conflict engendered between the large and small operators. Second, conflict forever will exist between the need to meet profit projections and achieving professional standards of care. The influx of private programs must occur only in conjunction with strong parent-consumer education programs and services—a mandatory component of state plans under the CCDBG.

NOTES

1.   Data was compiled as of January 1, 1990.

2.   The position paper of the Child Care Coalition published during the ABC debate states the following information on the lobby: "The Child Care Coalition is composed of three of the largest private proprietary child care providers in the nation: Kinder-Care Learning Centers, Inc.,: La Petite Academy; and Gerber Children's Center, Inc. Together we provide quality care for more than 200,000 children in forty-two states" (Child Care Coalition n.d.).

3.   Ann Muscari, vice-president of corporate communications for Kinder-Care, noted that consideration was being given to the possibility of accrediting "Kinder-Care at Work" centers as a pilot. Credentialing these employer sponsored centers might prove more attractive to employees who transfer from city to city and desire stability and reliability in their child care service (personal communication with Muscari 1990a; 1990b).

4.   For in depth information on the insurance crisis see the following references: "The U.S. Staggers Under the Burden of Soaring Insurance Rates," *Time* (March 24, 1986), pp. 3, 16–26. Mary Rowland "The Liability Crisis Hits Home," *Working Woman* (June

1986), pp. 104–106, 136–137.   Diane Feldman "Prices and Perks of Parenting," *Management Review* (January 1989), pp. 7–10. U.S. Congress, Select Committee on Children, Youth, and Families (House). July 18 and July 30, 1985. *Child Care: The Emerging Insurance Crisis.* Abby J. Cohen, Testimony by the Child Care Law Center before the Joint Investigative Hearing—Department of Insurance-Legislative Task Force on Child Care Liability (File No. RH-248) (Cohen 1986).

5.   Little data are available on proprietary curriculums. More comparative studies are needed to assess the differences among types of operations.   The new research and credentialing associations within the private sector should prove useful in evaluating quality of care within the private sector and between sectors.

6. Employer Sponsorship
and the
Economic Function

The description of the for-profit sector's sponsorship of child care services indicates a strong interactive relationship between child care entrepreneurs and industry. Corporate America, in various ways and to various degrees, has been involved in the delivery of child care services from the incipient stage of this contemporary movement. As with proprietary sponsorship, child care performs primarily an economic function under employer sponsorship. This economic function serves the productivity requirements of the sponsoring company by meeting felt and expressed needs of its employees.

A reading of the popular articles on corporate involvement in child care reveals a consistent concern among employers: productivity. Common themes and terminology seen in the popular articles and survey studies express employers' desire to recruit talented employees and reduce absenteeism, tardiness, and turnover among employees. If these goals are met, the company stands to achieve higher productivity. Therefore, within corporate America child care functions to bolster an increase in productivity and profits. Child care serves the "bottom line."

Employer sponsorship of child care began to proliferate in the early 1970s, although a few employers had been involved in such sponsorship earlier. Corporate sponsorship includes industry, business, health care organizations, public agencies, military establishments, and institutions of higher education. Such sponsorship involves both management and labor.

The impetus for employer involvement, and the realization of the economic function, arose from such combined factors as the economy, labor force trends, and changes in the tax laws. Testifying at hearings for the Comprehensive

Preschool Act of 1969, John Naisbitt of the Urban Research Corporation noted that the new interest in employer sponsorship stemmed from recent legislation to amend the Labor Management Relations Act, by allowing employer contributions to child care centers (U.S. Congress, Committee on Education and Labor 1969–70, 494). Businesses were allowed to deduct expenditures from their federal income taxes over a five year period for the acquisition, construction, or rehabilitation of child care centers to be used primarily by their employees (Magid 1983, 254).

The other two factors encouraging employer sponsorship in the late 1960s and early 1970s was the need for women workers in certain industries and the overall increase of mothers in the labor force:

There is ample evidence that the development of on-site industrial centers correlates with historical periods of high demand for female labor among particular types of industry and during critical times. Concomitantly, declines in the economy and labor demands have been the key factor in the demise of such operations. (*On-Site Day Care: The State of the Art and Models of Development* 1980, 11)

This trend within industry parallels the history of federal involvement in child care. Government legislation, for example, has coincided with war efforts to recruit women workers in the defense industry under the Lanham Act of 1941 and to maintain workers during the Depression through the federal Works Project Administration (WPA). When it was conducive to withdraw support for women workers, the federal government did so.

The current debate over employer sponsorship can be divided into four periods: World War II and Postwar (1941–1959); the New Frontier and Antipoverty Years (1960–1974); the Era of Demographic Change and Privatization (1975–1986); the "Family Friendly" Era (1987 to the present) (*On-Site Day Care* 1980, 11).[1] Prior to World War II, employers were involved in child care only minimally. The Lanham Act of 1942 served as an impetus to employers by providing funding for child care for children in "war impacted" areas; that is, where women were needed to replace men in "war-related employment" (Perry 1978, 9).

Six hundred thousand children were provided for in child care centers under the Lanham Act. The most noted centers during this period were built in Portland, Oregon, at the Kaiser Shipbuilding Corporation. The two centers operated from 1943–1945 and closed after the war. The Kaiser centers operated seven days a week, twenty-four hours a day, 364 days a year. They provided other supplementary services for the working mother, such as "carry home" dinners, shopping, and secretarial activities. In this capacity, these centers served a social service function. Fulfilling the economic function, Kaiser's Child Service Department claimed that the centers allowed for 1,246,773 additional production hours in one year (*On-Site Day Care* 1980, 11).

Industry sponsored child care had served a definite economic function during the war years. The provision of centers furthered the economy and the war effort by enabling and encouraging women to join the work force, thus functioning to change their social status. However, these functions were not embraced after the war. The country readapted the prevailing attitude that women belonged at home. Yet, in spite of this overriding sentiment and the withdrawal of government funding for child care, many women remained in the labor force. "The labor force participation rate of married women with children under 6 increased, from 10.8 percent to 24.2 percent between April 1948 and March 1966" (*On-Site Day Care* 1980, 11).

This upward trend of women into the labor force incited the development of child care centers in the late 1960s under various sponsors. In 1953, the Women's Bureau of the Department of Labor reported that there were seventeen "industrial nursery schools" as of 1950 (Perry 1978, 17). The Women's Bureau repeated surveys of industrial child care centers. These surveys were conducted on three different sectors: hospitals in 1970, industry in 1971, and universities in 1973.

Hospitals were the pioneers of employer sponsored child care. The Women's Bureau surveyed 3,000 hospitals with 100 beds or more. Of the 2,000 respondents, 98 had child care facilities. Nine had been in operation for at least fifteen years, with fifty-six operating between one and five years. The centers served skilled and professional personnel (Perry 1978, 18). Hospitals became involved in child care because of the high percentage of women workers and the need to compete for nurses (Perry 1978, 19–20).

The Wells National Services Corporation updated the 1970 Women's Bureau study. The study surveyed 113 hospitals identified in the original study or in later literature and found that out of sixty-five respondents only forty-four had child care centers. The 1960s had seen a severe shortage in nursing personnel, which can account for the earlier proliferation of on-site centers (Perry 1978, 18–20).

The Women's Bureau survey of private industry's sponsorship of child care centers in 1970 (published in 1971) found only nine companies that were operating centers. Eight years later, Kathryn Senn Perry found six more companies sponsoring centers at the time, all of which had predominantly women employees (Perry 1978, 20). Labor unions sponsored eight centers at this time, and six of these centers were under the sponsorship of the Amalgamated Clothing Workers of America (Perry 1978, 23–24).

In 1973, there were five public agency sponsored centers in the Washington, D.C., area. These centers usually received outside funding in the form of research and demonstration project money or funding for low income employees. The findings of the 1971 Women's Bureau survey into child care on university and college campuses revealed that out of a sample of 310 institutions there were 425 prekindergarten programs. Ninety of these were child care centers; the others being nursery schools, laboratory schools, or a combination of types (Perry 1978, 24).

These data indicate the existence of employer sponsorship in 1970. In 1978, Perry updated the findings of the Women's Bureau in her dissertation, "Survey and Analysis of Employer-Sponsored Day Care in the United States." She documented a decrease in the number of centers in the eight year period since 1970. In 1978, an estimated 8,419 children were enrolled in employer sponsored centers. This represented 2.6 percent of all children in centers based on 1975 data. Military institutions sponsored centers for 25,050 children in either full day or "drop-in" care for a few hours (Perry 1978, 95). Perry further found nine centers sponsored by industry, seven sponsored by unions, fourteen sponsored by government agencies, and seventy-five sponsored by hospitals. "All eleven industry-sponsored centers identified in 1970 had closed operation by 1978. Ninety-eight hospital-sponsored centers were identified in 1968, and that number decreased by 23 percent by 1978." Hospital sponsored centers peaked in number of openings in the late 1960s (Perry 1978, 96).

Several factors account for the decrease of centers under employer sponsorship by the middle of the 1970s. The economic recessions of the period caused company closings and layoffs. Therefore, the "bottom line" economic function that child care served under employer sponsorship was not needed. Management no longer needed centers to attract or retain a work force. Furthermore, layoffs decreased the demand for and utilization of existing child care services. The cost of maintaining a center increased with the decrease in the child to staff ratio, causing parents to rely on less expensive services (On-Site Day Care 1980, 14).

The decrease in the involvement of employers was related directly to the functioning of the economy and labor force participation. In addition to the recession and inflation, the rate of unemployment had changed: "As the rate of unemployment has increased, the employers have had less trouble filling positions and did not need day care as a recruitment incentive or as a service to keep young mothers on the job" (Perry 1978, 97). This effect was most apparent in the health care professions. Hospitals no longer needed to sponsor centers to attract and maintain a qualified staff.

The Economic Policy Council of the United Nations Association of the United States of America published a report in 1985, by the Family Policy Panel, *Work and Family in the United States: A Policy Initiative.* The report found that of the nation's 6 million employers only 1,850 provided any form of child care assistance (p. 16). The amount of employer sponsored child care services was quite limited; however, interest in such sponsorship peaked once again in the early 1980s.

The National Employer Supported Child Care Survey (NESCCS) updated Perry's 1978 study. Conducted in 1981–1982, the NESCCS identified 415 companies that supported child care services. The researchers, Sandra L. Burud, Pamela R. Aschbacher, and Jacquelyn McCroskey, found a growth of 395 percent in the number of companies with child care programs between 1978 and 1982: "The growth in activity from 105 child care centers in 1978 represents a four-fold increase. Even more dramatic is the twenty-fold increase during the same period in the number of programs in business and industry, from 9 in 1978 to 197 in 1982" (Burud, Aschbauer, and McCrosky 1984, 226). The types of companies providing services had changed. Hospitals no longer were the major supplier of child care services, although health care organizations still were a dominant force within employer sponsorship of child care. In 1978, hospitals accounted for 71 percent of the total number of employers involved; industry accounted for 9 percent; and government agencies or unions accounted for the remaining 20 percent. By 1982, industry and health care organizations each accounted for 47 percent, and public agencies and unions represented 6 percent (Burud et al. 1984, 5).

At present, hospitals are in the forefront of providing child care benefits and on-site care. According to a survey of 965 hospitals conducted by the American College of Healthcare Executives (Chicago) and the American Association of Healthcare Consultants (Fairfax, Virginia), two out of five provided or helped provide some form of child care for their employees. Of those that did not, 38 percent planned to establish benefits before the end of 1989. Of all the hospitals in the United States, 19.2 percent provided child care information and referral; 11.1 percent provided assistance with expenses; 14.2 percent allowed for arrangement of flexible working hours; 11 percent had on-site child care; 7.3 percent had facilities nearby; 10.5 percent offered child care for sick children. Those hospitals that provided child care benefits tended to be nonprofit operations located in midwestern cities of less than 250,000 with over 200 beds (Silverman 1989). The Conference Board's Work and Family Information Center estimated that out of the 1,077 companies that offered on- or near-site child care in 1989, 777 were hospitals.[2] Government agencies accounted for 100, and corporations provided 200 (Conference Board 1989).

The renewed interest in corporate sponsorship during the 1980s stemmed from policies of the Reagan administration. The 1981 Economic Recovery Tax Act (ERTA) allowed child care to become a nontaxable benefit that could be provided to employees by corporations. The Reagan administration provided an incentive for private sector involvement while reducing public funding by cutting the social services budget in 1981. A resurgence in corporate involvement in child care was seen in the popular press and continues to remain a popular topic for media coverage. The new interest of the 1980s in child care manifested itself in multiple, yet indirect approaches. On-site child care is only one option of child care assistance available through the workplace.

In 1984, The Bureau of National Affairs issued a special report, *Employers and Child Care: Development of a New Employee Benefit*. Employers began offering child care as a fringe benefit by making use of government tax provisions. The report found that "the number of employers offering some child care benefit to workers has doubled since 1982. But only about 1,000 employers provide child care assistance to their employees, representing only a tiny fraction of all U.S. firms" (BNA 1984, 3). Furthermore, the provision of on-site child care is the exception, rather than the rule. On-site centers are the most costly option open to an employer.

An updated survey by the Bureau of National Affairs (BNA) in 1986 found similar data. Organizations offering some form of child care assistance remained in the minority. The most popular form of assistance was information and referral programs, not on-site care. A survey of 424 employers found that only one-fourth provided some type of assistance (BNA 1987a; 1987b).

The Bureau of Labor Statistics conducted its first survey of employer child care practices in 1987, the results of which remain among the most reliable data (NCJW 1988, 3–4). The survey found that 2 percent of the nation's establishments with ten or more employees sponsor child care centers. An additional 3 percent offer financial assistance to be used specifically for child care. A total of 11 percent of employers provide some type of child care benefit, including direct provision and financial assistance (U.S. Department of Labor 1988, 1).

The pattern of companies that provide some type of child care to their employees is as follows. Large employers tend to be more involved than medium sized and small firms. The survey results revealed that 32 percent of firms with 250 employees or more provided benefits or services compared to 9 percent of firms with 10 to 49 employees. Medium sized firms provided 15 percent. The report indicated that government agencies were more involved in providing benefits or services than private industry, 9 percent to less than 2 percent (U.S. Department of Labor 1988, 1). Government agencies also were more progressive in the provision of child care information, referral, and counseling services than private firms. Yet, the private sector was as likely as the government to assist employees with child care expenses (U.S. Department of Labor 1988, 2). In 1990, a Gallup poll report indicated that only 10 percent of American workers had access to an employer sponsored child care center at or near their place of employment ("Few Workers Have Access to Work-Site Child Care" 1990, 110).

In "Prevalence of Employer-Supported Child Care," the Conference Board's Work and Family Information Center estimated that a total of 4,177 corporations were involved in child care in some manner. On- or near-site centers represented approximately one-fourth of the child care related expenses. Fifty percent of the corporate contribution was in the form of financial assistance. Fifty companies offered vouchers or discounts, and 2,000 companies provided a dependent care option within a flexible benefit plan. Fifty companies had provisions for family child care, after-school care, and sick child care (Conference Board 1989).

The Conference Board has monitored the trend in employer involvement in child care and family related polices. The 1989 report noted that the actual number of corporations involved in child care provisions was small, but the growth in the delivery during the last half of the 1980s was dramatic. In 1978, 110 companies supported child care in some fashion; in 1982, 600 companies were involved. By 1984, the number of companies involved jumped to 2,000 with expansion to 2,500 the following year. In 1988, 3,500 companies were supporting child care (Conference Board 1989). The Conference Board held a two day meeting in New York City in March 1990, the Work and Family Policies Conference. As of that date, 5,400 companies indicated providing some form of child care (Conference Board 1990). This rapid expansion into child care is attributed to a "variety of factors," including:

improvement in the economy; nontaxability of child care as a benefit; reindustrialization creating labor shortages; new emphasis on people-oriented management; changing worker attitudes and values; and most significantly, changes in the demographics of the work force. (Conference Board 1989)

The prevalence of industry's interest in the ever-expanding demand for child care provisions was evident in a two day conference held in New York City in February 1990, by the Institute for International Research, in conjunction with the Peat Marwick Executive Training Facility. The conference was entitled How to Develop Cost-Effective Health and Child Care Plans. The conference brochure identified child care as the benefit issue of the 1990s. A conference of this nature is historically significant because it represents a turning point in management's viewpoint regarding child care.   During a time of fiscal constraints, child care concessions were being viewed on par with health care benefits. The conference was intended to be a pro-active response to pressure arising from labor's expectations to receive benefits and management's need to remain competitive and productive.

Corporations are now conducting cost-benefit analyses on the implications of offering child care benefits by quantifying human resource costs (Collins 1988). A new business literature is emerging that quantifies the cost of the new "family friendly" policies, of which an array of child care benefits constitutes a major component. The economic function of child care is the criteria for a company's consideration and eventual implementation of the service. The impact of the service on children is not the focus of discussion or the basis on which strategic plans are formulated. Any concern for program quality follows the initial discussion of bottom line company figures. American policy making within the business sector and in government is pragmatic as opposed to the approaches taken by many European and Scandinavian countries. As one participant at the Conference Board's March 1990 meeting noted: "The U.S. business community often thinks of work-family as a problem to be managed so we can have employees on the job, on time, every day. Europeans see children as a resource and dependent care as an investment rather than a cost" (Wohl cited in the Conference Board 1990, 4).[3]

Most studies indicate that women intensive industries and organizations are the predominant sponsors of child care centers (Perry 1978; Magid 1983; Burud et al. 1984; Sallee 1986; U.S. Department of Labor 1988). Service oriented industries tend to employ more females than the goods sector, which includes manufacturing, mining, and construction. Service industries include, among others, transportation and public utilities; wholesale trade; retail trade; finance; insurance; and real estate. Service oriented industries provided more direct child care services and indirect benefits than the goods sector (U.S. Department of Labor 1988, 2).

Alvin L. Sallee (1986), identified six categories of companies that are involved in providing child care benefits:

(1) Companies that employ a high number of skilled workers or professionals whose job performance improves significantly the longer they remain on the job. An employee with small children is going to think twice about giving up the advantages of quality child care to take a job somewhere else.

(2) Companies that employ a large number of persons in fields where the demand for professionals exceeds the supply.

(3) Companies that employ a significant number of young women in areas such as law, research, or technical professions where their knowledge would quickly become outdated if the employee dropped out of the workforce to raise children.

(4) Companies that work in shifts. Most day care centers' hours correspond to the 6 to 5 workday and do not give a parent of small children who works an odd shift any type of option.

(5) Garment manufacturers, fabricators, and other businesses that employ a large number of female workers.

(6) Companies that compete with other corporations to employ members of young families in a community where there is a tight job market. (p. 12)

Employer sponsors of child care are clustered in the information and technology industries, as well as the previously mentioned services industry (Burud et al. 1984, 226; Magid 1983, 11). Newer industries and companies are willing to experiment with alternate plans to meet the child care needs of their employees; whereas, the older companies offer child care because they have an entrenched demand for women employees that encourages their interest in child care arrangements (Burud et al. 1984, 226–227). Firms involved in the production of family related goods have exhibited an awareness of their employees' family concerns and, therefore, have been among those in the forefront providing child care services (Friedman 1985a, 11). The Stride Rite Company, which produces children's shoes, for example, was a pioneer of the on-site child care movement.

LABOR'S VOICE

Among the leaders of workplace change are representatives of organized labor. Union sponsorship is one of a number of types of employer sponsorship; sponsorship can be by a single company, a group of companies forming a consortium, through a labor organization, or by means of a joint partnership between employees and management. In 1984, few solely union sponsored or joint union-management programs were in operation. Six participated in the National Employer Supported Child Care Project (Burud et al. 1984, 216). By 1990, unions had become much more active in the movement for employer sponsorship of child care centers and provision of child care benefits. Organized labor has consistently supported federal child care initiatives throughout the nearly quarter of a century movement. Unions remain active advocates for public involvement, but are negotiating simultaneously for child care provisions within specific industries.

Three women-dominated, substantial unions are mavericks among labor groups in the fight to establish child care provisions in the workplace: the Services Employees International Union (ASEIU); the American Federation of State, County, and Municipal Employees Union (AFSCME); and the Communication Workers of America (CWA) (Albert 1988). The International Ladies Garment Workers Union (ILGWU) and the Coalition of Labor Union Women (CLUW) are two other strong and historically influential labor organizations concertedly fighting for child care provisions. The process has been slow, but gained momentum over the years.

The Amalgamated Clothing and Textile Workers Union (ACTWU), formerly the Amalgamated Clothing Workers of America (ACWA), took the lead in the actual establishment of a union sponsored center. The ACWA opened their first center in 1969, and four more between 1969 and 1971 (ACWA cited in U.S. Congress, Committee on Labor and Public Welfare 1971, 487–488). In 1980, there were six ACTWU centers (*On-Site Day Care* 1980, 41), but a few subsequently closed due to plant closings and low attendance (BNA 1984, 804). Currently only two ACTWU centers are in operation. The original centers were closed due to changes in demographics. The ACTWU was a pioneer in sponsoring employment based care because the unique features of the industry lent itself to this type of model. Most of the centers were in rural areas where there was a large number of small employers within a district. The centers were funded through a joint employer-union fund negotiated by the union and administered jointly by labor and management. The fund was tax exempt with the employer contributing a percentage of the payroll (Waldron in Baden and Friedman 1981, 113; Jacobson 1986, 13).

The current ACTWU center in Knoxville, Tennessee, also serves multiple employers. The child care facility is representative of a joint effort of ACTWU and the Knoxville Cooperative Parish of the United Methodist Church. The center, Partners for Children Child Development Center, opened in 1989 after a 1988 partnership of the Southern Regional Joint Board of the ACTWU, and four inner city United Methodist Churches. The center is open to the community, and licensed to serve thirty children from age 2 1/2 to kindergarten entry. The Board of Directors is composed of an equal number of representatives from the churches and the union locals. The center enjoys a wide range of funding sources inclusive of business and philanthropic organizations. Partners for Children planned the expansion of its mission by developing an on-site center for the employees of the Forks of the River Industrial Park. The partnership intends to develop other child care programs in the future "to bring families and communities closer together" (personal communication with Kidwell 1990).[4]

In 1984, ACTWU was at the helm in spearheading a consortium model for child care at Grieco Bros. in Massachusetts when it helped establish the Merrimack River Child Care Center. The union supported the company's vice-president Tony Sapienza's interest in developing a child care center to reduce employee turnover. ACTWU was instrumental in funding the center, which is run as a nonprofit agency. Start-up funding came from Grieco Bros., the ACTWU, Polo Clothing Company, Lawrence General Hospital, the City of Lawrence, the Massachusetts Industrial Finance Agency, the Department of Social Services, and a number of private foundations. The center receives state subsidized slots and vouchers from the Department of Public Welfare (Fried 1987, 21).

As previously indicated, changes in demographics caused ACTWU centers to close over the years. Some of the midwestern centers were turned over to the communities when the union withdrew from sponsoring the service. Discretionary funds in union budgets were used to meet the needs of the aging membership (personal communication with Holcomb 1990). Changes in the demographics of union membership have presented utilization problems over the years.

The ILGWU's 1983 success in the establishment of the Chinatown Child Care Center is considered a historic breakthrough, illustrative of the consortium model of funding (Fried 1987, 22; Sweeney and Nussbaum 1989, 121–122; Levitan and Conway 1988, 21; Albert 1988, 45). The Chinatown center often is cited as an example of union activity in the child care arena because of the mass organizing effort of 3,000 Chinese-Americans. The unique composition of the union, employers, and government involved in the funding, as well as the garment district locale of the center, dramatize the tremendous need for the service that the center has met.

Mindy Fried (1987) profiled many instances of labor's tenacious involvement in the development of child care centers during the 1980s. Of historical significance at the onset of the 1990s is the organized effort of labor to put child care, and related issues of parental leave and alternate work scheduling that would help balance the laborer's family and work responsibilities, on the bargaining table. SEIU is at the vanguard of the fight for new family supportive policies, but is joined by many other prominent unions. In the 1989 "Summary of Union Child Care Activities," SEIU reported its involvement in twenty out of fifty examples of child care related union initiatives in twenty-three states. SEIU's endeavors are a part of a growing movement that, thus far, has included fifteen additional labor organizations as reported in SEIU's summary.[5]

The AFL-CIO has repeatedly supported federal child care legislation and backed the ABC and H.R. 3 bills. Labor groups split during the final stages of lobbying for H.R. 3 when vouchers for sectarian child care programs were included in the bill's final version. As highlighted in an earlier chapter, the labor organizations in the education sector withdrew their support of the legislation because of the allocation of federal money for sectarian child care programs under the certificate system. Nevertheless, organized labor has not wavered in its support of government involvement in child care. In fact, labor recognizes that the public sector ultimately is responsible for increasing and maintaining a system of child care services (Logan 1986; Fried 1987; CLUW 1988a; 1988b; Albert 1988; SEIU 1989d; Sweeney and Nussbaum 1989). CLUW's 1988 platform on child care called for active government involvement:

We do not believe that the solution can be reached short of federal legislation that provides funding for universal, comprehensive, quality child care. This federal legislation must provide for the right to child care, Head Start, early childhood education and after-school care. It must be available to all the children of our country. (CLUW 1988b)

In 1981, labor's involvement in child care was restricted primarily to hospital unions and public employee unions (Waldron in Baden and Friedman 1981, 113). In 1988, Levitan and Conway reported that child care had emerged within the intervening years as a recognized, legitimate bargaining issue. The new weight assigned to child care can be attributed to the expansion of two-earner families, union membership in the service sector, and greater attention given to female union members' concerns (Levitan and Conway 1988, 20).

This relatively new attention to women's concerns by the labor movement is symptomatic of two feminist issues: (1) the minimal percentage of women's representation in union membership, and (2) the dominant perception across sectors of society that child care is a problem particular to women. The combined factors of the increase in mothers in the work force; the heightened push to organize women and the service sector; and the dawning realization by society at large, and male union members specifically, that child care is a familial and collective concern have given the issue of child care long overdue recognition at the bargaining table.

Ed Clark, an international vice-president of ACTWU, however, has warned that for serious change to take place, child care must be strategically negotiated and supported by the members. Grass-roots efforts within the organization are needed before the negotiation process begins (Fried 1987, 31). Child care provisions must be considered a high priority so that they eventually will become as essential a part of the collective bargaining agreement as medical insurance, a decent wage, and defined work hours. Securing child care as a guaranteed benefit will involve a long, tortuous struggle that will be successful only if labor remains united over the severity of the need:

The success of unions which have pursued child care at the bargaining table has been limited, but in many ways accounts for the increase in the number of employers looking into child care. The negotiating process on this issue is extremely arduous and in many cases, where the union is able to overcome employer resistance, the result has been merely an agreement to set up a joint labor-management committee to study the problem. This is followed in many cases by years of struggle which may or may not culminate in the employer participating in the actual provision of child care services. Far more often, the result has been employer involvement in information and referral services or holding seminars on child care. (Logan 1986, 9)

The move to negotiate for child care provisions, through an industry by industry approach, however, could seriously undermine labor's commitment to promoting universal services, if a strong lobby for government involvement is not sustained. The mid-1980s saw much activity by organized labor, as is evident in their publications. AFSCME published *Negotiating about Child Care: Issues and Options* in 1984. The Coalition of Labor Union Women (CLUW) published a guide to bargaining for child care, *Bargaining for Child Care* (CLUW 1985). The February 1986 issue of *Labor Today* published sample clauses from several union contracts and reviewed the CLUW publication which included language from twenty-two American and Canadian unions. The Arnold M. Dubin Labor Education Center published Mindy Fried's *Babies and Bargaining: Working Parents Take Action* (1987). The Amalgamated Clothing and Textile Workers Union published *Bargaining on Women's Issues and Family Concerns: Clauses From ACTWU Contracts* in 1988. John J. Sweeney, president of the Service Employees International Union, and Karen Nussbaum, executive director of 9 to 5, wrote *Solutions for the New Work Force* (1989), excerpts from which are distributed by SEIU as part of a package of literature entitled *Work and Family*.

The labor movement has given voice to a concerted and organized effort to influence the workplace on child care matters. The Coalition for Labor Union Women sponsored a conference, The American Family Celebration 1988, in Washington, D.C., which was a political call for action to implement a National Family Policy. The 50,000 attendees represented labor, civil rights, religious, and women's rights groups. Labor has been behind child care legislation from the start, but it is forging ahead in the broader arena of balancing work and family life, as is management. Within the labor movement, child care functions as social reform because it is used as an organizing tool. Child care is igniting "new life" into labor's cause (Albert 1988, 46; Levitan and Conway 1988, 21).

The leverage child care carries was evident in the successful 1988 drive to organize Harvard University's nonteaching, white collar workers. "AFSCME committed 16 full-time organizers and nearly $1 million to the bitter showdown with management, and with a narrow 1,530 to 1,486 vote won the right to represent Harvard workers" (Albert 1988, 46).

TYPES OF EMPLOYER INVOLVEMENT

There are four basic categories, or types, of employer involvement in child care. The first and most popular form of assistance is through Information and Referral Services, in which the employer provides employees with information on existing child care programs in the community. The second category includes financial assistance programs, of which there are several variations. A benefit favored by employees is the federal Dependent Care Assistance Program (DCAP). In fiscal year 1988, DCAP cost the government a total of $3.4 billion. It constituted the largest source of government expenditure for child care (Mercer 1989).

DCAP is a nontaxable benefit. Employer and employees mutually agree to reduce the employee's wages by a predetermined amount, which is then placed in a Dependent Care Assistance Program fund. The employee may draw upon the fund for child care expenses and benefits by not having to claim this money on his or her federal income tax return. The employer benefits by not having to pay unemployment insurance or social security for that portion of the employee's paycheck which has been set aside into the DCAP (U.S. Department of Labor 1989, 32–37). Furthermore, the employer's costs in the implementation and administration of the program are minimal compared to other forms of child care, and this is the reason why financial assistance programs are the most popular form of employer involvement in child care.

Employers must follow rigid guidelines in setting up these plans. They can offer the DCAP as a separate benefit or as part of a cafeteria plan, and the plan must be written to include all employees as participants. Furthermore, the plan must guard against discriminating in favor of highly placed employees because the programs are tied to the individual's tax rate. Thus, the higher the salary, the greater the benefit (Murray 1985, 294):

The favorable tax treatment of employee child care benefits shows an even stronger slant toward higher-income families. Child care assistance plans, like other fringe benefits, are more frequently made available to workers with high incomes. In addition, workers with larger paychecks can afford to set aside more money, and their higher marginal tax bracket makes the exclusion even more valuable to them. (Levitan and Conway 1988, 14)

Murray (1985, 300–302) and the Women's Bureau of the U.S. Department of Labor (1989, 38–39) provide an overview of other federal tax provisions that relate to child care through the employer. First, employers can declare child care as a business expense if the provisions are provided to reduce personnel problems and enhance productivity. A second tax avenue for the employer is attained through capital expenses. Child care center property, such as the building, equipment, and the remodeling of a building, is depreciable.

Third, "start-up and investigatory expenses in acquiring or creating a new child care center may be amortized over a period of sixty months or more" (U.S. Department of Labor 1989, 38). A fourth means of maximizing tax benefits for the employer is the deduction of child care outlays as charitable donations. Additionally, corporations may engage in the establishment of nonprofit child care programs, which then are exempt from federal income tax if the organization is able to meet certain criteria. This avenue provides several options to an employer. Instead of establishing a nonprofit child care center under the individual corporation's auspice, many businesses prefer to collaborate with other businesses, or with organized labor, to fund a child care facility. Employees also may initiate formation of a nonprofit center, as has been demonstrated by unions.

Employers may further maximize their tax benefits through two other routes. Centers may be established by the employer's private foundation as long as the centers serve the wider community and do not give preferential treatment to or engage in "self-dealing" with the company's employees and their families. A final route for employers is to hire members of targeted groups for employment in the child care centers. An employer that hires from the groups targeted under the Jobs Training Partnership Act may declare a targeted jobs tax credit for certain wages paid to such individuals.

Tax credits are available to the employer also through state internal revenue systems (Trost 1989). In 1983, only four states offered tax incentives through credits to employers for providing child care services. In 1989, thirteen states provided a tax credit, and twenty-one other states had tax credit programs in pending legislation. Less than 1 percent of eligible companies are taking advantage of this credit. The low rate of usage is due, in part, to corporate tax liabilities needed to claim the credit. Other constraining factors include the expense of start-up and the additional administrative burden accrued from claiming the credit (Trost 1989).

The Child Care Action Campaign contends that state tax credits divert attention from the necessity of building up the supply of child care centers. CCAC proposes that employers could enhance the field of child care by supporting information and referral programs or funding a child care office within the departments of economic development at the state level. Because the federal tax credit reduces the amount of income subject to taxation, the state employer tax credit reduces the money the businesses owe in taxes, "dollar for dollar" (Trost 1989). Both the Act for Better Child Care of 1989 and the Early Childhood Education and Development Act of 1990 addressed the issue of tax incentives for employers to encourage their involvement in the delivery of child care services. Under ABC, businesses would have been eligible for grants or loans for the provision of child care benefits and services. H.R. 3 allocated $25 million in grants to be distributed by the Health and Human Services Secretary for start-up costs or for the cost of additional child care services. Higher priority would have been given to businesses with fewer than 100 full-time employees, and employees would have been expected to match the grant by 200 percent. Public-private partnerships were encouraged in both versions. ABC also included a provision for the revision of Internal Revenue Code Section 89. Such provision would invoke a one year delay in the application of the section, which discusses discrimination within certain employee benefit plans. H.R. 3 set a cap on the use of flexible benefit packages at family incomes of $90,000; ABC had no such provision (Willer 1990b; Sec. 114 in ABC; Title V in H.R. 3; Sec. 303 in H. R. 3). The final product contained in CCDBG does not include a separate provision for employer sponsorship, but does require the number of business partnerships in each state to be reported.

During hearings on the two bills in 1989, Norton Grubb raised an issue of tax equity. Grubb questioned the worthiness of providing tax incentives to corporations when the research clearly indicates that the provision of child care will benefit the company's productivity by reducing employee retention problems. He raised the unpopular notion that the federal government's sanctioning of business involvement through tax incentives has the latent consequence of promoting an inequitable service delivery system. When commenting on the need to involve the corporate sector, Grubb accepted the idea of encouraging business involvement, but expressed skepticism about the need and appropriateness of federal tax incentives:

I don't think we should hold out much hope that there will be a great deal of support coming from corporations for a long time. And I particularly think it would be quite inappropriate to try to institute special incentives for corporations, for example, through the corporate income tax, because I think that those would be really quite inequitable.

The people who would benefit from those would be people who work for large corporations, who are typically better paid and are not low income. They would be quite inefficient in the sense that they would reward a few corporations already providing early childhood and probably not induce many more to enter that area. So I think it is an area which has in California, as in New York apparently, not lived up to the hopes that many people have had for it. (U.S. Congress, Committee on Education and Labor 1989, 68)

Senator Christopher Dodd raised the equity issue surrounding corporate tax incentives during hearings on the ABC bill in 1988 (U.S. Congress, Committee on Labor and Human Resources 1988, 334–335). He questioned the wisdom of providing the incentives on several counts. First, he conjectured that if child care is a sound business move for an organization, then the business will venture forward without the federal carrot in the form of a tax credit. To reward business for a step that would be inherently profitable and, therefore, self-rewarding would be an unnecessary, inefficient, and inequitable allocation of federal funds. Second, he highlighted the data on employment patterns, at-risk populations, and current utilization of the tax credit to support his position that the record of business's involvement in child care suggests an insular nature of self-interest that excludes the population most at risk. This at-risk population not only needs child care now, but will become the labor pool of the near future. Industry is not rushing into urban areas with child care support. Corporate initiatives have been directed internally toward the "bottom line" of the company.

The third form of providing child care assistance to employees is an avenue to which Senator Dodd would like to see greater efforts directed, the support of existing child care programs in the community or the development of community based centers through the consortium model. Additional functions of child care are achieved through this type of involvement because the existing functions of recipient centers are supported. San Francisco has been a leader in the arena of promoting and establishing community child care programs through consortium efforts. A San Francisco ordinance was passed in the fall of 1985 whereby developers of projects of considerable magnitude were required to either provide space for child care centers or contribute to a city fund targeted at increasing the supply of centers to low and moderate income families (Kantrowitz 1986, 57; Massengill and Petersen 1988, 61–62; Micheli 1986, 133; Mooney 1988, 24; Sweeney and Nussbaum 1989, 117).

The ordinance concept is not without controversy. For example, Pittsburgh's Mayor Masloff backed such a concept, but met stiff public opposition. The *Pittsburgh Post-Gazette* printed the editorial "A Half-Baked Day Care Plan" (1990), which criticized the proposed mandate in favor of tax inducements and more thoughtful, deliberate planning. *The New York Times* reported strife among developers, condominium owners, and government regulatory agents over the permissibility and desirability of home operated child care programs within condominium developments (Brooks 1990).

Although the issue of family child care is not of the same magnitude as the issue of sponsorship of center based care, the apprehension over child care centers sponsored by developers or within planned communities is very real and most likely will spur legal action. A division between residents is drawn by those who bought into the condominium concept with the desire for "peace and quiet" (Brooks 1990). The special and conflicting interests of the aged and the young repeatedly emerge in debates over child care. Albeit intergenerational programs for elder and child care are developing as symbols of conciliation among the groups, age specific interest fights will persist over funding questions. This is evident with Title XX funding and will emerge in regard to questions of taxation of senior citizens for public school sponsored child care programs.

The corporate consortium concept is a viable option for employers who do not want the sole financial responsibility of a child care center. The consortium model appears whenever employer options are enumerated, because common funding of child care programs by multiple corporations is appealing and practical. Yet, the idea does not gain as much media attention as on-site and near-site corporate programs, which command higher visibility. The consortium concept fits the "public-private" partnership movement, but it actually runs against the grain of corporate culture as it necessitates that competitive companies enter into a partnership and work cooperatively.

California has set another example by establishment of the California Child Care Initiative in 1985, through the combined funding of BankAmerica, Pacific Telesis Group, twenty-two other corporations, and state and local agencies ("California Makes Business a Partner in Day Care" 1987, 100). The $700,000 pilot project was implemented to support the state's resource and referral agencies' attempts to recruit and train new and existing providers for licensure purposes. Another example of a joint effort by employers to solve a particular child care problem was evidenced in 1989, when seven large New York employers pooled their resources to support a service for employees when usual and customary child care arrangements become unavailable. Thus, the employers, under the guidance of the nonprofit resource and referral agency, Child-Care Inc., established emergency family based care for 13,000 employees in the New York City area and northern New Jersey. Factors resulting in utilization of the service would be the illness of a child, the unavailability of the usual care provider, and sudden school closings. Two licensed home health care agencies will provide the direct services (Lawson 1989).

The on-site or near-site center is the fourth and most heavily publicized, but most expensive, form of industry support for child care. As previously noted, on-site or near-site employer provided care is rare (Levitan and Conway 1988, 19; U.S. Department of Labor 1988; Conference Board 1989; BNA 1989, A-3; "Few Workers Have Access to Work-Site Child Care" 1990). In 1989, only 2 percent of American businesses provided on-site child care (BNA 1989). Hospitals are the major providers, followed by public agencies, universities, businesses with variable shifts, and corporations that have some public interest orientation (Conference Board 1989; BNA 1990b, A-15; BNA 1989, A-3; Levitan and Conway 1988, 19; U.S. Congress, Committee on Education and Labor 1989, 67; Fried 1987, 18–19; SEIU 1989b).

Norton Grubb and Alfred Kahn each testified as to the inactivity of corporate sponsors during the 1989 Hearings on Child Care. In addressing the private sector involvement in the delivery of child care in the state of California, Grubb testified:

Well, I think it is fair to say it has been slow in California, too, and not for lack of any efforts. There have been tremendous efforts to try to get corporations to fund early childhood programs. There is a very small number of them that do it. The same names turn up time and time again. In the last list I saw of the corporations providing early childhood programs at least half of them were hospitals, other kinds of quasi-public institutions, or corporations that have some sort of public interest bent to them, for example, Tom Hayden's Committee for Economic Development down in Santa Monica. So that the number of real true blue profit-making corporations that offer early childhood programs is pretty slim (U.S. Congress, Committee on Education and Labor 1989, 67).

Dr. Kahn emphatically argued that on-site child care has been and continues to be an illusion: "Company-based on site care will not meet a major part of the need. It has been talked about endlessly now since 1980, '81, actually since the mid-70s. The overall result has been modest to use a modest word" (p. 246).

CORPORATE MOTIVATION: ADVANTAGES AND DISADVANTAGES

The National Employer Supported Child Care Survey (NESCCS) analyzed the advantages and disadvantages associated with each type of assistance program (Burud et al. 1984).[6] Employers opt for different child care benefit options according to their needs and financial picture. Yet, there are common reasons why employers get involved in child care assistance per se. Given the changes in family structure and the composition of the work force, company involvement still stems from self-interest: "As family structures change, so does the composition of the work force. In order for business to attract and retain a productive work force, it has begun to consider the family needs of its workers" (Friedman 1985b, 4).

John P. Fernandez reported on his study of five large, technically oriented companies in *Child Care and Corporate Productivity* (1986). Fernandez documented the child care problems faced by employees and the costs of such problems to the companies. He concluded that child care problems do cost companies money; employer programs initiated to address these problems are costly, but financially beneficial to the company in the long term.

A survey by the National Council of Jewish Women's Center for the Child *Mothers in the Workplace* (1988), built from the three commonly cited baseline studies, Perry 1978, Magid 1983, and, Burud et al. 1984, with the explicit purpose of documenting the *actual* effects of employers' family policies, rather than the *perceived* effects. The study concluded that employers' diverse efforts to assist workers meet their child care needs in fact do make a positive difference. The NCJW survey found that employer support for child care per se had a greater impact on retention than the availability of health insurance and job guaranteed maternity leave. This policy had similar effects for professionals, managers, and workers in other occupational strata (NCJW 1988, 4). The NCJW survey was focused on retention patterns immediately following childbirth. The study suggests that further research examine the effects of child care assistance policies over the entire period of maternal child rearing.

In Renee Magid's 1983 survey for American Management Associations, *Child Care Initiatives for Working Parents: Why Employers Get Involved*, the data indicated that the initial motivation for employer involvement in child care assistance was economic. The Family Policy Panel of the Economic Policy Council (1985), Fernandez (1986), the Child Care Action Campaign (1988), and the Conference Board (1990) discuss the importance of employer sponsorship in relation to the competitive market at home and abroad. Companies are in competition and child care can become a deciding factor in the competitive game. Perry's 1978 study also indicated that employer support of child care rendered important economic benefits for the employer.

The National Employer Supported Child Care Survey (NESCCS) offers the most thorough account of measured benefits of child care involvement by employers. The economic incentive for corporate involvement is clear when seen in light of the measured variables: reduced absenteeism, tardiness, turnover, and quality of products or service. The concern for child care is very much productivity oriented with little mention of the quality of care or the impact of the care on the children. This is not to say that corporations do not seek to implement programs of high quality, but it does imply that the effect of care on the children themselves is a secondary concern.

The National Employer Supported Child Care Survey examined the question of program quality and variability. According to the study, employer sponsorship can affect the quality of the program positively or negatively. The employer can insist on setting high standards in all of the critical areas for quality assurance. The researchers have found that the level of financing is perhaps the greatest factor in determining quality. Child care programs need adequate levels of subsidization (Burud et al. 1984, 245). Programs risk being of poor quality when the company expects their employees of low and moderate incomes to pay without subsidization (p. 243). Too often, reports on company sponsored centers neglect to describe the nature of the funding, the degree of subsidization, and socioeconomic status of the clientele. More research is needed that would focus on criteria other than those productivity measures most frequently reported. Furthermore, whether employer sponsored centers comply with the professionally recognized NAEYC accreditation criteria should be included in any discussions on such sponsorship.

In a recitation of the measured benefits to the company in terms of productivity variables, the economic function is apparent. There are latent functions to employer sponsorship, however. Specifically, the multiple and interrelated stresses endured by employees and family members because of inadequate child care arrangements would be alleviated; child care then functions as a social service. With respect to the provision of on-site or near-site centers, the general quality of home life can reach a new level if employees have more time with their children due to a reduction in commuting time and the possibility of daily visits. Children attending on-site centers can further benefit by viewing their parents at work: "This perspective may reestablish the job role models that have disappeared in our industrialized society where children, separated from their parents, have difficulty developing pictures of what their jobs are like" (Burud et al. 1984, 240).

Employer sponsors with progressive vision connect the problems employees face in child care and elder care. By recognizing the broad problem of "dependent care" and designing appropriate strategies for meeting needs, employers achieve many gains. New developments in intergenerational programming, such as on-site care for both children and elders, should serve to break down age barriers in contemporary society. Children and seniors engaged in social interaction will achieve many benefits. Children will obtain refreshing conceptions of the aged, rather than stereotypic images. Seniors will enjoy the company of the children, and a sense of contributing to their development, which in turn provides a sense of self-worth at a time in their lives when they are most vulnerable to feelings of futility and unworthiness.

Another latent positive consequence of employer sponsorship is that key community leaders gain important knowledge about the status of children and children's services.   Ideally, having recognized the need for child care, employers can also become advocates for high quality programs and motivators for change in the delivery of care (Burud et al. 1984, 241–242).

Business management practices are susceptible to change as a consequence of sponsoring child care. Hiring trends are set in motion affecting women and other minority groups, thus furthering the cause of equal employment opportunities. Sponsorship "also reflects the individualistic character of our technically sophisticated society, providing benefits which have particular appeal to a certain group of employees" (Burud et al. 1984, 241). The social status function is at play because more women and minority people enter the work force as a result of the availability of child care.

Employer sponsorship has definite consequences for the child care market at large. On the positive side, private sector sponsorship can raise awareness about need and usage, impact regulations, and stimulate communication and coordination among child care programs (Burud et al. 1984, 238). Corporate sponsorship can positively affect parental choice by providing more options, or to the contrary, parental choice can become more limited, depending on the type of employer involvement. Reimbursement programs can widen the availability of programs, as long as the company does not impose numerous restrictions. Financial assistance programs can have a distinct affect on the general child care market of a community: "Reimbursements may indirectly affect long-term supply and demand trends as well. For example, corporate contributions to centers may reduce the market for in-house family day care and in the long run thereby reduce the supply of that care" (Burud et al. 1984, 239). Burud and colleagues' thesis about the impact employer sponsorship has on the child care market in the community and country at large, supports the thesis of this book, which is that competitiveness and conflict have existed and continue to exist in the delivery of child care to the detriment of young children.

One major drawback of employer sponsorship is that parents often feel locked into their present job and resist change for fear of losing their child care arrangements.   Additionally, corporations run the risk of becoming too paternalistic and overextending themselves into the lives of their workers at the expense of their employees' privileges to exercise free choice. This latent consequence is ironic because the issue of choice is the overall cry by diverse interest groups in the movement for an increased supply of child care facilities.

This interconnectedness between work and family merits further investigation and suggests that corporate policies of the past be closely examined.

Corporate child care initiatives of today are reminiscent of corporate practices during the Progressive Era when corporate welfarism took hold. At that time, sociological departments of companies offered social and recreational services ranging from mutual benefit societies, pension plans, stock options, company newspapers, sporting clubs, medical services, children's services, and cooking classes (Montgomery 1987, 237, 455). Corporate welfare policies during the Progressive Era emerged with an emphasis on personnel management and the establishment of sociological departments within industries. The movement of corporate welfare was rooted in the social service work of reformers outside of the corporate circle. These workers moved into the corporate sector when management became preoccupied with personnel problems of turnover and the desired assimilation of the immigrant labor pool (Montgomery 1987, 236–242).

The most active period of corporate welfare practices were the years 1916–1922, although these practices began at the turn of the century and continued throughout the 1920s. Labor militancy was correlated with the institution of corporate welfare policies (Montgomery 1987, 237, 454–455). Corporate welfare policies were implemented in part as a union busting strategy in an era when the state had retreated from backing organized labor's cause (Montgomery 1987, 453). The corporate welfare model assumed that any conflict that arises from labor originates with malcontents. The existence of a basic, underlying conflict between labor and management is buried under the assumption that the two sides share common visions and goals. This vision is intricately tied to any discussion on corporate involvement in child care provisions.

The current antiunion climate, coupled with the emphasis on privatization policies rather than pro-active public policies, lends support to the position that the tenor of today echoes past corporate welfarism. In fact, many social reformers of today are being lured into accepting the workplace as a major vehicle of change a phenomenon that occurred during the Progressive years:

Both the numbers of people brought together daily by the modern corporation and the coercive authority the corporation could wield over them made the workplace itself appealing to many social reformers as a more effective agency through which to change popular behavior than legislation or appeals to reason seemed to provide. (Montgomery 1987, 238)

Montgomery observed that the corporate welfare policies had begun in the late nineteenth century, but that the movement took on a significantly different demeanor in the twentieth century, when the emphasis was placed on the concerns of the new immigrants and individuals with social service backgrounds became actively involved. The corporate welfare movement focused specifically on the worker's family life and use of leisure time. By addressing the personal lives of their employees, corporate leaders intended to elicit loyalty to the company. It was at this juncture that the new professional manager emerged as an important role in labor relations (Montgomery 1987, 237–242). As previously mentioned, the contemporary movement for child care has brought with it a new professional, the work and family specialist-consultant.

Implicit in the concept of corporate welfarism is a paternalistic relationship between employers and employees. This dependency relationship, which also places the worker's personal life in the judgmental view of the employer, deserves more in-depth scrutiny in the contemporary movement for on-site child care. Inherent in the provision of child care is the employer's intended consequence of securing the employee's loyalty for an extended duration of time, depending on the number of eligible children in an employee's family, during the worker's (man or woman) child rearing years. Furthermore, the secured retention of an employee during the child rearing years presumably should lead to continued company loyalty, especially as the new corporate movement of cafeteria benefit packages caters to the "life cycle" of employees. Dependent care benefits that cover aged and ill relatives complement child care benefits in fulfilling the same needs of management.

As Alfred Kahn pointed out, on-site child care provisions are most appropriate when special circumstances exist, "where there are industries of special labor force needs as hospitals, where there are company towns where there are isolated factories related to where people live" (Kahn cited in U.S. Congress, Committee on Education and Labor 1989, 246). However, when corporate "benevolent attentiveness" is analyzed, ripples of discontent may surface in individual families straddled by a situation in which child care is provided by the employer, but other needed services or a sufficient income are not so provided. The AFL-CIO contends that "no worker should be forced to choose between economic survival and the welfare of his or her children" (AFL-CIO 1988).

The Coalition of Labor Union Women (CLUW) voiced apprehension in their 1984 treatise, *Child Care Resolution* that some employers have used child care as a union busting technique. Unions, on the other hand, envision child care as an organizing tool for the recruitment of women (Waldron in Baden and Friedman 1981, 114; Levitan and Conway 1988; Albert 1988). Furthermore, labor leaders warned that employer sponsorship, which in the early 1980s accounted for less than 1 percent of existing care and presently accounts for only 2 percent, should not be seen as the solution to the child care dilemma. For example, union spokespeople cautioned that the Reagan administration's thrust for private sector involvement should not disguise the need for government involvement:

The AFL-CIO and the Coalition of Labor Union Women have taken a formal position that while unions and employers should negotiate to establish child care programs, the ultimate answer to the child care needs of this nation are in government-subsidized, non-profit child care centers. (Waldron in Baden and Friedman 1981, 114)

The warning issued by CLUW and the AFL-CIO has not been heeded. Corporate sponsorship of child care, and for that matter elder care, has become increasingly "in vogue." The media has played a major role in promoting industry's claim to child care sponsorship. Sophisticated and entrepreneurial energy has been directed toward the corporate sector, as denoted in the growth of the management consultant groups discussed in the previous chapter. Institutes and organizations devoted to "work and family" issues have become quite popular. This directed attention on the corporate sector is merited, if the media and organized labor simultaneously communicate the implications that will result from child care's link with the workplace.

Two other negative consequences for parents can occur when companies offer on-site child care. First, many parents are faced with transportation problems. Some parents voice concerns about commuting to metropolitan worksites with their children if they have to take public transportation. Others express a preference for a neighborhood child care center so that their children develop playmates near their home (Perry 1978, 30–31). In such cases, parents seek child care that functions on the community level and offers a different kind of socialization experience than that which functions under the corporate sponsor. On-site centers tend to favor the involvement of one parent over the other in the transporting issue, which can be problematic for some families. Another major drawback of on-site centers is that they are susceptible to underutilization due to swings in the economy, as was illustrated in the profile of ACTWU sponsored centers.

The socialization function of child care has definite ramifications under company sponsorship. One of the major policy issues raised by such sponsorship is that of coverage. In some respects, employer sponsorship can serve either a broad population with a socioeconomic mix or a small, select population. The degree of coverage depends on the company's form of involvement. The risk of employer sponsorship is that only upper income groups within the company will be served if adequate subsidization is not provided. On the other hand, corporate contributions to community programs and reimbursements can assure a more evenly served population of all income levels (Burud et al. 1984, 239). On-site centers will offer the benefit of an economic mix of children only when both upper management and lower status employees choose to utilize the center.

The issues of eligibility and accessibility are of serious concern with employer sponsored centers for two reasons. First, the target population often is middle class children who are the offspring of professional and managerial workers (BNA 1984, 283). As Jane Bryant Quinn noted in 1981 after the Reagan budget cuts, "The children getting kicked out of the publicly funded day-care centers are not the same children likely to be helped by employer-sponsored services" (Quinn 1983, 159). Quinn commented on the "twin" initiatives of the Reagan administration that took funding away from public programs while encouraging private sector involvement through tax incentives. Employer sponsorship of child care set up a system for middle class children at the expense of low income children.

Perry (1978) found that most employer sponsored centers serve primarily skilled and professional employees. Out of a sample of thirty-eight civilian centers, 39 percent of the parents using the center were in supervisory or professional jobs; another 35 percent were white collar workers, and 18 percent were skilled blue collar workers. The remaining 8 percent were unskilled blue collar workers (p. 99).

The results of a Gallup poll reported in 1990 found that income and occupation were not predictors of corporate sponsorship of child care. Of the workers polled, those with incomes under $15,000 were as likely to report that their employer offered child care benefits as those earning more ("Few Workers Have Access to Work-Site Child Care" 1990). As reported, the Gallup poll data does not clearly differentiate the percentage of respondents that received benefits versus those with actual access to center based care through their employment. More research is needed on utilization patterns of employer sponsored centers by socioeconomic status and occupational status within a given industry. The SEIU did find that "large companies which provide comprehensive child care benefits usually do so at their headquarters location, not at branch plant locations." This results in a tilt in favor of the higher earners because they tend to be the ones at the headquarters site (SEIU 1989b). Thus, the composition and extent of the population served by employers is of particular concern.

The much touted American values of self-determinism and the right to exercise choice in the utilization of child care services suddenly are disregarded when attention is given to corporate sponsorship of such services. "Choice" is a middle class notion; the degree of choice an individual has in many matters often coincides with his or her economic position and occupation. Choice denotes the existence of flexibility in one's ability to maneuver within the system. Corporate sponsorship already has been shown to constrain employees of companies who have no viable option outside of the company to which they can turn for child care arrangements. Therefore, the concept of choosing among a range of child care options, which is a diehard position of many child care advocates, is no reality under corporate sponsorship.

This deeply felt desire for choice simply is shunted aside when emphasis is placed on the corporate sector as a primary sponsor of child care. The two-tiered system of child care that presently exists will only be perpetuated, and those with the lowest incomes will continue to have the least amount of choice in child care as they will not be a part of the corporate sector that will deliver a significant portion of the limited available care. This false notion of the existence of choice is evident in other corporate "family friendly" policies. The availability of nontraditional work schedules, whether through part-time, flex-time, job sharing, or compressed workweeks, is linked to both the nature of particular occupation and its prestige in society. More research is needed on the link between nontraditional work hours and job status. The trend suggests that higher paid women tend to have more flexibility than lower paid women (Deutsch 1990). However, economic class and professional status intervene in corporate attempts to accommodate both employee's personal needs and company needs. For example, part-time employment among lower status occupations is not usually linked to guaranteed benefits. On the opposite extreme, professionals who are availed the opportunity to engage in a reduced hour workweek cannot draw clear lines as to *when* professional obligations end for the day or the week (Deutsch 1990).

Many traditionally "flexible" jobs have never provided perks or benefits. Immigrant and minority women historically have labored at specific occupations that provided some flexibility in weekly hours, but little protection other than the minimal daily wage. Examples of such work include the following: domestic servants, laundresses, seamstresses, pieceworkers, harvesters, boarding house keepers, and custodians. To meet family and work obligations, lower income women navigated the traditional system of forty hour workweeks long before the current observable interest in implementing workplace reforms (Jones 1982; 1983; Kessler-Harris 1981; Yans-McLaughlin 1981; Tentler 1979; Strasser 1980; U.S. Department of Labor 1930; 1922; Anthony 1914). Gender, race, ethnicity, marital status, and motherhood have always restricted both the employment options available to women and their own desires. The influx of the middle class has brought pervasive, deeply rooted concerns of the lower classes to the forefront of the media and the corporate culture.

Again, practices during the Progressive period merit examination for comparative purposes. The current movement for in-home, off-site work is reminiscent of the historical practice for women and children laborers to engage in piecework at home. Industrial homework incurred new stresses for the family unit (U.S. Department of Labor 1922; 1930). Safeguards must be instituted that will protect the work standards gained during the Progressive years and thereafter. With all of the manifest advantages of the new pro-family policies come many latent consequences. Worker exploitation can occur easily when part-time pay is given for allegedly part-time work, but full-time work actually is required or when part-time workers are prohibited from receiving important benefits. The labor movement must take on these issues in a forward thinking fashion.

Advocates for changes in work arrangements need to carefully evaluate the implementation of reforms that would address multiple issues simultaneously. The development of flexible work schedules that would benefit the family unit could be economically harmful if other benefits were traded in exchange. Trade-offs would not be necessary, however, if the broad economic context of the desirable reforms is given due consideration. Changes in the workday and the workweek are legitimate reforms to pursue when their current statuses as institutions functional to the economic order are discerned. The length of time required for earning wages and the wage provided are functional to the system (Fishman 1987, 527).

The traditional American work ethic presumes the adherence to a workday consisting of eight hours and a workweek of forty hours. The career ladder rewards those who go beyond this minimum expectation or whatever floor in terms of hours is set for a particular occupation. Depending on the profession, economic and social prestige often are gained by those who excel in their accumulation of workhours. This pressure to put in more and more time at work, away from the family, is detrimental to the personal lives of many and furthers the stratification of society. This work ethic, the use of the minimum wage, and the use of both a minimum number of hours for the workday and workweek as terms and conditions of employment, either as contractual, statutory, or regulatory provisions, must be evaluated alongside the implementation of child care services, if the maximum benefits are to be achieved for individual workers, the family unit, and children. It is doubtful, however, that such a wide-ranging agenda will ever develop, because as Miller (1989) contends the implementation of universally available child care and flex-time would erode the capitalist and patriarchal system (p. 19).

Perhaps the gravest danger of employer sponsorship of child care is that a delivery system will be established similar to the present day employer-based medical insurance system, complete with all of the inherent problems and escalating costs. A very definite risk exists that the emphasis on private sector responsibility will link the attainment of child care to one's place of employment. As is the case with health care coverage, many people remain uncovered simply because they do not work for a company that offers the benefit. In 1986, 37 million Americans were without insurance. It was estimated that this population was growing by 1 million annually. Another 50 million people are reported to have inadequate coverage (Sweeney and Nussbaum 1989, 78).

The country could very well end up with a system of child care where a few are covered and the majority are not, especially as the trend in employer sponsorship is not keeping up with the need for child care. This problem of inequity was recognized in the early 1980s by pioneer researchers and management consultants in the field, Sandra Burud, Pamela Aschbacher, and Jacquelyn McCroskey of the National Employer Child Care Service Study:

Of community concern, however, is the capability of a new system of employer-supported child care to further differentiate the services available to the public. In the overall view it is important that there not be a child care "rich", who receive a child care benefit at work, and a child care "poor", who do not work for a company that offers child care or who are not yet employed (such as people in education or training programs). The issue of these unserved populations underscores the fact that employer support is only one part of the societal solution to child care needs. (Burud et al. 1984, 242)

In 1990, Sarah Rosenbaum, director of programs and policy at the Children's Defense Fund, compiled a report on the health status of American children in which she underscored the consequences of a health insurance system tied to the workplace. Rosenbaum emphasized three basic points. First, insurance status is correlated to income status. Children in employed families with below poverty incomes are four times more likely not to have employer provided health insurance coverage than those families above the poverty line. Second, the profile of the employer provided health insurance system has itself changed dramatically due to changes in labor trends and corporate policies. Non-college bound young adults increasingly are working at lower paying jobs, as well as at more part-time and seasonal work. These jobs tend to pay the minimum wage and fail to offer medical insurance coverage. This trend in young adult employment patterns operates in tandem with the increasing numbers of employers that do not provide medical coverage for employee's dependents, thereby excluding these young adults from coverage under their parents policies (S. Rosenbaum 1990, 14–15).

The third reason for the high numbers at risk for not having employer-based insurance coverage is that the modest funding increases in Medicaid do not offset the decrease in employer provided coverage (S. Rosenbaum 1990, 15).[7] Data on the health care status of American children, in conjunction with the reports on the drop in the bucket provisions for on-site child care, the high degree of positive media attention to the subject of employer sponsorship, and the twenty year span of time passed since contemporary interests in employer sponsored child care were kindled, strongly suggest that corporate sponsorship of child care is nothing more than a mirage for most American families.

The publicity given to employer sponsorship detracts from its negative consequences. Although the economic function is actualized under corporate sponsorship, attention too often is diverted away from other equally critical *economic* issues. The significance of child care's economic function on the global, corporate, and personal levels is not disputed. Yet, although the bottom line of the companies are being served through child care benefits, such benefits also have been buffeted over the past years by management practices detrimental to labor. As Sweeney and Nussbaum dramatically illustrated in *Solutions for the New Work Force: Policies for a New Social Contract* (1989), the United States has never seen a more unequal distribution in wealth since the war years than that seen at the end of the 1980s (p. 11). The authors contend that corporate policy makers have made choices that have been detrimental to the general work force. They challenge the more popular explanation for the problems facing the work force; that is, the change from an industrial-based to a service-based economy as the major cause for the decline in higher paying jobs and worker displacement. Instead, Sweeney and Nussbaum argue that corporate leaders were caught off guard in the 1970s when America began to lose its competitive edge in the world economy. At that point in time a policy path could have been selected that would have seen an investment in human capital and an upgrading of product quality. However, the alternate course selected was to compete in the world market through a reduction in labor costs (p. 19).

Sweeney and Nussbaum claim that this policy path was not only shortsighted, but a regressive move for labor because it was the first time in the postwar years that the living standard dropped. The low wage strategies, antiunion sentiment, and benefit reduction policies coupled with a withdrawal of government support for social services have succeeded in lowering the standard of living for the majority of working Americans. The economic recovery of the mid-1980s did not boost the middle class, but rather saw a polar distribution between the upper and lower classes. The stagnation of the 1980s necessitated two earners per family to maintain a lower middle class life-style. Sweeney and Nussbaum describe five strategies management instituted that have hurt workers:

wage reduction and concession bargaining, elimination of high-wage jobs and the concomitant increase in low-wage jobs, reduction in the value of the minimum wage, sex and race discrimination, and antiunion activity. All five strategies have lowered the living standards of low- and middle-income families while leaving those at the top freer to set their own wages and to restructure jobs and industries at will. (Sweeney and Nussbaum 1989, 36)

Policy changes must be implemented that address these issues to effect positive change in the standard of living for workers. Thus, the implementation of child care policies may be a valuable move for both labor and management, but it is only one response to a complex situation. Child care actually promotes the status quo under many corporate plans. The establishment of child care benefits placates employees in lieu of addressing wage and other hard line employment issues.

SUMMATION

In the final analysis of employer sponsorship of child care, the conclusion is reached that under such sponsorship child care functions primarily as an economic benefit to the company by serving as an incentive for the recruitment and retention of employees. Back in 1972 with the first upsurge in company interest, a few child care advocates voiced doubts about the role of the corporate sector in the delivery of child care:

Some child-care experts oppose employer sponsorship of day care altogether, complaining that companies are more concerned with profits than with the child's welfare. Says William L. Pierce, of the Child Welfare League of America: "The child becomes sort of a hostage, to see that the employe stays with the company." ("Latest Benefit to Employes" 1972, 66)

The bottom line of productivity over child welfare is a real concern. Literature on corporate sponsorship consistently acknowledges the primary motive of self-interest. In his conclusion to *Child Care and Corporate Productivity* (1986), Fernandez adeptly sums up the situation facing companies and the role child care plays:

Older male managers will not move forward as expeditiously as they should unless they understand and believe that child care problems and family/work conflicts cost their corporations a great deal of money in unproductive time and also that their own involvement is part of the solution. They need to recognize that this nation can ill afford, in the competitive world economy of the 1980s and 1990s, to run its companies in less than the most efficient, cost-effective manner. It is a given that if any significant part of a corporate human resource is not fully and productively utilized, it will become a liability to the company that, in the long run, cannot be ignored. The same executives need to recognize that the change in women's work status will increasingly affect their male work force. (p. 191)

With economic gain as the primary function of child care under corporate sponsorship, the functions of social service, education, social status, social reform, and socialization are secondary. Liberation-universalization, welfare reform, and religion are not functional under this sponsor. Child care does liberate women, but corporate sponsorship does not promote liberation of all social members equally. The liberation-universalization function implies that child care functions as a social utility available to all, a function not reached under corporate sponsorship.

When child care's secondary functions are scrutinized, the power of corporate America is quite visible. First, in regard to the education function, it is clear that the corporations provide much support in the delivery of high quality care, which has been linked to adequate funding levels. Corporations can upgrade programs, implement high quality programs, and support existing high quality programs within a corporation's community or the greater community.

Second, the corporate structure's influence on the socialization of children has multiple consequences and ramifications. If the on-site or near-site centers truly serve a range of children, representative of the entire worker strata, then families and children will have more opportunity for interaction than previous structural arrangements allowed. Furthermore, the child's disparate view of work and family roles will be addressed appropriately. In the small segment of on-site centers that encourage parents' active "lunchtime" or "nursing time" participation, children will have more time interacting with their parents. In the same light, intergenerational programs offer many positive consequences for the young, the old, and the family unit.

Another advantageous consequence of on-site operations is that the occupational role of child care workers is more visible to the mainstream work culture, which traditionally degrades such work. In the context of the corporate workplace, the demeaning social status of child care work cannot be avoided so readily. The social status function has many latent consequences because gender roles and hierarchical work positions will inevitably come into direct contact and, perhaps, conflict. The everyday occurrence of a highly placed woman manager dropping off her child to the care of a lowly paid child care worker spotlights the manner in which child care has functioned to advance "career" trained women and simultaneously suppress those willing and able to care for and educate children. Poorly paid, but highly competent child care workers also are professionally trained or in the process of gaining professional training, but they lack access to prestige or comparable worth remuneration.

Child care has dramatically performed a social reform function under corporate sponsorship. The last several years document the increased provision of child care benefits, in any of the discussed forms, as a precursor to the move toward the provision of family friendly policies of which there is a wide array. The corporations first saw child care as a female labor problem, but soon broadened their understanding of the "the problem" to see the issue as one of balancing work and family demands. The new policies have been offered to effect the intersection of work and family. Structural change has occurred in the corporate frame. In this instance, function has had an impact on structure.[8]

The goal is structural change in the family and the corporation. Major upheavals in the structure of work itself are needed. Management and labor must continue to examine and implement the innovative policies of flex-time, job sharing, compressed workweeks, and part-time scheduling. All of these changes in the structure of time must be complemented by increasing the supply and availability of high quality child care services and guaranteed, job protected parental leave policies. The delivery of child care is a limited means of solving a complex problem that permeates the ethos of our culture. Changes in the fabric of family life that would "balance" the changes in the structure of the workplace come haltingly, if at all. Deeply held cultural beliefs regarding gender, the role of work, the relationship of the old and the young, and the rearing of children are but a few examples of those being challenged by today's work ethic and environment.

A latent consequence of management's good faith venture into pro-family personnel policies is that said policies are often underutilized. The "bottom line" issues surface again from both management and labor's perspective. Workers often hesitate to capitalize on new policies if they suspect that their jobs or career potential are at stake. Managers are prone to make decisions based on bottom line concerns that have the potential of pitting worker against worker. Specifically, the worker who elects to take advantage of a parental leave or compressed workweek policy risks jeopardizing his or her reputation as a dedicated worker. Otherwise sympathetic managers are placed in a position of meeting the "bottom line" and look askance at untraditional work habits and patterns.

Change in customary or cultural expectations need the vigorous and conscientious support of both top executives and organized labor, because both parties are needed to implement such changes. The obstacle in the change process is that the two sides do not necessarily share the same view of the situation. As is the case in all of the sectors discussed in this book, conflict exists within the corporate sector. The glossy image painted by the media of labor and management joining hands to provide a jointly sponsored child care center does not communicate the greater and much more complicated picture.

Conflict in the instance of corporate sponsorship of child care exists between management and labor. The conflict is seminal to the very nature of the corporate culture and does not change because the media happens to report on isolated incidents of corporate initiative in the area of work and family issues. Rather, more attention needs to focus on the erosion of benefits and the marginal standard of living faced by so many American families. As is so often the case in American policy making, a singular policy is hailed as a solution to a complex situation. The relationship between work and family finally is being seen as a broad problem, rather than just the specific problem of finding child care and securing adequate arrangements. This emerging view of supporting middle class America's struggle to balance personal and employment needs must be linked to the alternate picture of marginal America. The practices played out in the corporate workplace need to be placed in a broader context.

The social service function exists under corporate sponsorship in the sense that child care is part of a trend, including the implementation of Employee Assistance Programs (EAP). Child care becomes a service in a range of "employee assistance" services that include, among others, counseling on marital problems, substance abuse, parenting, stress, and career development. These services developed during the Reagan administration when the private sector was asked to take on more social responsibilities, which traditionally had been performed by the public sector (Klemmack and Roff 1985). This particular function of child care becomes problematic if a company offers child care and thereby considers the broader problems of the employed parent to be solved.

Social service under employer sponsorship and social service under nonprofit sponsorship have similarities and differences. The range of services provided under each sponsor differ by the particular center; however, child care usually is only one service among many with employers that offer EAPs. Publicly supported centers often reach the family via the child care program, which acts as the hub of a web of services offered, as described in the research study of Kagan and Newton (1989). A major point of divergence in the functioning of child care according to sponsor is that the employer programs serve more of a middle and working class population; whereas, nonprofit sponsors generally serve low income families who are traditionally recipients of "social services." The services offered by both corporate and nonprofit organizations may overlap, but also diverge to address population specific needs.

Much is made over government intervention in family life, while little discussion is being given to the new attitude of paternalism by corporations. Historical research suggests that more heed should be given to the blurring of work and family lines, so that the latent consequences can surface and be addressed appropriately. A dimension of the employer-employee relationship clearly illustrated by history is that corporate interest in child care is directly linked to labor market trends. On-site child care, specifically, is offered when competition among employers is high, not when competition among workers for jobs is high. The promotion of on- or near-site centers appears risky over the long term. Centers will be established when there is a need, and then they will tend to close in a sporadic, industry dominated manner. The supply of child care will be uneven, and resources will be inefficiently utilized when centers close because a particular industry deems it is in its best interest to retreat from the delivery of care. This inefficient use of resources could be rectified by implementing the consortium approach to funding and sponsorship.

The primacy of the economic function in the delivery of child care through employer sponsorship cannot be overstated. The dominance of this function in relation to the other functions is overwhelming. The most irresolute issues of employer sponsorship center on the functions of liberation-universalization, social reform, and social status. The research suggests that the education function could be addressed positively through adequate corporate subsidization and leadership in any number of ways. However, the consequences of the secondary functions that child care performs under corporate auspices are acute, as are the consequences for not addressing the liberation-universalization function that would enable child care to function as a social utility.

Three pertinent points emerge from the research on corporate sponsorship of child care. First, child care performs an economic function under employer sponsorship, but this function often ironically diverts attention away from other pressing concerns of economic importance to workers and their families. Second, the preoccupation with the bottom line coincides with a lack of concern for assuring that programs first meet the needs of children. Last, the uncritical reliance on corporate sponsorship detracts from the need for increased public responsibility for children and families.

NOTES

1.   On-Site Day Care (1980) defined four periods: Pre-World War II (1920–1940); World War II and Postwar (1941–1959); New Frontier and Antipoverty Years (1960–1974); and, Current Centers (1975–1980). The research that forms the basis for this book indicates that the last fifteen years have been affected significantly by demographic trends and the Reagan administration's twin policies of promoting private initiatives and fiscal conservatism. This last period of fifteen years is presently being marked by a turn in corporate involvement in child care from minimal involvement on the part of corporations to "family friendly policies."

A clear break in corporate policies is seen at the end of the 1980s as the issues broadened to concerns on how to balance work and family life. This change in corporate focus, together with the birth of the Alliance for Better Child Care, and the alliance's related legislative initiatives that led to the passage of the Child Care and Development Block Grant Act of 1990, suggests the line of demarcation for a new era be set at the conclusion of 1987.

2.   The Conference Board is a not-for-profit business information service "whose purpose is to assist senior executives and other leaders in arriving at sound decisions." The board was established in 1916 (description from the Conference Board's 1987 publication, Family-Supportive Policies: The Corporate Decision-Making Process). The Work and Family Information Center is a division within the board.

3.   Faith A. Wohl attended the 1990 conference as the director of Work Force Partnering at Du Pont Company.

4.   Information about Partners for Children was sent by Mary Kidwell, the director of the program. The information was derived from the following items: letter, brochure, a statement of philosophy, and a description of the center and its development. The center's funding is derived from the following sources: ACTWU, Knoxville Cooperative Parish of the United Methodist Church, United Way, The General Board of Global Ministries of the United Methodist Church, Bike Athletic Co., Crystal Brands, East Tennessee Foundation, Knox Children's Foundation, local United Methodist Church groups and UMC women's groups, and private donations from parents, board members, staff, and others.

5.   Labor unions listed in the SEIU 1989 "Summary of Union Child Care Activities": American Clothing and Textile Workers Union (ACTWU); American Federation of Government Employees (AFGE); American Federation of State, County, and Municipal Employees (AFSCME); American Federation of Teachers (AFT); American Postal Workers Union (APWU); Communications Workers of America (CWA); International Brotherhood of Electrical Workers (IBEW); International Ladies' Garment Workers Union (ILGWU); International Union of Electronic Workers (IUE); National Association of Letter Carriers (NALC); National Treasury Employees Union (NTEU); the Newspaper

Guild (TNG); United Automobile Workers (UAW); United Food and Commercial Workers (UFCW); and United Steel Workers of America (USWA). SEIU also published a list of their child care activities. SEIU and AFGE publish quarterly newsletters that focus on contract language and current activities in the work-family arena (Jacobson 1986, 13).

6. Although the research was conducted in the early 1980s, it still is cited as one of three comprehensive national surveys. The 1989 publication by the U.S. Department of Labor, Women's Bureau, *Employers and Child Care: Benefiting Work and Family*, cites the three surveys by Burud et al. (1984), Magid (1983), and Perry (1978), (p. 10). The Conference Board's *Family-Supportive Policies: The Corporate Decision-Making Process* cites these three studies as the major national survey studies as well, but also reports on smaller research projects that examined work-family issues within a subset of companies. Kahn and Kamerman reviewed the research and analyzed the status of employer sponsored child care in *Child Care: Facing the Hard Choices* (1987).

7. Since the compilation of Rosenbaum's data, the 1990 OBRA adjusted the Medicaid and Medicare programs by increasing benefits to low income families in some areas and decreasing program outlays in others. Three aspects of the 1990 OBRA are relevant to this discussion: (1) Medicaid coverage was changed to cover poverty level children through age 19, rather than the previous limit of age 7 (DSG 1990a, 39); (2) when deemed more cost effective than Medicaid, states will be required to pay private insurance premiums for qualified family members of employees with health insurance coverage that can extend to dependents (DSG 1990a, 38–39); and (3) a child health insurance tax credit has been implemented based on the earned income tax credit criteria. The credit will enable low income families to purchase health insurance coverage for their children (DSG 1990a, 28).

8. Ellen Galinsky, cited in The Conference Board's summary of its March 1990 conference held in New York, "Work and Family Policies: The New Strategic Plan" (1990), has identified three stages of evolution for firms interested in developing programs to address the work-family dilemma (p. 3). In stage one, a company addresses the child care problem in the interest of affecting productivity. During stage two, companies target dependent care as the problem, in the interest of reducing retention and recruitment concerns. The final stage encompasses a concern for the career development of employees and the implementation of appropriate affirmative action plans. At this third stage, the company is concerned with projections of their potential employee pool based on demographic information.

7. Public School Sponsorship
and the
Education Function

The final contender for sponsorship of child care is the public school system. As with the other sponsors, public schools offer advantages and disadvantages for the delivery of child care. After analyzing the four previously discussed sectors, the school sector appears in a new light.

The latter half of the 1980s witnessed a reemergence of the overt debate over the role that public schools should perform in the delivery of child care. As shown previously, the schools have been omnipresent throughout the patchwork development of the American child care system. The potential that resides with the schools disturbs many of its competitors and challenges public school reformers. The schools bring significant influence to the sponsorship debate because of two unique features. First, schools are the only universalized delivery system in the United States. Second, schools are designed to provide a service expressly for children.

The most intense debate over sponsorship is generated over the public schools. Commentators have attributed this heated factionalism to long-standing divisions of professional traditions. To many opponents, the schools represent an entrenched establishment offering a rigid, systematic approach toward the education of children and youth. To others, the schools represent a threat; the greater the involvement of the schools in the delivery of child care, the smaller will be the consumer market for the proprietary and private nonprofit child care providers.

The age-old rift between the social welfare profession with its predominant social service function and the education profession with its social role as mass educator has set the stage for a more complex debate today. As noted in the first chapter, this deeply rooted division has been described as the care versus education debate. The discussion that follows will demonstrate how such a dichotomous split in the analytic framework oversimplifies a more subtle and complicated tension that persists in the public's perception of child care. This tension is reflected in the term *child care*, itself a term rich in multiple meanings that contribute to confusion within the early childhood community and with the public at large.

The debate over the school's role originated with the antagonistic relationship between the social service community and the educational community (Caldwell 1986; 1989b; Grubb 1987; Kagan 1989a; 1989b; Morgan 1989). The list of players in the debate over the schools has changed over the last two decades. School opponents no longer are represented primarily by members of the social service community. A reformulated early childhood community with roots in both the social service profession and the education profession, together with the for-profit and church providers joined hands with those already skeptical of the schools' overall abilities to educate children, which included many advocates representing minority groups, and opposed public schools as a main sponsor of child care and early childhood education.

Bettye Caldwell (1986; 1989b), an early pioneer in public school sponsorship of child care, acknowledges two dominant reasons for the adversarial relationship between the child care community and the education community, which support the thesis that the function of child care is dependent on the structure of the sponsoring institution: "The first basis for the adversarial relationship between day care and education relates to the concepts out of which each service pattern has grown and, if you will, to the way in which proponents of each service want the field to be identified" (Caldwell 1986, 38). Caldwell links the "care and protection" function of child care to the social services and the "educational" function to the schools. Although each of these sponsors has a separate history in the development of child care delivery in this country, the two functions are not mutually exclusive. "It is literally impossible to care for and protect young children without educating them, and vice versa" (1986, 38). Caldwell has been a long-time proponent of renaming the service *educare* and legitimizing a merger of services and traditions (Caldwell 1989b).

Due to this split in child care functions by profession, a stigma attached to the service that long kept educators and the larger public at bay. The welfare and social service system sponsorship of child care led the public to believe that the service was only for poor children from problem homes (Caldwell 1986; Grubb 1987; Steinfels 1973). Bettye Caldwell captured the severity of this division in her article, "Day Care and the Public Schools—Natural Allies, Natural Enemies" (1986). Caldwell attributes much of the conflict to the low esteem in which society holds both the social welfare profession and the education profession. The educational system is easy prey to much criticism for failing to educate its charges; the child care and social service community has been attacked for delivering poor quality care and undermining the family structure. Caldwell implored the rival groups to join together as allies, rather than struggle to prove dominance over each other, in the search for prestige and access to limited resources.

The tension over the delivery of child care is exacerbated by society's failure to provide adequate financial support for children's programs regardless of the program's auspice. Although strife between the education and social service community did not prevent formation of the Alliance for Better Child Care and the historic passage of comprehensive child care legislation in 1990, the issue of public school sponsorship remained a divisive factor during the 1987–1990 legislative debates and shaped the final outcome of the many years of lobbying activity.

The dramatic rise in the labor force participation by mothers has precipitated extraordinary changes in the structuring of child rearing arrangements in middle class households, which in turn has affected child care's structure-function relationships. Child care is emerging slowly as a mainstream service rather than a residual service for "the poor and downtrodden." Furthermore, the stigma attached to child care's social service function has waned. This demand of the middle class for child care services has pushed the schools into the delivery market and legitimized their claim to sponsorship.

The issue of whether the schools should become prime sponsors of child care first flared when the Child and Family Services Act of 1975 was introduced in August 1974. The Child and Family Services Act, had it not been vetoed by President Ford, would have authorized an expenditure of $1.8 billion dollars over a three year period for services to children, of which child care was included (Child Care and Family Services Act of 1975 [S. 626/H.R. 2966]; CQA 1975, 693; Fishhaut and Pastor 1977, 39).

Although the final bill listed a variety of sponsors, the public school constituency under the leadership of Albert Shanker, president of the powerful teachers union, American Federation of Teachers, AFL-CIO, had ardently pressed for the public schools to be the presumed prime sponsors. Shanker's stand divided the previously united coalition for child care (Steiner, 1976). In *The Children's Cause* (1976), Gilbert Steiner identified three subgroups of the child care advocacy community that had united in the late 1960s and early 1970s: (1) the cognitive developmentalists and educators; (2) the social service community; and (3) the community control activists. Steiner posited that the 1974 breach over the public school's role in the sponsorship of child care services seriously weakened the political base of the coalition that had successfully lobbied for congressional passage of the Comprehensive Child Development Act of 1971, which President Nixon vetoed. Unfortunately, history confirmed Steiner's theory. An organized alliance of child care advocates did not reappear until 1987 when the Alliance for Better Child Care was formed as a voice for the implementation of comprehensive child care legislation.

Steiner's first subgroup of the original 1970 coalition, the cognitive developmentalists and educators emphasized the education function of child care. These advocates were concerned most with the cognitive development of children in the early years and could cast their vote either way on the issue of public school sponsorship. Concerned with educational issues themselves, this group did not view alignment with the schools as threatening.

The second component, the social service community, aligned themselves on both sides of the debate and viewed child development as "primarily a problem in the physical care and supervision of children" (Steiner 1976, 245). Members of this constituency most valued the social service and liberation-universalization functions child care provides.

Windows on Day Care (Keyserling 1972) gave support to the idea of sponsorship by the public schools through its revelation of numerous problems within the prevailing child care scene. The study's data revealed the stark reality of the quality of available child care and called for increased public scrutiny. The proprietary centers were rated as providing the lowest quality of care. Thus, those advocates most concerned with the quality of care found in Keyserling's landmark empirical account reason to support public school sponsorship. On the other hand, the many child care workers who had strived hard to establish existing centers were unwilling to relinquish their arduously earned base to the public schools. They argued that the schools had only their own self-interest at heart and had enough to manage in the delivery of educational services to the older children. This group doubted the school's potential to deliver the desired quality of care (Steiner 1976, 246).

The third component of the earlier child care coalition were the community control activists. This group had ambivalent feelings about the role of the schools at the time that the Child and Family Services Act was introduced. Although this contingent perceived child care to be an instrument for social change in the sense that it could be "a way to provide depressed people a greater measure of control over their own destinies," the desire to promote that function of child care was not as pervasive in the mid-1970s as in the 1960s. Second, the many political sophisticates among this group of community control activists were savvy enough to conjecture that the passage of major child development legislation depended on a concentrated lobby, which was realized in 1971 for the passage of the Child Development Act, but was at odds three years later (Steiner 1976, 246).

Reservations about public school sponsorship were expressed by The Child Welfare League (which braced the social service function), The Children's Foundation (whose primary concern was nutritional), the Black Child Development Institute (which pushed for the inclusion of the social reform function), and Americans for Democratic Action (which had a general interest in child care). In spite of these differences in functional preferences among child care advocates, Shanker cultivated a cohesive association of advocates, including, the support of the AFL-CIO. At the 1975 AFT convention a resolution was passed calling for a national early childhood educational program (Steiner 1976, 247–248; AFT 1975).

Fifteen years later, the controversy over the school's role in child care continued, although the issue was not the subject of open debate until the latter half of the 1980s. The historical significance of its reemergence is most evident in the multitude of publications and the testimony before the Senate and House Committees on the Act for Better Child Care and the Early Childhood Education and Development Act.[1] There is a remarkable similarity in the arguments pro and con school sponsorship between the debate of 1974–1975 and the debate of the late 1980s. Despite the consensus building process of the 1970s, significant unresolved issues persisted. Today's key spokespeople have reiterated their former positions in a changed context. Shanker's cry for active involvement of the schools first met with opposition and then with silence during the 1970s and early 1980s. The demographic changes that occurred during the 1980s, coupled with the winds of reform in the public schools, provided Shanker with a firm platform from which to republish his position for school sponsorship. See "The Case for Public School Sponsorship of Early Childhood Education Revisited" (Shanker 1987) in *Early Schooling* edited by Sharon Lynn Kagan and Edward F. Zigler.

The winter of 1984 marked a turning point in a lengthy period of tranquility surrounding the issue. An unprecedented meeting of child care advocates and child development specialists convened outside of Minneapolis to work out positions on the festering controversy surrounding the issue of public school sponsorship of child care services: "For the first time in anyone's memory, the leadership of child care and early childhood education, educators and education policymakers sat down together to discuss the role of the public schools in child care" ("The Debate Begins" 1985, 172). The conference did not set any strategic plans, but served to "break the ice" (p. 173).

Another milestone occurred in 1985 when the National Black Child Development Institute (NBCDI) published a pamphlet on the role of public

school sponsorship, *Child Care in the Public Schools: Incubator for Inequality?*
NBCDI foresaw the potential of the schools for the expansion of child care and
sought to rekindle a debate on the issue before programs proliferated without a
sound policy foundation. Since the 1985 publication, the NBCDI published a list
of safeguards for implementation of early childhood programs for 4 year olds in
the schools (NBCDI 1987). The purpose behind the 1985 pamphlet speaks to the
vacuum in public policy discourse during the period from 1975 through the late
1980s. Conflict amongst practitioners existed, but policy makers and scholars
were not wrestling with the issue until *after* the implementation of various
programs under school auspices and when the demand for child care became so
obvious it could not be ignored. Whereas the legislation proposed in 1974–1975
was meant to be pro-active, the transpiration of time suggests that new policies
are more reactive in nature. The NBCDI 1985 critique highlighted the
intervening trends since 1974, which placed the spotlight on the schools as a key
delivery system for child care services in the 1980s.

The National Black Child Development Institute (1985) identified two
distinct models in early childhood education that have converged into public
school programs. These models explain the consequences of the structure-
function link and the conflictual history of child care services that has developed
into a two-tiered system based on socioeconomic class divisions:

One model is reflected in the Head Start type programs for poor families which grew out
of the social welfare movement. The other model is reflected in the lab
school/cooperative preschool type programs for upper middle class families which grew
out of the child study movement. (NBCDI 1985, 11)

The first model grew out of the 1960s' War on Poverty, which developed
compensatory educational programs for disadvantaged children. Project Head
Start, which originated during this time period, administered many programs
within public schools.

The second model "grew out of the child development movement which
started with the research of Dr. Arnold Gesell, and the clinic founded by him at
Yale University in 1911" (p. 11). Gesell's program inspired other university
laboratory schools, which then served as models for parent-run cooperative
preschools. These cooperatives were operated by underpaid teachers and
volunteers. A latent consequence of this program model was the exclusion of
low income families who could not volunteer their time or work for token
wages (pp. 11–12). Minority and low income groups did not enjoy the privileges
of university campus life or the luxury of time for cooperative volunteer
activities. The part-day preschools did not meet the needs of the poor or

working poor. Neither, incidentally, do the part-time programs offered today, although the poor and near poor are the targets of such current arrangements. Many early intervention efforts taking place in the states are only half-day programs, yet they are targeted for families in need of full-day services.

The contemporary child care movement has converged with the early childhood field for several reasons (NBCDI 1985; Grubb 1987; Kagan and Zigler 1987a; Kahn and Kamerman 1987; Mitchell, Seligson, and Marx 1989). First, the research on early learning that initiated the 1960s movement for compensatory education continues to lend support for policies that invest in children during their earliest years. In this respect, child care serves a preventive function, but this prevention is part and parcel of a comprehensive service delivery model that embodies the social service and education functions. As mentioned earlier in this book, the milestone Perry Preschool Project (Berruta-Clement 1984) delineated the benefits of early education for at-risk populations. The National Black Child Development Institute credits this research for defining "early childhood education" as a "social good," thus endorsing the liberation-universalization function (1985, p. 12).

A second reason for the convergence of the schools and early childhood education is the escalating number of white middle class parents who seek the benefits of early childhood education for their children (NBCDI 1985; Elkind 1987a; 1987b; Zigler 1987a; 1987b; Olsen and Zigler 1989). Interrelated functional and class differences come into play, as "[s]ome see early childhood education as a critical first step to an Ivy League education, others see it as the first step in an education that will lead their child out of poverty" (NBCDI 1985, 18).

The period between 1970 and 1980 realized a two-fold increase in pre-primary school enrollment of 3 and 4 year olds ("The Debate Begins" 1985, 172). The trend continued into the 1980s with the number of pre-primary school children rising from 4.1 million to 6.0 million from 1970 to 1986. The attendance rate for 3 to 5 year olds was 55 percent in 1985 compared to 37 percent in 1970. "The rate for 3-year-olds has more than doubled from 13 percent in 1970 to 29 percent in 1986" (Snyder 1988, 26).

This broad based middle class demand for early childhood educational programs has the effect of constraining the service of child care to its education function in the eyes of many consumers and some public school leaders. Zigler and Olsen (1989) emphasize the faulty assumption made by this population and others that earlier "educational" experience is beneficial to all children regardless of socioeconomic status. The early intervention literature contends that low income children at risk for school failure benefit from well-designed programs, but the research has been inappropriately generalized and popularized giving rise to the misunderstanding that middle class children benefit to the same degree as low income children. Middle class youngsters have not been shown to acquire the same beneficial effects as youngsters from low socioeconomic backgrounds, although all children benefit from high quality programs and suffer from poor quality programs (Olsen and Zigler 1989, 169; Clifford cited in U.S. Congress, Subcommittee on Children, Family, Drugs and Alcoholism 1989, 3). The popularized version of the research findings on compensatory programs often neglects to emphasize the critical variable of quality as a predictor of the program's benefit to its participants.

It is apparent that the third causal factor for the link of early childhood programs with public schools is obviously attributable to the exponential rise in working mothers who desperately need child care services. Olsen and Zigler (1989) argue that this need for child care converges with the middle class parents' desire for early education experiences for their children. In other words, the need for care arrangements for children before and after traditional school hours, which would provide a schedule compatible with the parents' workday, is perceived as a caveat for public school involvement.

One purpose of *Early Schooling* (1987b), edited by Sharon Lynn Kagan and Edward Zigler, was to tease out the misconceptions surrounding the increased demand for child care services and the "preschool" services being offered through the schools. Early childhood programs have proliferated under school auspices in the 1980s, but the majority of the initiatives have been the expansion of half-day programs (Mitchell et al. 1989, 241–243). The data from the Public School Early Childhood Study indicates that less than 10 percent of 1,681 programs in a survey of school districts fell into a child care category. By contrast, 70 percent of the district programs were three hours per day or less. Eighty percent of all of the programs operated according to the traditional school calendar year (p. 242).

The decline in public school student enrollment accelerated the linkage process throughout the 1970s because the schools' physical plants had much unused space. The current demographic picture no longer provides available space in public classrooms to fill the need for child care. Instead, many school districts are opening previously closed schools to meet the needs of the current crop of school-age children; other districts are confronting the problems of overcrowded classrooms (Marrison 1990; Rimer 1990). The availability of space in schools for child care varies by region, but the national trend indicates increased rates of student enrollment because baby boomers are now rearing their own children (CCAC 1988, 35; U.S. Department of Commerce, Bureau of the Census 1987).

A fifth antecedent to public school involvement in early childhood programs stems from the implementation of PL 99-457 (Bailey 1989; Gallagher 1989). The Education for All Handicapped Children Act Amendments of 1986 require that public schools assume the responsibility for the education of all 3- and 4-year-old handicapped children by the 1990–1991 school year. This statute sets a historic policy precedent of school responsibility for children in this age group. Specifically, the policy requires that children with special needs be placed in the least restrictive environment, which necessitates the integration of handicapped and nonhandicapped children. Thus, a paradox created by this federal law exists, wherein the schools which are not required to provide education for 3- and 4-year-old nonhandicapped children, must provide education for handicapped 3 and 4 year olds.

An obvious consequence of all these pressures on the schools to respond to the crisis in child care is that the stigma attached to the service, primarily because of its traditional link with the social work profession has weakened, significantly, and a change in functional emphasis has occurred. The emphasis placed on community involvement and social reform has been supplanted by more immediate concerns of day to day life that respond to pragmatic decisions. The NBCDI highlighted this shift in pubic perception and expressed its dissatisfaction with the trend in the following passage from its 1985 publication:

It is important to note that there has been a subtle shift among advocates in day care policy over the last decade. . . . The child care proposals of the early 70's focused on community-based programs to complement and aid the social and economic development of the family and community. . . . Today's child care proposals pay insufficient attention to child development and even less to community needs and cultural values that bear on development. Instead, proposals focus primarily on expedient methods of increasing the availability of day care slots to meet the demand. . . . Expedience may be replacing quality as a primary goal. It is significant that it is in discussion circumscribed by this limited perspective on child care that more and more mention is made of public school based early childhood programs. (NBCDI 1985, 14–15)

In this passage, the institute captured a significant change in the perception of child care's function by the general public and by the early childhood advocacy community. Less emphasis is being placed on the functions of social service and social reform (NBCDI 1985; Moore and Phillips 1989) and more on establishing the liberation-universalization and economic functions. Child care no longer is seen as an instrument for social change, but as a facilitator for parental employment.

This change in function coincides with a change in sponsoring institutions. Those who advocated community sponsored centers that would function as instruments for social reform are not the same people advocating public school sponsorship today. The latter generally do not envision child care as an instrument of social change when linked with the public schools. Many proponents of the schools as sponsors, however, do affirm the potential of social reform through public schools (Kagan and Zigler 1987a, 222–228; Zigler and Finn-Stevenson 1989; Viteritti 1989; Macchiarola 1989). Such divergent views of the schools will be developed further.

Another significant impetus for public school sponsorship of early childhood services was the marked decrease in federal money available for child care. State educational budgets became attractive alternatives to federal subsidies (NBCDI 1985; Grubb 1987; Kagan and Zigler 1987a; Kahn and Kamerman 1987; Mitchell et al. 1989). The expansion of early childhood services through the schools is occurring on a state by state level. The conclusions of a national research project (Mitchell et al. 1989) confirms this trend and traces the active role of the schools with its 1989 publication.[2] The landmark federal legislation passed in the 101st Congress maintains the jurisdictional power of state legislatures through the block grant plan for funding, but it did not result in a federal mandate to strengthen the position of the public schools in the child care delivery system. The states and individual communities must continue to wrestle with the sponsorship issue as "hard choices"[3] will be made on resource allocation.

POSITIONS IN FAVOR OF SCHOOL SPONSORSHIP

In 1976, the American Federation of Teachers published a manual for its members stating its position in favor of prime sponsorship of child care by the public schools. *Putting Early Childhood and Day Care Services into the Public Schools: The Position of The American Federation of Teachers and an Action Plan for Promoting It* still states AFT's position. The 1976 manual, which grew out of a resolution of the membership at a 1975 national conference, continues to be quoted; and Shanker has reiterated the same justifications for school sponsorship. To his advantage, Shanker now is able to refer to the widespread state legislative movement, local initiatives, and exemplary school based programs to bolster his argument for the schools as the primary sponsor of child care services. In response to critics, he has softened the tenor of his plea by stressing the willingness of school proponents to adapt to the safeguards demanded of them for the implementation of high quality early childhood programs. Furthermore, Shanker has gained the support of pivotal interest groups, policy makers, and scholars. The National Education Association (NEA) (1989) and the National Association of State Boards of Education (NASBE)

(1988) have rallied to the schools' cause. Alfred Kahn and Sheila Kamerman (Kahn and Kamerman 1987; Kamerman 1989), with their keen economic and international perspective, also favor a more active role for the schools. Edward Zigler has developed a model program for school sponsorship referred to as the *School of the 21st Century* (Zigler 1987a; 1987b; 1988; Zigler and Ennis 1988; Trotter 1988; Zigler and Finn-Stevenson 1989; Fiske 1990c; Lawson 1990a; Cohen 1990e).

Morgan (1989) set forth the three primary policy positions on public school sponsorship presently under debate as they have developed from competing interest groups:

The major turf issues occur between for-profit centers and schools (and not-for-profit centers), between centers and family day care; and between support for existing programs versus the start of new ones in schools. Some for-profit providers do not believe that not-for-profit centers should be permitted to exist, and vice-versa. The for-profit centers have challenged the schools' right to offer care and education programs for young children. In some states family day care is also rejected by center providers, who incorrectly see it as competition. In other states, center and family day care dovetail well, and are often offered under the same auspices. (Morgan 1989, 43)

The debate over the schools centers on whether they can successfully deliver high quality early childhood programs. The first faction opposes school sponsorship because they believe that the needs of young children are incompatible with the schools' current educational approach. The second group admits that some schools are operating exemplary programs, but claims the majority will need safeguards to implement high quality programs. The third position asserts that in time the schools will voluntarily adopt the appropriate standards and need not be hindered by safeguards (Morgan 1989, 45).

The Bank Street–Wellesely research (Mitchell et al. 1989) represents a landmark in the debate because it put to rest any lingering notion that the schools encroachment into the delivery of child care could be prevented. Although the data indicated that school involvement is aimed primarily at the provision of half-day services for 4 year olds, it nevertheless documents the turning point in the relationship between the schools and the years of early childhood. The study underscored the incremental fashion in which early childhood is entering the public schools. Parents are speaking with their feet despite theoretical discussions on the advantages and disadvantages of school sponsorship. The development school-based initiatives began on the state level before OBRA 1990 and will continue in spite of the language in the final version of the Child Care and Development Act, which downplayed the role of the schools.

The much acclaimed reports by the Child Care Action Campaign (1988) and The National Research Council of the National Academy of Sciences (Hayes et al. 1990) defend the diversity of the present system. The Children's Defense Fund and the National Association for the Education of Young Children advocate policies that would upgrade the availability, affordability, and quality of child care, but do not advocate full-fledged sponsorship by the schools. A common theme throughout the years of hearings on ABC and H.R. 3 was the populist desire for choice. Organizations, providers, consumers, and legislators have heralded the advantages of a system of mixed providers.

Perhaps the most controversial position has been taken by Edward Zigler, director of the Bush Center in Child Development and Social Policy. He has been an advocate for his position within the confines of the federal legislative debate and outside of this debate on a grass-roots level with state-based initiatives. Zigler's model of the Schools of the 21st Century has become a lightening rod for controversy on the role of the schools. The concept of Zigler and his colleagues, Matia Finn-Stevenson and Karen Linkins, of a "full service" school overlaps with the vision of Bettye Caldwell, although there are points of divergence between their respective views (Caldwell 1989b; Olsen and Zigler 1989; Olsen 1989). Caldwell herself established a public school sponsored child care program in Little Rock, Arkansas, in 1969 that operated through 1978 from which was developed the Kramer model (Caldwell 1986, 35–36; Caldwell 1989a).[4] In order to best understand the advantages and disadvantages of the school as prime sponsor of child care, the arguments of these different factions will be examined in detail, beginning with Shanker's original position in 1976. Shanker and his colleagues at AFT initially cited two of the aforementioned reasons for prime sponsorship of child care by the public schools: the escalation in the numbers of working mothers and the expansive knowledge base regarding the importance of early educational experiences. Resting their case on these two fundamental principles, the AFT also addressed the preventive role child care can play in attacking the problems of latch key children and child abuse and neglect (AFT Task Force on Educational Issues 1976, 2–4). This preventive role is a component of the social service function.

This early position included recognition of the union's vested interest due to a drop in student enrollment that led to fewer classes, a need for fewer teachers, and the closing of school buildings. In 1976 two qualified teachers existed for every job. Between 1965–1973 elementary and secondary enrollment dropped 13 percent, which created 7 million vacant spaces nationwide (AFT Task Force on Educational Issues 1976, 4). This trend continued into the 1980s, together with the increasing number of mothers of young children entering the labor market. Given the decreasing number of students and an overabundance of teachers, the AFT advocated utilizing the schools' existing resources to expand the availability of child care services. They envisioned retraining teachers, adding new teachers, and using the available space. This argument for backing the expansion of the school's role in the field of early childhood generated considerable criticism. Shanker had created a new function for child care, "preserver of teachers' jobs." When "revisiting" this earlier argument for public school prime sponsorship of child care in the 1987 essay, Shanker was without the benefit of those teacher-enrollment trends of the 1965–1975 period.

Although the demographics of school enrollment had changed, Shanker prevailed in utilizing demographic conditions to bolster his position by underscoring the inadequacy of the current delivery system in meeting the demand for child care services. He emphasized the latent consequences of public polices that promoted an inequitable system of early childhood services based on family income rather than children's developmental needs. Shanker's words reflected themes that run throughout this book: (1) the current fragmented, flawed system of delivering child care is a direct consequence of implied and expressed policies that represent influential ideological beliefs about class and the allocation of resources; (2) child care performs multiple functions; and (3) children's needs are not the wellspring of American social policy regarding child care:

One result of both the overt and implicit public policies on early childhood education is that the supply of neither public nor private programs of high quality is adequate to the demand. The other, related result is a series of inequalities: access to child-care programs of any sort is related to the ability to pay; access to good programs depends on the size of a family's income; and, within the category of quality programs, there is a dual system, one for the rich, the other for the poor—and catch-as-catch-can for those who fall in neither category. Clearly, too, the wealthier a mother is, the greater her opportunity to avoid the wrenching choice between meeting the need or desire to work outside the home and meeting the needs of her youngsters; both interests can be accommodated.

As a matter of public policy, the contradiction between enabling mothers to work and enabling children to thrive can, of course, be reconciled. It is, after all, a product of history and public policy, and both are shaped by human decisions. (Shanker 1987, 55)

In 1976, the AFT maintained that the present child care system was of overall poor quality due to inadequate licensing standards and enforcement practices. The predominant tendency to classify child care as a function of welfare reform was called to task: "As long as public day care continues to be defined as a poverty program geared to work incentives or tied to income levels, it will probably continue in a custodial vein, there being little pressure from the middle class mainstream to upgrade and broaden it" (AFT Task Force on Educational Issues 1976, 7). The union contended that linkage with the schools would facilitate a move away from viewing child care as primarily welfare reform, with its custodial care stigma, toward the educational function of child care. Linkage with the schools would promote the liberation-universalization function by ensuring accessibility to the service for children and their families from all socioeconomic classes.

Shanker (1987, 59–63) summarized the schools' position for prime sponsorship and identified four key arguments in favor of the schools serving as the hub of an early childhood delivery system, which includes full day child care services.   First, the schools offer an existing, experienced administrative structure through which a myriad of uncoordinated early childhood programs could become unified.   Second, the schools are universally available and accessible. Third, the schools have the capability of coordinating the wide range of related services.   In other words, Shanker envisions the school coordinating medical, nutritional, and social services.   Bolstering his argument, Shanker underscored the public school's track record in maintaining safe, clean environments and providing services for children with special needs.

Quality controls already are built into the educational system, thus forcing the both consumers and the providers to apply these controls to child care. The schools also provide a fish bowl environment where little can be hidden from the public eye.   In 1976, the AFT pointed out that the methods and procedures for implementing controls regarding certification standards, building codes, and health standards already exist and would merely need to be applied to the child care programs (AFT Task Force on Educational Issues 1976, 13).

Shanker's fourth major reason (1987) for backing public school sponsorship concerns the "staffing" problem surrounding child care services. The alignment with the schools upgrades the economic and social status of child care workers. An association with education carries with it more public prestige, and union membership boosts salaries.

The early childhood field already is rife with a myriad of career paths. The classic National Day Care Study (Ruopp 1979) documented the critical importance of explicit training and actual experience in early childhood education for the development of high quality teachers–caregivers. Practitioners currently enter the field from varied economic, social, and educational backgrounds. NAEYC has attempted to deal with the dual objectives of assuring high quality teaching and supporting the fluid entry into the field by minority people through endorsement of a career ladder (Bredekamp 1984, 19; 1989; Willer 1988). Policy analysts have suggested utilizing the different levels of the career ladder to staff early childhood classrooms in a cost-effective manner by having lead teachers with higher credentials than the assistants or aides (Grubb 1987; Zigler 1987a; 1987b; 1988; Olsen and Zigler 1989; Granger 1989; Clifford and Russell 1989).

Zigler and Caldwell, who share many of the same baseline perspectives on the favorable role public schools could perform in the delivery of child care services, remain divided on the approach to staffing. This controversy became the subject of a public debate in an article, commentary, and rebuttal published in the June 1989 issue of *Early Childhood Research Quarterly*. In the article, Deborah Olsen and Edward Zigler offered a review of the all-day kindergarten movement and recommended reforms. Rather than concentrating efforts on extending the kindergarten day and risk the expansion of child care into overly academic schedules, Zigler and his colleagues advocate a new concept of full-day programming. They recommend hiring college trained early childhood certified teachers in the morning and CDA trained teachers in the afternoon (Olsen and Zigler 1989, 181).[5] Zigler's plan calls for a split in the day that is marked not only by a change of staff but a change of curricular emphasis. Olsen and Zigler claim that children aged 3–5 need all-day care, but do not need more than a half-day of educationally planned curriculum:

What we propose specifically, is supplementing the formal school day with nonmandatory day care that extends until the early evening. This, we believe, is an effective and practical way of providing children with the academic, social, and recreational experiences necessary for development while meeting the needs of working parents. (Olsen 1989, 268)

Caldwell contends that Zigler's model is a throwback to the old pattern of viewing child care and education as separate functions. Zigler's model, in Caldwell's view, is condescending to many early childhood professionals who share her perspective that the adult-child interactive process is "educare." She sees splitting the day between care and education as an artificial distinction and a regressive move for the early childhood field (Caldwell 1989a, 261–266).

School sponsorship for child care services has implications for state standards on teacher education and preparation. Although a movement is underway across the country to upgrade the quality of early childhood professional education, early childhood certification practices for kindergarten and prekindergarten teachers remains a formidable challenge. As of 1989 the state variation in early childhood certification practices fit the following profile: "Fifteen states and the District of Columbia provide for certification; twenty-one endorse kindergarten specialties within the general elementary certificate; and fourteen have no unique regulation of kindergarten teachers" (Fromberg 1989, 397–399).

Having identified the manifest consequences of public school sponsorship (Shanker 1987; AFT Task Force on Educational Issues 1976): universalization; coordination among early childhood programs; integration of education, health, and social services; quality control; and the professionalization of staff, the AFT (1976) identified some latent consequences. Several of these consequences would evolve naturally from public school sponsorship, others are areas that demand a concerted effort to meet the challenges of critics and to insure that the results are positive.

A natural consequence of school sponsorship would be convenience. Families with children spanning early childhood into the elementary years could utilize one facility or near-by facilities. By housing the programs in the schools, parents will have the convenience of having all of their children in one place. They will also have the opportunity to contact the school for information on child care, rather than embarking on a random search for available centers (AFT Task Force on Educational Issues 1976, 13; Zigler and Finn-Stevenson 1989).

Continuity between early childhood and the elementary years would be another positive consequence of public school sponsorship of early childhood programs. "Continuity between early childhood and elementary educational programs should be as normal and routine as continuity between second and third grades. In most educational settings, however, this is definitely not the case" (Caldwell 1986, 36). Caldwell claims that current practices are disjointed and cause dysfunctional changes in terms of auspices, funding, location, size, philosophy and curriculum, and in the training background of personnel. Furthermore, the exchange of student records is either nonexistent or extremely rare.

Shanker and his proponents acknowledge several administrative areas in which the schools would need to make adjustments to assure positive consequences from the linkage of child care with the schools. One area for change is the length of the school day and school year. The school calendar would need to accommodate full-day, year-round scheduling. Such adjustments involve the possible hiring of more staff, salary adjustments, and a possible increase in the administrative staff (AFT Task Force on Educational Issues 1976, 14). Caldwell (1986) addressed the need to change the school calendar and daily hours. The operating schedule is anachronistic because the school year originally was designed around an agricultural society where children were needed at home for certain chores at certain times of the day and months of the year. It behooves a modern, technological, and overwhelmingly urban society to adjust the school calendar again to keep pace with the needs of contemporary families. The Bank

Street–Wellesley Public School Early Childhood Study found that the schools have gained experience in delivering half-day prekindergarten programs, but do not have experience in delivering full-day, full-year services (Mitchell et al. 1989, 72).

Although the issue of parent involvement was not specifically addressed in Shanker's 1987 article, the 1976 position statement by the AFT conceded that the schools would have to aggressively seek a high level of parent involvement, which is recognized as a necessary component of sound early childhood programs. The 1976 position statement emphasized that schools are democratically controlled, and in its ideal such control implies the potential for parent involvement.

This democratic tax base for the schools makes child care a responsibility of all taxpayers. Child care becomes a collective responsibility as well as a parental responsibility. The fact that schools are operated through democratic control sets the school apart from all of the other competing sponsors and holds them publicly accountable. Thus, theoretically the schools under local control provide a base for the social reform function of child care.

Once in control, the schools must learn to be more flexible in their administrative abilities. When "presumed prime sponsorship" was argued in the 1974–1975 debates, it implied that the schools would have the authority with which to operate centers, but that they would not always elect to exercise that power. It was also anticipated the schools would operate in conjunction with existing centers as an umbrella agency. Thus, they would have been able to collaborate with the many state and local agencies serving community needs (AFT Task Force on Educational Issues 1976, 14). The researchers of the Public School Early Childhood Study documented the many collaborative efforts currently in practice across the country and concluded by pressing for a collaborative and integrative delivery model. Their profile of state practices illustrates the conundrum of funding streams that prevent easy collaboration (Mitchell et al. 1989).

Kahn and Kamerman (1987), Grubb (1987), Kagan and Zigler (1987a), and Zigler and Finn-Stevenson (1989) have each pressed for a collaborative conception of the school's role. Collaboration among agencies and integration of services are the goals of the 1990s as evident in the Child Care and Development Block Grant, discussed in greater detail in Chapter 2. This plea for cooperative efforts across professions, government levels, and agencies bespeaks a well-entrenched interagency struggle. Shanker (1987), too, pledged to work with other agencies:

The school system also can work with other agencies to ensure that plans for preschools are coordinated with existing or anticipated day-care programs. The point is that public school sponsorship of early childhood education does not require uniformity or rigidity. School districts would be free to expand and vary their services to meet local needs or fund other agencies or even non-profit organizations that were providing high-quality services. There is also no reason why, at the state or local level, the decision could not be made to provide incentives for home care or extended maternity leaves. The goal is quality, flexibility, and coordination. (Shanker 1987, 60)

The greatest danger of school sponsorship is that the schools might simply extend their present curriculum into their delivery of child care services without taking into consideration the special needs of early childhood. AFT claims they are aware of this risk and will counteract it. They go so far as to say that a latent consequence of early childhood programs within the schools would be that the continuity, which derives from the linkage, will positively affect the entire school program (AFT Task Force on Educational Issues 1976, 15).

Although not as vocal nor as adamant as the American Federation of Teachers Union in the earlier debate in the 1970s, the National Education Association (NEA) was a key player in the debates over ABC and H.R. 3. NEA has consistently supported the schools role in the delivery of early childhood services. During the legislative hearings on the Child and Family Services Act, NEA put forth a positive position for public school sponsorship. Speaking on behalf of the organization during legislative hearings, then president James A. Harris, articulated the NEA's belief that the nation must move toward providing "voluntary universal early childhood education and care" (U.S. Congress, Committee on Labor and Public Welfare 1975, 1231). He argued that the schools are "one of the strongest, most visible, most viable institutions in our society" (p. 1232). The NEA claimed that the schools have demonstrated their commitment and ability to bring together other institutions for a common goal, such as Head Start. Harris noted that there was bias against the schools housing Head Start from its inception, but that in 1975 30 percent of the programs were within the schools.[6] Harris viewed the democratic aspect of the schools and their local operating base as advantageous (p. 1232).

In *Early Childhood Education and the Public Schools*, in June 1990, the NEA came forward with a strong statement for states:

to mandate the availability of early childhood education programs in the public schools for all three- and four-year olds. States also should encourage and support efforts by community agencies to identify and place in such programs children who can most benefit from the services provided. (NEA 1990b, 9)

Included in the NEA's position booklet are seven reasons favoring school sponsorship and ten standards for implementing quality programs (NEA 1990b, 8–10). The reasons for public school involvement include those listed in this discussion thus far and the following several additional reasons (p. 8). First, the structure of the schools enables "many services to be provided in an economical or efficient fashion." Second, the public school work force is "the most stable and highly credentialed work force in pre-K-12 education." Third, the schools are engaged in systematic "restructuring efforts which necessarily will require consensus building and broad community involvement." Finally, the schools serve as "an acknowledged socializing agent." The reasons listed by NEA acknowledge the multifunctional aspect of child care by identifying the following functions linked to the school structure: education, socialization, social service, social reform, social status, and liberation-universalization. The NEA standards for the implementation of high quality school-based programs for 3 and 4 year olds cover the following areas: parent involvement, the delivery of a full range of services, staff training, compensation, funding, appropriate assessment techniques, the integration of child care and education, and the need for coordination (pp. 9–10).

The National Association of State Boards of Education (NASBE) published *Right from the Start* toward the end of 1988. The publication was the culmination of a national task force on early childhood education initiated as a means of uniting two movements with overlapping goals: the movement for school reform and the movement to establish a cohesive national early childhood delivery system. The findings of the task force called for a fundamental change in the basic structure of the schools.

Right from the Start recommends the establishment of early childhood units in the schools that would serve children aged 4–8. These units would be premised on five tenets: (1) the implementation of developmentally appropriate practices (DAP); (2) improved assessment; (3) responsiveness to cultural and linguistic diversity; (4) partnership with parents; and (5) training and support for staff and administrators (NASBE 1988, 9). The task force also called for collaboration among agencies and across government levels.

In keeping with NEA and NASBE, the Council of Chief State School Officers posited a position on early childhood services in the coming decade. Gordon M. Ambach, the executive director of the council, listed seven imperatives among which was included the expansion of early childhood services through the structure of local or state boards of education. The boards would have to possess the authority to contract with other agencies so that a multiple delivery system could be maintained (Ambach 1989, 7).

The National Association for the Education of Young Children's 1986 position statement on the criteria necessary for assuring "developmentally appropriate practices" in early childhood programs has been widely embraced by child care advocates. DAP has become the bedrock of discussions on delivering high quality early childhood programs. All of the previously mentioned proponents of school sponsorship accept the criteria set forth by DAP and commit to standards to assure its implementation.

The tension in early childhood circles is not over the definition of high quality programs, but whether the schools can make good on their stated objectives. Grubb and Lazerson produced an important work, *Broken Promises: How Americans Fail Their Children* (1982), which provides a reflective analysis of social programs for children that failed to meet the desired program goals. Given this reality, many children's advocates remain skeptical of the schools' abilities to deliver developmentally appropriate programs in spite of the influential organizations supporting the promulgated reforms, hence the subtitle "Between Promise and Practice" of Mitchell, Seligson, and Marx's *Early Childhood Programs and the Public Schools* (1989).

POSITIONS AGAINST PUBLIC SCHOOL SPONSORSHIP

The stance of Marian Wright Edelman and her coalition in the early 1970s favored community control for child care; and, therefore, the coalition shied away from public school sponsorship, which would have involved state boards of education and large, inflexible district bureaucracies. The coalition endorsed the social reform function of child care as well as the social service and education functions.

The contemporary position of the Children's Defense Fund reflects the imprint of this earlier orientation. CDF led the fight for the Act for Better Child Care (S. 5), which did not have a free standing title for school-based care. The House bill, the Early Childhood Education and Development Act (H.R. 3) included a separate title for school-based expansion, which CDF and allied organizations opposed.

Neither the Children's Defense Fund or the National Association for the Education of Young Children have come forward with a position in favor of presumed prime sponsorship for the schools or in favor of an increased degree of responsibility for service delivery by the schools. Rather, as evidenced in an article by former NAEYC president, Ellen Galinsky, published in the September 1990 issue of *Young Children*, the role of prime sponsor by the schools is notably downplayed. Galinsky wrote in favor of the diversity of the present system. Albert Shanker alluded to both the influential power of NAEYC, and its antagonism toward the public schools when he stated:

> Less philosophically complex but even more controversial than questions about the nature and purpose of early childhood education is the issue of sponsorship. Historically, the battles over turf have been between the public schools and community-based organizations, between elementary educators and early childhood educators. The transcendent interest in restoring early childhood education to the national agenda has submerged these differences, but the attacks on public schools heard at the 1986 annual meeting of the National Association for the Education of Young Children suggested that a renewal of old antagonisms is not out of the question. (Shanker 1987, 47)

In the voices raised against public school sponsorship of child care, several common themes prevail. Those against such sponsorship favor a more diverse, pluralistic system. Opponents do not see the school system as being able to provide for the very special needs of the younger population. They see an inherent conflict in the organizational structure of the schools and the developmental needs of small children and their families.

The 1976 AFT position statement that education leaders understand the developmental needs of the young and are willing and able to make adjustments does not alleviate the fears of those opposed to school sponsorship. Fishhaut and Pastor (1977) criticized the AFT position paper for taking "a view of the public schools that is simplistic and idealistic." They argued that the union unrealistically portrayed the school system as a rational organization stationed in the center of community life, capable of flexible programming and accessible to parents (p. 40).

Young children need programs that are individualized and informal. Critics of the schools worry that the traditional, restrictive curriculum of the present system of education will move downward into the early years (Sugarman in Sugarman, Martin, and Taylor 1975; Grubb and Lazerson 1977; Fishhaut and Pastor 1977; Greenman 1978; Elkind 1987a; 1987b; Rust 1989). Unlike the more optimistic supporters of public school involvement who see early childhood programs functioning within the schools as an element for change in the school system itself, Fishhaut and Pastor argue that the "dominant genes" of the school system will prevail over the "recessive genes" of early childhood curriculum (1977, 47). In other words, the predominant education function of the schools will suppress all other functions of child care. Grubb and Lazerson (1977) cite as historical examples of this trend occurring: the California Children's Centers and the kindergarten movement.

The California Children's Centers, an outgrowth of those centers that began under the Lanham Act during World War II, are a unique phenomenon in the history of child care. California placed these centers under the Department of Public Instruction and continued to provide funding after the withdrawal of financial support under the Lanham Act. The state funded the programs until 1957 at which time the centers became permanent recipients of the state's education budget (Grubb and Lazerson 1977, 13). Examination of the centers over a period of time, led Grubb and Lazerson to conclude that linkage to the public schools had negative connotations on several issues. They describe one impact on the content of early childhood programs in the following manner:

It is thus our view that the Children's Centers are becoming increasingly suffused with the values and norms of the elementary grades. Notions of accountability to the State Department of Education, to district administrators, and to local elementary schools have become much stronger in the past five years. Indeed, the most likely trend is that the methods and goals of the elementary school will be extended downward to child care. We believe this will increase the stress on bureaucratic procedures, orderly classrooms, rote instruction, and conformity. (Grubb and Lazerson 1977, 25)

Grubb and Lazerson, among others, perceived of the following negative consequences of school linkage on the "staffing" problem: (1) the move is costly; (2) early childhood teachers tend to jump ship from their present non-school employment to gain the better income; and (3) elementary teachers who lack early childhood training and experience may conceivably step down to teach the early years (Grubb and Lazerson 1977; Modigliani 1988; Kagan cited in U.S. Congress, Committee on Education and Labor 1989, 95; Granger 1989).

Grubb and Lazerson's (1977) analysis of the link between California's child care services, known as the Children's Centers, and the schools revealed manifest and latent consequences that resulted from new certification policies. The increase in number of credentialed teachers as a result of the link tended to correlate with higher operating costs and a greater emphasis on traditional elementary pedagogy. The authors forewarned that the trend in certification could inhibit the entry of minority people into the field of early childhood (Grubb and Lazerson 1977, 22). The alternate training routes that result in associate degrees and child development associate credentials would not be honored in the school system. Such avenues are less costly and, therefore, more available to minority people.

Jule M. Sugarman, former Head Start director at the Children's Bureau in the Office of Child Development, shared the concerns expressed by Grubb and Lazerson and blamed the structure of the schools for this trend of bureaucratization that prohibits the implementation of developmentally appropriate child care within school walls. In contrast to the AFT, Sugarman regards the physical plant itself to be intimidating and inflexible. The size of a school building implies the need for a "certain order and discipline and time table" (Sugarman, Martin, and Taylor 1975, 125).

Other structural variables have provoked conflicting views on the school's potential to deliver high quality child care. A clear example of structure affecting function is the exemption status that some states provide child care centers sponsored by educational institutions. Although the CCDBG will affect the use of exemptions, at the time of its passage twenty-nine states fully or partially exempted child care centers under school sponsorship from regulation (CDF 1990d, 2).

Another unique structural consequence of school sponsorship is the unionization of public school employees. Many remain skeptical of the unions' ability to adapt their organizational structure to the functional demands implicit in the delivery of child care (Sugarman, Martin, and Taylor 1975; Grubb and Lazerson, 1977; Fishhaut and Pastor, 1977). The long hours of child care present scheduling problems for union members (Sugarman, Martin, and Taylor 1975, 124).[7]

In their study of the California Children's Centers, Grubb and Lazerson (1977) found that the unions were interested in the centers as a new source of membership. In balance, they also found that the strength of the unions enhanced the status of the centers within the school district. Unions have the positive potential of increasing the status and wages of child care workers. Certain programming issues, such as child-adult ratio and shift hours, are negotiable through union representation and collective bargaining (p. 24).

Sugarman raised three other issues of concern regarding the viability of school sponsorship that persist today as points of contention: parent-school relations, financing, and the already over-burdened role of schools. Schools frequently are criticized for having poor lines of communication with parents, especially minority groups (Fishhaut and Pastor 1977; Greenman 1978; Lightfoot 1978; NBCDI 1985; 1987; Bowman 1988; Moore and Phillips 1989). The social service and social reform functions dominant in child care in the 1960s and early 1970s risk elimination under school sponsorship. Parents, especially minority parents, too often are disenfranchised from the system. Fishhaut and Pastor (1977) see a formality and distance set by the manner in which policy is made within a school district. Boards of education are very remote from the workings of an individual classroom:

The section of the AFT report on parental involvement begins with the statement that "public education is a collective rather than an individual function" (1976, p. 91). It points to the fact that policy is determined by local school board members who are elected to represent the community. Adequate representation is surely questionable when one considers the inner-city schools in relation to an entire school system. Election of a board requires money to finance a campaign and discretionary time to devote to participation, not to mention required know-how. It must also be stated that the role of the school board in relation to the operation of a single classroom is almost nil. When early childhood proponents speak of parental involvement, they are reflecting concern about the special nature of programs for very young children. The role of the teaching adults in the child's life (especially in the long hours of a day-care program) is certainly more intense and perhaps more important than in a typical classroom. (Fishhaut and Pastor 1977, 45)

Parent involvement in the earliest years implies active daily participation by parents in the lives of their children within the child care setting. It also means that parents should be involved in establishing policies for the center. Community activists have recognized parent involvement as a component part of the social reform function. Community control advocates doubt that social reform is possible through the schools.

Representatives from the Day Care and Child Development Council of America testified during child care hearings in 1978 that child care workers understand that they supplement the parental role, but educators see themselves as experts who as a consequence of this perception usurp the primacy of the parent's role (U.S. Congress, Committee on Human Resources 1977-78, 751). School opponents argue that distinct differences exist between the structural organization and policies of child care centers and schools. The schools are regarded as child directed; whereas child care center are viewed as family directed (U.S. Congress, Committee on Human Resources 1977-78, 753; Grubb and Lazerson 1977; Lazerson 1971; 1972a; 1972b; Greenman 1978). The schools' organizational structure presents a drawback in the move toward delivering child care services through its auspices. Child care workers by the very definition of the job are concerned with the whole child for eight to twelve hours a day. Schools are concerned with "part of a child's life and day" (U.S. Congress, Committee on Human Resources 1977-78, 751). The schools' ability to perform such nontraditional tasks as diapering, toilet training, preparing meals, and developing satellite family day care homes is challenged by opponents of school sponsorship (p. 752). There is a danger that specific services will be dropped or undeveloped, such as infant care (Greenman 1978, 10).

The social service function is at risk when child care is under school control because educators traditionally have been taught to teach the child without regard for the family unit. The single-minded nature of the American educational system that stresses cognitive development over affective development departs from sound early childhood practice that focuses on the whole child and considers the child in the context of the family. The social service function of child care not only emphasizes a holistic approach to the learning process, but recognizes that basic familial needs must be met to assure adequate functioning of all family members. The Head Start model is the foremost example of a comprehensive service for young children and their families.

The degree to which child care should perform a comprehensive service is debated by both sides of the school sponsorship issue because policy concerns regarding coverage are implicit in the nature of comprehensiveness. In an era of fiscal constraint and great need most people would argue that the populations most in need must be targeted as recipients for social services. Distribution issues are then raised as to the definition of risk and need. Nevertheless, if a mainstream, universal system of delivery for early childhood and parent support programs is desirable, then the social service function is most appropriate and needs to be implemented through a sliding scale fee system. A link with the schools complicates these already difficult policy issues.

Another argument against designating the schools as primary sponsors of child care is the contention that they already are overburdened (Macchiarola 1989, 172–173). First, schools are failing at their education mission. Second, the schools should not be asked to take on responsibilities that should rest with other social institutions and families. Historically, schools have gradually taken on more and more special tasks, such as driver education, health education, teen parenting, and drug education. School proponents counter that schools must deliver support services and special services; otherwise, the needs of children will go unserved. The school's role in society has changed for two significant reasons: a high school diploma is a prerequisite to future employment and other social institutions have lost their effectiveness. The family, church, neighborhood and community groups, and other religious and social institutions no longer play as central or formative a role in the lives of young people (Macchiarola 1989, 172).

One of the strongest arguments against expansion into the schools is that it would generate uncontrollable costs. Investing in a school system based delivery system of child care has definite financial advantages and disadvantages (Grubb 1987; Kahn and Kamerman 1987; Kagan and Zigler 1987a; Clifford and Russell 1989; Granger 1989; Zigler and Finn-Stevenson 1989). The general consensus is that a shift in policy toward financing child care through the educational system would be costly. The trade-off in cost would be the increased socioeconomic status of early childhood personnel, thereby upgrading the quality of the service for the children and their families.

Grubb (1987), Clifford and Russell (1989), Granger (1989), and Zigler and Finn-Stevenson (1989) have carried out cost-benefit analyses and conclude that a range of options exists as to the level of funding needed or desired. These analysts suggest that funding options are available, but decisions need to be formed as to the model chosen for implementation. Clifford and Russell (1989) suggest that four models exist for upgrading child care in general. These models differ on several criteria: child-staff ratios, group sizes, staff qualifications, staff compensation, and program necessities. The four models vary in cost along a continuum in which the superior model meets the highest criteria in quality standards as defined by NAEYC's accreditation standards to a model which represents current minimum standards.

The ability to fund child care through the schools does exist, the choice is whether Americans want to expend their resources in this direction. All of the cited researchers contend that public school sponsorship is a viable option; the funding issue should not be viewed as an impossible obstacle to overcome. Older arguments about the long-term benefits to society generated by investment in the young are raised at this particular juncture.

Proponents of school sponsorship suggest that a mixed system of funding be initiated at first between all levels of government, parents, and business, which over time has the potential of resulting in a universally available, tax based system.[8] Zigler's School of the 21st Century Model includes the two-tiered staffing pattern discussed earlier as a cost saving strategy, a strategy that Grubb (1987, 65) also raised as a viable approach. Head teachers with more educational background would earn more than their assistants.

Opponents deride the concept of expanding child care programs through the schools as too expensive and inequitable. Yet, Zigler and Finn-Stevenson (1989) ascertain that the current $2 trillion investment in the public school system would provide the most logical, efficient, and cost effective approach to expanding child care services. The in-kind savings would be high as existing buildings and personnel could be utilized. Zigler (1987) proposes a sliding fee schedule for child care services. The federal government's role would be to target funding to districts with high percentages of low income families.

Regardless of the viability of funding options within the schools, an issue of equity permeates all such discussions. A system of public financing is currently in place that distributes funds inequitably across locales because the public school system's property tax base discriminates against low income families and neighborhoods. Current reform initiatives are addressing this inequity through state legislative action and through the legal system (Suro 1990).[9] For school sponsorship to achieve its ideal potential, a restructuring of school taxes must be achieved.

Nevertheless, the problem of financing child care is not confined to the issue of public school control. As indicated throughout this book, providing adequate funding to ensure high quality programs is a pervasive problem across the five sectors because of deep-seated American beliefs. Conflicting values are at stake about the role of the state in family matters and ideas about raising other people's children. Divisiveness also exists over the definition of a floor of support for families in need.

The issue germane to school control most rife with emotion is pedagogical in nature. Critics of the school contend that the constraints placed on delivery incumbent in the massive, bureaucratic administrative structure will prohibit the implementation of developmentally appropriate practices. The reason that safeguards are offered by both diehard school proponents and those willing to concede more territory to the schools is that an evident risk exists as to whether the teacher-directed, didactic model of learning will extend downward to the early years. Will the structure of the public school dominate the multifunctional aspect of child care? Will the function of child care effect the structure of the intransigent bureaucracy? These are some of the questions that merit further examination and possible solutions by looking to the kindergarten movement of the past, with its policy implications for the present.

The most conclusive empirical data to date (Mitchell et al. 1989) about current public school early childhood programs suggests that the delivery picture across the country is uneven. When examining how well the liberation-universalization function operates within the school system, the study revealed that the state funded programs are primarily serving at-risk children with other programs being offered on sliding fee scales (pp. 147–161). Regarding the social service function, early childhood programs in the schools vary in their delivery of comprehensive services and the degree to which they involve parents (pp. 234–261).[10] The Head Start model was used as a base of comparison and often is used by policy makers as a model. According to Head Start, comprehensiveness includes health, nutrition, social services, and parent involvement (pp. 236–237). Mitchell, Seligson, and Marx's definition of comprehensiveness, based on Head Start, coincides with the definition of the social service function, which throughout this book has been defined as the "array of services" provided in addition to the education function. Transportation has become an important additional support service.

The education function seemed to vary greatly throughout the thirteen sites visited (pp. 211–233). The researchers compared the diversity within the public school sector to that found outside of the schools. A wide range of philosophical approaches were evident across all observed sites with no easily observable pattern. The hierarchical bureaucracy had some effect on the choice of curriculum, but each classroom teacher offered a distinct personal mark during the actual implementation of the given pedagogical approach. Mitchell, Seligson, and Marx (1989) concluded that public school sponsorship has offered a mixture of programs that vary in quality, but the structure administering the program made a significant difference in the service itself: "The form and structure of program administration at the school district level appears to have major influences on the nature and quality of the services delivered to children and families" (Mitchell et al. 1989, 73).

In "Day Care in the Schools? A Response to the Position of the AFT," James Greenman (1978) elucidated the functional differences in the "day care model" and the "schooling model." He referred to the classic dichotomous split in viewing child care and early childhood education. According to Greenman, early childhood education is a piece of child care, but child care is not necessarily a component part of an early childhood program—one encompasses the other.

Greenman argued that public school priorities are not on the family, but on the community. Schools design programs to educate without parental approval and expect parents and children to accommodate the schools. The schools' emphasis is on attainment of knowledge and skills at designated levels. He describes the schools as "monothetic," meaning that "children are all on the same road with the same destination" (p. 6). Social reform does not function within schools because they are invested in maintaining their own structure and prescribed education function. In contrast early childhood educational programs range on a continuum from "idiographic to monothetic" (p. 7). Greenman differentiates between an early childhood classroom model and a traditional elementary classroom model on the basis of teaching style. Elementary school classrooms prescribe to an educative paradigm involving one teacher or a teacher operating with aides. The child care center model is additive and more on the lines of a collective work group, less hierarchical (p. 8).

Greenman's concern with the existence of two separate paradigms for the teaching-learning relationship is important, as is his concern that the concept of nurturance is missing from the elementary school paradigm. He flagged the importance of the socialization function of child care. Greenman moved beyond the circumference of the classroom and examines the relationship between the school as a social institution and the role of the state. He contended that child care centers are institutions of the home and family, whereas schools are responsible to state mandates. Greenman foresaw a definite crossroads in the rearing practices of this country. The choices in deciding on child care delivery necessitate decisions about the primacy of the family versus the primacy of the state (p. 7). In Greenman's idealized vision of child care, parental control and involvement is implicit. The child care staff is there to assist the parents (p. 8): "Parent control of schools may be controversial, but parent control of childrearing is an American tradition. If day care is more closely aligned to the latter, then parent or parent/staff control should not be so controversial" (p. 10).

Greenman has linked structure and function. He at once highlighted the child rearing function of child care and asserted that alignment with the schools has broad ramifications. Placing child care under the jurisdiction of the educational institution is sanctioning the involvement of the state in the child rearing process. Similar arguments have been made over simply increasing public expenditure for child care. The 1971 Comprehensive Child Development Act was vetoed because President Nixon feared the "sovietization" of American children. Vestiges of these antistate sentiments remain in the political system, were evoked during testimonies on ABC and H.R. 3, and are manifest in the legislation that emanated from all of the debate.

During the first large scale public debate (1969–1971) child care was characterized by those opposed as being antifamily. Consensus was found in the later debate (1987–1990) because child care was framed as supportive to the family. In *Within Our Reach: Breaking the Cycle of Disadvantage* (1988), Lisbeth and Daniel Schorr contended that conservatives and liberals can find common ground in advocating policies that support the family, the institution that both sides view as central to the American way of life. According to Greenman's analytic framework, an autonomous child care center is friendlier to the family than the domineering public schools. The school represents the state, which in turn is viewed as a threat to the family's influence.

The socialization function of child care is much more controversial than manifest issues of financing and pedagogy. The debate over child care is a debate over the power to raise the nation's children (Taylor cited in Sugarman, Martin, and Taylor 1975, 118–119). Granting additional power to the school transfers power away from parents (p. 119). Skeptics fear that the educational system would work against the needs of children and would inhibit well-intended reforms.

Testimony and positions abound that challenge the notion of striving for a uniform delivery system as a national goal. Even those who strive to make child care universally accessible shy away from the school system as the basis for delivery. Proponents of school sponsorship argue that the schools are the only means for assuring the liberation-universalization function of child care. Does school sponsorship represent the only alternative for providing universal accessibility to child care services, or will a multiple sponsor model reach that goal? The issue of choice and the protection of pluralism, which has been an obvious issue in the analysis of the advantages and disadvantages of the other sectors' claims of right to deliver child care, appears again in the context of the school's role.   This issue of pluralism and cultural identity is of particular importance to the minority community and warrants further discussion.

SPECIAL CONCERNS OF THE BLACK COMMUNITY

As stated earlier, the National Black Child Development Institute (NBCDI) expressed the need to take a strong position on public school sponsorship of child care.   NBCDI shares many of the general concerns voiced by others opposed to such sponsorship.   NBCDI's involvement in developing legislation for child care can be traced back to some of the first congressional hearings held in 1971 on child care legislation.   At the hearings on the Comprehensive Child Development Act of 1971, Evelyn Moore, executive director, and Maurien McKinley argued the case for community control of child care on behalf of the NBCDI (U.S. Congress, Committee on Labor and Public Welfare 1971, 367). They envisioned child care as a catalyst for total community development.   This social reform function was encompassed in the notion of community control of centers through active parent participation.   Moore and McKinley were interested in promoting cultural awareness and black pride within their community.

Four years later, in 1975, Evelyn Moore testified on behalf of NBCDI during congressional hearings on the Child and Family Services Act of 1975. She promoted the social reform function of child care by advocating the "strengthening of black family life within the context of community development" (U.S. Congress, Committee on Labor and Public Welfare 1975, 1262). NBCDI's proposed delivery system favored states and municipalities with nonprofits as the second choice (p. 1263).   It did not want sponsorship placed in the hands of the public schools.   Speaking to black concerns about the Child and Family Services Act in an essay in *One Child Indivisible* Moore (1975) wrote, "Until the public schools can become more responsive, I do not think they ought to be given the entire responsibility in this new piece of legislation" (p. 175).

In *Child Care in the Public Schools: Incubator for Inequality?* NBCDI (1985) makes some specific points regarding the impact school sponsorship would have on the black community.   In her preface to the 1985 position statement on child care, Evelyn Moore, the executive director, points to the past as precedent for the concerns of the black community:

The past is precedent to this discussion. In many of our nation's cities, Blacks have inherited the failures of public policy: decrepit housing, inadequate public services, and empty municipal coffers. In urban public schools, once again, Blacks stand to inherit institutions and programs abandoned by the mainstream of our society. Are we compounding the error by assigning the youngest of our children to a system that has yet to prove that it can work for Black children? How are we to assure ourselves that the public schools can develop the skills and techniques necessary to nurture Black talent at its most fragile and formative stage? Who has looked deeply into the movement and can assure us that we are not consigning our Black babies to what may turn out to be nothing more than diaper ghettos? (p. 5)

NBCDI acknowledged the crisis condition of child care in 1985. The previous quarter of a century had not served the needs of minority children and their families well, causing the crisis in child care to be most acute in the black community for the following reasons (NBCDI 1985, 8–10). Again, let it be stated, child care is not a new problem among blacks; it was not until child care became a white, middle class problem that action was taken.

Black women historically have worked outside of the home. In most cases, mothers relied on relatives to care for their children. As is the trend across cultures, black families are losing their support system because relatives also are joining the work force and unavailable to care for the young.

Blacks have always needed child care, but in the last two decades they have had to compete for child care slots with other groups. Until 1990, the competition had been particularly stiff, because less federal money had been available to subsidize centers and provide benefits to those in need. Due to the cutbacks in social services under the Reagan administration, that is, AFDC, Title XX, and the Child Care Food Program, many more black families had less disposable income to use for child care. Data collected at the time of the 1985 NBCDI publication indicated an increased gap between rich and poor and between black and white. Black families were left at a disadvantage when they were left behind in the economic recovery of the early 1980s:

While the white median family income has increased, the Black median family income has fallen. While the poverty rate among white children dropped between 1983 and 1984, the poverty rate among Black children hit an all time high—51.1 percent. These economic constraints put Black families at an enormous financial disadvantage just when they are forced to purchase child care services. (NBCDI 1985, 9)

The child care market in the black community was affected by the Reagan budget cuts and the insurance crisis of the middle 1980s, when centers were forced to close or raise their fees. These combined factors narrowed an already limited child care market for black families.

In spite of these trends, the black community in 1985 did not want to turn to the public schools as the answer to the child care crisis. The community's level of trust was low and level of concern high, especially as it is projected that urban schools will be predominantly minority students by the turn of the century. "In the next fifteen to twenty years, most urban public schools will be between 48 percent and 65 percent minority" (NBCDI 1985, 18). NBCDI cited dismal statistics on the status of black children's experiences with the public schools as measured by illiteracy rates, drop-out rates, suspension rates, percentages placed in special education classes, and college enrollment rates (NBCDI 1985, 18–19). Given available data, there is a very real concern that public school based early childhood programs and child care would serve the black community inadequately (NBCDI 1987; Moore 1987; Bowman 1988; Moore and Phillips 1989).

The National Black Child Development Institute posited that an inherent conflict exists between the structure of the schools and the needs of black children and families, particularly in the case of early childhood programming (NBCDI 1985, 20). Several concerns voiced by NBCDI echoed issues raised by others. The black community is very much concerned that parents will be left out of the picture if schools become involved (p. 20). They also are skeptical that appropriate teaching methods will be used with young children (p. 21). They fear that the social reform function so crucial to the black struggle will be eliminated under school sponsorship.

Another concern among advocates for black children focuses on the socialization function of child care because of the schools' tendency to socialize children according to white middle class standards. The black community would like to ensure a better match between the socialization process within school and that of the black community (NBCDI 1985, 21; Bowman 1988; Moore 1987; Moore and Phillips 1989). NBCDI further asserted the position that student testing and teacher training methods of the schools have built-in biases against blacks; therefore, NBCDI does not want their youngest population subjected to these biases (NBCDI 1985, 22).

In 1985, NBCDI concluded that it "cannot and will not support wholesale proposals for public school child care" (p. 26). It perceived the movement to do so as politically expedient, but not grounded in a well-rounded understanding of the enveloping child care crisis. The institute advocated a system of child care that is diverse, of high quality, responsible, and culturally sensitive. They cautioned against the assumption that public school housing of child care programs implies public school control because schools can house centers without controlling them. The institute pleaded for more public debate and analysis of the issues raised in their report.

Two years after the 1985 statement, NBCDI published *Safeguards: Guidelines for Establishing Programs for Four-Year-Olds in the Public Schools.*

The intervening years indicated that the move forward into the public schools was inevitable and, therefore, demanded a framework from which to build programs deemed appropriate for minority children. NBCDI cited four reasons for the participation of blacks in early childhood programs sponsored by public schools (1987, 1). First, a high percentage of the children served by the existing public school based early childhood programs are black because the programs are targeted at "at risk children," a majority of whom are black. Second, 67 percent of black mothers participate in the work force. Third, black families seek educational experiences for their children. Fourth, public school programs offer free or income determined services. The following passage synthesizes the thinking of the minority community in 1987:

The National Black Child Development Institute (NBCDI) has a record of support for the public schools and their teachers. As advocates for Black children, such support is mandatory—because it is here that the vast majority of Black students will be found long into the 21st Century. Still, as the public school systems add to their responsibilities the needs of yet another constituent—the very young, it is incumbent upon us to address some concerns to which this trend has given rise. These concerns emerge from past public policy in general and from trends in education which have drastically affected the lives of countless Black children. In many of our nation's cities, Blacks have inherited the failures of public policy: decrepit housing, inadequate public services, and empty municipal coffers. (p. 1)

Within the black community anti-public school sentiment turns the debate to the weighing of advantages and disadvantages between the schools and nonprofit, independent for-profit, and church sponsored centers, As illustrated in earlier chapters, the for-profit chains and corporate sector fail to include a high percentage of the minority low income population in coverage. Evelyn Moore and her colleagues confront the sponsorship dilemma head on and justifiably persist in agitating for structural change in the organization of the schools (Moore 1987; Moore and Phillips 1989; Bowman 1988). The black community cannot withdraw from the school reform movement; but it can (1) continue to demand structural changes in the educational system as demonstrated in the list of ten safeguards and (2) highlight the multifunctional aspects of child care so that safeguards protect those functions desirable to the community within the school structure.

THE SCHOOL OF THE TWENTY-FIRST CENTURY
AND THE
CONCEPT OF COMMUNITY CONTROL

Over the protracted years of debate, opponents of public school sponsorship have held fast to the concept of local control that they envision as the vehicle for the social reform function of child care. The interrelationship between the federal, state, and local levels of government become cumbersome and controversial when public school sponsorship is discussed. Local control advocates prefer funding to pass from the federal government directly to local organizational entities, both public and private nonprofit (Sugarman 1989; Edelman cited in U.S. Congress, Committee on Labor and Public Welfare 1971, 520-550). In addition to desiring control over allocation decisions, parents and educators prefer to have as much local autonomy as possible over pedagogical policies. State boards of education vary in the degree to which they delegate control to the district level.

Debates over which level of government should gain power were intense during the 1970s and in hearings on the Child Development Act of 1971 and the Child and Family Services Act of 1975. Since that time there has been a retreat from the federal to local distribution practice preferred by community control advocates. Instead, concentrated power has been granted to the states for the dispersion of funds (Kahn and Kamerman 1987; Sugarman 1989). The reliance on block grants has granted considerable discretion to state agencies.

This investment in the jurisdictional power of the states was reaffirmed in the debates over ABC and H.R. 3., as evident in the resultant block grant approach and the National Association of Governors' success in preventing the drafting of federal standards for child care centers. The block grant component was a part of both H.R. 3 and S. 5. Yet, the former bill's first two titles presumed a distribution of resources according to existing administrative structures, Head Start and the public schools. The separate title approach of H.R. 3 was problematic for community control advocates, who feared any legislation that granted more power to the schools and believed that the coordination of existing programs would be better served according to the Senate's approach in S. 5.

In spite of the failure to include a school-based title in the final legislation, the reality has been that states have moved ahead in the delivery of child care and half-day early childhood programs through the public schools. This movement, which combined child care demands and school reforms, was well underway on a state by state basis before passage of the Child Care and Development Block Grant Act (Bridgman 1985c, 1; "The Debate Begins" 1985,

173; Grubb 1987; Mitchell et al. 1989; Kahn and Kamerman 1987; Council of Chief State School Officers 1988).

The outcome of the debate over sponsorship on the federal level as evident in the CCDBG is open for interpretation. On the one hand, the legislation clearly indicates that the schools were not chosen as the seat of a national delivery system. The intent of the legislators was to honor the existing diversity of the current system. The claims of the proprietary and religious sectors were viewed as too prominent and pervasive to negate or challenge by granting a majority of funds or authority to the schools. According to this interpretation, the debate over sponsorship was resolved against the schools.

The alternative interpretation views an unresolved debate by arguing that the federal government only deferred the decision about sponsorship to the states and perhaps to the consumers themselves. The states must design plans that designate lead agencies, of which state Boards of Education are strong contenders. Each state will build from its own unique history of agency involvement.

Consumers will influence policy decisions regarding sponsorship because they were given much clout in the new legislation. A major thrust of the legislation was to ensure parental choice across income levels. It is likely that middle class communities will utilize public school programs when such programs are available and of high quality. Lower income communities will avail themselves of existing public school early childhood programs, which already have begun within the schools. These utilization patterns will only encourage more growth within the school sector. Those states with well-developed school-based programs before the passage of the 1990 legislation will continue to strengthen and expand the existing delivery base.[11]

Given these indicators of continued public school involvement regardless of the failure of a specific federal mandate to establish a school-based delivery system, the analysis here turns to the viability of the local school becoming the hub of a child care delivery system. Because local educational agencies undoubtedly are tied to state Boards of Education and the powers of such boards vary across the nation, this variance in practice needs to be taken into consideration as a factor influencing school based reform efforts. The variation in state education boards and state interagency coordination mechanisms suggests that any grass-roots concept risks bastardization in the reform process, yet also has the potential to respond to idiosyncratic needs of specific communities.

Edward Zigler (1987c; 1988) proposed a model program, the School of the 21st Century, to facilitate expansion of child care services through the public schools. The concepts underlying the model pose solutions for many of the issues at conflict over the sponsorship of child care. Dr. Zigler's vision of the school embraces the concept of community control so dear to the hearts of 1960s–1970s liberals and Deweyan education reformers.   The model also provides a mechanism for the coordination of a wide range of community services through the school serving as the focal point of a delivery system.

Zigler's concept of the School of the 21st Century, which he developed with the assistance of his colleagues Matia Finn-Stevenson and Karen Linkins, envisages a "full service" school that operates throughout the calendar year and for the full working day.   The model includes five specific services: (1) a program for 3–5 year olds; (2) before- and after-school programs; 3) a parent education–home visitation component modeled after the Missouri Parents as Teachers (PAT) program; (4) an information and referral service for specialized care demands; and (5) a satellite infant–toddler family child care network that receives technical assistance and support from the schools.   These five services would be provided through the school system, but as a separate system within the school, administered by an individual well-grounded in child development (Zigler and Finn-Stevenson 1989, 324–325).

Zigler's model is open to the involvement of other community agencies and flexibly conceptualized to be implemented from a state or local initiative.   The School of the 21st Century is to be constructed in response to the particular needs of a community and can be implemented in piggyback fashion by building from existing services.   Funding for present on-site implementation of the model comes from a variety of sources.[12]

As of fall 1990, the School of the 21st Century has been implemented in six different states with interest expressed from many other states and district superintendents.   The six states currently involved in the implementation process are Wyoming, Missouri, Colorado, Connecticut, Oklahoma, and North Carolina. Initial steps in the implementation process have begun in Ohio, Iowa, and Texas with additional states expressing preliminary inquiries.   Each locale has developed the model to meet the particular needs of the community.   Every implemented model has built from a unique set of circumstances, which represent the varied manner in which the concept can take hold.   Funding patterns vary by utilizing state revenues, local revenues, corporate donations, foundation grants, and fees on a sliding scale.

Missouri's 21st Century model is located in Independence County, a middle class community outside of Kansas City.   It has thrived because of the statewide commitment to the Parents as Teachers Program, which served as a catalyst for the implementation of the Zigler model.   The PAT program is in operation throughout the Missouri public school system and a foundation for the expansion of the 21st Century concept into districts other than Independence County, such as St. Louis.   The state has instituted statewide public funding for PAT that contributes to the development of the Independence County full service school district.

The School of the 21st Century was initiated in Independence County in 1988 by the superintendent of schools. The model involves all of the district's thirteen elementary schools. The before- and after-school component is in every school; whereas the all-day preschool program is open to all in the district, but operates in only two of the elementary buildings. The other two components of the 21st Century model already existed in the school district and were used to piggyback on the other services. The Independence County school district implemented the family child care network through a developmental process with providers, teachers, the PTA and participants in the PAT program.

Independence is experimenting with a follow-through elementary curriculum component to the preschool service and developing an intergenerational program using grandparents as volunteers in the early childhood programs. The district has further responded to community needs by innovatively linking the preschool needs with adolescent needs. A work study program for high school students was instituted that enabled the adolescents to work at the child care centers. Funding for the services of the full service schools derive from the state legislated funds for PAT in addition to foundation grants and parent fees.

The School of the 21st Century model also operates in the Lake County School District R-1 based in Leadville, Colorado, and is administered by the Lake County School District in conjunction with an advisory board. Administrators are certified by the Colorado Department of Social Services or the Department of Education, and program leaders meet standards set by the Department of Social Services. This Colorado model is an example of a district initiated implementation process in a region that has suffered from a depressed mining economy and relies on the ski industry for revenue. Under the leadership of the district's superintendent, the city established the model under the name *The Center* and offers child care services to families that work odd hour shifts in the tourist industry. An elementary school building that had been abandoned because of the population decrease from downsizing in the mining industry was utilized to offer these new services. The superintendent had commenced offering child care services before contacting Dr. Zigler and his team, but then expanded the services offered to include both the family network and Parents as Teachers component.

The Leadville Center developed around the unique needs of the low socioeconomic community. The parents leave for work at 5:30 A.M. when they commute to one of two mountain passes and conclude the day at 6:30 P.M. Early childhood services were developed to strengthen the abilities of the children by implementing the High/Scope curriculum for the 3–5 year olds. A follow-through curriculum program has been incorporated into the elementary schools. By 1989, the Colorado district was operating a full service school and offered the five core services. The district continued to expand outreach services by targeting pregnant teens and by offering nutritional services.

Leadville achieved this full service operation by capitalizing on a number of financial sources. The project began with a large community development grant and a second grant from Lake County. Capital improvements included removing asbestos from buildings, upgrading the heating system, and renovating buildings to assure accessibility for the handicapped. Family paid tuition accounts for approximately 70 percent of the program's operating budget. The state Department of Social services provided funds for child care services for single parents and the Mountain Valley Development Center contributed for mainstreaming children with special needs. The remaining funding was secured from a combination of local foundations, civic groups, businesses, local and state agencies, and Jobs Training Partnership.

Laramie County School District No. 2 in Wyoming exemplifies the flexibility of the School of the 21st Century model because of its rural characteristics. Laramie's 21st Century School began with the vision of the district superintendent who secured seed money from the state Department of Education. The initial funding was supplemented with contributions from ten corporations that provided grants for a three year period. In addition to these start-up funds, the services depend on parent fees. Laramie has achieved the full service concept by building on the existing child care and information and referral services in the community. The geographical vastness of the district, which has a radius of several hundred miles, placed special demands on the development of a system of services. For example, the information and referral service utilizes an 800 number to promote free access to parents who otherwise would have been charged long distance telephone charges.

The state of Connecticut at the time of this writing operates three full service schools in rural, urban, and suburban districts, with five or six new sites projected to open in 1991. The state's Department of Human Resources is responsible for distribution of the operating funds and coordinates plans with the state's Department of Education. Connecticut has the unique attribute of being the first state to legislate funds for the development of 21st Century Schools. The Connecticut General Assembly passed Public Act No. 88-331 to initiate the model in the three school sites with an appropriation of $350,000 for the first year, and $500,000 annually thereafter. Connecticut refers to the model as the *Family Resource Center* and calls the Parents as Teachers program *Families in Training* (FIT). In keeping with the flexible, community oriented goal of the School of the 21st Century model, Connecticut is developing two additional services to address the literacy needs of adults and counter the increased trend in teen-age pregnancy. In this context, child care services function as a bridge to other adult oriented services facilitating parent-child interaction. The comprehensiveness and flexibility of the Zigler model enables child care to perform the social service and social reform functions, in addition to the education, socialization, and economic functions.

In Tulsa, Oklahoma, the model has developed under unusual circumstances. Tulsa's large urban population of 374,900 and the extensive involvement of the city's Chamber of Commerce, which is spearheading the project, offers untested possibilities for business-government partnership in the delivery of child care services. During the fall of 1990, the Metropolitan Tulsa Chamber of Commerce sponsored a group of twenty-six citizens composed of business, education, and civic leaders to confer with Zigler and his colleagues at Yale University's Bush Center in Child Development and Social Policy. They also had the opportunity to meet with Connecticut legislators to discuss Connecticut's implementation of the Schools of the 21st Century.

Tulsa's business and education leaders have discussed funding the program with an extension of a local sales tax. The preliminary funding projection of $10 million is to be split between public funds and a sliding fee system. Public money would be used to build or renovate buildings, subsidize programs for 30 to 40 percent of the 3- and 4-year-old population, and fund the Parents as Teachers program. Parent fees on a sliding scale would subsidize other costs. Tulsa's School of the 21st Century is expected to begin in at least eight of fifty-six elementary schools in September 1991 (Cohen 1990c; Lawson 1990a, B-5).

Commentators suggest that Zigler has "broadened the mission" of the schools (Lawson 1990a). The School of the 21st Century infuses an old debate with new opportunities and initiatives. Zigler's model transforms the debate by cloaking the school structure with new functions. If the role of the school can be perceived as much more than educative in nature, then the tenor of the debate must change because its opponents have long been preoccupied with the concern that the education function will override all other functions of child care under school sponsorship.

Controversy over public school based child care has revolved around fears that the schools would harm children's development, that parents would lose control over selecting their children's type of caregiving, that costs would be prohibitive, and that competitors would be forced out of business. Schools are perceived by some to pose a threat to the religious, social service, welfare reform, and social reform functions of child care.

The social status, economic, socialization, and liberation-universalization functions clearly are functional under school auspices. Most commentators acknowledge that the socioeconomic status of caregivers would rise. School sponsorship offers a greater chance for the socioeconomic integration of children than any of the other sponsors, except the corporate; albeit the socialization of children will vary by district.

The social service function has potential under school sponsorship, despite its critics, particularly, if coordination with other agencies takes place. Zigler's full-service school offers a model for the actualization of the social service function. Opponents of school sponsorship repeatedly voice concern that school linkage would destroy the social reform function. They argue that parental control would be placed in jeopardy by the power of the bureaucracy, and this lack of parental control would affect the actual day to day planning of the child care programs. Critics further contend that this loss of parental control goes hand in hand with a loss of political control on the local level, which in turn stifles community activism. Advocates of school sponsorship counter that social reform is possible because of the community base of the schools and the democratic system of governance.

The administrative issues of standard of care, scope of coverage, and cost have been discussed throughout this section in explaining positions on the debate over school sponsorship. One of the most adamant arguments in favor of the public school sponsor is that it is a well-established system with the technical skill already built into it by which to deliver the service. Advocates argue in favor of the centralized system's effectiveness and efficiency. They claim that the standard of care would be high because it is under the scrutiny of the public eye and trained personnel.

By realizing the social status and liberation-universalization functions, there are certain administrative consequences. The upgrading of caretaker salaries presents a trade-off on the issue of delivering the service in the most cost-effective manner. The cost of delivery would rise with school sponsorship, but there also would be a tax base through which to finance the system. This tax system necessitates adjustment to assure equity and stability. The benefit of increased caregiver status is a concomitant increase in program quality. Research confirms that quality of care varies with low turnover rates, which in turn is dependent on socioeconomic status (CCEP 1989).

The strongest argument in favor of the schools as prime sponsors of child care is that with them resides the potential for creating and delivering a publicly funded, universally available system of child care in the United States. The liberation-universalization function could best be addressed under school sponsorship. The public school system is the only service universally available in the United States; therefore, such sponsorship suggests the potential for universally available child care. With this gain of universality, comes the risk that child care would become compulsory.

Many of these conflicts over functions and their consequences mirror conflicts present in the kindergarten movement. Sponsorship was at issue for the kindergarten, before its eventual link with the public schools. The eventual control of the kindergarten by the schools has important implications for current trends in child care and would elucidate the centrality of various arguments for and against the various sponsors.

An analysis of the kindergarten movement is fitting for two other reasons. First, as noted by Olsen and Zigler (1989) and Kagan and Zigler (1987a), the demands for school based early childhood programs and all-day kindergartens are interconnected with the demand for child care services. The child care and kindergarten movements are merging with one another, both are at crossroads. Second, reference has been made to the kindergarten movement throughout the debate. An in-depth analysis of that movement could pinpoint key issues and suggest specific courses for further policy development.

NOTES

1. The following publications are a sample of those that appeared in the late 1980s on the issue of public school involvement in child care services: *Early Schooling* (Kagan and Zigler 1987); *Early Childhood Programs and the Public Schools* (Mitchell, Seligson, and Marx 1989); *Right from the Start* (National Association of State Boards of Education 1988); the Spring 1989 issue of *Teachers College Record*, "The Care and Education of Young Children: Expanding Contexts, Sharpening Focus," edited by Frances O'Connell Rust and Leslie R. Williams; the Winter 1989 issue of *Theory into Practice*, "Public Schooling at 4?" edited by Richard M. Clifford and Sally Lubeck; and the October 1989 issue of *Phi Delta Kappan*, "Early Care and Education: Reflecting on Options and Opportunities," edited by Sharon L. Kagan.

2. For an in-depth analysis of school based early childhood programs refer to this definitive study, *Early Childhood Programs and the Public Schools* (1989), by Anne Mitchell, Michele Seligson, and Fern Marx. The survey study was a joint project by Wellesley Center for Research on Women and Bank Street College of Education; it spanned the years 1986–1987.

3. Term borrowed from Kahn and Kamerman's *Child Care: Facing the Hard Choices* (1987).

4.   Many of the major components of the program are still in operation, although not in the original Kramer building. The program is referred to as the *Kramer Model* and cited as an example of the viability of the public school and child care link.

5.   *CDA* represents the child development associate degree awarded to Head Start teachers after the completion of competency based training. Zigler pioneered both Head Start and the CDA training program.

6.   As of 1989, approximately one-fifth of all Head Start programs throughout the nation were operated by public schools (Mitchell et al. 1989, 50). This represented a decrease of 10 percent over a period of almost eleven years.

7.   For an updated position statement by Jule M. Sugarman on the financing of children and youth services, see "Federal Support Revisited" in *Caring for America's Children: Proceedings of the Academy of Political Science* (1989), vol. 37, no. 2, edited by Frank J. Macchiarola and Alan Gartner for the Academy of Political Science.

8.   For in-depth analyses of the economic picture for school-based care, readers are referred to Clifford and Russell (1989), Grubb (1987), and Granger (1989). The mixed system of funding has been suggested by Zigler (1987c) and Kahn and Kamerman (1987). Other examples of funding models are cited in (Mitchell et al. 1989) and Morado (1989). Business is also viewed as a valued partner. As previously noted in this book's section on employer sponsorship, corporations have devoted resources to the establishment and maintenance of public facilities and should be encouraged to continue to do so.

9.   Before his retirement, Representative Hawkins introduced legislation on January 23, 1990, commonly referred to as the Fair Chance Act (H.R. 3850), which would address the problems inherent in the national approach to financing public education. The bill was referred to the Subcommittee on Elementary, Secondary, and Vocational Education.

10.   In Mitchell et. al., see Table 10-1 (pp. 239–40) for a comparison of six states' prekindergarten programs and public school operated Head Start programs on the degree to which comprehensive services are being delivered.

11.   For information on state initiatives before the 1990 legislation, see Grubb 1987; Mitchell et al. 1989; Morado 1989; Kahn and Kamerman 1987; Gnezda 1987.

12.   The profiles of 21st Century Schools in operation at the time of this writing were obtained in a telephone interview with Karen Linkins on October 22, 1990, and in descriptions found in the Bush Center in Child Development and Social Policy's *The School of the Twenty-First Century*. In the Oklahoma and Missouri models, two articles also were consulted as additional sources to Linkins and the Bush Center publication: Deborah Cohen's (1990c) "Tulsa Business Officials Leading Drive for Citywide School-Based Child Care"; and Carol Lawson's (1990a) "In Missouri, Schools Open Their Doors to Day Care."

PART II

THE KINDERGARTEN DEBATE

8. The Context of the Past Debate

The child care movement and the kindergarten are both at crossroads. Each tradition must grapple with dilemmas inherent to it, yet that overlap and demand common policy responses. The specific issues facing parents and teachers of kindergarten children are rooted in the history of both child care and the kindergarten. Of these issues, three deemed critical today are the result of past policy decisions in the development of the modern kindergarten. The choices that eventually will be made have ramifications, not only for the kindergarten, but also for the delivery of child care and should be considered within the context of the child care debate itself.

Educators on the practice, research, and policy levels are sifting through academic literature and public sentiment to arrive at decisions regarding (1) the appropriate age of entry for kindergartners, (2) the appropriate length of day, and (3) the appropriate curriculum content. These critical decisions can be best informed when the implications of past policy decisions are brought to light. When scrutinizing the roots of today's dilemmas in the delivery of both the kindergarten and child care, it becomes apparent that policy decisions of the past set the framework within which these contemporary predicaments arise. Solutions to the delivery problems cannot be resolved adequately without recognizing the merger of two traditions into a new social program ripe for efficient and effective delivery.

With this perspective in mind, the book shifts its focus from the contemporary debate over the delivery of child care services to the debate over kindergarten sponsorship during the Progressive Era. The prevailing conception of the contemporary kindergarten often is falsely assumed and unquestioned. The kindergarten too often is perceived as a static institution. This notion fails to take into consideration the institution's turbulent, formative past.

The kindergarten now commonly known as the first tier in an American education possesses three prominent attributes that contribute to the present day quandary over how best to deliver child care. First, the kindergarten is a public service. Second, the kindergarten is a commonly accepted one year institution. Third, the kindergarten is considered a half-day program. The "full-day kindergarten" represents a relatively recent phenomenon and is a break with the commonly accepted norm.

By revisiting the kindergarten's past, it becomes apparent that this institution, which is pivotal in the child care debates, must be stripped of present-day assumptions and viewed in a totally new light. When comparing the present turn of the century climate to the previous turn of the century climate, startling similarities and differences appear with important policy ramifications. The context of the times are radically different, but the problems of grappling with the delineation of collective responsibility for guiding the growth and develop-ment of the nation's young children remains the same, although almost a century has past. The tension over who is to assume responsibility for whom continues to persist as a social dilemma.

The enactment of the Child Care and Development Block Grant of 1990 is a testimony to the uniqueness of the contemporary time period. The two periods, 1880–1920 and 1969–1990, are markedly different politically and socially. The contrast of these respective historical periods and ongoing human problems create the framework for informing policy decisions over the delivery of child care services.

The kindergarten, like child care, performed multiple functions under various sponsors before its eventual link with the public schools. Interestingly, the kindergarten served functions that child care now performs, except for the function of welfare reform. An additional function of the kindergarten was vocational education, but for our purposes it shall be included as part of the educational function.

The kindergarten debate occurred during the years after the Civil War and before World War I, but peaked in the Progressive Era of 1880–1920. In the preface to *Child's Garden, The Kindergarten Movement from Froebel to Dewey*, Michael Steven Shapiro (1983) aptly describes the movement as a "social-educa-tional movement, a collective attempt to bring about change in American society by reforming its educational institution" (p. ix). The kindergarten explicitly functioned as social reform and education. The kindergarten and its crusaders were very much a part of a wider social movement sweeping the country.

In the years after the Civil War the nation's attention was given to the development of industrial and human resources. There was a new demand for higher education and new interest in the basic sciences and the newly organized social sciences. The country also exhibited an increased awareness of the arts

(Vandewalker 1923, 39). Within this context the idea of the kindergarten took shape in the United States.

Weber (1969) identified influential forces in the movement for kindergartens as "animal spirits of a youthful democracy, disintegration of established religion, the stirrings of a new humanitarianism, and the dissemination of a genuine idealism" (p. 36). She pointed to two primary phenomena of the times. One was the idealistic philosophy that prevailed in the field of education, which viewed the child in a new and more positive light. The second was the "burgeoning humanitarian interest which embraced all manner of philanthropic kindergartens" (p. 36).

Shapiro posited the thesis that the change in the American view of child rearing consisted of three elements and that these elements each influenced the development of the kindergarten. First, the country was changing its view away from Calvinistic teachings toward a more Evangelical perception. Second, the associationalist psychology of Locke was being replaced by the new faculty psychology. Third, the philosophical orientation of Rationalism was replacing the Scottish Common Sense Philosophy (Shapiro 1983, 2). By 1860, Americans were questioning the functions of early childhood education. The functions of the family and the school also were being reexamined. The Calvinistic view of the child was not as encompassing, leaving the door open to European influences (Shapiro 1983, 16).

Under the Calvinistic perspective, children were viewed as the inheritors of man's depravity. A sense of fatalism prevailed in the idea that a child was preinclined toward grace or evilness. Contrary to this thinking, the then emerging views of Rationalism acknowledged the impact of parents in the upbringing of their children. The development of a moral sense and the training of the faculties were new challenges for parents and educators (Shapiro 1983, 7–8).

In contrast to the severe teachings of Calvinism, the movement of New England Transcendentalism, which began in the 1830s, offered a romantic view of the child. The New England Transcendentalists recognized the potential of the child to transcend his or her original limitations. The child was given the honor of being a "symbol of human potential" (Shapiro 1983, 11). The early Transcendentalists (1830–1869) were not well received by American parents. They had tremendous difficulty in accepting the movement's premise that spiritual self-knowledge was a central objective to early education. Searching for a middle ground between the extremes of Calvinism and Romanticism, American reformers and their followers were open to the teachings of European theorists and practitioners, in particular Friedrich Froebel (Shapiro 1983, 16–17).

Friedrich Froebel (1782–1852), the German born father of the kindergarten, shared transcendentalist ideas. Elizabeth Peabody (1804–1894), a member of the New England Transcendentalists, became enamored with Froebel's theory of education and pioneered its acceptance in the United States (Shapiro 1983; Ross 1976).

In addition to the Transcendental movement in the middle of the nineteenth century, the Progressive movement for reform at the turn of the century encompassed and carried the kindergarten movement forward. The child saving movement and scientific philanthropy of the period formed a foundation for kindergarten crusaders. The Froebelians were tied to the progressive reform movement through a number of commonly held beliefs. The reformers of the period, of which the kindergarten crusaders were a subgroup, shared the following views: (1) the city was seen as an artificial environment that contrasted sharply with country life; (2) the family was the focus for reform; (3) the environment was in need of reform; (4) the child represented hope for the future; and (5) education functioned to liberate both parents and their children (Lazerson 1972b, 38–39).

Progressives, as mentioned earlier in the discussion of the day nursery movement, credited the environment as the causal factor in character development; therefore, the new urban-industrial areas were determining factors in the delinquency of youth and the plight of the poor. In active pursuit of social reform, child savers aspired to alter the environment and remove the child from detrimental influences. Within the child saving movement itself, reformers debated the best means of saving the child. "By the 1880s, two approaches—institutional and family—dominated the discussions of charity workers" (Shapiro 1983, 91). The institutional approach that grew out of the Jacksonian era favored placing children within an institution; whereas the family approach advocated placing the child with a family in the country (Shapiro 1983, 91).[1]

The methodology of reform was guided by the new approach to charity known as *scientific philanthropy*. Scientific philanthropy spanned the years 1873–1893 and evolved into a movement of preventive social work, which in turn formed the basis of the reforms of the Progressive Era (Bremner 1956). Scientific philanthropy rejected the accepted practice of charity, which was to give direct relief to those in need. In lieu of individuals giving directly to the poor, charity organizations were founded:

The immediate purpose of the charity organization societies was to promote co-operation and higher standards of efficiency among the numerous groups already engaged in dispensing relief. Their method of operation was to secure registration of all applicants for public or private assistance, to investigate the need and worthiness of all persons seeking aid, and to encourage friendly visiting of the poor by volunteer workers drawn from the higher walks of life. The ultimate goal of the societies was to husband the charitable resources of each community so that money or other aid, instead of being dissipated on persons who did not really need material help, would be available in sufficient quantity to provide adequate assistance for all deserving cases. (Bremner 1956, 169)

The kindergarten fit easily into this idea for several reasons. First, it was a service, not direct relief. Second, it provided personal contact with the people served. And third, it helped the child grow into an "industrious" adult, which was an overarching goal of scientific philanthropists. They wanted to help the downtrodden learn to care for themselves and contribute to society.

The awakened emphasis in intellectual circles on the new discipline of psychology also furthered the cause of the kindergarten movement. The early efforts of the kindergartners were supported by the leader of the child study movement G. Stanley Hall.[2] This child study movement, which began in the 1880s as an outgrowth of the interest in the new psychology, influenced the course of the kindergarten movement (Shapiro 1983). The movement was based on the empirical study of children:

The child-study movement was, first and foremost, an attempt to improve the physical health of children by bringing current educational practices in line with children's "natural needs". Before the turn of the century, Hall and his followers were only marginally concerned with adolescence, the stage of the life cycle for which they are best remembered today. Instead, Hall's main interest was to use behavioral-science knowledge to create a science of pedagogy. (Schlossman 1976, 441)

In this context, the kindergarten had an education function.

In 1883 Hall's initial two-year survey of Boston kindergarten and primary children was published (Shapiro 1983, 107); a survey that relied on the questionnaire method of inquiry and popularized its use (Schlossman 1976, 441). Kindergarten children were those most often studied. The child study movement, like the kindergarten movement, caught the attention of professionals and lay people. Each group of followers held the child as the focus of attention and analysis.

Three other forces of the period contributed to the popularity of the kindergarten movement and set the background for public debate. The impact of industrialization was felt in two ways pertinent to the kindergarten. First, industrial life had changed the division of labor between the sexes. Mothers were relegated to the home and had more responsibility for raising their children:

Though American women had always borne and reared children, motherhood prior to the nineteenth century had not assumed a transcendent value in American culture. It was the patriarch who kept a "stern fatherly eye" over the flock, subduing the will, educating, and guiding toward spiritual conversion, and preparing the child for a vocation. An industrializing economy was dramatically changing the division of labor within the household by the nineteenth century. The household had become a place where the children stayed before they began school or work and where the husband rested after a day of labor. With the father absent from the home for long periods of time, the primary responsibility of childrearing and early instruction by 1830 was assigned to the mother. . . .

With a virtual monopoly over her children's time, mothers were now responsible for both the instructional and recreational activities of the home. (Shapiro 1983, 9)

Froebel's philosophy elevated the maternal role, so that the new status enjoyed by middle class mothers was congruent with his ideal maternal figure. His emphasis on motherhood confirmed the new social trend among the middle class.

Froebel believed that "modern industrial society had separated the roles of 'mother' and 'woman' previously bonded in primordial union" (Shapiro 1883, 25). He believed that the division of roles affected both upper and lower class women. In Froebel's perspective, upper class women abandoned their motherly duties to wet nurses, governesses, and teachers. In contrast, working women were forced to leave their children in child care settings. Therefore, both classes suffered from "poor child management." Froebel envisioned the emancipation of women coming from changes in child rearing practices and early childhood education rather than in the political arena (Shapiro 1983, 25). Thus, the kindergarten elevated the social status of mothers and teachers of the young.

The second historical trend that influenced the development of the kindergarten was the dramatic influx of immigrants during the late 1800s and early 1900s, which caused much social unrest and urban congestion. The immigrant mothers did not find themselves enjoying middle class status, but Froebel's philosophy addressed them and their families as well. As will be further developed in later sections, the kindergarten met many of the perceived needs in the immigrant communities. It was exactly this population of immigrants and urban poor that the kindergarten crusaders tried to reach. Within this immigrant community, the kindergarten performed social reform and socialization functions.

A third force that enveloped the kindergarten crusade was the fervor for general educational reform (Vandewalker 1923; Lazerson 1971; Tyack 1974;

Smith 1961). The country as a whole was moving away from traditional modes of pedagogy. Higher levels of education also were undergoing change, but the kindergarten movement addressed the needs of the younger children aged 3 through 6 and advocated more innovative methods of education in the latter half of the nineteenth century. Later in time, kindergartners were joined by the Progressive educators led by John Dewey, whose vision has had a wide-reaching impact on all of American education, past and present. Writing in the midst of this time period, Vandewalker (1923) described a receptivity to change in educational methodology sweeping the country.

Educational reform was one of the major objectives of the Progressive Period (Smith 1961). In discussing the "impulse to educational reform," Smith writes that the "institutions traditionally relied upon to educate the young—the family, the church, the apprenticeship system and the public school—seemed inadequate" as the country faced the problems of mass immigration and industrialization:

Social workers laboring to protect the classes most deeply affected by social disorganization—the Negro, the indigent child, and the immigrant—were understandably the first to realize the dimensions of the crisis and the necessity for reform. Idealistic and essentially conservative, they turned naturally to educational remedies, especially those which promised to rejuvenate rather than to replace traditional institutions. For these reasons, one can learn more about the origins of progressive education from the literature of charity than of pedagogy, and more from the story of privately-sponsored than of public schools.

What the proponents called until around 1910 the "new education" combined three elements: vocational training or "education for life", the child-centered school and social reform. (Smith 1961, 181)

Education for life became the task of vocational programs whereas the kindergarten provided a new method of teaching the young child. The social settlement movement of the 1890s strived for social reform by establishing community centers that placed particular value on education. The kindergarten movement became a part of this social settlement movement:

An army of idealistic, college-bred men and women demonstrated first in fact and later in theory that an educational center, linking learning with both individual and community needs, could regenerate a neighborhood and so contribute to the reformation of city and national life. (Smith 1961, 182)

THE PHILOSOPHY OF THE KINDERGARTEN

The kindergarten was the innovation of the German idealist Friedrich Froebel. He established the first kindergarten in Blankenburg in 1837 (Ross 1976, 3). Froebel was the son of a pastor whose mother died when he was very young. After having explored various career paths, Froebel committed himself to education reform (Peabody 1875, 12–14).

Froebel's theory of education rested on a religious interpretation of the world and assumed a spiritual outlook. Thus, imbedded in the work of Froebel and his followers was a deep sense of religion and religious purpose:

Froebel's thoughts on religion pervaded his entire philosophy. According to him, all life was based on what he called the eternal law of unity, that is, the interconnection of all things in life. God was the supreme or "Divine Unity" and the source of all subsequent unity. Education, in the most general sense, was the process of leading man to a conscious appreciation of those principles. Froebel spoke of religion in a broad, non-sectarian sense, and he referred frequently to the concept of Christian love, meaning love which was a conscious reflection of the divine origin of man. He wanted the child to learn to appreciate God through observation, reflection, and activity, not through dogmatic religious teaching. (Ross 1976, 4)

Froebel addressed his attention to the earliest years of life, infancy through age 6, believing that they were formative; thus, his writings were directed toward mothers and kindergartners. The kindergarten itself was designed for children aged 3 through 6. He conceived of a new social institution designed to bridge the experiences of these young children between home and school (Shapiro 1983, 21–22):

The kindergarten was to be an institution where the child could congregate with his peers outside the restraints of the family and the school. At the same time, the protective gardenlike atmosphere of the kindergarten would guard the child against the corrupting influence of society and the danger of nature. In the child garden, the mental, physical and social faculties of the child could be cultivated, unfolded and ripened. In the end the term "kindergarten" signified for Froebel more than an institution—it was an approach to early child training. (Shapiro 1983, 22)

Froebel designed a program of education that was revolutionary for its time. He based the program on the philosophy that children learned by doing and rejected traditional, didactic education. The term *kindergarten* exactly described his vision, which was to create a garden for children. The children thrived under the attentive care of the gardener, the "kindergartner."

Froebel felt that the teacher was pivotal to the success of the program. He designed a very explicit curriculum that was divided into three components: (1) the gifts; (2) the occupations; and (3) the games and songs (Ross 1976, 5–7). All teachers were carefully trained to implement this curriculum.

The explicitness of Froebel's system provoked a wide schism among the kindergarten crusaders as the campaign expanded. As is true with many movements built around the writings of one person, a group of kindergartners chose to interpret Froebel's work in a more liberal and updated manner; whereas purists adhered to a strict, dogmatic interpretation of the master's work. The philosophy of Froebel eventually became "Americanized" as the following discussion on the campaign for kindergartens and the issue of sponsorship will reveal (Good and Teller 1973, 194–195; Shapiro 1983).

A CHRONOLOGICAL SKETCH
OF THE
HISTORY OF THE KINDERGARTEN, 1855–1914

The history of the kindergarten is the story of an institution that began on a small scale as a private institution for a select population and evolved into a public institution for a universal population. The evolution involved many different sponsors, but could be classified into three primary types: the private sponsor that charged tuition or restricted itself to a given group of children; the associations that provided free charitable or missionary programs; and the public schools (Vandewalker (1923, 78). Each sponsor served a particular population; and, as will be seen, the kindergarten fulfilled multiple functions under these various sponsorships. Smith (1961) comments on the origins of the kindergarten: "Modern students who see in the public kindergarten a luxury which only middle-class suburbs can afford, will be surprised to discover that the early spread of the idea owed much to the humanitarian work which earnest women did among the poor" (p. 188).

Writing in 1907, Vandewalker subdivided the history of the kindergarten movement. The first period was labeled the *Period of Introduction*. This period was further divided into the period of the German kindergarten, 1855–1870, and the period of Americanization, 1870–1880 (p. 9). The second period was known as the *Period of Extension*. The first decade of this period, 1880–1890, saw the kindergarten meet with general public acceptance. After 1890, the kindergarten endured factionalization within the movement and criticism from without as it became a part of public schools (p. 10). The 1880s were referred to as the

Association Decade; whereas the 1890s were the *Public School Decade* (Vandewalker 1923, 184).

As the kindergarten movement continued beyond Vandewalker's work, it appears logical to recognize a third period from 1900–1914 and refer to it as the *Period of Public School Adaptation and Transformation*. By 1914 every major city had kindergartens (Ross 1976, 83).

The kindergarten was introduced to America by German emigres leaving Germany for political reasons in the middle of the 1800s. Shapiro breaks the German influence into two waves: 1848–1860 and 1860–1872 (p. 44). The first group of Germans were familiar with Froebel's teachings, but not trained as kindergartners. The second group were actually trained by Froebel and his followers.

The first wave of German emigres left as a consequence of the European Revolution of 1848 and brought with them a feeling of social liberalism (Weber 1969, 20). The earliest kindergartens in the United States emerged from the German-English academies of the 1860s and 1870s (Weber 1969, 20; Vandewalker 1923, 12). These academies were private, bilingual schools established by cultured Germans in large American cities in the decade of 1850–1860 (Vandewalker 1923, 12) and served a wealthy, fee paying class (Blow 1897, 934; Weber 1969, 22). The kindergarten most often credited as being the first in America was established by Margarethe Schurz in her hometown of Watertown, Wisconsin in 1855–1856 (Shapiro 1983, 31; Vandewalker 1923, 13; Boone 1889, 333; Jenkins 1930–31, 48; Ross 1976, 2).

The New England Transcendentalists, who in fact were exponents of German Idealism for the American community, were responsible for introducing the kindergarten to the general population (Vandewalker 1923, 26). Further interest in the kindergarten was ignited by Dr. Henry Barnard in 1854 when he provided the first public expression of the kindergarten's value (Fisher 1905, 689). Barnard had attended the International Exhibit of Educational Systems and Materials in London in 1854 (Vandewalker 1923, 14; Fisher 1905, 689). On his return, he spoke to the Connecticut governor about his impressions and wrote an article on kindergartens in the *American Journal of Education* (Vandewalker 1923, 15). Later, as commissioner of education, Barnard suggested to the United States Senate in 1868 and to the House of Representatives in 1870 that the kindergarten be the first level of school entry in the District of Columbia's school system (Fisher 1903, 689).

Barnard kindled Elizabeth Peabody's interest in the kindergarten and she became one of the strongest pioneers of the movement (Vandewalker 1923, 16). Peabody established the first public kindergarten in Boston in 1860 (Vandewalker 1923, 12; Ross 1976, 2; Weber 1969, 25)—1870 according to Blow (1897, 932) and Garland (1924, 23). Peabody's school lasted only a few years due to financial difficulties; yet, after the closing of the school a new group of patrons, Boston philanthropists, took up the cause of the kindergarten (Garland 1924, 23).

Kindergarten associations were formed under this philanthropic sponsorship in the 1880s. Through these associations, a functional change occurred. The general aims common to the associations included providing help and advice to mothers, establishing kindergartens and advancing the kindergarten cause, and carrying out a needed social service function. Due to the array of aims, membership in the associations crossed social class boundaries (Vandewalker 1923, 58). The association members established free kindergartens for the select population of poor children:

The past thirteen years have been memorable for the free kindergarten movement in the United States. Previous to that time, the work was largely private, experimental, and within the limits of the well-to-do classes. "Kindergarten" was the shibboleth of the few. (Mackenzie 1886, 48)

Before 1870 the kindergarten was of little academic or public interest, but within a decade it was the subject of much discussion in educational circles (Good and Teller 1973, 192). In 1873 the kindergarten became part of the public schools in St. Louis; by 1880 St. Louis had fifty public kindergartens. Other cities followed the lead of St. Louis with rapid expansion occurring after 1890 (Good and Teller 1973, 195). Until 1890, "there were about as many children in private as in public kindergartens, but by 1900 the latter was forging ahead and the combined enrollment of both had increased from about 30,000 in 1890 to about seven times that number in 1900" (Good and Teller 1973, 195). The Centennial Exposition in Philadelphia in 1876 stands out in the history of the kindergarten as an instrumental factor in popularizing it. Kindergarten materials and practices were on exhibit for the purview of the public (Vandewalker 1923, 18–19; Shapiro 1983, Ch. 5). Five official and two unofficial kindergarten exhibits were set up for the 10 million people that attended the Centennial (Shapiro 1983, 66).

At the turn of the century there were kindergartens in thirty states (Read and Patterson 1980, 48). Two thirds of the 4,500 programs were privately sponsored by humanitarian organizations, churches, missions, and philanthropic agencies. The trend toward the private sector kindergarten was soon reversed. In 1912 the United States Commissioner of Education cited a total of 6,400 kindergartens in 900 cities with 312,000 children enrolled. The public kindergartens constituted 85 percent of the total number of programs (Ross 1976, 90).

One impetus for the growth of kindergartens was the development of organizational support. The National Education Association (NEA) actively condoned the development and expansion of the kindergarten idea. In addition to the NEA, specific organizations were established to promote the work of the kindergarten. Peabody started the Froebel Institute of America in 1877. In 1892 the International Kindergarten Union (IKU) was formed (Wesley 1957, 162). The IKU's charge was to gather and disseminate knowledge of the kindergarten movement, to unite all of the kindergarten interests, to establish other kindergartens, and to elevate the standard of the training of kindergartners (Haven 1908, 119).

By 1915 three nationwide organizations were serving the kindergarten cause: the IKU, the National Congress of Mothers, and the National Kindergarten Association. In 1918, the IKU had 18,000 members and was considered the third largest educational organization in the world (Lazerson 1972b, 41). The IKU eventually merged with the National Council of Primary Education to form the Association for Childhood Education in 1930 (Lazerson 1972a, 23).

The expansion of the kindergarten in the United States involved a transformation and adaptation of Froebel's original ideas. Froebel's kindergarten was Americanized (Vandewalker 1923; Shapiro 1983; Good and Teller 1973; Weber 1969; Ross 1976). It became less class structured (Shapiro 1983, 42–44) and less mystical (Good and Teller 1973, 194). American theorists and practitioners expanded on the actual philosophy of Froebel, but a number of other outside pressures influenced the kindergarten, too. School supply houses encouraged the use of new and more materials; children became involved in housekeeping activities; attention was given to health habits and rest needs; free lunches often were supplied; and the use of English supplanted German songs (Good and Teller 1973, 194–195) "The American took the place of the Froebelian kindergarten. It followed Froebel's spirit rather than his set form" (Good and Teller 1973, 195).

Kindergartners increasingly became divided over their interpretation of Froebel. In 1900 those that held a conservative view were in the majority (Weber 1969, ix). In 1913, a "Committee of Nineteen" edited a nonconclusive report on the controversy. It was divided into three sections written by three different authors representing three views. Susan Blow wrote for the conservatives; Patty Smith Hill for the radical perspective; and Elizabeth Harrison took a moderate position. The radical perspective eventually became the dominant mode of implementing the kindergarten because of the movement to train kindergartners in settings other than the specialized kindergarten training schools. Universities and normal schools met the new demand for kindergartners by offering teacher certification (Weber 1969, 121–122).

NOTES

1.   The institutional versus familial debate is ongoing today in relation to the placement of troubled and at-risk children and youth.   The differentiation of institutional and familial settings also plays a large role in the debate over child care, especially in regard to infants and toddlers.

2.   Hall was the most popular psychologist in the late 1800s and the president of Clark University; he was responsible for placing the study of children into the curriculum of universities.   He also was responsible for encouraging the study of children at home and school.   His following came from the ranks of educators and mothers (Schlossman 1976, 441).

   Kindergartners refers to the kindergarten teacher or kindergarten administrators.

9. Private Sponsorship of Kindergartens

As previously noted, the kindergarten originated as a private institution rooted in the German-English communities and the Transcendentalist circles of the nineteenth century. Sponsorship of the kindergarten then branched out:

The three main branches of kindergarten work in America are the private kindergarten, the charity kindergarten, and the public kindergarten. Each of these has an interesting history and has exercised its specific influence in shaping the work and in forming public opinion in regard to the educational and social value of the system. (Fisher 1905, 690)

However, as reported in a study of the kindergarten for the commissioner of education in 1903, growth in the private sector did not compare with the dramatic expansion of kindergartens under philanthropic and public school sponsorship (Fisher 1905, 690).

This lack of development was attributed, in part, to the poor training and incompetence of the private school kindergartners. The most capable teachers sought employment for higher salaries outside of the private sector. The kindergartners in the private settings, which catered to children from "chosen homes," were criticized for allowing their charges to run the program instead of assuming and maintaining control (Fisher 1905).

The private kindergarten began with Elizabeth Peabody's model program and spread from Boston to New York. The kindergarten expanded further as a component of other private institutions, such as Mrs. Shaw's school in Boston. Many of these programs were set up as two year programs with the second year providing a transition to the primary school. Private kindergartens' primary function was educational. They implemented a traditional Froebelian curriculum to an exclusive population. These schools were successful because of their incorporation into a larger system of education. The principal performed a key role in effecting a positive attitude from the parents. The kindergartens attached to schools were so highly regarded by the providers that they often were maintained despite financial loss incurred for the overall operation (Fisher 1905, 690–691).

"Women of means" were enthusiastic supporters of these kindergartens and formed the Froebel League in New York. These women wanted to see kindergartens for children of all social and economic classes because they recognized the potential developmental benefit the service availed their own class as well as for the poor. They supported the liberation-universalization function of the kindergarten. Yet, others of the wealthy strata did not attribute value to the kindergarten. Instead, they felt that their children were well cared for at home. These critics envisioned school as a place where traditional subjects should be taught through traditional methods (Fisher 1905, 691).

In a "Discussion" in the National Educational Association's *Journal* (Langzettel 1903), the special function the kindergarten performed in the private sector was described: "The private kindergarten belongs largely to the child of the rich, and it is here perhaps that it is to do its most important work" (p. 405). According to Langzettel, the children of private kindergartens were one-third larger in size than other children, one-third more developed intellectually, but one-third behind in dramatic expression and creativity. Thus, these children could benefit from the kindergarten and, in particular, its socialization function.

Private kindergartens offered more freedom in the area of program design than kindergartens under other sponsors, because the program did not need to comply with a large system. Consequently, kindergartners within private schools did not gain the benefit from supervision provided within a larger system, but they did have the opportunity to select an environment of choice (Langzettel 1903, 405).

Kindergarten under private sponsorship had the privileged function of saving the wealthy children from indulgence and weak family management (Troen 1972, 227–228). In this regard, the kindergarten performed a social service function for the wealthy by meeting their children's needs. Yet another function of the private kindergarten was its ability to serve the young ladies of the rich by providing them work as kindergartners. The kindergartens became way stations between the home and matrimony. Kindergartens functioned as finishing schools, thus serving a social status function (Troen 1972, 227–228). For example, Mrs. Shaw opened a training department alongside her kindergarten "in the hope that young women would study the kindergarten in order to better prepare themselves for work in the home" (Fisher 1905, 691). The teaching profession in general was still frowned on by many because it often led to spinsterhood. Yet, the kindergarten was perceived as a noble vocation because motherhood was sanctified. Kindergartening was viewed as a service to God and was blessed by the church (Ross 1976, 52–53):

In the 1880s, kindergartening provided a solution for many young women seeking a life outside the home. . . . Parents, however, often felt more at ease at the prospect of kindergartening, since the stress kindergartners laid on the responsibilities and beauties of motherhood contributed heavily to its general social as well as parental acceptability. (p. 52)

The kindergarten had several other functions within the private domain. It provided children with the "classic" kindergarten education, thus serving an education function. Kindergartens also served as finishing schools for wealthy young women and as compensatory programs for wealthy, overprivileged youngsters, thus serving the social status and socialization functions, respectively. Additionally, the kindergarten served the education and social service functions with the parent body, teaching them the responsibilities of motherhood (Fisher 1905, 691).

Although most of these private programs served the upper classes, those that were a part of other institutions often served other classes as well, such as the kindergarten of the Ethical Culture School in New York City. Nevertheless, the consequence of private sponsorship was that only a select population of children was served. The kindergarten crusaders believed in the universality of the kindergarten, but many of the early kindergartens in fact were for the elite, taught by women of culture to the cultured class (Lazerson 1971, 45). A class conscious Boston newspaper of the early 1870s forecast, "So long as kindergartens remain private schools with the price of tuition fixed at from sixty to a hundred dollars per year, they will be of little real importance" (Lazerson 1971, 45). The quality of the programs within the private sector seemed to range from the purest of Froebelian kindergartens with highly trained teachers (Fisher 1905, 690), to the ineffectual kindergarten under the direction of a poorly trained or mercenary kindergartner (Good and Teller 1973, 192; Wiggin and Smith 1896, 12; Fisher 1905, 690).

10. Free Kindergartens

After the Philadelphia Exposition of 1876, the kindergarten was hailed as a child saving agency (Vandewalker 1923, 19). True to the noble mission of Froebel, kindergartners shifted their attention away from the private sector and devoted considerable energy to serving the poor by establishing "free" kindergartens, which were also known as *charity kindergartens*. Vandewalker captured the implication of this move:

Before its general acceptance by the school system could be expected, an important work still needed to be done in its behalf. The movement needed to be illustrated on a large scale in strategic localities and the value of the kindergarten as a child-saving agency demonstrated. To meet this need a new agency came into existence in all the larger cities, and in many of the smaller ones—the kindergarten association. (Vandewalker 1923, 55)

The leaders of these associations, who were from the middle and upper classes, were appalled by the conditions of urban life and turned to the kindergarten as a means of remedying the situation (Ross 1976, 30). In this context the kindergarten functioned as social reform.

Shapiro (1983) classifies the free kindergarten crusade as occurring from 1873–1893 (p. 85). The associations that sponsored these free kindergartens were private, voluntary groups that supplied the initial funding (Shapiro 1983, 96). The immigration and labor problems of the 1880s inspired those of means to undertake the kindergarten cause. Comfortably situated members of society feared that the ignorance of the poor would spread throughout the social system. Rather than analyze the economic determinants, the well-to-do assumed that the poor needed special training to better themselves. The kindergarten became the means of providing this training (Shapiro 1983, 88). Thus, social reform would occur through education, in particular vocational education. The progressive belief in the power of education to promote change was manifest in the free kindergarten movement. The kindergarten served an education function, as well as a social reform function.

The Americanization and democratization of the new immigrants were primary consequences of the new urban kindergarten founded by these associations. In other words, the socialization function was manifest and directed. Industrialization and massive immigration had an impact on the cities, causing overpopulation and slums. In 1890 "The City Waif" appeared in the journal *The Kindergarten*, describing the plight of the urban child and the redeeming value of the kindergarten (Jameson 1890). The kindergarten was heralded as an institution that would meet the needs of these "waifs," as well as "foreigners," by providing socialization and social service. The influential editor of *Century* magazine, Richard Gilder, wrote "The Kindergarten: An Uplifting Social Influence in the Home and the District" in the *Journal of Proceedings and Addresses of the National Educational Association* (1903). Gilder sang the praise of kindergartens for their work with the immigrant family and community. The kindergarten was seen to have very positive effects on the children, the home and the community. The kindergarten provided "a strong common interest that binds together socially many antipathetic nationalities" (p. 392).

Many authors of the period described the importance of the kindergarten in bringing the foreigner into the mainstream (Mabie 1905; Spencer 1910; Wiggin and Smith 1896). The kindergarten embodied ideal democratic principles and socialized the young into the democratic and American spirit. In addition to this "Americanization" of the urban masses, some crusaders included "Christianizing" as a goal (Sturges 1901, 238): "In the kindergarten the wee ones are early led into the English tongue, American ways, and Christian influence. As a wedge into the homes and an avenue to the parents' hearts, the kindergarten is indispensable" (Allen 1913, 113). The ideology of the free kindergarten movement was rooted in evangelical Protestantism, as well as scientific philanthropy. Christian benevolence was a guiding force in the entire thrust of the movement. There was a belief in salvation within the nurturance of the family (Shapiro 1983, 86, 96). If the socialization function was pervasive, the religious function also was evident.

The function of the kindergarten as a means to impress specific social values on the young changed with the prevailing ideology of the times. With the onset of scientific philanthropy, kindergartens served the goals of collective social reform, rather than the goals of the Transcendentalists who sought change in society through change in the individual. The new philanthropy placed the emphasis on reforming the environment because the child was seen as a victim of urban decay. If left to the influence of the slum, the child could easily become a delinquent (Shapiro 1983, 91). In the pursuit of social reform, the kindergarten functioned to prevent delinquency.

The movement for free kindergartens expanded the base of the general kindergarten movement. This new structure, the kindergarten association with its child saving mission, also broadened the functions of the kindergarten. The original educational function of the kindergarten was supplanted by the philanthropic, which included the functions of social reform and social service (Shapiro 1983, 86; Vandewalker 1923, 19; Lazerson 1971). New members joined the ranks and assumed leadership positions in the associations. These new members were philanthropists, charity workers, and reform editors. With the new association members, the movement broadened dramatically and reached new populations (Shapiro 1983, 86).

The associations first set out to provide education, food, and clothing, but expanded to provide other community services. In this capacity, the kindergarten functioned as a social service. Free kindergartners and association members initiated home visits, evening classes for fathers, and afternoon classes for mothers (Shapiro 1983, 96). They also incorporated the teaching of cleanliness and discipline to the children (Shapiro 1983, 85):

The free kindergarten would also serve as a community center for adult education classes and home-visit programs. By reaching the child at an early age, free-kindergarten adherents hoped to eliminate the problems of urban poverty, help the immigrant mother, save the child, and improve the nation. (Shapiro 1983, 85)

The associations often took over the work of other agencies or extended the work of others. For example, they took over the services of the YWCA in San Francisco. In Louisville and Philadelphia, the association worked alongside the Children's Aid Societies (Shapiro 1983, 96). The New York Association claimed that it was not a relief agency, but served as a referral agency (Waterman 1907, 464). Some associations also conducted kindergartner training classes (Shapiro 1983, 149).

By 1890, 115 free kindergarten associations in the United States were sponsoring 223 schools and serving 14,987 children (Shapiro 1983, 98). In describing the pioneer work of Kate Wiggin in California in "The Free Kindergarten of the Pacific Coast," Shinn (1890) described three classes of children served. Shinn referred to one class as children of petty tradespeople where both parents worked, "old-clothes men, small saloon keepers, rag-dealers, tailors." The second class were the children of employed fathers and at-home mothers: "[The] father is employed as a peddler, tin-mender, etc. or as a day laborer, and the mother remains at home, making more or less successful attempts to care for her children, and often assisting somewhat in the support of the household, by taking in sewing or washing" (Shinn 1890, 97). The third class of children, according to Shinn's hyperbolic turn of speech, were those of "absolute criminals" (p. 97).

Free kindergartens functioned to meet the special needs of the urban community (Ross 1976; Shapiro 1983). Shapiro labeled the kindergarten the cornerstone of urban neighborhood reform (p. 100). One of the chief services added to the kindergarten for the purpose of better serving the needs of the children and families were home visits. Kindergartners would visit the homes of their students in the afternoons (Ross 1976, 29; Shapiro 1983, 101).

These home visits forged a vital link between home and school. The kindergartners would explain the kindergarten program and "tactfully" teach nutrition, hygiene, and child rearing (Ross 1976, 29). At first, the home visits were intended to convey Froebel's teachings, but were extended into these other unchartered areas (Shapiro 1983, 101). Home visits not only served Froebel's intent that mothers learn and practice his theory, the visits also brought the modern "scientific" ways into the home (Shapiro 1983, 101). The kindergartner "worked in social services in the afternoons to help unemployed parents seek jobs and to get free medical and dental care for children and their families" (Read and Patterson 1980, 48).

As a further extension of these home visits, kindergartners began to offer mothers' meetings. These meetings involved lectures on housing, marketing, child care, health, and community facilities (Shapiro 1983, 101). Mothers' meetings became central to the associations and served a social status function by raising the status of mothers through the elevation of motherhood. More specifically, kindergartners tried to communicate to the working class mothers the importance of their mothering. They impressed on them that caring for children was the most noble of jobs a woman could undertake and one that demanded serious study and commitment.

The glorification of motherhood to the downtrodden, confined urban mother by upper and middle class kindergartners illustrated the class differences among the women. How the mothers interpreted their role and the role of the kindergarten is left ambiguous in the literature on the early kindergartens, but the social support offered by the meetings was widely acclaimed. As can be imagined, the mothers welcomed and relished the social interchange between themselves and with the kindergartners (Shapiro 1983; Ross 1976).

In addition to the primary social services, associations remained flexible in responding to the community and expanding their outreach by offering idiosyncratic services. For example, the Silver Street Association taught bed making, dusting, and marketing to 12–14-year-old girls (Shinn 1890, 98). Some kindergartens served the needs of working mothers by opening early in the morning and offering breakfast to the children. In many instances, meeting basic physical needs often superseded the original kindergarten goal of providing an early educational experience (Shapiro 1983, 99–100).

The "child saving" aspects of these free kindergartens were obvious. The child was taken out of the home and placed in the clean and caring "children's garden." The deprived home was reached through the mothers' meetings, home visits, and through the child who brought the daily lessons of the kindergarten back to the family. "The slum child, then, was seen as a wedge into the urban neighborhood. The education of the child was only the first step in a program of urban neighborhood reform" (Shapiro 1983, 100).

The kindergarten also was acclaimed because of its preventive function. Unlike remedial charities of the times, the kindergarten intended to prevent the vices of urban life by concentrating on the impressionable, young child. Supporters of free kindergartens voiced grandiose claims that the kindergarten would prevent children from becoming criminals and paupers (Ross 1976; Shapiro 1983; Newton 1886; Hufford 1899; Mackenzie 1886; Cooper 1882; Waterman 1907).

In addition to these many functions attributed to the free kindergarten, other functions came into play that were specific to the period, culture, and locale. For example, in some southern villages, the kindergarten was seen as taking on a special role in the lives of the miners because it provided contrast to their humdrum lives (Hanckel 1911, 283). In Ironwood, Michigan, it was reported that the kindergarten was regarded as a second home for the miners' children and the place where they could learn English (U.S. Bureau of Education 1914, 98).

The kindergarten was used to address racial inequities in the South. It was viewed as an institution that addressed the "race problem" and the "race question" (Cary 1900; Murray 1900; Claxton 1900). Writing as a black, Murray pleaded for the provision of kindergartens for her race. She felt it would answer the needs of black children as well as white children and would benefit the nation; she believed in its social reform function.

In contrast to the needs of lower class children met by the kindergarten, the free kindergarten served one other function. For the upper class women, the free kindergarten provided an education. It broadened their interests and their understanding of life by introducing them to the problems of the urban poor. Moreover, Froebel's pedagogy transformed their views about education and creativity. By suggesting new courses for study, the kindergarten actually had an impact on the character of education in women's colleges (Vandewalker 1923, 124).

The free kindergartens served many functions, but their overriding thrust was as a child saving agency with all of the implications of the social reform and social service functions. The population served was the poor; although, upper class women benefited from the mothers' meetings and association membership, too.

As early as 1907, it was recognized that the various sponsors of the kindergarten speeded the progress of expansion and allowed for different emphasis on the functions it performed (Vandewalker 1923). Disadvantages with the multiple sponsorship system also were evident (Vandewalker 1923, 125). The dysfunctional aspect of the philanthropic sponsorship by associations was that the public began to associate kindergartens with day nurseries (pp. 125–126). Viewed in this light, the kindergarten was denigrated for lacking an educational content:

Many mission kindergartens unfortunately justify this impression. The large number of children frequently enrolled, much too large for effective work, the economy exercised in the use of material, the low salaries paid, these and other conditions that too frequently prevail in philanthropic work, have done much to obscure the real educational value of the kindergarten. (Vandewalker 1923, 126)

The tendency of kindergartners to work for low wages was a significant disadvantage of the philanthropic kindergartens (Vandewalker 1923, 126). This trend established a negative precedent difficult to break away from and that caused problems when the public schools became involved with kindergarten sponsorship. "The kindergartners' services therefore did not reach a true valuation in the educational labor market" (Vandewalker 1923, 126).

The quality of the kindergartner also was problematic in the philanthropic setting. Vandewalker asserted that the training of the kindergartners in these situations often was inadequate. This lack of quality was due to the large number of kindergartner trainees. Not only were the training standards not set high enough, but often the instructor was not of a high caliber. The theoretical work of Froebel often was lost in the transmission process by instructors' tendencies to overemphasize the practical work of the kindergarten (p. 127).

The free kindergarten movement did not stop with association sponsorship, but moved into other arenas:

Enlivened by new ideas and new members, free kindergartners began to explore new institutional settings for social and educational reform; before the conclusion of the debate, they had placed free kindergartens in orphanages, reform schools, church missions, public schools, and social settlements. (Shapiro 1983, 86)

The kindergartens of the church, social settlement, corporation, and public school will be explored in greater detail to determine the consequences of such sponsorship. Despite its drawbacks, association sponsorship altered the original educational function of the kindergarten and widened the population served.

11. Kindergartens Under the Sponsorship of Social Settlements, Churches, Corporations, and the Women's Temperance Union

SOCIAL SETTLEMENT SPONSORSHIP

As mentioned earlier, the kindergarten movement was linked to the social settlement movement; the two movements shared common goals and philosophies. In fact, the social settlement was known as a kindergarten for adults (Shapiro 1983, 105; Hofer 1895, 54; Vandewalker 1923, 108). A social settlement was a community house that had informal education as its focal point. The schools within the settlements were assigned "a creative social function" (Smith 1961, 182).

Smith (1961) reviewed successive issues of the *Bibliography of College, Social, University, and Church Settlements* (first published in 1895) and found that "virtually all the [settlement] houses established kindergartens, mothers groups, and boys and girls clubs in the first months of their existence" (p. 200). Vandewalker noted that the 1905 edition of the *Bibliography* indicated from incomplete data that there were 200 settlements of which over 100 included kindergartens among their agencies (p. 111). "The settlement movement gave the kindergarten movement increased impetus: all settlements maintained one or more kindergartens at some time during their existence" (Ross 1976, 45). The kindergarten and its offshoot programs such as playgrounds, vacation schools, and summer kindergartens quickly became permanent features of social settlements (Shapiro 1983, 105). Vandewalker (1923) remarked on the nature of the kinship between social settlements and kindergartens, as follows: "So akin are the social settlements and the kindergarten in spirit that several head residents of settlements were originally kindergartners, and several well-known settlements began as mission kindergartens and became settlements by the natural extension of their work" (p. 107).

There were significant differences between the free kindergartners and the settlement workers, however. Settlement workers generally lived in the neighborhood of the settlement, whereas the kindergartners tended to commute to the neighborhood where the kindergarten was located. Settlement workers more often were unmarried and devoted to the cause of social reform, whereas kindergartners tended to work only as an interlude before marriage. Furthermore, settlement leaders, such as Jane Addams, departed from Froebel's romantic view on individual deliverance and looked to collective change. Addams also felt that adults should be the focus of settlement work, not children (Shapiro 1983, 103–104). Kindergartners felt that social reform began with children.

As Shapiro points out, a social settlement was in essence the outgrowth of a merger of several agencies performing different functions, of which the kindergarten was only one. He identified a trend in the history of the kindergarten in which the settlements eventually absorbed the functions of the free kindergartens (pp. 102–103). The kindergarten lost its special identity and became a component of the settlement house.

Settlement houses were training grounds for kindergartners (Hofer 1895, 53–54; Ross 1976, 45). The settlements deepened the kindergartners' understanding of the life of the urban child (Hofer 1895, 53–54; Vandewalker 1923, 112). Settlement sponsorship spread the work of Froebel to a new population of college educated men and women. The settlement trained kindergartners and crusaders would effect change with new interpretations of Froebel. The traditional kindergarten ideals were recast by those outside the original kindergarten culture. Jane Addams and her followers would apply the teachings of Froebel to adult life (Vandewalker 1923, 109–111). "By its adoption of the kindergarten the settlement has interpreted it to the public in a larger and higher sense" (p. 111).

The settlement was viewed as a very favorable sponsor of the kindergarten (Vandewalker 1923; Lazerson 1971). Settlements aimed to meet the total needs of the community, as kindergartens aimed to meet the total needs of the child. Settlements did not have any additional motive in sponsoring the kindergarten, as did other sponsors. Vandewalker compared the settlement's sponsorship motives to those of the church, which had a dogma to inculcate; to those of the associations, which had the mission of converting the public to the kindergarten cause; and to those of the Women's Temperance Union, which sought to prevent alcoholism (p. 108). Lazerson (1971) considered the settlement kindergarten to be the most articulated definition of the kindergarten ideal (p.50).

The relationship between the social settlement and the kindergarten was free of tension. The symbiotic nature of structure and function was clear in this relationship, each had an impact on the other. The kindergarten functioned within the settlement to harmonize and socialize individual families (Lazerson 1971, 50). It also served as an initial attraction for families to the settlement.

The settlements did not change the function of the free kindergarten except to use it to build a wider forum in the community at large. However, settlement sponsorship did have a significant impact on the organization of the kindergarten associations because settlement sponsorship eventually prevailed over association sponsorship and encompassed the associations' functions. Under settlement sponsorship kindergarten work was one service among many. The children and their families no longer were the key target population; instead, the adults and the neighborhood as a whole were targets for social reform by settlement workers.

THE RELIGIOUS FUNCTION AND CHURCH SPONSORSHIP OF KINDERGARTENS

Church sponsorship of the kindergarten was a natural and expected occurrence, particularly as Froebel's philosophy presumed a strong religious base. Froebel sought to achieve a unity of the individual child with God and God's work. When describing Froebel in *Kindergarten Principles and Practice* (1896), Kate Douglas Wiggin and Nora Archibald Smith wrote, "He declares that his system is founded upon religion and must lead to religion, and, again, that he works in order that Christianity may become realized" (pp. 77–78).

This religious perspective pervaded kindergarten work within and outside of church sponsorship. The religious element existed on two levels. First, a specific mission of teaching religion per se existed. Second, on an overall level kindergartners practiced with a spiritual predilection and proclivity that was not specific to any one sect or creed. There was a deep sense that the kindergarten functioned to guide the child's moral and spiritual development:

The kindergarten, too, cultivates the religious nature in a manner suitable to childhood, and the principles on which this training is based need no interpretation by a kindergartner, but can be understood and developed by any thoughtful, earnest woman. This religious nurture has nothing whatever to do with sects, and need be objected to by none, for it is an awakening of the spiritual nature, a development of the powers of love, reverence and aspiration, and a turning of the soul toward God, as the flower to the sun. (Smith 1898a, 21)

Wiggin and Smith (1896) describe the essence of moral training as the cultivation of "a devotion to righteousness" (p. 119). The work of the kindergartner was to be a continuation of the mother's work of guiding the child, who is innately good, to a life of goodness (Wiggin and Smith 1896, 108–127).

Good and Teller (1973) attributed Froebel's religious concepts and, in particular, his concept of the formation of the child as similar to an act of Godlike creation, as having a profound impact on the history of the kindergarten:

The introduction of this concept had important effects upon the history of the kindergarten and not least in the United States, where the reformers, philanthropists, and the churches became its early promoters. (Good and Teller 1973, 193)

Such promoters found in the kindergarten a means of reforming their world and promoting their beliefs. This underlying sense of religious purpose infused kindergarten work, but it did not mean that direct religious teaching was a part of all kindergartens. Kindergartners in general did not advocate a particular religious creed or dogma (McCarty 1898, 948; Ross 1976, 27; Wiggin and Smith 1896, 108–127).

The most prominent kindergartner who advocated religious teachings through kindergarten work was Sarah B. Cooper (Ross 1976, 26–29; Shapiro 1983, 93–95). Cooper was a bible teacher who adapted kindergarten practices to her Sunday school work with children in San Francisco in 1878. Cooper's work was attacked by the Presbyterian deacon and elder James B. Roberts. She withstood a heresy trial because the Presbytery of San Francisco believed that her kindergarten program was not within the dogma of the church. Cooper's classes were seen as sacrilegious because children were "playing" and because Christ was not the subject matter of their activities. In 1881, Cooper was charged by the Presbytery of San Francisco for "teaching 'allegorical and mythical interpretations of the scriptures' and holding 'sentimental and humanitarian views not in accord with the orthodox creed of the Presbyterian Church'" (Shapiro 1983, 94). Shapiro claims that Cooper's trial brought attention to the kindergarten movement, severed the free kindergarten work from the church, and brought the kindergarten into the slums. Cooper eventually was cleared of the charges and joined a Congregational Church where she continued her kindergarten Bible classes (Shapiro 1983, 95). She organized and presided over the Golden Gate Kindergarten Association and supported free kindergartens through the efforts of her Bible classes (Fisher 1905, 695) for adults from many denominations (Ross 1976, 26).

Religion and morality were taught not only indirectly, but also directly as reports of kindergartners indicate. Kindergarten programs often had bible stories and prayers (Hansen 1904, 154–155; "Bible Study in the Day Schools" 1904, 30; Sturges 1901, 237; Shapiro 1983, 80). Wiggin and Smith advocated morning prayers, which were to be sung or read aloud, and moments of silence. Prayer was to be that "which only voices love and gratitude, reverence and aspiration, and so is appropriate for any creed and for any religion that looks up to God as the power that ruleth all and worketh in all" (Wiggin and Smith 1896, 118). In writing about the work of the kindergarten-settlement Peabody House, Brown (1901) acknowledged that direct religious instruction could not be given to those of the Jewish or Roman Catholic faith (p. 67). The religious function of the kindergarten existed outside of church sponsorship, but church sponsorship placed religious instruction in a primary role. The church also saw its role as promoter of social regeneration being implemented through kindergarten work (Newton 1881, 705). The Reverend R. Herber Newton, pastor of Anthon Memorial Episcopal Church in New York City, was a leader in the church's involvement in the kindergarten movement.

Newton opened a kindergarten in his church in 1877 with the help of women in his congregation. The kindergarten was a free kindergarten for children of all denominations that was open eight months a year, five days a week, from 9:30 to 1:00. Newton believed that the most formative years were those before age 7 and, therefore, wanted to reach the young at this crucial stage of their development (Ross 1976, 20–21):

The most valuable period of childhood for formative purposes is unclaimed by the State. The richest soil lies virgin, unpreempted, free for the Church to settle upon and claim for the highest culture. It is no new secret that the most plastic period lies below childhood, in infancy proper. (Newton 1881, 708)

Vandewalker, in discussing mission work of the church, relates a conversation she had with a Catholic priest who shared Newton's perspective on the importance of the early years. The priest is reported to have quoted a traditional Catholic belief in the primacy of the early years of life:

We Catholics catch our people young and they never get away from us. We hold that if we can have the care and guidance of a child under seven years of age, it will always come back to the church in after years, in every important crisis of grief or joy in life. That is why our great church is unaffected by the godlessness that alarms others. We make Catholics of little children, and they never cease to grow as the twig is bent. (Vandewalker 1923, 101–102)

The kindergarten represented a frontier for the church. It was a natural vehicle for fulfilling church missions. Yet, Vandewalker claims that the church did not realize this potential, for if it had there would not have been a need for social settlement sponsorship (p. 83).

The kindergarten served the same magnetic function under church sponsorship as it did under the social settlement. It was a means of building up a church's population and neighborhood. It also acted as a stimulus to all aspects of church life, such as the home, Sunday school, and the involvement of mothers (Vandewalker 1923, 83–84).

Mary J. Chisholm Foster's comprehensive work on the church's involvement in the kindergarten, *The Kindergarten of the Church* (1894), identified some key reasons for church involvement in the kindergarten movement. The church, first of all, was sensitive to the new educational methods of the period, including kindergartens. Second, the traditional one day a week of religious education on Sunday was an insufficient amount of religious instruction. Finally, the early years were seen as the most formative (pp. 41–42). Foster cited Bishop Lawrence of the Protestant Episcopal Church who identified three missions of the church that the kindergarten could help promote: to advance the intellect of its members; to address social problems of the day; and to advance the personal and spiritual development of its members (Foster 1894, 58).

Foster further identified and elaborated on the difference between the German approach to education, which was the springboard for Froebel's pedagogy, and the American approach to education. The Bible was a more basic component of the general education in Germany than in America, where public education, under the doctrine of separation of church and state, must not impart religious instruction. Foster inferred that, "The Church only is free to employ and to use the kindergarten idea in its widest scope and in the comprehensive meaning of its reforms" (1894, 53).

Foster built a case for church involvement in kindergarten work by reference to Froebel's writing and philosophy. She underscored the religious base to Froebel's work and his emphasis on building up the family, which is a mission shared by the church (1894, 73). The church and the family, through the kindergarten, were destined to prepare the young for life. The kindergarten was to be a prototype of society offered by a church that had no class distinctions. The kindergarten and the women's organizations of the church were seen to be an important and natural mix (Foster 1894, 55, 57, 96). Mothers' meetings and the women's groups of the church shared common agendas.

Foster advocated a church kindergarten that had trained kindergartners, who in turn trained assistants. The trained assistants and mothers then also could work in the Sunday school. The emphasis on training workers was to maintain the high quality and intactness of Froebel's system (Foster 1894, 115–116). At the end of her book, Foster provides the report of the director of her church's kindergarten. This director described her kindergarten work where, "a systematic course of religious instruction, with a daily Bible study, is combined with the best features of the kindergarten" (p. 218). A church kindergarten was not the same as a kindergarten that simply was housed in a church, because Foster herself recognized the latter did not necessarily provide religious instruction (Foster 1894, 218).

The exact number of church kindergartens was not recorded. In 1897, the commissioner of education reported 400 kindergarten associations and over 60 of these were church associations (Vandewalker 1923, 58, 77–78). Others divided kindergartens into those supported by public funds and those not so supported. Of the second category, there were two divisions: the private, fee charging kindergartens intended for a given social class and the charitable or missionary kindergarten. There were about 1,500 charitable or mission kindergartens, and within this group, there was an estimated 300 church supported kindergartens. Various auxiliary organizations of the church also sponsored kindergartens (Vandewalker 1923, 78–80).[1]

All denominations were involved in kindergarten sponsorship with Episcopalians in the lead: Roman Catholics, Lutherans, Jews, Friends, Swedenborgians, Unitarians, Christian Scientists, Methodists, Baptists, Congregationalists, and Presbyterians (Vandewalker 1923, 79). In some cases church sponsorship preceded public school sponsorship. For example, the diocese of New Orleans supported a kindergarten and training school for five years before the public schools assumed responsibility for the program. The willingness of churches to become involved in kindergarten sponsorship varied according to the church's sense of mission (Vandewalker 1923, 80–81). Church involvement in the kindergarten spread further through the work of missionaries, who established many kindergartens throughout the world at the turn of the century (Vandewalker 1923, 88–96).

The most readily apparent function of the kindergarten under church sponsorship was evangelical in nature. Vandewalker referred to the writings of Reverend Edward Judson in *The Institutional Church*. Judson discerned the kindergarten as the vehicle for reaching the new masses of immigrants. The Sunday school served this purpose, too, but it did not offer the greater number of hours provided by the kindergarten. Judson had high hopes for the church kindergarten:

If we would redeem the children the church must have her day school. Let her have a kindergarten which will embrace children from three to seven. These are too young to be admitted into the public schools and here is a providential opportunity which the church has of gathering them into her fold day by day. Let her employ a devout and trained kindergartner who shall not only educate the child's mind and body with the charming symbolic exercises of the kindergarten, but will tell each day a little of the story of the life of Christ, and teach the children Christian prayers and hymns. (Judson cited in Vandewalker 1923, 82)

The kindergarten and the church affected one another in often subtle ways. In "A Bohemian Kindergarten in Baltimore" (Conliff 1909) is a description of the effect the kindergarten had on immigrant parents who were nonbelievers. It was observed that "free thinker" families would send their children to the kindergarten, even if they themselves did not attend church. The parents would then send their children to Sunday school, because "having the kindergarten in the Sunday school room, they feel they belong there" (Conliff 1909, 78).

Sponsorship by the church recruited families for the church and influenced the family in the ways of the church through the children. The kindergarten affected the church's structure by effecting change in the teaching methodology of the Sunday school (Vandewalker 1923, 86–87; Foster 1894, 114). Church sponsorship highlighted the religious underpinnings of Froebel's philosophy and elevated the religious function of the kindergarten to a primary role.

MINOR SPONSORS OF KINDERGARTENS: WOMEN'S CHRISTIAN TEMPERANCE UNION AND BUSINESSES

In her history of the kindergarten movement through 1907, Vandewalker devoted a small section to the role of the Women's Christian Temperance Union (WCTU). The union was devoted to wiping out the influence of liquor and gave the kindergarten the function of preventing alcoholism from spreading to the next generation. Vandewalker described two goals of the WCTU: (1) "to acquaint mothers with fundamental principles of child rearing," and (2) to stimulate mothers to work on behalf of the kindergarten cause (p. 104). Froebel's philosophy of educating mothers on methods of child rearing were capitalized on by the women of the WCTU. The social status function thus was served by the WCTU through its concern with the status of mothers. Approximately twenty kindergartens were established in twenty large cities by the WCTU in the 1880s, with two such kindergartens in Chicago (p. 105).

The WCTU put forth considerable effort on the local, state, and national levels to legislate for the establishment of kindergartens in the public schools. The WCTU's kindergarten in San Jose eventually was adopted by the public schools. The WCTU efforts helped pass legislation that provided for the incorporation of kindergartens under the state school systems of Vermont and Michigan in 1887 and 1891, respectively. The kindergarten was such an important part of the WCTU's work that a special kindergarten department was established to carry out and coordinate efforts on behalf of the cause (pp. 105–106).

The Progressive movement of corporate welfarism did not neglect the kindergarten either (Vandewalker 1923, 112–124). Echoing present-day business concerns for productivity, Vandewalker reports that the welfare work undertaken by business leaders was intended to attract better workers and ensure a better product. The economic function was of primary concern:

Closely allied to settlement work in many respects is the welfare work now being undertaken by many larger business firms with the cooperation and for the benefit of their employees. Employers are beginning to recognize—apart from any moral concern that they may feel for those in their employ—that clean and wholesome conditions of labor will attract a better class of workers and produce more and better work than will the opposite; in consequence a general improvement in factory conditions is taking place. (pp. 112–113)

The kindergarten was one of the new benefits offered to the employee of large companies, "[t]o increase the happiness and efficiency of the worker, provision must be made for the welfare of his children" (p. 114).

One of the most recognized kindergartens was that run by the National Cash Register Company of Dayton, Ohio. The kindergarten was established by the president of the company, Mr. Patterson, with the intent of setting an example for the community in the hopes that the schools would eventually offer the service. Patterson wanted to train future workers and ingratiate the company with his employees. By 1903, the city of Dayton had a complete system of kindergartens as the result of National Cash Register's example. Patterson was such an avid devotee of kindergartens that he promulgated a rule that by 1915 no one could be hired by the factory who had not had kindergarten training (pp. 114–116).

The National Cash Register Company provided the kindergarten in conjunction with playgrounds, gardens, clubs, and other classes. Children of all ages were included by the activities, and at least 100 children used the kindergarten. The kindergarten and other activities were held in a model cottage called the *House of Usefulness*, which acted like a settlement house on company grounds (pp. 113–114).

The Colorado Fuel and Iron Company of Pueblo also was cited by Vandewalker as "the business firm that must be awarded the banner for the extent to which it has adopted the kindergarten as a feature of its welfare work" (p. 116). The company owned forty coal, manganese, and iron mines and coke camp properties in Wyoming, New Mexico, Colorado, and Utah. It employed

15,000 employees who spoke at least twenty-seven different languages. A complex welfare system existed within the company as a result of a kindergarten established in one of the mining camps in 1892 by the wife of the general manager of the company, who later became the president (pp. 116–117).

The welfare system was run under the company's "Sociological" department. By 1903, thirteen kindergartens in thirteen different localities were serving about 500 children. Some of the kindergartens were in specially designed buildings and others were housed in schools. With one exception, the kindergartens were held in the morning giving the kindergartners' time in the afternoons for club work and activities for older children (p. 119).

Much of the work was directed toward the special needs of children who did not speak English (p. 120). The kindergarten methodology was adapted to reach these children. Two benefits were cited by a report issued by the company's "sociological" department. The all-around development of the child was supported at the most impressionable age, and the particular needs of foreigners were met through the socialization and social service functions. The kindergarten served to further their "social betterment" (p. 121).

The kindergarten was seen by the Colorado Fuel and Iron Company as a means of entering the homes of the newcomers to promote a trusting relationship (p. 121). Kindergartners were encouraged to have a knowledge of Spanish or Italian. The company recognized that the children of its workers usually attended school only through eighth grade and saw the kindergarten as a way of extending the child's school life by one or two years (p. 122).

Cotton mill companies took on the kindergarten cause in the South. Vandewalker cites incomplete data, but lists approximately ten companies that provided kindergartens for their mill workers (pp. 122–123). O'Grady (1911) described the mill kindergartens and remarked on the variance in their quality. These mill kindergartens functioned as social reform by attracting illiterate families into the educational system. The mill's operatives often did not send their children to school because they could not read or write themselves, but the kindergarten lured them with its emphasis on handiwork and play. The parents liked the emphasis on handiwork because they felt it would prepare their children for later employment. Kindergartners encouraged the children and their families to stay in school once they were enrolled in the kindergarten (O'Grady 1911, 130).

Not all company sponsored kindergartens were solely the product of company initiative. Vandewalker specifically pointed out that the kindergartens of the Georgia Eagle and Phoenix Company in Girard and Phoenix City were partly attributable to the initiative of the workers. She posited that this was the first known educative venture initiated by labor. The kindergartens were financed by the company inclusive of the kindergartners salaries (pp. 123-124).

This historical overview reveals that corporate sponsorship maintained the multiple functions of the kindergarten. The structure of the sponsor was strengthened through sponsorship of the kindergarten and its position correlated with increased productivity and placated workers. The social service function of the kindergarten was important under this sponsor as was the educative function. The WCTU claimed the kindergarten for its social reform function of preventing alcoholism. Under WCTU sponsorship, the kindergarten also served a social service function. Interestingly, the WCTU was a strong advocate of public school sponsorship because the kindergarten's accomplishments had universal appeal.

NOTES

1.   Some of these auxiliary organizations were the Young People's Society of Christian Endeavor, King's Daughters, Young Women's Christian Association, Young Women's Guild, and Young Men's Guild (Vandewalker 1923, 79-80).

12. Public School Sponsorship
of the Kindergarten

This final chapter on the kindergarten debate describes the campaign for public school kindergartens and the ramifications of this linkage on the functions of the kindergarten. By the time kindergarten crusaders turned to the schools, the kindergarten had proven to serve multiple functions that varied by sponsor. Contrary to the child care movement of today, the schools did not aggressively court the mantle of kindergarten sponsorship. Rather, kindergarten crusaders turned to the schools as the solution to an escalating problem of delivering the kindergarten to the masses.

The eventual adoption of the kindergarten by the schools continued the pattern by which the American system of schooling had developed—from the top down. For example, primary grades were added after the high school grades and the kindergarten was added after the primary. The present system of age grading was established in 1860 with the primary linked to the upper grades in 1854 (Vandewalker 1923, 3–4).

The campaign for public school adoption of kindergartens spanned two decades, 1890–1910 (Shapiro 1983, 131). The number of children served by kindergartens had increased dramatically in the 1880s from 31,227 to 143,720 (p. 132). The free kindergarten associations no longer could meet the demand; they simply did not have the finances nor the organizational structure to satisfy the pressing public need. The financial situation was acute and demanded prompt solutions. The funds of the so-called kindergarten angels were being depleted and the contributions of the middle class members of the associations were becoming more scarce. Leaders of the free kindergarten movement, including private benefactors, recognized that the private kindergartens had met a social need that now demanded public support (Shapiro 1983, 131–133).

Not only was there a lack of funding, but the lay boards were forced to respond to a broader market with the many complications that accompany growth in service delivery. Furthermore, the paid kindergartners who had replaced the volunteers needed supervision, which the associations could not offer. The associations reorganized themselves by separating management issues from daily operational issues and began to develop new managerial skills (Shapiro 1983, 132–133).

Intent on maintaining existing programs and achieving universal status, kindergarten associations began an all-out campaign for public school sponsorship of the kindergarten. Those that carried the banner for public school sponsorship included long-time kindergarten advocates and other activists committed to education and social reform. The campaigners grabbed onto the social reform function of the kindergarten with the intent of simultaneously assuaging the plight of the urban poor and the problems of the urban schools (Shapiro 1983, 131–133).

In spite of any problems exhibited in the schools, public school sponsorship of the kindergarten was widely embraced as an ideal remedy for the fumbling kindergarten associations and as the mechanism for achieving the goal of universal kindergarten coverage. In discussing the contribution of social settlement workers in the push for public school involvement, Smith (1961) observed: "As the magnitude of the task of restoring health to both individuals and neighborhoods sank in upon them, however, they began to look more and more for help from the public school" (p. 201). Kindergarten crusaders envisioned the public school as the solution to the problems facing the kindergarten movement They assumed that in turn the kindergarten would offer new life and new functions to the entrenched elementary curriculum.

Public schools became receptive to the idea of kindergarten sponsorship only after the waves of education reform had moved the public educational system away from its strict didacticism toward a more hands-on and informal approach to learning (Vandewalker 1923). A major impetus in readying the schools for the acceptance of the kindergarten was the contribution of Dr. E. A. Sheldon, who founded the Oswego Normal School and introduced the principles of Pestalozzi. The introduction of drawing and manual training to the elementary curriculum also provided the schools with a fresh and receptive perspective to the idea of sponsoring kindergartens (Vandewalker 1923, 4–6).

The idea of public school sponsorship of the kindergarten was first introduced as early as 1867 when Elizabeth Peabody petitioned the school committee of Boston to establish kindergartens in the schools. The committee rejected her initial request, but did establish an experimental kindergarten in 1870, which eventually closed in 1879 due to lack of funds and interest (Ross 1976, 12). The leading educator, Henry Barnard, was reported to have petitioned the United States Senate in 1869 and the United States House of Representatives in 1870 for the incorporation of kindergartens into the schools (Committee of 19 1924, 65). Nevertheless, it was not until 1873 that the first public school kindergarten was established in St. Louis, Missouri (Ross 1976, 13).[1]

Shapiro identified a specific pattern to the campaign for public school kindergartens in many of the large cities (pp. 133–134). First, the press exposed the corruption of public school programs linked to political patronage and the need for reform. Then, the free kindergartners, municipal reformers, and the press drew attention to the advantages of the free kindergartens. The kindergartens were depicted as operating spirited, child oriented programs in contrast to the rigid teacher directed programs of the schools. Kindergartners were held up as prototypes of dedicated, selfless teachers committed to the welfare of the urban children, including the immigrants. Finally, the campaigners pressured the municipal government to investigate the situation of the schools, kindergartens, and other child saving agencies with the hope that the unveiling of the problems in the schools and the solutions offered by the kindergartens would motivate efforts toward reform.

The campaign for public school kindergartens occurred in the context of a media highly influenced by liberal and influential editors, as well as muckrakers. In 1892, Joseph Mayer Rice, a pediatrician, educator, and journalist, conducted his renowned survey of American cities, which was later published in the popular periodical of the time *The Forum*. Rice sharply criticized the schools' methodology and rigidity and charged them with corruption, but praised those schools that had incorporated the kindergarten (Shapiro 1983, 134–135). The press, in general, furthered the public school campaign for several reasons:

> To the editors of the liberal press, educational and political reform seemed to go hand in hand. The campaign for the public adoption of free kindergartens seemed an appropriate response in at least two ways. First, the community service ideal of the free kindergarten would be a healthy antidote to the self-interest of political bosses. Second, the stress on innovative teaching techniques might provide a model for the reform of the stale teaching techniques of the primary teacher. The most enthusiastic editors also argued that the public-service ideal of free kindergartens might provide a good example for the reform of other municipal services, especially police and health care. (Shapiro 1983, 135)

Although the great majority of kindergarten advocates endorsed public school sponsorship, a minority greeted the new movement with trepidation, concerned that such sponsorship would result in a loss of functions traditionally associated with the kindergarten. Sarah Cooper, who had been associated with church sponsorship and became a leader of the free kindergarten movement in California, voiced apprehension that the kindergarten under public school auspices would suffer from budget cuts and politics (Shapiro 1983, 135–136). However, Ross (1976) indicated that Cooper did support the idea of public kindergartens as a means of preventing crime and as a positive experience to ensure the wholesome development of children from all classes (pp. 84–85). Other opponents of school sponsorship worried that the religious aspect of Froebelianism would be lost in the public schools (Vandewalker 1923, 51).

Although critics eventually blamed school sponsorship for negative changes in the kindergarten program, there was little initial debate among kindergartners about the need for public school involvement. Instead, there was a strong joint effort to promote such sponsorship in the hopes that more children of all classes would be reached:

Although some kindergartners may have had qualms about whether the quality of their efforts would be maintained once sponsorship passed into the public schools, almost all of them engaged in strenuous efforts to achieve this aim. By 1914, they had achieved their goal in good measure, since every major city in the United States had municipal kindergartens. Success, however, both fulfilled and disappointed their expectations. (Ross 1976, 83)

Kindergarten crusaders utilized many arguments to support their position in favor of public school sponsorship. Many of the same arguments used to establish philanthropic kindergartens were recycled because the child saving movement was behind the new push for public school adoption. Ross (1976) cites the president of Baltimore's Board of School Commissioners, who "urged municipal kindergartens for those children whose parents could not rear them properly and who otherwise would be neglected and left to develop bad habits" (p. 83). The familiar goals of saving the children from slums, providing industrial preparation, and preventing crime were rationales for school involvement. The envisioned school-based kindergartens would provide a much needed social service function.

There were arguments in favor of the schools that were specific to the school as the sponsoring institution. In discussing Boston's history of adopting the kindergarten into its public schools, Lazerson (1971) stated: "The rationale for accepting this responsibility emerged in two areas, one involving the relationship of preschooling to social reform, the other focusing on early childhood education as a prerequisite for future success" (p. 58). In an address to the Educational Commission of Chicago, in the *Report of the Educational Commission of the City of Chicago* (1898, 195–204), Edmund J. James of the University of Chicago spoke of the increasing tendency in society at that time to assign more responsibility to public institutions in the raising of the young, which had previously resided with the family, the church, and the street: "One of the great questions now before the educational world is this: Can the family properly look out for the education of the child until its sixth year, and if it can, does it actually do so, or can we insure its doing so?" (p. 196). James further noted that the question was really a question of timing: When should public education begin?

James highlighted several key points in the argument for public schools to expand their reach to include the kindergarten. First, the kindergarten was seen as an institution that could bridge the home and school while providing for the child's development before the primary years. Second, the early years were becoming recognized by educators as the most valuable in shaping the child, both intellectually and socially; yet, the potential of those years was wasted. Third, the kindergarten was needed across classes. Kindergarten was becoming recognized as a right for all children and thereby equated with all of public education.

In addition, private enterprise could not and would not supply the kindergarten adequately to meet the demands placed on it. Finally, economic conditions did not permit the majority of students to remain in school beyond the tenth grade; therefore, the additional years in school would increase the total number of years in school for the majority and result in a better society. In conclusion, James commented that the kindergarten was a "logical and necessary complement to our present system of free public education" (p. 203).

The most significant issues surrounding public school adoption of the kindergarten concerned the universalization of the right to receive a kindergarten education and the role of the school in influencing the youngest members of society:

The state has no right to assume the duty of giving an education, unless it provides the best possible training and culture for its children. . . . If the Kindergarten be truly the most stimulating educational process at a certain period of a child's development, then all children are entitled to its advantages. (Hughes 1894, 749)

In this sense, the public school system could widen the population served by the kindergarten. The school was considered an elixir in that it would afford coverage the free kindergarten associations and settlements could not provide.

Less idealistic and more practical arguments were also proffered to support public school involvement with kindergartens. The Progressive Era was marked by its emphasis on bureaucracy, professionalization, and efficiency. It was argued that public school control of the kindergartens would allow for centralization and better management.

An example of this pragmatic philosophy is represented by the "Cleveland plan" of school management. Under this plan implemented in 1894, the school system was divided into two departments: the supervision of instruction and business affairs (Shapiro 1983, 136–137). The kindergarten was included in Cleveland's plan to reorganize the system of education in the city: "The Cleveland Commission hoped that the kindergarten itself might serve as a safeguard against future public-school corruption by humanizing and Christianizing urban public education" (Shapiro 1983, 137).

Citywide investigations into charges of graft within cities' educational systems reached similar conclusions as in the case of the 1898 Harper Commission of Chicago. One of the several conclusions reached by the Harper Commission was that kindergartens should be incorporated into the Chicago public school system. Kindergartens would function "to improve the overall quality of instruction and provide a first rung to the ladder of Chicago's educational institutions" (Shapiro 1983, 136).[2]

The eventual adoption of kindergartens into the Chicago school system was an outgrowth of the relationship between philanthropists and the schools. Similar cooperative efforts took place in other urban areas. Actions were taken by many other large cities during the late 1880s through the turn of the century to incorporate into the educational system the free kindergartens supported by philanthropists and associations (Shapiro 1983, 136; Ross 1976, 88; Fisher 1905, 702). By 1903, New York had 362 public kindergartens, Philadelphia had 197, and Boston had 92 (Fisher 1905, 702).

Progress in the adoption of kindergartens by the schools was occurring on the state level as well through the examples of Wisconsin and Minnesota, which had established kindergarten departments in state normal schools in 1880 (Vandewalker 1923, 191). In 1891, the National Education Association came forward advocating the adoption of the kindergarten by the public schools (Vandewalker 1923, 192–193). NEA recommended that kindergartens be a part of all school systems and petitioned for establishment of a kindergarten department within the Bureau of Education. The NEA also promoted the kindergarten cause by offering technical assistance to states in drafting laws that would enable the growth of kindergartens in the public school sector and publishing articles (Committee of 19 1924, 14).

Despite the positive commitment of many forces, formidable obstacles were encountered in the campaign for public school adoption of the kindergarten. Cities outside of the major urban areas were leery of the expense and the idea of centralization. States established barriers by requiring local districts to fund the kindergartens (Shapiro 1983, 138). Vandewalker provided two central reasons for the "slow march" of kindergarten progress in the schools. First, the cost was perceived as prohibitive, especially when compared to the primary grades, because the kindergarten required specific materials and a low teacher to child ratio. It had been Froebel's original intention to have classes of fifteen children (Vandewalker 1923, 184–185). The second obstacle facing the kindergarten crusaders were the state laws. Most states did not permit spending funds for children of kindergarten age (Vandewalker 1923, 187).

The National Kindergarten Association (NKA) was formed in 1909 specifically for furthering the kindergarten crusade. NKA was an outgrowth of the former New York Free Kindergarten Association, which had been so successful that New York activists hoped for an impact on the kindergarten movement nationwide (Shapiro 1983, 138). Under the leadership of John Dewey, the president of the NKA in its incipient stage, the association organized itself with business and political acumen to achieve its sole purpose of promoting the kindergarten. It led a national campaign "to remove legal barriers and promote mandatory establishment of public kindergartens through changes in state laws or constitutions" (Shapiro 1983, 139).

The leaders did not come from the kindergarten classrooms or supervisory level; instead, the NKA was composed of professional public relations people. The association conducted local surveys and provided consultation to interested parties. Additionally, it implemented several promotional strategies, such as press releases and field demonstrations in public schools, orphanages, hospitals, asylums, and factories (Shapiro 1983, 139).

Savvy from its start, NKA's leaders built alliances with other government and private organizations concerned with the welfare of young children: the NEA, the General Federation of Women's Clubs, and the National Council of Women. It had the unmatched support of the U.S. commissioner of education, P. P. Claxton, who established a kindergarten division within the Bureau of Education. The NKA worked through this division by publishing and circulating promotional materials, including films. NKA was devoted to propagandizing the need for public kindergartens (Shapiro 1983, 139).

From 1892–1913, thirteen states enacted new statutes or adopted various amendments to existing legislation for enabling the institution of public kindergartens statewide. Three states used the petition process. In 1916, only three states had mandatory establishment of kindergartens despite the popularity of the kindergarten on the local level (Shapiro 1983, 139–140). By 1903, forty-five states had reported supporting public kindergartens, with Oklahoma declaring to establish kindergartens within a year (Fisher 1905, 703). In 1903, one source indicated that over 440 cities had public kindergartens. The five states with the largest number of kindergartens were New York (86), Wisconsin (71), New Jersey (56), Michigan (43), and Massachusetts (34) (Vandewalker 1923, 195). The ready acceptance of the kindergarten into the public school system was so dramatic that by 1908 the National Society for the Scientific Study of Education devoted two issues of its journal to the subject of coordinating the kindergarten with the elementary curriculum.

Free kindergartens usually were incorporated into the public schools by a vote or simple procedural action on the part of city councils. Although the concept of a publicly supported kindergarten met with relatively little conflict, logistical issues of "absorbing" the "teachers, children, and classrooms posed more complex administrative problems" (Shapiro 1983, 140). The successful implementation of the kindergarten into the public school system most often rested with the leadership capabilities the superintendents (p. 140).

Shapiro posited that superintendents of major school systems played pivotal roles in the adoption of kindergartens by the public schools. Although legislative action on the state level was required to formally legalize the process of incorporating kindergartens into schools, the actual implementation depended on the power, interests, and personalities of school superintendents. A change in administrative styles, nevertheless, was evident in the period from 1870–1890. Charismatic and committed administrative leaders of the kindergarten movement turned more and more to the teachings of the new managerial science that exacted changes in the delivery of the kindergarten (Shapiro 1983, 140–141).

THE SIGNIFICANCE OF THE ST. LOUIS EXAMPLE

The prime example of the kindergarten's attachment to the schools is best illustrated by the history of the St. Louis kindergartens, which were the first to become part of an American public school system. The adoption of the kindergarten by the public schools in St. Louis in 1873 was credited to the inspiration of William T. Harris, superintendent from 1868 to 1880 (Weber 1969, 28; Troen 1972, 213), and Susan Blow, a local kindergartner who became a leader in the movement. Harris eventually became United States commissioner of education from 1889 to 1906 (Weber 1969, 28; Troen 1972, 213).

St. Louis had a large immigrant population during the period 1860–1870, and a considerable proportion of this population was German. The German constituency facilitated the adoption of the kindergarten in St. Louis because they first supported "local neighborhood kindergartens and later provided a base of popular support for the introduction of the kindergarten to the public school" (Shapiro 1983, 45). The introduction of the kindergarten into the schools was inspired by Harris's "block reports" (Troen 1975, 100). In 1868 Harris conducted a survey of the city neighborhoods with the intent of assessing the educational needs of the children. The survey reported the class, ethnicity, and age of attendance. Harris was appalled to learn that children from the slums were receiving far less of an education than their counterparts in other areas of the city. Children of working parents often were receiving a minimum of three years of schooling because they started at age 7 and left at age 10 for paid employment. Superintendent Harris was distressed about the potential long-term effect this inequity would have on society (Shapiro 1983, 48–49).

Harris embraced the kindergarten as a means of removing slum children from the streets. While rescued from the streets, the children would benefit from a program that would prepare them for the elementary curriculum and provide them with an industrial education in preparation for life itself (Troen 1973; 1975; Weber 1969; Shapiro 1983). Unlike traditional Froebelians, he did not want to extend Froebel's influence into the home or the primary school. He saw the function of the kindergarten as a transition from the home into the school; it was auxiliary to the school system (Shapiro 1983, 88; Weber 1969, 29–30).

Harris parted ways with Elizabeth Peabody's transcendental view of the kindergarten as liberator of the individual child for a better future. Instead, he saw the kindergarten as a means of maintaining the status quo by providing children with an avenue into school and the world of work (Troen 1973; Weber 1969; Ross 1976; Shapiro 1983). In essence, Harris viewed the education function of the kindergarten as primary with the social status function as secondary. He believed that the kindergarten would responsibly prepare children for the work world and that working class children would then attain working class status.

Harris's original intention of solving an attendance problem by reducing the legal age for entry into public education to age 3 was resisted in 1872 by a school board that cited the already overcrowded conditions of the schools as its reason for denying his plea (Shapiro 1983, 50; Troen 1975, 100–101). Harris not only hoped to lower the age of entry into public schooling, but he also pressed to reach all socioeconomic classes of children by transforming the kindergarten into a public institution. The child saving function was clear to

Harris.   Kindergarten would remove children from their native, destructive environments and place them into productive, preparatory environments.   The poor were saved from the evil influences of the street, and the children of the upper classes were rescued from their indulgent homes and ignorant caretakers (Troen 1975, 112; Shapiro 1983, 59–60; Weber 1969, 29).

Harris's view of social reform encompassed this conception of child saving. His vision of the social order was conservative, but he strived to strengthen the position of each child in the system.   While meeting the needs of all classes of children, the kindergarten would also further Harris's goal of maintaining the social order:

The kindergarten had come to offer something to all the city's children. It would help the tenement child grow up a moral person, properly disciplined and capable of taking his place in the home or the city's factories; and it would develop the rich child's character and creative powers so that he might take his place in the direction of the community's affairs. This view presupposed that children of different classes would have different futures for which the schools must equip them. For all classes the kindergarten idea represented the belief that urban living required a new public agency to assist in the "transition between life of the Family and the severe discipline of the School." (Troen 1972, 228)

"Harris believed that the role of the school was to adjust the child to society, not to create a new social order" (Ross 1976, 15).   The socialization function of the kindergarten captured Harris's attention.

In St. Louis, critics complained that the kindergarten was Germanizing the city schools and that it was a frill the system did not need.   Others contended that it usurped the role of the family.   Additional criticism ranged from seeing no benefit in it to blaming it for making a child "untractable" for the primary grades.   Some arguments centered on the difficulty of securing appropriate kindergarten teachers (Shapiro 1983, 54–55; Troen 1972, 225; 1975, 70–71, 110).

A legal attack was directed at the St. Louis kindergartens in 1878 when 3,000 citizens signed a petition calling for abolishment of such kindergartens on the basis that they violated the state's age of entry into public school requirement and departed from the mission of the schools to deliver a traditional education (Troen 1972, 225–226; 1975, 110).   The kindergarten was then considered a part of the public school system.   The petition was rejected by the board of education, but legal battles continued through the court system from 1878 to 1883 (Troen 1975, 110).   Three courts upheld the board's decision, but in 1883 the Supreme Court of Missouri ruled against the board on the issue of the age of entry.   The high court's decision necessitated a board compromise whereby the age of admission to kindergarten was raised to 5 and a fee of $1 a quarter was charged for 5 year olds, but not for 6 and 7 year olds (Troen 1972, 226; 1975, 111-112).[3] This court decision had ramifications for the role of the kindergarten in the St. Louis public schools:

This prevented the board from carrying out its mission of reclaiming younger children from the pernicious influences of the city's streets and slums. In effect, these pioneering efforts to meet the problems of the post-Civil War industrial city were checked by a legal document drawn for a smaller and less complicated society, the St. Louis of 1833. This turn of events dramatically showed how far the city's educators and school managers had progressed in redefining their responsibilities to the community; it also demonstrated the persistence of a more conservative view of public education. (Troen 1972, 227)

The education function of the kindergarten was sanctioned, but the social reform function was not.

Volunteers were responsible for much of the growth in the number of kindergartens throughout the St. Louis school system during the early years. This volunteer-based system changed rapidly in a short space of time. In 1876-1877, 150 women volunteered their services. In 1877-1878, 139 women volunteered. By the 1878-1879 school year, there were only 65 volunteers. The decline in the number of volunteers was due to the professionalization of assistants. In 1877 volunteers began to be awarded teaching certificates on the completion of a special exam, and the certification enabled them to receive a salary (Troen 1972, 224; 1975, 108-109). This shift away from volunteers to a certified staff changed forever the social status of the kindergarten worker. Kindergartners gained a professional status, but lost the extra help of volunteer staff who facilitated the delivery of high quality programs and low adult-child ratios. The professionalization of kindergartners closed the doors to the many women interested in volunteering.

The St. Louis system of providing kindergartens through the public schools was judged a remarkable success and became a model for other cities. This model, with the education function as primary, was copied all over the country. Susan Blow, writing in *Outlook* in 1897, claimed that the kindergarten experiment in St. Louis was significant on a national level because it proved that the kindergarten could function as an integral part of a school system. The St. Louis kindergarten demonstrated that the kindergarten was the first stage of public education (Blow 1897, 935). As Shapiro has observed: "At its peak, the Saint Louis experiment created a system of free urban public kindergartens, an occupational subculture, and a wide base of public support" (p. 63). For these reasons, the incorporation of kindergartens in the St. Louis public school system represents a critical step in the history of the kindergarten movement throughout the United States.

CRITICISM AND EVALUATION OF PUBLIC SCHOOL KINDERGARTENS

For the most part, public school kindergartens were evaluated favorably by members of the education community in the years following linkage: "Despite some negative reaction, schools seemed to evaluate their kindergartens in essentially positive terms, as letters from primary teachers, supervisors and school superintendents bore out some of the numerous claims for the kindergarten" (Ross 1976, 90). Generally, the education function was used as the criteria for judging the program's impact. Negative commentary came between 1890 and 1900 from the new psychologists who found fault with the methodology of the kindergarten. Other criticism originated from art teachers and physical education instructors, who questioned the total use of the kindergarten curriculum as a basis for their subjects (Vandewalker 1923, 243).

At the onset of the expansion of the kindergarten into the schools, primary school teachers and principals were apprehensive, concerned that kindergarten children would not meet the expectations of elementary school (Blow 1897, 934). Surveys taken of primary school staff after the kindergartens had been in existence for various periods of time indicated, however, a majority of positive responses regarding the effect of the kindergarten experience on children (Merrill 1898; Holden 1905; U. S. Bureau of Education 1914).

For example, a survey taken in 1905 of 6,000 teachers across the country by Francis Holden indicated that 100 percent of those surveyed responded favorably to the statement, "Kindergarten training is good preparation for school studies" (Holden 1905, 391). Holden summarized his own work: "An impartial survey of the facts unquestionably leads to the conclusion that the verdict of the teacher, so far as it is given in this study, is unanimously in favor of kindergarten training as a preparation for grade work" (p. 395). One can see how the education function was used as the criteria for evaluating the kindergarten's early success.

A 1913 survey of superintendents, primary school supervisors, and first grade teachers in 127 cities was conducted by the commissioner of education. Again, the overwhelming response was favorable to the kindergarten experience (U. S. Bureau of Education 1914, 93). In this national survey the socialization function was also set as an evaluation criterion, together with the education function. Comments were solicited as well regarding the liberation-universalization function of the kindergarten. On the whole, the superintendents did not think that the kindergarten was necessary if mothers were available in the home, if the income level was average, and if the children had access to the out of doors. They did see a need for the experience of kindergarten in congested neighborhoods (U. S. Bureau of Education 1914, 97–103).

The superintendents attributed the kindergarten experience with connecting the parent to the school and installing a positive attitude about school in the young child. They claimed that first grade teachers wanted kindergarten trained children in their classrooms. Assistant superintendent A. E. Kagel of Milwaukee wrote, "We consider the kindergarten indispensable for all classes of children. It is here that the child gets his first lesson in democracy and social obligation" (U. S. Bureau of Education 1914, 102).

The majority of respondents felt that the kindergarten prepared children academically and socially for primary level work. Others felt that the socialization function was negative because the children were more difficult to teach than their non-kindergarten trained peers, as they were used to the informality of the kindergarten program. This opinion was evidenced in Frederic Burk and Caroline Frear Burk's survey of the Santa Barbara kindergarten experience, *A Study of the Kindergarten Problem in the Public Kindergartens of Santa Barbara, California, for the Year 1898–1899*. The Burks reported that the primary teachers in the study felt that kindergarten trained children were more difficult to teach.

The U.S. Bureau of Education analyzed approximately twenty-four surveys of kindergartens in twenty-four cities over the years 1915–1926. Mary G. Waite synthesized the surveys' results in *The Kindergarten in Certain School Surveys* (1926). Waite found that taken as a whole the kindergartens were functioning as well as other parts of the school system and that the kindergarten positively affected the primary curriculum. In a reciprocal fashion, she also observed that kindergarten methods had changed as a result of the connection with the primary.

It is interesting to note for purposes of this work that Waite's review indicated a change in functions in the kindergarten after adoption by the public schools. The kindergartens became an intricate part of the elementary schools. Waite discussed the need for further unification in the training of kindergarten and primary school teachers. She set as goals the setting of unified objectives for children aged 4 through 6 and the establishment of kindergarten as the first year in school life (Waite 1926, 2–3).

By 1926 most of the children attending kindergarten were 5 years old, although some were 4 years old. In contrast to Froebel's mixed age grouping of children, the public school kindergartens grouped children by ability (Waite 1926, 10–11). She described three types of kindergartens, which varied by the quality of the physical setting. On evaluating the curriculum, Waite found little consensus regarding kindergarten objectives (pp. 26–27) Waite did point out that the kindergarten curriculum served an "Americanization" function:

The kindergarten has always understood the necessity for beginning Americanization with the very little children. Through emphasizing the need for visiting the children and their mothers in their homes, as well as through the classroom activities and the teaching of English, the kindergarten helps to give children of foreign parentage something like a fair start. (Waite 1926, 28)

In this capacity the kindergarten performed the socialization function as well as the education function: socialization in the sense that the children were gradually set into a mainstream mold; education in the sense that academic readiness was the goal of the program. Waite pointed out a primary function of the kinder-garten when discussing the needs of teacher training:

One of the important functions of the kindergarten is to prepare children to do the work prescribed for the first grade. If the kindergarten is to fulfill this function the teacher must be thoroughly acquainted with primary principles and activities. (Waite 1926, 29)

The thrust of the survey was that there should be greater unification between the kindergarten and the primary school. This desire for unification elevated the education function over all other functions. Waite pointed the way to this unifi-cation by proposing that the training of primary and kindergarten teachers be consolidated. She proposed that there should be opportunities for all teachers to take common courses of study. In Waite's judgment supervision should be by someone who was in charge of both the kindergarten and the primary grades (Waite 1926, 41). As the professionally trained educator became the model for kindergartners and their supervisors, the social work aspect of the kindergartners' jobs was greatly diminished.

Waite (1926) concluded that, although more scientific investigation of the kindergarten experience was advisable, there was a definite need for more kindergartens because less than one-eighth of all children between 4 and 6 attended (pp. 42–43). She recommended expansion of the kindergarten because of the advantage of three functions. First, the kindergarten prepared children for the educational demands of the primary grades. Second, the kindergarten socialized the children in terms of their language, creative thinking, and interactive play abilities. Third, the kindergarten could function as a social utility by providing needed and additional years of schooling (p. 44). In sum, the kindergarten was seen to have affected the primary school:

The surveyors believe that one great value of the kindergarten lies in its suggestions for other grades in the school system. They also believe that hundreds of primary schools have changed their methods and subject matter because they have accepted the principles of kindergarten education. The kindergarten, they believe, has helped to soften formalism and to create a joyful spirit of achievement in many elementary school-rooms. (Waite 1926, 38)

PUBLIC SCHOOL STRUCTURE'S EFFECT ON THE FUNCTION OF THE KINDERGARTEN

In addition to the loss of a religious function, the connection of the kindergarten with the schools resulted in many other functional changes. In *Origins of the Urban School* (1971), Marvin Lazerson put forth his thesis that the link of the kindergarten to the public schools resulted in the loss of its social and urban reform functions as well as the extinction of other distinct features. As a consequence of this link, the kindergarten's focus no longer was on the child and the slum home, but on the child in school. Kindergarten was seen as a preparation for school, which was a much narrower function than that of urban reform (Lazerson 1971; Weber 1969; Ross 1976; Shapiro 1983).

Lazerson (1971) argued that certain processes emanating from the structure of the school system made the kindergarten simply an adjunct of first grade (p. 65). First, the economic restraints of the large school systems placed the kindergarten in a position of compromise. Kindergartners needed to adapt to less than ideal situations regarding class size and materials acquisition. Second, the attempts to introduce kindergarten methods into the early primary years compromised the kindergarten because it was then thought that the kindergarten program in its entirety was introduced into the schools, whereas in reality isolated principles of a whole were implemented.

The Progressive Era's ideals of efficiency, bureaucratization, professionalization, and scientific management had their impact on the kinder-garten. On the positive side, kindergartners found themselves less isolated within the schools. As Shapiro comments, the "lure of professionalization" was attractive after two decades of isolation. Some kindergartners believed that sponsorship by the schools provided a desirable career ladder (Shapiro 1983, 144).

The lack of isolation and increase in prestige demanded a trade-off in autonomy for the kindergartner and the kindergarten program. School administrators sought to create an efficient, centralized, and unified system of education. To achieve this end, the kindergarten and its functions needed to be altered in several notable ways.

The kindergarten that first joined the public schools came without uniformity in regard to the age of the children, standards for admission, qualifications of the teachers, and the selection of curricular materials (Shapiro 1983, 141). Kindergartens, under association sponsorship, varied in the delivery of their program according to neighborhood needs, "The neighborhood orientation of the kindergarten, once its chief strength, was now under attack" (Shapiro 1983, 141). Linkage with the schools changed the delivery of the service into an established, predetermined service that did not respond to the quirks of each neighborhood served. In this regard, the social service function was diminished.

Superintendents had a three step plan for the reorganization of the kindergarten (Shapiro 1983, 141-142). They sought to achieve a smoothly operating, continuous system of education that began in the kindergarten and followed an efficient organizational pattern through high school. It was not in the interests of the administrators to maintain a separate kindergarten department. In their minds, the kindergarten units provoked disharmony and unjustified expenses.

In the first step of the superintendents' reorganization plan, the kindergarten director was to be placed under more control and supervision. Thus, the power and prestige of the kindergarten director was usurped because the superintendent wanted centralized control (Shapiro 1983, 143). In the eyes of the superintendent, the director only perpetuated the kindergarten as a separate unit from the primary school. Directorial duties, such as visiting individual classrooms, training staff, and visiting homes in the afternoons, were eliminated (p. 144).

Shapiro claimed that the dismissal of the kindergarten director reflected a shift in power from women to men in school administration. This shift was indicative of a change in the social status function. While the corps of kindergartners gained professional status, former kindergarten leaders lost their power base. For example, St. Louis lost Susan Blow in 1885 when Edward H. Long, then superintendent, requested a joint training program for kindergarten and primary school staff. Blow would not agree to such a change in her program. After her departure, Long put the kindergarten under the authority of local principals (Shapiro 1983, 142-143). Some school systems created a new position for a supervisor of the kindergarten *and* primary school. Others had the director act as an advisor to the Board of Education. By 1910 the authority of the kindergarten director was gone entirely. "Only a vestige of the training function of kindergarten directors remained after World War I" (Shapiro 1983, 144).

The removal of kindergarten directresses eroded the influence of the old kindergarten leadership. Some kindergartners who had been dissatisfied with the power exerted by their fellow kindergartners looked forward to the administrative changes with optimism. "Many public kindergarten teachers welcomed the administrative changes because they feared the hegemony of kindergarten directors more than the authority of school superintendents" (Shapiro 1983, 144).

After changes were made to the administrative structure of the kindergarten, charity work was eliminated as a kindergarten function. Arguments were proffered that education and social welfare were now two separate "professions." At first, many superintendents were supportive of the mothers' meetings aspect of the kindergartners' work. In Boston and Philadelphia, home visits and mothers' meetings were continued for over a decade after the adoption of the kindergartens into the schools:

In Cincinnati kindergarten philanthropy continued until 1912, when public teachers were still visiting more than 2,000 homes each year; similar programs were conducted in Queens and Brooklyn (New York) until 1905. But the rationale of the programs had changed. School superintendents were less interested in extending their influence into neighborhood social concerns than in preparing children for primary instruction. (Shapiro 1983, 145)

The social service function was virtually eliminated when double session kindergartens were established. Double kindergarten sessions, one in the morning and one in the afternoon, were initiated to reduce the cost of educating the kindergarten child. Volunteers and assistants were eliminated and teachers were assigned double loads:

The most significant change brought about by double sessions was the declining involvement of kindergartners in community affairs and the crippling of their social work functions. While everyone continued to consider the ideal kindergartner a social worker as well as a teacher, the ideal rang hollow when the kindergartner had to work in school each afternoon. (Ross 1976, 93)

Shapiro reports that after 1895 there was greater concern for economy within the public schools. The "charity" programs were sacrificed and scrutinized in the interest of cost efficiency. Critics argued that the kindergarten equipment was expensive enough. Citing Lazerson's review of Massachusetts's school history, Shapiro noted a 30 percent cost increase in educating a kindergarten child between 1889 and 1909 (Shapiro 1983, 145). The kindergarten was vulnerable to budget cuts because it served the youngest children and was not yet fully recognized for its liberation-universalization function.

In the final step of the superintendents' three step plan for the reorganization of the kindergarten, the curriculum and teaching methods were standardized and aligned with the primary curriculum and staff. "Together the proposed changes comprised an agenda for the active transformation of the kindergarten" (Shapiro 1983, 142). This transformation of the kindergarten was not accomplished without the customary battle of competing interest groups. Although public school sponsorship was welcomed by the majority of kindergarten crusaders in the late 1890s, kindergarten practitioners were subjected to many compromises. Diehard Froebelians conceded many practices in a thirty year period, 1890–1920, as was evident in the superintendents' three-step plan.

Tension already had existed within the kindergarten movement because of factional disputes over pedagogy. With public school involvement, new players were brought into an ongoing debate. Kindergartners once detached from the stranglehold of bureaucracy, now faced guidelines imposed on them by outsiders. When employment was found within the jurisdiction of the schools many kindergartners found themselves in conflict with administrators and other teaching staff.

Administrative issues that surfaced with public school sponsorship included proficiency requirements for entry into first grade, use of school building space, standards for hiring of kindergarten teachers, and curriculum objectives. Certification of the kindergarten teacher presented many problems because there was tremendous resentment among the primary teachers who had longer training requirements and longer work hours (Shapiro 1983, 147).

Public school sponsorship encouraged the move away from private kindergartner training schools toward university training. When public schools first became involved in kindergarten sponsorship during the 1890s, there was a lack of qualified kindergartners to teach in the expanded service (Shapiro 1983, 147). Because there were no state standards on certification of kindergartners, public school officials had to invent training requirements (Shapiro 1983, 148).

A variety of approaches were taken by superintendents and school boards to solve the certification problem. In some cases former free kindergartners were grandfathered into certification compliance, in other cities examinations or relatively short training courses were established for the explicit purpose of quickly satisfying the demand for kindergartners (Shapiro 1983, 147–148). Colleges, universities, and normal schools offered in-service and summer training courses. Summer courses also were provided by "old-school Froebelians" (Shapiro 1983, 148).

By the turn of the century superintendents, leading educational reformers, and some kindergartners were voicing discontent with the training provided by the private kindergarten training schools, many of which were sponsored by established kindergarten associations (Shapiro 1983, 149). A struggle to control kindergarten teacher preparation then ensued from 1893 to 1920 between normal schools and universities and within the universities' departments of education

(Shapiro 1983, 151–171).[4] The battle over teacher preparation courses mirrored the larger battles between strict Froebelians and liberal kindergartners, who increasingly became more influenced by those outside the traditional kindergarten circle. The distinct features of the kindergarten gradually were blurred with the features of the primary school through the new training courses and because of superintendents' desires to achieve a unified program.

The pressures within the school system for managerial efficiency and standardization caused the kindergarten to became an institutionalized bridge between home and school. One of the major consequences of public school linkages was evidenced in the age of entry criteria.

As exemplified in the profile of the St. Louis kindergartens, many states had to adjust their statutes to serve younger children. Most public kindergartens began by serving children aged 4 to 6 (Bloch, Seward, and Seidlinger 1989). To fit the pattern of the graded primary school and budgetary constraints, the kindergarten eventually served children for one year rather than several. As evident in today's kindergarten, the three year age span between 3 and 6 that Froebel targeted as the population to be served by the kindergarten was compacted into one year. The original multiple functions to be carried out over a three year period were eliminated, reduced, or significantly compressed in the interests of implementing the education function in the most efficient manner.

It is evident that the structure of the public school affected the function of the kindergarten. The kindergarten was markedly different before becoming attached to the schools. School sponsorship affected the population served, the hours of delivery of the service, the scope of the service, and the content of the service. The education function was the beneficiary of much attention by public school administrators, whereas the social service and social reform functions were offered little financial or administrative support. The kindergarten program functioned as an educational service, but the actual curriculum changed over time in tandem with new teacher training requirements.

THE EFFECT OF THE KINDERGARTEN'S FUNCTION ON THE STRUCTURE OF THE PUBLIC SCHOOL

The impact that the kindergarten had on the primary department is variously reported as little or none to tremendous. Most commentators, however, attribute some change in the primary curriculum and approach to the kindergarten's influence (*Report of the Education Commission of Chicago* 1898; Claxton 1900; Fisher 1905; Vandewalker 1923; McKenny 1908; Waite 1926; U. S. Bureau of Education 1914; Wesley 1957; Weber 1969; Troen 1975; Ross 1976).

Writing in *NEA: The First Hundred Years*, Edgar B. Wesley (1957) attributes to the kindergarten the   introduction of broad concepts into the elementary school's approach to education. He capsulized the underlying values of the kindergarten that were built on in the primary school as direct experience learning, self-activity, self-expression, group cooperation, play as a mode of learning, and the use of freedom rather than constraint. The decline of whipping and the growth of child welfare clinics also were attributed to the influence of the kindergarten's philosophy (p. 164).

Vandewalker was realistic in her appraisal of the integration process and acknowledged that the changes brought about by the kindergarten were also attributable to the influences of other movements of the times such as the art and manual training movement, the child study movement, and the Herbartian movement (p. 211).[5] Looking back on the changes in 1937, Alice Temple also saw a force of related influences acting on the primary school. She credits the thinking of Pestalozzi, Froebel, Parker, and Dewey with bringing "progressive" change to the schools (Temple 1937, 362). The kindergarten was one factor in moving the schools away from a didactic and formal structure.

The other major effect that the kindergarten had on the public schools was related to mothers' meetings. These meetings evolved into the Parents and Teachers Association (PTA). Fisher (1905) describes a new function of the school that was attributable to the kindergarten. She noted that the kindergarten made the school into a social and educational center. Mothers could congregate at the school and partake of meetings that provided them new avenues for social and educational exchange (p. 703):

The traditional holding of mothers' meetings also awakened the school's interest in community involvement. Increasingly, primary teachers began to hold mothers' meetings of their own, sometimes together with the kindergartners. Although the school did not achieve the degree of neighborhood concern that the kindergarten had, it did develop interest in closer ties with the home. The kindergartner's meetings with parents involving them in their children's education were forerunners of the modern Parent Teacher Associations found in most school districts in the United States today. (Ross 1976, 99)

The school adapted the function of the mothers' meetings through the Parent Teacher Association. However, as the historians cited here have noted, far-reaching social service and social reform functions of the kindergarten were lost on linkage with the school. The focus was no longer on the child and his or her home and neighborhood; instead, the child alone was seen in relation to the school's academic mission:

No longer did kindergarten teachers establish direct contact with their pupils' families; no longer did they work directly to close the gap between the immigrant or rural parents and their Americanized or urban child. In short, kindergartners lost much of their opportunity to express their humane concern for social welfare that had characterized the free kindergartens of the late nineteenth century. (Ross 1976, 99–100)

FUNCTIONAL CONSEQUENCES OF PUBLIC SCHOOL SPONSORSHIP

Linkage with the public schools resulted in functional losses with one substantial functional gain. The primary gain under school sponsorship was that the liberation-universalization function was fully realized. The kindergarten was finally available and accessible to many more children of all classes.

Under public school sponsorship, the education function reigned in conjunction with the socialization, social status, and liberation-universalization functions. The social service, social reform, and religious functions were almost completely relinquished. Vestiges of social service remained in the form of the Parent Teacher Association.

The kindergarten's attachment to the public schools elevated kindergartners to a new, more highly regarded professional status. With this gain came a loss in keeping the service open to volunteers. Consequently, without these volunteers the children received less individualized instruction. The new social status was acquired by accepting new state training and certification standards. These new routes for becoming a kindergarten teacher pleased the powerful public school administrators, university professors, and a radical faction of the old kindergarten guard, but disheartened those that continued to hold fast to Froebel's original tenets.

Unlike the discord engendered by school sponsorship over the social status function, the socialization function enjoyed a smooth transition into the public school domain. Socialization within the schools was directed and not left to chance. Children were socialized to fit into the regimen of the school system with all of its many expectations. They also were socialized into the "American" way of life with much emphasis on learning English.

As the kindergarten became more institutionalized under the schools' auspices, it increasingly served a more purely educational function. The longer it was a part of the school, the more its secondary functions were erased. The dominance of the school's educational and socialization functions in society at large overshadowed other functions the kindergarten had before linkage.

The overall objective of the schools was to create a unified elementary department. Any original function of the kindergarten that hindered meeting this goal was eliminated. In the process of change, the close-knit community of kindergartners was forced to fit into the larger and more impersonal framework of the public schools.

NOTES

1.   It is of historical significance to note that Missouri is presently a leader in the movement for school based child care and family services.

2.   Other recommendations included revamping the board of education in number and quality; "increasing the powers of the city superintendent of education"; and "appointing a business manager to oversee school contracts" (Shapiro 1983, 136).

3.   A fee system had been introduced in 1876–1877. A dollar per quarter charge was assessed those who could afford to pay. Those students who could not pay were excluded from the fee; 40 percent of the attending population did not pay. In the 1878 school year all children were admitted free. In 1881 the final step in extending the kindergarten to all children was taken when the black children in the segregated schools were offered kindergartens (Troen 1972, 223).

4.   See Chapter 9, "Froebelians at the University," of Michael Shapiro's *Child's Garden* (1983). See also Marianne N. Bloch, "Becoming Scientific and Professional: An Historical Perspective on the Aims and Effects of Early Education," in *The Formation of School Subjects: The Struggle for Creating an American Institution*, edited by Thomas S. Popkewitz, pp. 25–63, (New York and Philadelphia: The Falmer Press, 1987).

5.   The German philosopher Johann Friedrich Herbart influenced American educational thinking during the years 1890–1910. Herbart stressed the importance of character development through meaningful curriculum development. "Herbartians" formalized a five step process of curriculum design that emphasized the correlation of subjects (Tanner and Tanner 1990, 56–57).

PART III

CONCLUSION

13. Policy Implications

LEVELS OF DEBATE

This analysis has examined the debate over sponsorship of child care services and the consequences of various policy options. The debate has taken place on three levels. First, controversy over sponsorship has been on a fundamental, ideological level, striking at people's core values and belief systems. The issue of sponsorship envelopes perennial questions about how society delegates responsibility for its youngest members. Although these questions have been asked for generations, new answers are urgently needed as society heads into the twenty-first century. It is necessary to examine the basic institutions of society that uphold the social fabric for their existing and potential contributions to the children. The institutions of family, church, and school are juxtaposed with the legal, economic, health, and social service systems. The very idea of expanding beyond the family for a solution to the child care problem ignites much strife because adults are in conflict over their own priorities in arriving at a decision about where and how to provide care for the young. This debate is forever present, below the surface, laden with the many conflicting values left unarticulated. The perpetual problem of arranging care for children becomes manifest in the inevitable decision making process over the appropriate emphasis to place on various institutional settings.

The second level of the debate presumes this ongoing tension and conflict, but centers on the practical solution of the problem through policy implementation. Sponsorship has been an obstruction in the twenty year child care debate, but has taken on different facades. In the first congressional debate over the Comprehensive Child Development Act of 1971, the polemic focused on which level of government ultimately should be in control of the resources for the delivery of child care services. The final act, later vetoed by President Nixon, embraced the community control model rather than a state control model. Federal funding was to flow to smaller, rather than larger units of government.

The second federal debate of the mid-1970s revolved around the appropriateness of the schools as a presumed prime sponsor. During the recent third debate, the focus of the debate shifted to the appropriateness of the role of religious institutions as sponsors and revolved around the issue of separation of church and state. The controversy over sponsorship also involved disputes over which congressional committee would control the new service and which level of government would set the standards of care. This conflict over standards has only been shifted to the state level where interest groups will continue the battle. At every turn over the years, sponsorship has been at issue.

The research for this book suggests, however, that institutional control has been an issue and a stumbling block, and the role of the school in particular has implicitly and explicitly shaded the particular debates and the overall debate. The school's role was explicitly questioned in the 1974–1975 debate, but factored in to the other two federal legislative disputes. During the first go around under President Nixon, children's advocates who favored the community control model did so because they resisted the idea of state agencies, including state Boards of Education, setting policies and distributing funds:

Marian Edelman saw child development as the Child Development Group of Mississippi where the Head Start program had been, in her words, "perhaps *the* most important social catalyst for change in the state. It helped poor parents understand new ways of having an effect on their children's education." Child-care legislation turning control of services over to the states would have meant, she feared, control by the public schools. "In Mississippi and other southern states this action would have meant the end of parental involvement for the poor." Because she deemed that outcome intolerable, Edelman undertook to mobilize support on behalf of community control. (Steiner 1976, 100–101, citing Edelman's interview by Rochelle Beck and John Butler, "An Interview with Marian Wright Edelman," *Harvard Educational Review* 44 [February 1974]: 68); emphasis in the original

At the next juncture, a few years later, this latent animosity became manifest when the schools overtly vied for prime sponsorship.

In this last debate, which resolved itself with the block grant approach in conjunction with a specific tax plan, the presence of the school was again overshadowing. The resultant policy, in favor of certificates for the utilization of sectarian child care programs, not only comments on the importance of religion in American life and in child rearing in particular, but is further indicative of a policy germinated from a negative regard toward the current and potential role of the public schools. The CCDBG represents a strong statement by federal policy makers against a pro-active role by the public schools in the delivery of child care. The fact that Title II of H.R. 3, the school based provision, was not included in the compromise measure is telling.

During the drafting process, alliance members had to make a critical decision. Marian Wright Edelman, along with her lead lobbyists Helen Blank and Amy Wilkins and their followers within the alliance, resolved to support the inclusion of the certificate and sectarian components. This decision was grounded in a political appraisal of the situation, but the decision also was rooted in the deep historical schism between many child care advocates and public school proponents. Edelman supported the United States Catholic Conference and Orthodox Jewish constituency because she believed that their alliance in the battle for child care was of paramount importance in obtaining passage of the bill and the endorsement of a president who repeatedly had threatened to veto legislation that did not appease conservative and religious interests groups. Edelman also knew that churches constituted approximately one-third of the existing child care programs, thereby providing an infrastructure to promote and expand upon. Cognizant of the implications of the permissive church-state language, the drafters included a severability clause in the act because constitutional challenges appeared inevitable. It was the position of CDF and its allies that church-state questions should not prevent the passage of much needed child care legislation.

Nevertheless, given all of the political rationale for the course of action selected by the majority of the alliance, the animosity between the education and social work professions played a determining factor. Edelman chose to ally herself with the religious community, rather than with the education community. On the basis of this analysis, it is conjectured that the ramifications of school sponsorship appeared more threatening than the ramifications of religious sponsorship. One can only speculate at the political power base that would have been created had Edelman, the mainstream religious groups, and other members of the coalition allied themselves with the key education groups (AFT, PTA, and NEA) over the issues of church and state. Although the majority of religious organizations within the alliance opposed the sectarian provisions, they accepted Edelman's assessment of the political climate. Only a few religious groups allied themselves with the Coalition for Public Education (see Appendixes H and J).

The severance of the alliance left deep wounds in the heretofore allies. The selection of the politically expedient route by CDF and other alliance members, which condoned the certificate and discrimination provisions, provoked conflict within the alliance. Members of the coalition, including the education groups and those who were more neutral on the school issue, refused to compromise on issues of church-state separation and religious discrimination. Critics of the legislation view the inclusion of sectarian programs in the certificate program to be unconstitutional and the provisions allowing religious discrimination in hiring and admissions to be a setback in civil rights.

The lack of unity among alliance members over these issues denotes several forces persistent in shaping the debate. For one, the idea of religious institutional sponsorship was most threatening to the interests of the school proponents. Yet, the education groups were open to provisions for religious institutional involvement, as long as their programs had no sectarian content and did not discriminate in any way. They were divided among themselves as to the points of compromise. The NEA and the PTA did not want any voucher program with or without the sectarian component. The AFT, which was more willing to compromise on the idea of vouchers, drew the line on supporting passage of the bill when the sectarian provisions were added.

Another determining factor in the debate was that the education organizations could not congregate enough political clout to push Representative Hawkins' bill through Congress. In its original construction, H.R. 3 included a separate title for public school based child care and lacked the religious provisions. The design of H.R. 3 clearly contrasted with the intent of ABC, which had been drafted by alliance members. The introduction of Hawkin's bill offered an alternative vision of a national response to child care that ran counter to the advocacy community. Neither the significance of the structures or the functions it promoted satisfied the majority of the alliance. Public school proponents could not override the antischool, pro-religion and pro-consumer choice sentiments.

The history of earlier debates contributed a third force to the process of drafting and successfully passing the 1990 legislation. Edelman's long experience as a child care advocate gave her a perspective that invoked the memory of the anti-child care campaign during the 1975 debate, when conservative groups launched an aggressive mail and media assault against the "sovietization" of American children (Pierce 1976, 187). During the 1971 debate, a column by James J. Kilpatrick denigrating child care as state-controlled communes was widely circulated among key legislators and administrative staff members (Steiner 1976, 115). In the 1989–1990 debate, Edelman could have conjectured that Catholics and Orthodox Jews would lobby assertively against any child care bill that did not include their desired provisions, whereas the education groups would remain relatively silent. Edelman's political savvy and long-time leadership steered the alliance in politically safe directions.

The political and procedural machinations within the congressional committees were another force in both spurring the legislative process along and stalling the initiatives at critical junctures. Leaders in both the House and the Senate at once complicated and furthered the cause of child care.

Society wrestled with conflicts over raising its youngest members in the legislative arena. New social policy was thrashed out in response to a pressing social problem. This problem of caring for young children while their parents work already was being confronted on a practical level at which more debate has occurred.

This practical level of debate over child care sponsorship stems from the crossroads faced by the merging traditions of child care services and the kindergarten. Each tradition needs to adjust to new demands that overlap. The increased utilization of child care services by the middle and lower middle class suggest that it be considered a service independent of its social service–public welfare system base. This need to deliver a newly conceptualized service sets the stage for competitive claims to the unchartered turf. Meanwhile, the kindergarten tradition is forced to adapt to the child care demands superimposed upon it.

At the same time that child care is undergoing change, the kindergarten is continuously evolving from its own roots. The kindergarten's history is shaping its contemporary problems as it continues to develop throughout the fifty states. States currently are readjusting their statutes regarding age of kindergarten entry, the mandatory requirement that school district's offer kindergarten, and mandatory attendance in kindergarten (Education Commission of the States 1989; NAEYC Survey 1989). The antecedents to these policy decisions stem directly from the kindergarten's initial link with the schools at the onset of the twentieth century.

This study utilized several frameworks, including functional analysis, conflict theory, and an historical perspective, to tease out the consequences of policy options in these debates over sponsorship regarding the basic societal concerns about children, the appropriate role of the schools in providing the service, and the professional claim to the merging of the kindergarten and child care services. In response to the subliminal debate, child care has been presented as a multifunctional service because of the multiple aspirations adults place on rearing the next generation. These functions have been demonstrated to vary in their dominance according to the structure from which they are sponsored.

The historical perspective indicates that the questions of today are not new, but reignited questions of a previous debate over what to do with the young. Further analysis of the varying positions on sponsorship reveals an underlying tension. Implicit throughout the debate is the dichotomy of public versus private responsibility. This dialectic demands a response in every historical period. The solutions are specific to each epoch, not permanent. Such basic social problems as rearing the next generation do not get resolved and fade away, but instead are recast in new contexts.

The story of the Alliance for Better Child Care illustrates the premises of conflict theory. Coalition politics were necessary for the passage of the historic child care legislation of 1990. The actual fight for comprehensive child care legislation began twenty years earlier with Marian Wright Edelman actively piloting a coalition venture then, too. A collective voice of diverse interest groups was inevitable to override the power of conservative elements in the administration and Congress. The congregated power of these interest groups succeeded in getting the child care legislation through Congress and past the administration as part of the Omnibus Budget Reconciliation Act of 1990. The final language of the child care component of the 1990 OBRA reflects the many compromises and negotiations that had occurred along the way.

In 1976, Gilbert Steiner hypothesized that the political climate had been ripe for the 1971 legislative bill, but that the bill had been poorly constructed (pp. 116–117). He contended that the opportune moment would be a long time in arriving again. Thus, when the Act for Better Child Care (S. 5) and the Early Childhood Development and Education Act (H.R. 3) reached the conference agreement stage of a tortuous process, and time was pressing forward in one of the country's most tumultuous congressional sessions, Edelman and her team pushed relentlessly. The alliance had worked on the bill for three years, only to see it stripped out of a 1989 legislative agenda. The political ripeness of 1990 can be attributed to the bipartisan, middle class claim to child care as an issue and President Bush's precarious popularity amid the deficit reduction turmoil and Persian Gulf crisis. The language finally constructed as the milestone child care legislation is correctly heralded as historic, but it simultaneously embodies the ethos of conservative times and is far less comprehensive than the earlier vetoed Comprehensive Child Development Act of 1971.

The multifunctional nature of child care incited much of the conflict over the legislation, as did the issue of turf. The analysis of the contemporary movement highlighted the turf issues and the intertwining functions of child care. The debate over child care has been framed to proceed beyond the commonly held perception of the territorial rift attributed to the social work profession's "custodial care" function and the education profession's "education" function. Conflict theory informed the analysis by illustrating that institutional competitiveness carried the debate beyond the idea of an early childhood community challenging a didactic elementary education community. The dissension over child care involves five sectors of society competing for a service with at least nine functions. By analyzing the structure-function relationship of each sponsor, the consequences of the link become clearer.

CONCLUSIONS DRAWN FROM THE CONTEMPORARY ANALYSIS

The contemporary analysis indicates that each of the five sponsors offers advantages and disadvantages for the delivery of child care services. At this point in history a resolution to maintain a multiple sponsor approach to the child care dilemma has been arrived at on the federal level. Nevertheless, the block grant approach necessitates further allocation decisions, by means of a state plan that needs to be presented to the Secretary of Health and Human Services, as to the selection of a state's lead agency and grant recipients. The sanctioning of demand side economics through the certificate and tax credit approaches have given much credence to parental choice. Although the multifunctional aspect of child care has been retained by opting for the multiple sponsor delivery system, the selection of providers by state planners and parents will present ramifications for individual consumers, and society at large, on the basis of sponsor.

The Child Care and Development Block Grant has not moved the system farther away from the criticized socioeconomically segregated, two-tiered system in existence at the time of its passage. The low income target population of the block grant, the restructuring of the earned income disregard, and the Child Care Entitlement provision perpetuate the welfare reform function of child care and further the goals of the Family Support Act of 1988. These recent legislative initiatives substantiate the function child care performs in breaking the dependency on the welfare system. However, the emphasis on consumer choice rather than on the provision of child care facilities maintains a system of inequitably available child care centers. The degree to which the supply of child care centers will both increase and meet the needs of all classes will be tested with a reliance on market theory.

The waning nonprofit sector, composed of private nonprofit and public welfare sponsors, has been given a chance to revive its claim to child care services under the 1990 act. Whether this renewed mission will maintain the nonprofit sector's competitiveness remains to be seen. The private for-profit sector rejoiced at the outcome of the debate because the act included most of the major provisions for which they had lobbied. Tax credits, certificates, state standards, and the block grant approach enabled the proprietary sector to continue their business without sustaining undue hardship. They attained the opportunity to gain more consumers and receive grants to upgrade their services.

The state standard mandate has implications for some private providers, but the leeway in time before the standards are set and the possibility of receiving funding for improvement to offset the obstacles faced in meeting any new standards. The designation of state rather than federal standards supports proprietary interests. Large chains and many independent proprietary providers already comply with state standards and will lobby for their positions on defining standards at the state level. Family child care providers and some independent providers will withstand more difficulties in meeting the health and safety standards.

The imposition of standards will have ramifications across the sectors. Because some states currently exempt centers under religious institutional sponsorship or public schools from all or some state standards (Adams 1990; CDF 1990d; Kagan 1987, 17–18), bringing centers into compliance with new standards will affect the delivery capability of some sponsors, at least for an interim period. The consequences of the state standard provision of the CCDBG are unknown at this time, but should benefit children. The imposition of state standards represents a compromise between the present minimal standards and children's advocates desire for professionally recognized federal standards.

The CCDBG does not include a special provision for employer sponsored child care, except in the encouragement of partnerships that must be tallied in a state's annual report. The "bottom line" function of child care was recognized on the federal level. Law makers realized two important points about corporate child care. First, the existing tax incentives can suffice as inducements for employers to provide child care services, because the services themselves already benefit the company's productivity. Second, although there is much interest in employer sponsorship, it is apparent that the solution to the child care crisis is not through the provision of on-site child care centers. On-site centers are most beneficial in very circumscribed settings.

Employer involvement in solving the child care problems of employees must come from consortium efforts to support communitywide programs and through a restructuring of the workplace through noninstitutional arrangements. The workday and workweek need to be reexamined along with pay scales and the minimum wage. Important, the fight for family leave policies must continue within the corporate and government domains.

The strong sentiment about the role of the church in the provision of child care is undeniable. The religious function of child care has been given tremendous credence in this contemporary debate and its resolution. The church has not made the mistake it made in the past debate over kindergartens when it failed to appreciate the virgin territory offered by the new kindergarten programs for cultivation and inculcation of religious beliefs (Vandewalker 1923). Had religious institutions foreseen the extent to which the kindergarten would expand during the earlier era, they would have fought to retain their claim (Vandewalker 1923).

A focused examination of who supported the prevalence of the religious function in the contemporary debate, reveals a few key points about the function of child care, the role of religious organizations, the tenor of the times, and the division of power among competing interests. The implementation of a certificate program that could be used for sectarian child care is grounded in two basic ideological beliefs. First, child care involves acculturation to cultural beliefs, which include religious beliefs. Many parents seek to emphasize religious identity during the early years and, therefore, the other functions of child care must serve in either a complementary or secondary fashion. Proponents of sectarian-based care had to separate the education function from the religious, social service, and socialization functions to support their case, which argues that the establishment of the certificate program does not violate the First Amendment. Moderates drew a distinction between the provision of direct grants from the state to religious institutions and the use of certificates for the purchase of sectarian care under religious auspices.

The use of certificates for child care sprang forth from the religious ideological persuasion, but also from a second set of assumptions based on the primacy of choice. The right to parental choice in selecting child care has been a consistent and dominant theme throughout the debate of the last three years. The emphasis on choice was begun earlier in the late 1970s, when Alan Cranston introduced the Child Care Act of 1979, and the 1980s did not counter this trend. In fact, the importance of choice has influenced the school reform movement as choice gradually is being permitted within the public educational system. This issue of choice within the public school system is rife with controversy and disputed alongside the child care debate. States are implementing and debating policies that enable parents to choose schools for their children outside of their home neighborhood or district (Celis 1990a; 1990b; De Witt 1990; Fiske 1990a; 1990b; Wells 1990b). This American allegiance to the ethic of choice steered the debate over child care and was expressed candidly in the Child Care Statement of Managers included in the Conference Report on OBRA 1990:

The purpose of this block grant program is to give parents a variety of options in addressing family child care needs. Additionally, this provision is intended to build on and to strengthen the role of the family by seeking to ensure that parents are not forced by the lack of available programs or financial resources to place a child in an unsafe or unhealthy child care arrangements . . .

The managers believe that parents should have the greatest choice possible in selecting child care for their children. Thus, parents assisted under section 658E(c)(3)(B) would have complete discretion to choose from a wide range of child care arrangements, including care by relatives, churches, synagogues, family providers, centers, schools, and employers.   All such providers may be paid through grants, contracts or through certificates provided to the parents. (*Congressional Record* 10-26-90, H 12691)

The conference committee members, known as the managers, furthered parental rights and responsibilities by mandating unlimited access to their children's centers.   Although emphasis was placed on consumer choice, providers competitive interests were also protected.

The American adherence to choice is ever the more earnest when the rearing of children is of concern.   This ethic unified child care advocates and made for unusual bedfellows.   Proponents of choice included proprietary providers, Catholics, Orthodox Jews, and libertarians.   The belief that parents should be able to choose their child's form of care cut across lines of religion, political persuasion, gender, organizational ties, class, and race.   The dominance of this ideology over other values that were at stake coalesced the alliance and enabled the alliance's success in passing legislation.   This deeply held belief in choice is rooted in libertarian thinking, which values the individual's rights and abilities to exercise his or her freedom in the decision making process.   Implicit in libertarian thinking is an emphasis on the individual versus the collective and the assumption that one is a free agent.   This perspective fails to take into account class differences and negates public responsibilities for children.   The significance of this ideology that manifests itself in the CCDBG will be addressed further in the following discussion comparing the kindergarten debate to the contemporary debate.

Before moving on to analyze the implications of the kindergarten movement, the relationship of the public school structure and the service of child care needs to be examined at this conclusion of many years of intense discord over the school's claim to sponsorship.   The comparison of the five sectors competing in the contemporary debate revealed negative consequences for each sponsor.   The social service–nonprofit sector is at once responsible for the current gap in services and the stigmatization of child care because of the dominance of the welfare reform function.   Employer sponsorship was shown to advance the profitability of specific industries without furthering the overall supply of child care.   The dominance of the economic function within this sector created new problems for employees while addressing the work-family balance dilemma.   Furthermore, the discussion of this sector spotlighted latent problems with the economic order and employer-employee relations.

Private for-profit sector sponsorship of child care also revealed negative reverberations from overemphasizing the economic function of child care.   The discussion of proprietary sponsorship brought into focus the incongruity of delivering high quality care and the profit motive.   A central critique of the proprietary sponsor is the manner in which the social status function of child care operates. The low wages and high turnover rates of proprietary staff raise serious questions about the rightful role of for-profit providers. The chains were shown to be a separate category with unique consequences for the delivery of child care. In this light, the socialization function of child care becomes more provocative. When the responsibility of care for America's young is granted to chain operations, debate ought to be more vocal.

The consequences of religious organizational sponsorship has been stressed throughout the debate and in this analysis. The certificate program alone is not the only point of controversy. The so-called nondiscrimination clauses in the final act have serious ramifications for the coverage of children and the hiring of caregivers. As of this writing, insufficient safeguards are in place to guard against children being prohibited from care on the basis of religion or an otherwise competent worker being refused hire because of religious beliefs. When the supply of care is low, it is possible that a family's choice may be religious care or none at all. In some geographical areas children of a religious minority could be effectively prohibited from securing care arrangements because the majority religion dominates the market. Religious discrimination may have the effect of restricting, rather than expanding, choice. In the coming years regulations should provide additional guidance and clarification on some of the church-state issues. One fact remains certain, court challenges can be expected on the constitutionality of the legislation. Inevitably, the issues of church and state will continue to be problematic in the delivery of child care.

The public schools offer a viable alternative to all of the other sponsors, yet they were not provided with more power or control than any of their competitors. The nature of the block grant does not strengthen the school's ability to compete for funding over any other sector. Although some would argue that the schools have an edge on the amount of funding reserved for early childhood education and latchkey programs. The consequences for the school's stake in sponsorship will vary by state plans, which in turn will be influenced by state histories. Regardless of the CCDBG, which targets the population with incomes below 75 percent of the median state income, schools will still need to react to the demographic changes in their surrounding neighborhoods. Parents from all socioeconomic classes in turn will assess the school's role in providing care for their children as compared to other available providers.

The schools were shown to advance the education function, the liberation-universalization function, the economic function, the social status function, and the socialization function. They were revealed as the only sponsor that could deliver child care as a social utility. This universal attribute of the schools is considered by some an asset, to others of no special consequence, and to critics a reason for concern that child care would become compulsory and prohibitively expensive. School detractors assert that the schools will overemphasize the education function at the expense of all other functions. This concern over the consequences of linkage with the schools led to the analysis of the kindergarten movement, including a debate over sponsorship of the kindergarten.

IMPLICATIONS OF TWO HISTORICAL PERIODS

Both the similarities and differences between the present and the past debates are pertinent to the policy development process. The historical contexts are significant because they define the parameters of the debates and highlight the obstacles that need to be surmounted at specific points in time. The current era is marked by three trends converging on the delivery of child care. First, a school-education reform movement surrounds the whole issue initiated in part by a public panic stricken over the accountability of schools. This sweeping movement of reform engulfs the early childhood years from two sides while compensatory education once again is hailed as a nostrum. On the one side, the preschool years are given renewed attention with shades of the War on Poverty years of thinking. On the other side, the first grade curriculum is pushed down into the kindergarten under the guise that more "academics" *sooner* is better, causing much consternation among educators as they debate the appropriateness of curriculum content for young children.

Parents in their anxiety about attaining a competitive edge for their children turn to earlier schooling. Compounding the pedagogical dilemmas placed on the kindergarten, an overlapping group of parents caught up in the second historical trend of demographic and workplace changes, turn to the kindergarten year as a salvation after many years of scrounging for child care. The kindergarten day represents a reprise from child care problems, but necessitates adjustments in the standard half-day kindergarten program; thereby, the traditional half-day kindergarten is pushed to become an all-day program.

This push for all-day kindergartens by working parents is symptomatic of class differences and presents new problems for children. The disparity in the class system becomes evident when parents from dissimilar economic brackets turn to the schools at different points in their children's lives. Middle and lower class families turn to the kindergarten for help with child care when their child reaches the designated age for kindergarten entry required by their respective state. In contrast, upper class parents tend to start their children a year later. Concerned about the controversy over appropriate age of entry, which has some professionals claiming that children close to the cut-off date (summer birthdays) are at a disadvantage, the wealthy buy a year of time. They purchase private care and "schooling" arrangements. A detrimental social cycle is set in place whereby privileged children gain the much sought competitive edge by becoming the oldest in their cohort group. These affluent children gain further advantages by being placed in high quality private care arrangements before or during kindergarten.

The third trend affecting the child care crisis is the sense of impotency gripping the nation over the effects of global competition. The education reform movement is linked to this trend as Americans are intimidated by the advances of the Japanese and Germans, among others. Much scrutiny has been directed at the educational system and the business world. While the schools become the targets of reform in the interests of developing a more competent work force, the corporations target child care as a means of recruiting and retaining high quality workers.

If the Alliance for Better Child Care and the strength of the Children's Defense Fund are symbolic of contemporary times, a resurgence in child saving could mark the 1990s.[1] Previous decades have had an aura of aged saving with the emergence of the American Association of Retired Persons and the leadership of Representative Claude Pepper. If child saving is to take hold, the problems surrounding child care will be only a parcel of the package of tragic child welfare problems facing the nation as a result of the increased number of drug exposed infants, infants infected with AIDS, youths lost to drugs and gang warfare, and high rates of poverty with its associated consequences.

The Progressive Period was a time widely remembered for its commitment to child saving. The kindergarten cause, like child care, was one crusade among many. In sync with the tenor of today, Progressive reforms also were directed at the schools and the workplace. Reforms in the schools sprang from two movements, the move toward efficiency and bureaucratization and the diametrical thrust for the implementation of John Dewey's "progressive" philosophy. Concurrent with school reforms, the workplace reforms of the Progressive Era propelled industrialization and efficiency.[2] Most important, the early twentieth century is known for the strong labor movement that initiated many of the workplace reforms.

Here lies one of several notable differences between the contemporary period and the past. The labor movement of today lacks the fervor of the earlier years. This lack of voice has ramifications for child care, in spite of the commitment exhibited in the alliance by many key labor groups. The second crucial difference between the periods is the contrast in prevalent ideologies. The early part of this century embraced a melting pot ideology compared to the last part of the century commitment to pluralism.

The discussed valuation of parental choice is part and parcel of a pluralistic desire to maintain diverse cultural identities, which departs from the earlier goal of merging cultures into an "American" identity. This stark contrast in thought between the two periods is heuristic for understanding policy implications. Where the Progressives forged ahead in meeting common human needs, pluralists of today steadfastly defend differences at the risk of jeopardizing the attainment of solutions to basic human problems. Compromises are engaged only so far as they do not overstep cultural and institutional boundaries, unfortunately the needs of children often are left somewhere in the middle of all of these lines of demarcation.

The kindergarten crusade was distinctly different than the crusade for child care because it was motivated by an articulated philosophy. This philosophy at once unified the crusaders and directed their efforts at reform. The Froebelian base of the movement was undeniable, even after the divisions occurred among the Froebelians in their interpretation of Froebel. The child care crusade of the last twenty years lacked this base and comprises many more diverse elements. The articulation of "developmentally appropriate practices" by the National Association for the Education of Young Children (Bredekamp 1987) only recently has engaged a common denominator among factions of the child care advocates.

The kindergarten movement was clouded in a romanticism and spiritualism that the hardboiled world of the 1990s only mocks. Child care workers are less optimistic about the impact of their labor and often combat such brutal realities in the lives of children that flowery thoughts of gardens are farfetched. Kindergartners, like their day nursery counterparts, did teach in the new urban slums amidst deprived immigrant families in dire environments, but the spiritual underpinnings of Froebel brought an outlook to their daily jobs that the child care movement of today does not offer. There is no cohesive, seminal, or uplifting philosophy guiding contemporary caregivers. Nor is there any gain in social or economic prestige from child care travail.

The Progressives were deeply committed to reforming society and the kindergarten served this goal. The social reform function of child care prevailed in the early years, 1968–1973, but has since yielded to the pragmatic and entrepreneurial aspects of the economic function. The impulse to use child care for social reform was present in the activist movement of the late 1960s and during the feminist movement of the early 1970s. The interest in social reform since has been overshadowed by the more practical economic function as more and more women enter the work force. Even among women, child care is no longer the means to social reform, but rather a means of maintaining a job and the status quo. As the National Black Child Development Institute (1985) stated, the issues of community control and activism no longer shape policy.

Given the differences in the two historical periods, it becomes more understandable why the Progressives opted for the schools to sponsor the kindergarten and why contemporary actors concluded a twenty year debate with a block grant–tax credit, multiple sponsor approach. Nevertheless, as resolutions to social debates are temporary, two themes remain. First, the current federal resolution has only deferred the decision to the state level; and second, the course of the kindergarten has distinct lessons to offer, despite the differences between time periods.

The "melting pot" ideology naturally embraced the schools for sponsorship because the schools readily brought everyone into the mainstream and a unitary, newly designed American system. The kindergarten's socialization function of "Americanizing" immigrant children was shared by the schools. The pluralistic bent of our times precludes the ready acceptance of one function or sponsor over another.

This contemporary aversion toward "melting" into one stream clarifies the antagonism exhibited toward the schools, but simultaneously reflects back all the advantages of the schools that are being abandoned and all that is deleterious in our chosen course of action. If pluralism is the dominant ideology, the schools are at once a threat and a solution. The unitary system of the public schools does not satisfy the separatists' goals. However, in dialectical fashion, the public schools offer a common meeting ground for diverse cultures to sound out differences and to learn to cohabit.

Deep beneath the calls for choice and pluralism are the base sentiments of racism, class snobbery, and religious discrimination. The choice to be separate on the basis of class, race, or religion too often covers a distrust or ignorance of another's culture. With this tendency toward separatism, liberalism in the America of 1990 forsakes the public schools. Yet, ironically the analysis of the contemporary movement in the first part of this book, which compared the benefits and losses of functions by sponsors, revealed that the public educational system has much to offer that the other sectors do not.

THE CONSEQUENCES OF PUBLIC SCHOOL SPONSORSHIP

The schools function as a meeting ground for diverse cultures and promote the socialization function so necessary in a pluralistic, democratic society. This function too often is neglected and left latent. The schools also would elevate the socioeconomic status of caregivers.

Strikingly, the schools are the only sponsor that provides for the liberation-universalization function. Although Mitchell, Seligson, and Marx (1989) and others contend that *universal access* can be achieved through a multiple sponsor system of mixed public and private funds, the schools remain the only sponsor that presently assures universal delivery. In other countries, the social welfare system is utilized to assure universal coverage, but the American social welfare system is historically confined to serving the low income population.[3]

The kindergarten movement demonstrated that over a relatively short period of time public school sponsorship assured an adequate supply of kindergartens across socioeconomic classes. School sponsorship most likely could assure the same for child care. The story of Head Start is equally analogous, but reveals the negative consequence incurred from *not* looking to the schools as a primary system for program delivery. After twenty-five years, Head Start failed to reach its target population, although the Augustus F. Hawkins Human Services Reauthorization Act of 1990 should rectify the existing gap in service delivery for the half-day Head Start programs. Zigler, an instrumental leader in the Head Start movement, is now supporting school based child care.

Under school sponsorship, the service of child care would be open to the public eye and easily accessible. Rather than selecting public schools that are unmistakably in the forefront of social life, the managers of the block grant and all of the many advocates behind the final language of the bill, chose to select an alternate course of action. The ambiguity surrounding the designation of lead agencies at the state level and the emphasis on parental choice left parents in the position of scurrying around an undefined system, dependent on information and referral agencies, to find and secure appropriate care. In one sense, this delegation of authority to parents abdicates public and fiscal responsibilities of the collective. In another sense, the emphasis on choice symbolizes a lack of trust in collective decision making over the care of the young.

The story of the kindergarten verified many of the problems associated with school sponsorship and painted a very realistic appraisal of the consequences of such sponsorship. The analysis of the contemporary debate infers that the negative consequences of public school sponsorship are not any more negative than the consequences of its competitors. The school, however, has the distinction among the sponsors for being the bastion for public dispute. The school sustains the most criticism because it is the only universal system in the country. Schools also must withstand the spotlight when any problem exists regarding children and youth. Furthermore, that the school is the only universal delivery system in the American culture highlights its value system, which starkly contrasts with the values perpetuated by the other four sponsors.

CRITICISM LEVELED AT THE PUBLIC SCHOOLS

As there has been a need to filter through the mixed demands for child care, there is a pronounced need to decipher the mix of criticism aimed at the schools and properly categorize that which is significant to the child care dilemma. The overpowering outcry of discontent with the schools is steeped in fears about high illiteracy rate, high dropout rates, and low scientific performance among American youth. There is deep apprehension that American students are failing to achieve a level of competency that would permit a functioning society, both on the political and economic level. These concerns are legitimate and reflect the thinking of a cross section of the population.

The second set of criticism moves beyond the outcome of the educational system by turning its focus on that which is happening within the school walls. Apprehension exists about the safety and motivation of students. The crisis in families and cities is compounded within the schools where drugs and gangs gain control. The multiple problems of working mothers, single parent households, unemployment, inner city crime, AIDS, fiscal crisis, and teen parenting among others are confounded in the schoolday as teachers and students attempt to focus on the teaching-learning process. Critics of the schools are skeptical of the school's power and willingness to cope with yet another service such as child care.

A third set of critics debate the pedagogy of schools. The nature of these criticisms are locale specific, due to the variation in curricular approaches implemented in the schools. Further criticism reproaches the public school system for failing to provide parents with the opportunity to choose the program of their choice.

Beneath all of these negative assessments of the public schools lies an ambiguity within our culture toward the idea of public care for the under 6 population. The contemporary climate that emphasizes choice, pluralism, and the business model reflects a subliminal conflict over the provision of public education and universal child care. Inherent in the conflict is an erosion of support for the basic assumptions that sustain the American institution of public schools. Individuals and organized interest groups are confused about the legitimacy of spending hard earned money on other people's children. Although the concern for "other people's children"[4] always has been a source of conflict in American society, it recently took a new and frightening turn, exacerbated by the debate over child care services.

The choice between public and private responsibility for the care and education of young children was resolved through a mixed public and private funding approach. CCDBG represents a significant move away from the Reagan years of privatization, but continues to emphasize the individual family's responsibility in securing care. The low income target of the block grant supports the importance of the welfare reform function and perpetuates a two-tiered system of delivery. The income eligibility criteria and the amount of funding appropriated restrains the act from meeting child care needs of the middle class.

When moving past the rudimentary conflict over public versus private responsibility of care to assess the weight of the various functions of child care, each institution's overall function in society at large needs to be considered. The structure-function analysis indicated a strong connection between the institution's social role and the manner in which child care is manifested under that sponsor. Policy planners in essence will be selecting functions of child care when they designate grant recipients.

History suggests that, for pragmatic purposes, the schools inescapably will assume the new role of caregiver to the prekindergarten population; therefore, time and discourse should be expended on creating high quality school-based programs with issues of turf set aside. Due to the lack of federal policy until 1990, the many nonprofit, nonsectarian child care programs in existence at the time of the legislation unquestionably should benefit from federal funding directed at upgrading and maintaining the quality of the programs, but expansion efforts ought to include the schools if those functions of child care that the schools promote are desirable. When child care is linked to the schools, particular attention should be devoted to the social service and social reform functions, which are at risk in the structure-function relationship.

The nonprofit sector and overlapping religious sector easily could be enlisted to complement the schools by providing care for the under 3-year-old population. Family child care networks could be developed through the coordinated planning of the schools and these two sectors as Zigler and Finn-Stevenson (1989) have suggested and Kahn and Kamerman (1987) imply. The employer sector has tremendous potential for contributing resources to community based settings and closing gaps in service delivery, such as evening care and the care of ill children.

As discussed in Chapter 7, children aged 3, 4, and 5 with special needs are expected to be serviced by the public schools under the mandate of PL 99-457. They also are expected to be placed in the least restrictive environment. States are encouraged through an incentive system to establish programs and screening mechanisms for children from birth to age 3. This statute sets a policy precedent with practical implications from which to build services for all prekindergarten and kindergarten children under school sponsorship and the coordination of other agencies.

Public schools must contend with the entrenched private sector. Like the public schools, both the proprietary sector and the parochial schools present specific sponsorship dilemmas. Proprietary providers constantly must contend with the profit versus quality dilemma. Religious organizations must deal with all of the problems associated with church and state entanglement due to the need to monitor compliance with the appropriate regulations. Whether sectarian or nonsectarian in content, religious organizations have the added burden of monitoring their programs to guard against church-state and discrimination violations. The private and parochial sectors were granted much discretion under the 1990 statute. If the public schools should start to dominate a child care market, these sectors will compete as private education already competes with the public schools.

Both the contemporary and past debates demonstrate the intricate relationship of structure and function. Although the function of the kindergarten did have spinoff effects on the structure of the elementary curriculum, the structure of the schools definitely transformed the kindergarten. Opponents of school sponsorship find verification for their skepticism in the negative consequences of school linkage on the functions of the kindergarten. The kindergarten sustained serious losses under public school sponsorship and the education function superseded all secondary functions to a great degree. The Parent Teacher Association, the universal delivery of the program to the masses, and increased socioeconomic prestige for kindergartners were positive attributes of school association. The loss of the social service and social reform were negative consequences. Although more controversial, the religious function also was lost on school linkage.

The kindergarten story indicates that structure clearly has an impact on function. Plans to expand high quality, early childhood programs through the schools should be targeting reforms at the basic structure of the school. Rather than focusing on the program itself which has been extremely well articulated by the National Association for the Education of Young Children in DAP and other competitive models such as Montessori, High/Scope, Bank Street and Distar, policy should be directed at implementing structural changes. The 1988 report, *Right from the Start*, by the National Association of State Boards of Education (NASBE) is a maverick position statement. All of the lists of safeguards presented earlier in the text by the different interest groups can be traced to lessons of the kindergarten. A comparative analysis of the different safeguards does not reveal major points of contention.[5]

Referring back to Gwen Morgan's categorization of the three positions on public school involvement—not desired, accepted with safeguards, accepted without the need for safeguards—this book's research findings support the middle path. Schools need to be engaged as key players in the provision of child care, but safeguards in the form of structural changes must be implemented. If the multifunctional aspect of child care is to be assured, with the education function in balance with the other functions, then the organization of the schools must change.

The changes that are necessary for the early childhood years are also necessary for the elementary years. The National Association for the Education of Young Children defines early childhood as the years from birth through age 8. This issue of continuity of program structure around the individual child through his or her school experience has long been an issue championed by Bettye Caldwell. The concern for continuity includes a holistic perspective that sees children in a familial context of being a sibling. Planning programs for children should include a long-range perspective that includes the developmental span of the individual child, the maintenance of a cohort group, and the ability to include siblings in the developmental program. The attachment of early childhood to the schools facilitates transportation problems of parents and encourages family communication.

A latent consequence of not moving forward with child care in the schools is that not only is the idea of public education questioned, but the whole school age population is left in a lurch. The changes needed in the earliest years are the same changes needed in the primary years. NASBE recognized these twin agendas and attempted to harness two reform movements with common goals into one.

LESSONS FROM THE KINDERGARTEN: SAFEGUARDS

The look back in time to the kindergarten confirms these two agendas for reform and unveils the locus of some of the problems' origins. It is not sufficient to conclude that linkage with the schools will unavoidably cause the same problems for child care as in the past such linkage had on the kindergarten. Kindergartners and kindergarten crusaders during the Progressive Era did not enjoy the hindsight available today as crossroads are faced by policy makers. It seems cavalier and simplistic to avoid the schools as sponsor, instead the past should be used as fertile ground for the construction of safeguards and policy decisions. Knowledge of the past can incur a deliberated policy that shifts events and chains of reactions from occurring in an ensconced path to a newly inaugurated path. Whereas kindergartners of the past stumbled into the schools, today's advocates and planners have the option of more deliberation.

Several themes from the past debate that reappear in the contemporary debate intimate specific areas for policy development. Distinctive practices of the kindergarten before school sponsorship need to be retrieved. The most crucial reform that would promote change through restructuring would be to move forward with NASBE's proposed early childhood units in the schools. These units could include 3 year olds like the multiage groupings of the original kindergarten. The 3-year-old population seems to be a very vulnerable group whenever contemporary policy directions are debated. The Early Childhood Education and Development Act (H.R. 3) was criticized for not specifically considering 3 year olds in either the school-based title or the block grant title aimed at infants and toddlers. The present trend of public school involvement in early childhood is targeted at half-day programs for 4 year olds (Mitchell et al. 1989).

Early childhood units would simultaneously address the child care problem for prekindergarten children aged 3, 4 and 5; address school-age care problems on the site of the school; attack the appropriate age of entry dilemma because children would be in multiage groups; encourage individualized teaching on the part of teachers who would be forced to assess individual growth patterns; encourage cooperative learning from children; and offer family style age groups in an era that succumbs to age stratification and institutionalized patterns of separating siblings. The early childhood unit would protect the early childhood theoretical orientation while establishing a model program for the primary department to imitate. A division for early childhood designed in a comprehensive manner is much less susceptible to the dominance of the general school structure than its counterpart of a one year add on.

These units would reinstate the need for the "kindergarten director." In Zigler's model, the leader of the full service early childhood operation is the "liaison" person. The Bank Street–Wellesley report on public school involvement in early childhood programming asserted the pivotal position that leadership performs (Mitchell et al. 1989). According to the authors, administrative leaders trained in early childhood development and pedagogy make a significant difference in the realization of high quality programs, as does the organization of the administrative structure. One of the disadvantages of school sponsorship in Zigler's model and in other school based programs is that the position of liaison person or early childhood unit administrator most often would need to meet state Department of Education administrative standards. This certification standard could have the opposite effects of ensuring a high quality staff in the long term while prohibiting from participation those early childhood leaders presently without the certification.[6]

The early kindergartens (kindergartens that served mixed ages) had directresses concerned solely with the kindergarten child. These lost practices could have safeguarded the original intent of the kindergarten. Shapiro (1983) flagged the role gender played in the suppression of these practices. The predominantly female kindergarten directresses were seen as expedient positions by male superintendents who were ignorant of or disinterested in the methodology of Froebel or his followers. When Superintendent Harris introduced the kindergarten into the St. Louis schools, he had an overriding agenda that envisioned the kindergarten as a preparatory bridge to the academic world. He did not emphasize the intrinsic value of that time in childhood, but saw it as a means to the more academic stage.[7]

Right from the Start (NASBE 1988) does not share Harris's limited "means to an end" perspective. Harris's position, however, does share some of the compensatory education perspective, which suggests that certain populations are more at risk than others. Compensatory education theory is but one of several different research threads that focus on the early childhood years and from which the plan provided by NASBE builds.

The implementation of early childhood units under the leadership of administrators trained in early childhood theory are not the only necessary safeguards. Safeguards must be implemented that assure adequate parent involvement so crucial to the well-being of young children. The old family focus of the kindergarten needs to be reinstated with the modern ecological understanding of development. Policies emanating from Head Start and the field of special education that mandate parent involvement, parent representation, and parent decision making powers need to be incorporated into the early childhood units and elementary school experiences. Head Start recognizes the different levels of parent involvement also considered in the early days of the kindergarten. A movement for strengthening parent and school relations is underway, exemplified by the work of James Comer in the New Haven public schools, the Missouri Parents as First Teachers program built from the work of Burton White, and the Harvard Family Research Project under the direction of Heather Weiss, to name but a few.[8]

The kindergarten strategy of home visits must be rekindled and implemented in a collaborative approach with social agencies.[9] The acceptance of home visits by vast numbers of teachers or their unions is unrealistic to expect, but relations between school and home can be instituted and strengthened in numerous ways. This goal of linking home and school to meet the multifaceted needs of children and their families necessitates coordinated efforts on the part of many professions.

Support for the PTA that grew out of the kindergartners' mothers' meetings must be actively encouraged. Consideration should be given to recruitment problems across classes and cultures. The PTA is in the process of adapting itself to the demographic and social changes of modern life. To be a viable institution it needs to develop programs around the work schedules of parents.

Beyond the many ways of involving parents in the daily lives of their children, structural changes must occur in the institutions training teachers–caregivers and administrators. In the great appeal for coordination among agencies, the departmental divisions in higher education have been spared the spotlight. The kindergarten story and the more contemporary evolution of early childhood departments within schools of education underscore the need for interdisciplinary training of practitioners. The new early childhood educator, reminiscent of the normal school kindergartner, needs to develop a social work perspective. On another level, the social welfare and education researchers need to share lenses and communicate in more forums. The social welfare contribution to the field of early childhood has been supplanted by the field of developmental psychology, which informs both social work and education. The social welfare tradition should not be excluded in building the new early childhood services in this country. Everpresent animosities, which were exhibited during the recent legislative debates on child care, are destructive and counterproductive to the spirit of coordination. The social work tradition needs to imbue the early childhood community with a sense of history and politics; an understanding of how social problems develop; and strategic knowledge about how to coordinate and integrate diverse agencies. The social work tradition provides a broader framework than early childhood pedagogy; it includes the familial and social context within which children thrive. The education profession provides a preventive and developmental model that child care has adopted as it moved away from the social work focus on pathological families. With all the multiple social problems within which child care functions, traditional social work knowledge is useful.

The kindergarten began as a flexible concept, but became an entrenched school based model with new fiscal restraints that affected the quality of the programs. The current debate over child care has been preoccupied with the definition and imposition of quality standards. It is essential that the schools be brought into this debate and held accountable for assuring higher than minimum quality standards. The schools must become models that raise the competitive grounds for the private sector. Lazerson's study of the Massachusetts kindergartens underscored how cost efficiency and cost containment in large bureaucracies affect new programs, especially those targeted at the young. The new voice of advocacy and the rumblings of child saving, along with rich research bases, must hold back these tendencies. Helen Blank (1985) and Gwen Morgan (1985) correctly include among their listed safeguards stipulations about maintaining small class sizes and low teacher-child ratios.

As the list of safeguards spirals, critics of the schools again decry the costliness of any endeavor to expand the school's reach. Education reform has been placed high on the nation's domestic agenda, but budgetary concerns are forever present. Fiscal concerns are real, but not unsurmountable especially if turf issues are renegotiated so that limited resources, as well as squandered and untapped resources, are used collectively.

MODELS FOR POLICY IMPLEMENTATION

Vandewalker wrote in 1907 about the "slow march" of the kindergartens into the schools. The evolution of a universally accessible, multifunctional child care system will also entail a "slow march" into the schools. Zigler's model of the Schools of the 21st Century offered a guidepost and foretold the path that this march will take, now that the federal government has redirected the debate back to the states.

The states have jurisdiction over the schools and can take the lead in implementing beneficial changes. Many of these changes will include reforms in state statutes, as were implemented during the kindergarten movement. Zigler's model simultaneously presumed the revelations of the kindergarten's history and recognized the impending variables of the contemporary child care debate. The model he and his colleagues offered is helpful to counteract the negative consequences of school linkage because it is comprehensive in nature. Well-intended state Board of Education policy makers who have expended some time contemplating the many facets of the child care–early childhood debate, but are more focused on general school reform, risk implementing the shortsighted 4 year old, half-day preschool programs and all-day kindergarten programs, which address only part of a multifaceted problem. Too often the solution to a social problem exacerbates other problems or misreads the problem. Such is the case in the extension of days and programs that fill up the extended amount of time that children spend in group care with academics (Carmody 1989, 20; Elkind 1987b; Olsen and Zigler 1989). The School of the 21st Century is a well-conceived model that does not extend academic work traditionally geared to older children down into the early years.

A publicly supported universal early childhood system is achievable through the School of the 21st Century model. However, at this stage in history the model is proposed as a fee-based system in which parents pay according to income level. Allocation decisions are to follow the precedent set by Chapter I of the Elementary and Secondary Education Act of 1965 by distributing federal money to districts that serve disadvantaged populations. Building on the traditional state and local systems of financing education, Zigler proposes targeting limited federal resources to those most in need, a policy advocated by the Alliance for Better Child Care throughout the debates on the CCDBG.

The 21st Century model is in sync with the current climate of thinking—the coordination and integration of agencies and funding sources. The model presupposes idiosyncratic district and state histories of program development. In this regard, Zigler embraced the old neighborhood concept of the early kindergartners who were committed to social reform. The concept of neighborhood must be safeguarded. Once the kindergarten became a part of a centralized bureaucracy during the Progressive Era, the service lost its flexibility to respond to the unique needs of specific neighborhoods.

Zigler and his colleagues proposed a model that responds to existing programs by "piggybacking" on them. The full-service school avoids the trend of duplication. The mission of the 21st Century School is to bring families into a system that offers multiple services in an easily accessible manner.

When Zigler first introduced his model he centered his argument on the old community control notion or social reform function of child care, too often viewed as mutually exclusive to public school control:

Parents do not need children who read at age four, but they do need affordable, good quality child care. The most cost-effective way to provide universally available—again, not compulsory—care would be to work from the school. I am advocating a return to the concept of the community school as a local center for all the social services required by the surrounding neighborhood. (Zigler 1987b, 258)

In *Early Schooling* (1987), Bertha Campbell, the retired head of the New York State Education Department's Bureau of Child Development and Parent Education, wrote: "There is an unfortunate perception that Head Start and day-care programs are locally controlled and belong to the people, whereas schools are bureaucratic organizations that pay only lip service to parental involvement" (p. 73). Schools originally were conceived as community-based programs autonomous of state and federal influence. Over time the state and federal role has grown greater. Local schools have lost control in many areas, but to degrees that differ by state. A lack of community control is related to this imposition of federal and state mandates, but also symptomatic of the relationship of the educational system's bureaucracy and parents. Parent participation also differs by district according to size and the composition of the population.

Disenfranchised and apathetic parents, as well as the process by which communication flows between school and family, need to be the focus of reforms. In this quest for reform, the schools have become the victims of the misguided perception that other sectors of society can provide better services for the young or offer community control in a more idealized form. Whether the youngest are better served under one auspice or another is one question, but it is undeniably tied to the whole issue of how the public schools need to be revived for all children.

Writing from his experiences with large, urban school systems, Joseph P. Viteritti, a former special assistant to the chancellor of New York City schools and director of a transitional team for the superintendent of Boston public schools, in "Urban Governance and the Idea of a Service Community" (1989), presented a clearly articulated, historically based rationale for a service oriented, community controlled school. Viteritti proposed a reorganization of the urban school system based on two major strategies: (1) to invite participation on the "street level" by community members, and (2) to operate with school-based management. In keeping with the Zigler model, Viteritti conceived of the school as a focal point for community services with a network of services emanating from the local school. Viteritti's "school-based service center" is offered as a model for at-risk adolescents, but his concept includes the entire restructuring of the urban school system and the system's relationship with local government. He encourages the inclusion of an educational commissioner within the City Hall cabinet of agency executives, all of whom are appointed by the mayor who is then held politically accountable for the appointee's activities. In Viteritti's vision, the school system is "an integral part of a complex network of services designed to accommodate the greater needs of children" (p. 119).

The political and managerial structural reforms would enable the school to function differently in the community. Building on effective schools research and the experience of those urban systems that have tried school-based management, Viteritti claimed that a new vitality can flow through the schools on a street level and offer the additional needed services. The goal is to create an atmosphere of cooperation among parents and professionals over the issue of service delivery without the encumbrance of unnecessary politics that are bartered at a level removed from the lives of school participants. Parents will become engaged at the building level when services are available and the decisions are made within the shared domain, rather than at a distant district level.

Viteritti traces the history of the urban school system from the era of Progressive reforms that had adapted the scientific management model. His thesis is that the Progressive apolitical, bureaucratic model must be revamped for urban youth who rely on government for health, recreation, social, and protective services (Viteritti 1989, 114). The separatism of the educational system in society has left the school isolated from all of the other primary institutions serving children:

The separatism of schools has meant that public institutions where children spend most of their time are not part of the formal network of agencies that are capable of providing a variety of important services. Thus, cooperation and coordination among service providers becomes difficult. (Viteritti 1989, 114)

The schools are the vital link to urban children and must be coordinated and integrated with other social agencies. Boundaries of professional jurisdictions are destructive to the goal of delivering needed services.

Effective schools research is at odds with developmental research (Walsh 1989). Again, competing interest groups and entrenched professional traditions inhibit progress toward education reform. The perspective of early childhood advocates does not include the suggested reforms of those outside of their discipline. Conversely, effective schools researchers and administrators often fail to hear the voices of early childhood educators and developmentalists. These conflicting viewpoints, initiated in the earlier debate over kindergarten sponsorship, need to enter a stage of negotiation and compromise. *Right from the Start* (NASBE) and the National Education Association's 1990 position statement on early childhood and the schools are harbingers of this stage.

In "Changes in Kindergarten: Why Here? Why Now?" which discusses current policy trends in Virginia's kindergartens, Daniel J. Walsh (1989) arrived at a conclusion similar to that reached in this book:

The issue of what society should do and expect in the early years of public schooling is an important and complex one. In addressing this issue, early childhood educators must resist the temptation to be myopic. To argue that such-and-such is bad because it is happening in preschool or kindergarten, or to argue that certain practices may be appropriate for educating older children but not for young children (e.g., Elkind, 1986) ignores the reality that many of these practices are inappropriate for any child. (p. 389)

Walsh reviewed curricular changes over the years and the competing research bases that inform policy. Germane to this analysis over sponsorship of child care is the notion that policy initiatives often are misguided. The concerns about the impact schools will have on child care's functions is legitimate, but identifying the school as the problem is not sufficient.

POLICY DIRECTION: STRUCTURAL REFORMS

Now is the time to direct our energy to systemic reforms that will benefit children in the early childhood years as well as children in the elementary years. The contemporary analysis of the five sectors offering child care highlighted the advantages and disadvantages of the schools; the second analysis of the kindergarten movement highlighted the areas in need of safeguarding and reform. Both movements confirmed the impact of structure on function, thereby indicating that concern over function should be tackled by examining the structure.

Both Zigler and Viteritti offered models that focus on structural arrangements, in contrast to much of the early childhood literature that instead focused on function by emphasizing curriculum and program content. Viteritti and Zigler's structural reforms retained the image of a network of services germinating from the school. Zigler and Viteritti's services delivered the education, socialization, social status, economic, social service, social reform, and liberation-universalization functions of child care. Cognizant of apprehensions by "community control" advocates about school sponsorship of child care, both reformers contended that cooperative community action could be achieved through their models.

To achieve the maximum benefits of child care's multifunctional nature, the link between the service and the sponsor must be examined carefully. When the analysis has pointed to the potential of the schools, the structure of the school and the school's role in society at large too often become impediments that halt effective dialogue. The analysis of the contemporary debate indicated that the schools are on equal footing with other sectors as to respective gains and losses, but that each sponsor places different degrees of emphasis on the various functions of child care. Value judgments as to the importance of different functions will determine the selection of sponsors. If the functions that the schools offer are desirable, then more resources and policy attention should be directed at the schools. If the socialization, liberation-universalization, education, and social status functions are valued then schools should still be considered as key sponsors of the service, as long as the consequences of sponsorship are addressed in a comprehensive manner and structural reforms implemented. Deliberated plans for action could build the social service and social reform functions into the delivery model offered by the schools. Comprehensive approaches, such as found in the School of the 21st Century model or Viterritti's street level social agency school, begin with an understanding that traditional views of the school's structure and overall function in society demand to be challenged.[10]

On net balance, the schools are the strongest contender of the five alternatives for collectively assuming responsibility for children. The other sectors cater to different assumptions about responsibility and emphasize functions other than those associated with public school sponsorship; that is, religious, economic, welfare reform, social service.[11] Public schools provide the only egalitarian means of caring for the young. They offer the potential of creating a universally available and accessible system. The legislation that resulted from the recent 1987–1990 debate indicated that embracing the liberation-universalization function of child care, however, is not foreseeable in the near future.

A system of early childhood programs delivered through the public schools was envisioned by Canadian social analyst Hollis Joe (1981). His proposal promoted the liberation-universalization function of child care and offered a unique method for funding a school-based system. In Joe's perspective children are regarded as national resources and the responsibility of the public. He argued that the rewards of children benefit the collective and, therefore, should be a collective responsibility. Writing from a feminist perspective, Rothman (1989) also contended that the costs of child care ought to be envisioned as a societal responsibility, otherwise children would be viewed as burdens borne by individuals and families (Rothman 1989, 103).

The congressional debates over child care have framed the service as a private good, but according to Joe (1981) child care cannot be viewed as a private good for four reasons: (1) the upper and middle classes will be the only classes capable of affording high quality care; (2) private industry will provide the service only where profit is possible; (3) it is not the type of service for which long-term demand can be accurately predicted and, therefore, would not respond quickly to immediate increases in demand; and (4) the purchasers of the service are not the actual consumers (Joe 1981, 99). In Joe's model child care is considered a public utility and financed accordingly, with the service delivered and administered through the public school system.

Joe proposed the institutionalization of a "Human Resources Development Tax," which would be a progressive tax on industrial profits. In his scheme, the financial burden of the service of child care would be split equally between general tax revenues and the progressive industrial profit tax. Although Americans balk at such a suggestion, Joe offered an alternative funding scheme that conforms to the findings of this research. He identified the unique attributes of the schools and the responsibility of industries to look beyond their own specific interests.

Zigler has projected that Americans eventually will accept a tax for child care when the unrest over labor force participation by mothers is set aside (Zigler 1987, 14). Until then, he advocates the sliding fee schedule with a mixed funding source. Albeit high quality child care is expensive, the fiscal concerns over child care can be overcome. Parents and the general public need to be educated as to the variation in degrees of available quality care. Most important, the political will must be summoned to rally forward with child care beyond the reach of the Omnibus Budget Reconciliation Act of 1990.

Turf will continue to block pro-active policies, but a vision of cooperation and coordination is consistently being expressed as desirable by representatives of diverse persuasions. Partnerships will arise when common goals are defined. The conflict over who ultimately is responsible for children undergirds the entire debate, which has become embroiled in the more base concerns over who profits from a service: corporations, providers, the economy, the family unit, or the children? The nation once again must entertain the question that appeared during the kindergarten movement: At what age should universal public education begin? The new movement adds the following questions: At what age should universal public child care begin? Is there a difference? What do we as a nation want to achieve through our child care system?

The multifunctional nature of child care must be pushed further in the public's mind so that the ramifications of policy directions become visible. The latent consequences of certain sponsor-function links could prove detrimental to the nation's best interests in assuring the competency, well-being, and cooperative spirit of the next generation.

When considering how child care functions for adults, it cannot be overemphasized that the use of child care as a bridge to balance work and family commitments is only a partial solution to the challenges of working and raising children at the turn of the twentieth century. Changes in the workplace and workday must accommodate the natural desires of parents and children to be together, and for parents to carry out all of the other household responsibilities that they shoulder. Whatever solutions are adopted, the delivery of child care must be offered in conjunction with changes in the financing of the service so that caregivers are not undervalued or exploited. Child care offers an institutional solution, but must be delivered in tandem with corporate and government family leave policies and novel work scheduling policies.

Society is grappling with new arrangements in work and family life that are placing modern pressures on old institutions. The service of child care and the kindergarten are at crossroads. It is hoped that the new institution which merges the historical traditions will be clearly articulated and that the needs of children supersede the competing needs of institutions.

NOTES

1.   Dr. T. Berry Brazelton, along with many others, initiated the organization, Parent Action in 1988 and then reorganized it in 1990. The purpose of the group is to lobby on behalf of families (Lawson 1990a).

2. A theme common to both periods is the tenuousness of the school superintendent's position during times of rapid change, urban unrest, depleted budgets, and technological pressures for efficiency. Shapiro (1983) remarked on the tendency of superintendents to rely on new managerial skills. According to "Beseiged Urban School Chiefs Are Dropping Out" (Daley 1990), many modern day superintendents of large urban school districts are either retiring from their positions or seeking new employment. In an attempt to counter the pressures bombarding superintendents, the University of Pennsylvania began a special training program for superintendents. The one year program instructs those interested in superintendencies on a wide range of related issues: social work, employment trends, health issues, labor relations, community relations, and finance (Daley 1990, 13).

3. For cross cultural comparisons of child care systems, see Kamerman (1989); Kamerman and Kahn (1989); Tietze and Ufermann (1989), and Clinton (1990). A discussion on the restricted, residual nature of the American public welfare system is beyond the scope of this book.

4. *Other people's children* is borrowed from Sheila M. Rothman, "Other People's Children: The Day Care Experience in America," *The Public Interest* 30 (Winter 1973), pp. 11–27.

5. Although there is a disparity on how closely aligned different perspectives are in the field of early childhood, the field seems to have gathered enough strength recently to plunge forward into the schools with a platform from which to advocate changes. This platform is a necessary vision to guide the process and confront the system so that a direction is in sight for pro-active planning.

6. Certification standards for early childhood programs under state Departments of Education, or for that matter state Departments of Social Services, need to be developed with utmost consideration given to the design of an appropriate course of study, one that is interdisciplinary in nature.

7. Shapiro (1983), Mitchell et al. (1989), and Linkins (1990) have emphasized the vision and leadership abilities of administrators as key factors in the success of implemented early childhood programs.

8. See Deborah Cohen, "Parents as Partners: Helping Families Build a Foundation for Learning," *Education Week*, (May 9, 1990), pp. 13, 15, 20.

9. The idea of home visits dovetails the development of family-based child care settings. Linkage with other agencies could promote better home-school relations. As one example, the October 1990 issue of the Children's Defense Fund's newsletter described a program undertaken by a library system known as Project LEAP (Library's Educational Alternative for Preschoolers), which involves librarians visiting family care

providers and centers with books and curriculum packages. The home-school link needs to be coordinated with other social services.

10. Structural reform of the school system to deliver high quality child care can be carried out within the general aura of interest in education reform. Several national school-based projects are underway that focus reform efforts on structural changes: (1) the Mastery in Learning Project (2) the Coalition of Essential Schools; (3) the National Network for Educational Renewal; and (4) the High Success Program on Outcome-Based Education. (For an explanation of each project, see "The Danforth Foundation Links Four National School-Based Projects" in *Doubts and Certainties*, the newsletter of the NEA Mastery in Learning Project, 4, no. 10 (June 1990), p. 4.) In addition to these projects, another example of coordination and use of the schools as the forum for delivering services is exemplified in the mission of the nonprofit Cities in Schools organization. The Cities in Schools project is a nationwide program founded in 1977 and currently operating in fifty cities. The program delivers social services via the elementary school building and provides home visitors to prevent at-risk youngsters from dropping out of the system (Marriott 1990b).

11. The economic function and the socialization function operate under all of the sponsors, but the economic function is most pronounced under for-profit and corporate sponsorship. The schools actualize the familial level of the economic function for consumers of child care. Under school sponsorship, the economic function also operates on the organizational level because the schools gain financial rewards from child care operations and hire more staff as a result of offering the service.

Appendix A

Charter Members of the Alliance for Better Child Care, February 1987

American Academy of Pediatrics
American Federation of State, County, and Municipal Employees, AFL-CIO
American Federation of Teachers, AFL-CIO
American Psychological Association
American Public Welfare Association
Association of Junior Leagues
Child Care Action Campaign
Children's Defense Fund
Child Welfare League of America
Coalition of Labor Union Women
Communications Workers of America, AFL-CIO
Family Resource Coalition
General Board of Church and Society of the United Methodist Church
Girls Clubs of America, Inc.
International Ladies' Garment Workers Union, AFL-CIO
National Association for the Education of Young Children
National Black Child Development Institute
National Council of Churches, Child Advocacy Office/Ecumenical Child Care Network
National Council of Jewish Women
National Council of La Raza
National Council of Negro Women
National Education Association
National Organization for Women
National Parent-Teacher Association
National Women's Law Center
Service Employees International Union, AFL-CIO
United Church of Christ, Office for Church and Society
Women's Equity Action League
Women's Legal Defense Fund
YWCA of the USA, National Board

Source: National Association for the Education of Young Children

Appendix B

Members of the Alliance for Better Child Care, April 14, 1988

Amalgamated Clothing and Textile Workers Union
Amalgamated Transit Union
American Academy of Child and Adolescent Psychiatry
American Academy of Pediatrics
American Association for Marriage and Family Therapy
American Association of Classified School Employees
American Association of Psychiatric Services for Children
American Association of University Women
American Council of Nanny Schools
American Federation of Government Employees
American Federation of Labor and Congress of Industrial Organizations (AFL-CIO)
American Federation of State, County, and Municipal Employees, AFL-CIO
American Federation of Teachers, AFL-CIO
American Home Economics Association
American Jewish Committee
American Orthopsychiatric Association, Inc.
American Postal Workers Union, AFL-CIO
American Psychological Association
American Public Welfare Association
Americans for Democratic Action
Association for Regulatory Administration in Human Services
Association of Junior Leagues, Inc.
Bakery, Confectionery, and Tobacco Workers International Union
B'nai B'rith Women, Inc.
BPW/USA
Bread for the World
Camp Fire, Inc.
CATALYST
Catholic Charities, U.S.A.
Center for Child and Family Studies of the Far West Lab
Center for Law and Social Policy
Center for Women Policy Studies
Child Care Action Campaign
Child Care Employees' Project
Child Care Law Center

Child Care Nutrition Program Sponsors' Forum
Child Welfare League of America
Children's Defense Fund
The Children's Foundation
Church Women United
Christian Children's Fund, Inc.
Church of the Brethren
Citizen Action
Coalition of Labor Union Women
Committee for Children
Communication Workers of America, AFL-CIO
Community Nutrition Institute
Conference of Mayors
Council for Early Childhood Professional Recognition
Council for Exceptional Children
Council of Chief State School Officers
Department for Professional Employees, AFL-CIO
Division for Early Childhood/Council for Exceptional Children
The Elementary School Center
Epilepsy Foundation of America
Family Resource Coalition
Food Research Action Center
Future Homemakers of America
General Board of Church and Society of the United Methodist Church
General Board of Global Ministries of United Methodist Church
Girls Clubs of America, Inc.
High/Scope Educational Research Foundation
Industrial Union Department, AFL-CIO
International Ladies Garment Workers' Union
International Union of Electronic, Electrical, Salaried, Machine and Furniture Workers,
     AFL-CIO
Lutheran Office for Government Affairs
Mexican American Women's National Association
NA'AMAT USA
National Association of Child Care Resource and Referral Agencies (NACCRRA)
National Association for Family Day Care
National Association for the Education of Young Children
National Association of Community Action Agencies
National Association of Commissions for Women
National Association of Early Childhood Specialists in State Departments of Education
National Association of Elementary School Principals
National Association of Hospital Affiliated Child Care Programs
National Association of Letter Carriers

National Association of Social Workers
National Association of School Psychologists
National Association of the State Directors of Child Development
National Association of Working Women—9 to 5
National Black Child Development Institute, Inc.
National Center for Clinical Infant Programs
National Child Abuse Coalition
National Coalition for Campus Child Care, Inc.
National Committee for the Prevention of Child Abuse
National Community Action Foundation
National Community Education Association
National Congress of Parents and Teachers
National Consumer League
National Council of Catholic Women
National Council of Jewish Women
National Council of La Raza
National Council of Negro Women
National Council of the Churches of Christ, Child Advocacy Project
National Council on Family Relations
National Education Association
National Head Start Association
National Jobs with Peace Campaign
National Jewish Community Relations Advisory Council
National League of Cities
National Network of Runaway and Youth Services
National Organization for Women
National Puerto Rican Forum
National Urban League, Inc.
National Women's Law Center
National Women's Political Caucus
The Newspaper Guild
NOW Legal Defense and Education Fund
Office and Professional Employees International Union
Parent Cooperative Preschools International
Presbyterian Church (U.S.A.)
Public Employee Department, AFL-CIO
Save the Children
School Age Child Care Project
Service Employees International Union, AFL-CIO
Society for Research in Child Development
Southern Association on Children Under Six
Union of American Hebrew Congregations
Unitarian Universalist Association of Congregations in North America

United Auto Workers
United Church Board for Homeland Ministries
United Church of Christ

Source: Children's Defense Fund

Appendix C

The Following Members of the Alliance for Better Child Care
Endorsed The Act for Better Child Care as of January 23, 1989

Amalgamated Clothing and Textile Workers Union
Amalgamated Transit Union
American Academy of Child and Adolescent Psychiatry
American Academy of Pediatrics
American Association for Marriage and Family Therapy
American Association of Classified School Employees
American Association of Psychiatric Services for Children
American Federation of Government Employees
American Federation of Labor and Congress of Industrial Organizations (AFL-CIO)
American Federation of State, County, and Municipal Employees, AFL-CIO
American Federation of Teachers, AFL-CIO
American Home Economics Association
American Orthopsychiatric Association, Inc.
American Postal Workers Union, AFL-CIO
American Psychological Association
Association for Regulatory Administration in Human Services
Association of Junior Leagues, Inc.
Bakery, Confectionery, and Tobacco Workers International Union
BPW/USA
Bread for the World
Camp Fire, Inc.
CATALYST
Center for Child and Family Studies of the Far West Lab
Center for Women Policy Studies
Child Care Action Campaign
Child Care Employees' Project
Child Care Nutrition Program Sponsors' Forum
Child Welfare League of America
Children's Defense Fund
The Children's Foundation
Church Women United
Christian Children's Fund, Inc.
Church of the Brethren
Citizen Action
Coalition of Black Trade Unionists

Coalition of Labor Union Women
Committee for Children
Communication Workers of America, AFL-CIO
Community Nutrition Institute
Council for Exceptional Children
Council of Chief State School Officers
Council of Jewish Federations
Department for Professional Employees, AFL-CIO
Division for Early Childhood/Council for Exceptional Children
Elementary School Center
Epilepsy Foundation of America
Family Resource Coalition
Food Research Action Center
Future Homemakers of America
General Board of Church and Society of the United Methodist Church
General Board of Global Ministries of United Methodist Church
Gray Panthers
High/Scope Educational Research Foundation
Industrial Union Department, AFL-CIO
International Ladies Garment Workers' Union
International Union of Electronic, Electrical, Salaried, Machine and Furniture Workers, AFL-CIO
Lutheran Office for Government Affairs
NA'AMAT USA
National Association for the Education of Young Children
National Association of Commissions for Women
National Association of Letter Carriers
National Association of Social Workers
National Association of the State Directors of Child Development
National Association of Working Women—9 to 5
National Black Caucus and Center on the Aged, Inc.
National Black Child Development Institute, Inc.
National Coalition for Campus Child Care, Inc.
National Committee for the Prevention of Child Abuse
National Community Action Foundation
National Consumer League
National Council of Negro Women
National Council of the Churches of Christ, Child Advocacy Project
National Council on Family Relations
National Council on the Aging, Inc.
National Federation of Federal Employees
National Head Start Association
National Network of Runaway and Youth Services

National Puerto Rican Forum
National Women's Law Center
National Women's Political Caucus
The Newspaper Guild
Office and Professional Employees International Union
Parent Cooperative Preschools International
Parents Action Committee
Public Employee Department, AFL-CIO
Rainbow Coalition
Save the Children
School Age Child Care Project
Service Employees International Union, AFL-CIO
Society for Research in Child Development
Southern Association on Children Under Six
Union of American Hebrew Congregations
United Auto Workers
United Cerebral Palsy Association, Inc.
United Electrical Workers' Union
United Food and Commercial Workers International Union
United Steelworkers of America
Volunteers of America
Women's Legal Defense Fund
YWCA of the USA, National Board

Source: Children's Defense Fund

Appendix D

The Following Organizations Endorsed H.R. 3
as of September 27, 1989

A. Phillip Randolph Institute
African Methodist Episcopal Church, Women's Missionary Society
Alpha Kappa Alpha Sorority, Inc.
Alternative Schools Network of Chicago
Amalgamated Clothing and Textile Workers Union
Amalgamated Transit Union
American Academy of Child and Adolescent Psychiatry
American Academy of Pediatrics
American Association for Marriage and Family Therapy
American Association of Classified School Employees
American Association of Psychiatric Services for Children
American Association of School Administrators
American Association of University Professors
American Association of University Women
American Civil Liberties Union
American Federation of Federal Employees
American Federation of Government Employees
American Federation of Labor and Congress of Industrial Organizations (AFL-CIO)
American Federation of State, County, and Municipal Employees, AFL-CIO
American Federation of Teachers, AFL-CIO
American Home Economics Association
American Jewish Committee
American Jewish Congress
American Orthopsychiatric Association, Inc.
American Planning Association
American Postal Workers Union, AFL-CIO
American Psychological Association
American Vocational Association
Americans for Democratic Action
Association for Regulatory Administration in Human Services
Association of Junior Leagues, Inc.
Bakery, Confectionery, and Tobacco Workers International Union
B'nai B'rith Women
BPW/USA
Bread for the World

Camp Fire, Inc.
CATALYST
Center for Child and Family Studies of the Far West Lab
Center for Women Policy Studies
Child Care Action Campaign
Child Care Employees' Project
Child Care Nutrition Program Sponsors' Forum
Child Welfare League of America
Children's Defense Fund
Church Women United
Christian Children's Fund, Inc.
Church of the Brethren
Citizen Action
Coalition of Black Trade Unionists
Coalition of Labor Union Women
Committee for Children
Communication Workers of America, AFL-CIO
Community Nutrition Institute
Concerned Nutritionists for Better Child Care
Council for Exceptional Children
Council for the Great City Schools
Council of Chief State School Officers
Council of Jewish Federations
Delta Sigma Theta, Inc.
Department for Professional Employees, AFL-CIO
Division for Early Childhood/Council for Exceptional Children
Elementary School Center
Epilepsy Foundation of America
The Episcopal Church
Family Resource Coalition
Food Research Action Center
Future Homemakers of America
General Board of Church and Society of the United Methodist Church
General Board of Global Ministries of United Methodist Church
Girls Clubs of America, Inc.
Gray Panthers
High/Scope Educational Research Foundation
Industrial Union Department, AFL-CIO
International Ladies Garment Workers' Union
International Union of Electronic, Electrical, Salaried, Machine and Furniture Workers,
    AFL-CIO
Knights of Peter Claver, Women's Auxiliary
League of United Latin-American Citizens

League of Women Voters of the U.S.
Lutheran Office for Government Affairs
MADRE
Martin Luther King Jr. Early Learning Center
Mexican American Women's National Association
NA'AMAT USA
National Association for Family Day Care
National Association for the Advancement of Colored People
National Association for the Education of Young Children
National Association of Child Care Resource and Referral Agencies (NACCRRA)
National Association of Commissions for Women
National Association of Elementary School Principals
National Association of Letter Carriers
National Association of Secondary School Principals
National Association of Social Workers
National Association of State Boards of Education
National Association of the State Directors of Child Development
National Association of Working Women—9 to 5
National Black Caucus and Center on the Aged, Inc.
National Black Child Development Institute, Inc.
National Coalition for Campus Child Care, Inc.
National Coalition for Public Education and Religious Liberty
National Committee for the Prevention of Child Abuse
National Community Action Foundation
National Conference of Black Mayors, Inc.
National Congress of Parents and Teachers
National Consumer League
National Council of Jewish Women
National Council of Negro Women
National Council of Churches of Christ
National Council on Family Relations
National Council on the Aging, Inc.
National Education Association
National Federation of Federal Employees
National Head Start Association
National League of Cities
National Network of Runaway and Youth Services
National Pan-Hellenic Council
National Parent Teachers Association
National Prenatal Association
National Puerto Rican Forum
National School Boards Association
National Schools Public Relations Association

National Urban Coalition
National Urban League
National Women's Law Center
National Women's Political Caucus
The Newspaper Guild
Office for Church and Society, United Church of Christ
Office and Professional Employees International Union
OICs of America
Parent Care
Parent Cooperative Preschools International
Parents Action Committee
Presbyterian U.S.A.
Progressive National Baptist Convention, Women's Department
Public Employee Department, AFL-CIO
Rainbow Coalition
Save the Children
School Age Child Care Project
Service Employees International Union, AFL-CIO
Sigma Gamma Rho Sorority
Society for Research in Child Development
Southern Association on Children Under Six
Southern Christian Leadership Conference
Union of American Hebrew Congregations—Religious Action Center
Union of Electrical, Radio and Machine Workers of America
United Auto Workers
United Cerebral Palsy Association, Inc.
United Church Board for Homeland Ministries
United Church of Christ Coordination Center for Women's Issues
United Church of Christ, Office for Church in Society
United Electrical Workers' Union
United Food and Commercial Workers International Union
United Methodist Church, Department of Human Welfare General Board of Church and
    Society
United States Student Association
United Steelworkers of America
Volunteers of America
Washington State Office of the Superintendent of Public Instruction
Woman's Convention, Auxiliary to the National Baptist Convention, U.S.A., Inc.
Women's Legal Defense Fund
YMCA of the USA
YWCA of the USA, National Board

Source: Children's Defense Fund

Appendix E

Members of the Alliance That Signed a Letter Dated February 22, 1990, Supporting H.R. 3

A. Phillip Randolph Institute
African Methodist Episcopal Church, Women's Missionary Society
Alpha Kappa Alpha Sorority, Inc.
Amalgamated Transit Union, AFL-CIO
American Academy of Child and Adolescent Psychiatry
American Academy of Pediatrics
American Association for Marriage and Family Therapy
American Association of Classified School Employees
American Association of Psychiatric Services for Children
American Association of University Professors
American Federation of Government Employees, AFL-CIO
American Federation of Labor and Congress of Industrial Organizations (AFL-CIO)
American Federation of State, County, and Municipal Employees, AFL-CIO
American Federation of Teachers, AFL-CIO
American Home Economics Association
American Jewish Committee
American Jewish Congress
American Orthopsychiatric Association, Inc.
American Planning Association
American Postal Workers Union, AFL-CIO
American Psychological Association
Association of Junior Leagues, International
Bakery, Confectionery, and Tobacco Workers International Union, AFL-CIO
Black Women's Agenda
Bread for the World
Business and Professional Women, USA
Camp Fire, Inc.
Center for Women Policy Studies
Child Care Action Campaign
Child Care Employees' Project
Child Care Nutrition Program Sponsors' Forum
Child Welfare League of America
Children's Defense Fund
The Children's Foundation
Christian Children's Fund

Church of the Brethren
Church Women United
Coalition of Black Trade Unionists
Committee for Children
Communication Workers of America, AFL-CIO
Community Nutrition Institute
Concerned Nutritionists for Better Child Care
Council for Exceptional Children
Council of Chief State School Officers
Council of Jewish Federations
Department for Professional Employees, AFL-CIO
The Episcopal Church
Family Resource Coalition
Federally Employed Women
Food Research Action Center
General Board of Global Ministries of United Methodist Church
Girls Clubs of America, Inc.
Gray Panthers
High/Scope Educational Research Foundation
Industrial Union Department, AFL-CIO
International Ladies Garment Workers' Union, AFL-CIO
International Union of Electronic, Electrical, Salaried, Machine and Furniture Workers,
    AFL-CIO
Jack and Jill of America
Knights of Peter Claver, Women's Auxiliary
League of United Latin-American Citizens
League of Women Voters
Evangelical Lutheran Church in America, Lutheran Office for Government Affairs
MADRE
Mexican American Women's National Association
National Association for the Advancement of Colored People
National Association for the Education of Young Children
National Association of Child Care Resource and Referral Agencies (NACCRRA)
National Association of Commissions for Women
National Association of Letter Carriers, AFL-CIO
National Association of Working Women—9 to 5
National Black Caucus and Center on the Aged, Inc.
National Black Child Development Institute
National Committee for the Prevention of Child Abuse
National Community Action Foundation
National Conference of Black Mayors, Inc.
National Consumer League
National Council of Jewish Women

National Council of Negro Women
National Council of the Churches of Christ
National Council on Family Relations
National Council on the Aging
National Federation of Federal Employees
National Head Start Association
National League of Cities
National Network of Runaway and Youth Services
National Puerto Rican Forum
National Rainbow Coalition
National Urban Coalition
National Urban League
National Women's Law Center
National Women's Political Caucus
Newspaper Guild, AFL-CIO, CLC
Office for Church and Society, United Church of Christ
Office and Professional Employees International Union, AFL-CIO
OICs of America
Oregon School Employees Association
Parent Care
Parent Cooperative Preschools International
Progressive National Baptist Convention, Women's Department
Public Employee Department, AFL-CIO
Save the Children
School Age Child Care Project
Sigma Gamma Rho Sorority
Southern Association on Children Under Six
Southern Christian Leadership Conference
Union of American Hebrew Congregations
United Auto Workers, AFL-CIO
United Church of Christ Coordination Center for Women's Issues
United Electrical Workers' Union
United Food and Commercial Workers International Union, AFL-CIO
The United States Conference of City Human Services Officials
The United States Conference of Mayors
United Steelworkers of America, AFL-CIO
Volunteers of America
Woman's Convention, Auxiliary to the National Baptist Convention, U.S.A., Inc.
Women's Legal Defense Fund
YWCA of the USA, National Board

Source: Alliance for Better Child Care

Appendix F

Organizations Opposing the Ford-Durenberger Amendment to
Exempt Certificates from Section 19(a) of the
Act for Better Child Care

AFL-CIO
American Civil Liberties Union
American Ethical Union
American Federation of State, County and Municipal Employees, AFL-CIO
American Federation of Teachers, AFL-CIO
American Jewish Committee
American Jewish Congress
Americans United for Separation of Church and State
Anti Defamation League of B'nai B'rith
Child Care Employee Project
Child Welfare League of America
Children's Defense Fund
Church of the Brethren, Washington Office
Church Women United, Washington Office
Communications Workers of America, AFL-CIO
Council of Chief State School Officers
Council of Jewish Federations
International Ladies Garment Workers' Union
Lutheran Office for Governmental Affairs, Evangelical Lutheran
      Church in America
Mennonite Central Committee, Washington Office
NA'AMAT
National Association for the Education of Young Children
National Association of Elementary School Principals
National Council of Churches of Christ
National Council of Jewish Women
National Education Association
National Federation of Temple Sisterhoods
National Jewish Community Relations Advisory Council
National PTA
National School Boards Association
National Women's Law Center
People for the American Way
Presbyterian Church (U.S.A.), Washington Office

Unitarian Universalist Service Committee
United Church of Christ, Office for Church in Society
United Food and Commercial Workers International Union
United Methodist Church, Issue Development and Advocacy Unit,
      General Board of Church and Society
United Methodist Church, Office of Public Policy in Women's
      Concerns, Women's Division
Union of American Hebrew Congregations

Source: Children's Defense Fund

Appendix G

Members of the National Coalition for Public Education[1]

American Association of School Administrators
American Association of State Colleges and Universities
American Association of University Women
American Civil Liberties Union
American Ethical Union
American Federation of Teachers
American Jewish Committee
American Jewish Congress
American Vocational Association
Americans for Democratic Action
Americans for Religious Liberty
Americans United for Separation of Church and State
Baptist Joint Committee on Public Affairs
B'nai B'rith Women
Council of Chief State School Officers
Council for Exceptional Children
Council of the Great City Schools
Florida State Department of Education
International Reading Association
Jewish Labor Committee
Labor Council for Latin American Advancement
NA'AMAT USA
National Association of Elementary School Principals
National Association of Partners in Education
National Association of Secondary School Principals
National Association of State Boards of Education
National Coalition of Title I/Chapter I Parents
National Coalition for Public Education and Religious Liberty
National Congress of Parents and Teachers
National Council of Jewish Women
National Council of La Raza
National Education Association

---

1. Updated partial list of coalition members as of September 12, 1989.

National Head Start Association
National Jewish Community Relations Advisory Council
National Organization for Women
National School Boards Association
National School Public Relations Association
Service Employees International Union, AFL-CIO
Student National Education Association
Union of American Hebrew Congregations
Unitarian Universalist Association of Churches in North America
United States Student Association

Source: National Coalition for Public Education

Appendix H

Members of National Coalition for Public Education
That Signed the March 2, 1990, Letter to All House Members

American Association of School Administrators
American Association of University Women
American Baptist Churches, U.S.A.
American Civil Liberties Union
American Federation of Teachers
American Humanist Association
American Jewish Committee
American Jewish Congress
Americans for Democratic Action
Americans for Religious Liberty
Americans United for Separation of Church and State
Anti Defamation League of B'nai B'rith
Aspira Association, Inc.
Baptist Joint Committee
B'nai B'rith Women
Church of the Brethren—Washington Office
Church Women United
Council of Chief State School Officers
Council of the Great City Schools
Council of Jewish Federations
Evangelical Lutheran Church in America, Lutheran Office
    for Governmental Affairs
General Conference of Seventh-Day Adventists
Hadassah, The Women's Zionist Organization of America, Inc.
Jewish Labor Committee
Mennonite Central Committee, Washington Office
Mexican American Legal Defense and Education Fund
National Association of Elementary School Principals
National Association of School Psychologists
National Association of State Boards of Education
National Conference of Puerto Rican Women
National Coalition for Public Education and Religious Liberty
National Council of Churches
National Council of Jewish Women
National Education Association

National Organization for Women
National Parent Teacher Association
National School Boards Association
Presbyterian Church (U.S.A.)
Service Employees International Union
Union of American Hebrew Congregations
Unitarian Universalist Association of Congregations
United Church of Christ, Office for Church in Society
The United Methodist Church, General Board of Church & Society,
    Issue Development and Advocacy Unit
United Synagogue of America
Washington Ethical Action Office, American Ethical Union
Washington Office of the Episcopal Church

Source: National Coalition for Public Education

Appendix I

Organizations That Signed and Circulated a Flier Opposing the
House Bill After the Defeat of the Edwards Amendment

Baptist Joint Committee
American Association of School Administrators
American Association of University Women
American Civil Liberties Union
American Federation of Teachers
American Jewish Committee
American Jewish Congress
Americans United for Separation of Church and State
General Conference of Seventh-Day Adventists
National Association of Secondary School Principals
National Coalition for Public Education and Religious Liberty
National Education Association
National Organization for Women
National Parent-Teacher Association
National School Boards Association
Union of American Hebrew Congregations

Source: National Coalition for Public Education

Bibliography

I. NONGOVERNMENTAL SOURCES FOR THE CONTEMPORARY AND HISTORICAL PERIODS

Abelson, Reed. 1987. "Rocking Horse Offering Armed at Expansion." *Philadelphia Business Journal* 6 (October 12): 10–11.

Adams, Gina C. 1990. *Who Knows How Safe? The Status of State Efforts to Ensure Quality Child Care.* Washington, DC: Children's Defense Fund.

Adler, Felix. 1904. *A Statement of the Aim of the Ethical Cultural Society.* Ethical Pamphlet No. 6. Philadelphia: American Ethical Union; reprinted. 1910.

Adler, Felix. 1983. "A New Experiment in Education." *Princeton Review* 11 (March): 143–157.

Agudath Israel. 1988. Memorandum to members of the Senate Committee on Labor and Human Resources and members of the House Committee on Education and Labor, by David Zwiebel and Morton Avigdor (July 20).

——— 1989a. Letter to all U. S. senators, by Rabbi Morris Sherer (June 2).

——— 1989b. Memorandum to all members of the U. S. Senate, by David Zwiebel and Abba Cohen (June 2).

——— 1989c. "Choice in Child Care Pressed by Agudath Israel in U. S. Senate." News Release (June 13).

——— 1989d. Letter to Representative Stenholm by Abba Cohen (September 28).

——— 1989e. Letter to all House of Representatives members by Abba Cohen (October 2).

———— 1989f. "Parental Choice Amendment Suffers Setback in House." News Release (October 6).

———— 1989g. Letter to House-Senate conferees. (November 8).

———— 1989h. Memorandum by David Zwiebel (November 8).

———— 1990a. Letter to Representative Thomas S. Foley by Abba Cohen (March 22).

———— 1990b. "Agudath Israel D.C. Office Takes Lead Role in House Fight for Religious Child Care." News Release (March 26).

———— 1990c. Memorandum to House of Representatives Leadership (March 29).

———— 1990d. "House Victory on Child Care Should Spell Millions in Aid for Religious Families." News Release (April 4).

Albert, Jan. 1988. "The Union Fight for Child Care." *Working Mother* (November), pp. 45–48.

Allen, W. A. 1913. "The Stranger in Our Midst." *Home Mission Monthly* 27 (March): 113–114.

Almy, Millie. 1982. "Day Care and Early Childhood Education." In *Day Care: Scientific and Social Policy Issues*, ed. Edward F. Zigler and Edmund W. Gordon, pp. 476–496. Boston: Auburn House Publishing.

Amalgamated Clothing and Textile Workers Union. 1988. *Bargaining on Women's Issues and Family Concerns: Clauses from ACTWU Contracts.* New York: ACTWU Research Department.

Ambach, Gordon M. 1989. Stanley Elam lecture at the Educational Press Association of America Conference 89, National Press Club, Washington, DC, May 18.

American Federation of Teachers Task Force on Educational Issues. 1976. *Putting Early Childhood and Day Care Services into the Public Schools: The Position of the American Federation of Teachers and An Action Plan for Promoting It*. Washington, DC: American Federation of Teachers.

American Federation of Teachers. 1975. Position on Early Childhood Programs. Washington, DC: American Federation of Teachers, pp. 69–71.

American Federation of State, County, and Municipal Employees, AFL-CIO. 1984. *Negotiating about Child Care: Issues and Options.* Washington, DC: American Federation of State, County, and Municipal Employees, AFL-CIO.

American Federation of Labor and Congress of Industrial Organizations. 1988. "A National Need: Adequate Child Care for Working Americans."*AFL–CIO Legislative Fact Sheet.* no. 100–17 (June 17).

Americans United for Separation of Church and State. n.d. "The Act for Better Child Care Services: Summary of a Church-State Analysis."

Americans United for Separation of Church and State. n.d. "Additional Comments on the Proposed Act for Better Child Care Services," prepared by Lee Boothby.

Anthony, Katharine. 1914. *Mothers Who Must Earn.* West Side Studies. New York: Survey Associates, Inc. The Russell Sage Foundation.

Apple, R. W., Jr. 1990a. "Bush Hints at Rise in Top Tax Rates, Then Backs Away." *Education Week* (May 9), pp. A1, A11.

——— 1990b. "Government Itself Is the Big Casualty." *The New York Times* (October 25), p. A11.

Association for Childhood Education. 1939. *History of the Kindergarten Movement in the Southeastern States and Delaware, District of Columbia, New Jersey and Pennsylvania.* Atlanta: Association for Childhood Education.

Baden, Clifford, and Dana E. Freidman eds. 1981. *New Management Initiatives for Working Parents: Reports from an April 1981 Conference.* Boston: Office of Continuing Education, Wheelock College.

Bailey, Donald B., Jr. 1989. "Early Schooling for Children with Special Needs." *Theory into Practice* (Winter): 64–68.

Barber, John, Miro Cernetig and Ashley Geddes. 1986. "Parents, Jobs, and Children." *Maclean's* (November 10) pp. 46–50.

"Bargaining for Child Care." 1986. *Labor Today* (February): 3–6.

Barringer, Felicity. 1990. "Census Report Shows a Rise in Child Care and Its Costs." *The New York Times* (August 16), p. A10.

Basch, Mark. 1986. "Kinder Care Learning Centers Plans to Acquire Florida Thrift." *American Banker* (May 21): 2.

Bellm, Dan. 1987. "The McChild Care." *Mother Jones* (April), pp. 30–38.

Berger, Joseph. 1989. "Social Ills Pull Educators' Concern to New Issues." *The New York Times* (September 6), p. 22.

Berruta-Clement, J. R., L. J. Schweinhart, W.S. Barnett, A. S. Epstein and D. P. Weikart. 1984. *Changed Lives: The Effects of the Perry Preschool Program on Youths through age 19.* Monographs of the High/Scope Educational Research Foundation, 8. Ypsilanti, MI: High Scope Press.

"Bible Study in the Day Schools." 1904. *Home Mission Monthly* 19 (December): 30–31.

Black, Algernon David. 1960. *The Meaning of Ethical Culture.* New York: American Ethical Union.

Blank, Helen. 1985. "Early Childhood and the Public Schools: An Essential Partnership." *Young Children* (May): 52–55.

——— and Amy Wilkins. 1986. *State Child Care Fact Book 1986.* Washington DC: Children's Defense Fund.

——— Jennifer Savage, and Amy Wilkins. 1988. *State Child Care Fact Book 1988.* Washington DC: Children's Defense Fund.

——— and Nancy Ebb. 1989. "CDF Criticizes Proposed Child Care Regulations of Family Support Act." Guest Editorial, *Ecumenical Child Care Newsletter*, 7 (May–June): 2, 7.

Bloch, Marianne N. 1987. "Becoming Scientific and Professional: An Historical Perspective on the Aims and Effects of Early Education." In *The Formation of School Subjects: The Struggle for Creating an American Institution*, ed. Thomas S. Popkewitz, pp. 25–62. New York and Philadelphia: The Falmer Press.

Bloch, Marianne N., Deanne Seward, and Patricia Seidlinger. 1989. "What History Tells Us About Public Schools for 4-Year-Olds." *Theory into Practice* (Winter): 11–18.

Blow, Susan. 1897. "The History of the Kindergarten in the United States." *Outlook*, pp. 932–938.

Blow, Susan. 1900. *Kindergarten Education*. Albany: J. B. Lyon Co.

"A Boom Ahead for Kid-Care Companies." 1984. *Changing Times*. 38 (August); pp. 37–38.

Boone, Richard G. 1889. *Education in the United States: Its History from the Earliest Settlements*. New York: Appleton and Co.

Boston, Rob. 1988. "To Raise up a Child...The Impending Battle Over Church, State and Child Care." *Church and State* [Boston] (March), pp. 4–6.

Bourne, P. G. 1972. "What Day Care Ought to Be." *New Republic* (12 February), pp. 18–23.

Bowe, Claudia. 1986. "The Urgent Crisis in Day Care." *Cosmopolitan* (November), pp. 298–302, 360–361.

Bowman, Barbara. 1988. "Are Public Schools Insensitive to the Needs of Blacks? Yes, Indeed!" In *Shaping the Future for Early Childhood Programs*, pp. 60–63. Ypsilanti, MI: High Scope Press.

Boyer, S. 1971. "Day Care Jungle; Legislation, Federal Programs, and New Proposals." *Saturday Review* (February 20).

Boyle, Kathy. 1990. "Child–Care Center Opens on Hospital Campus." *HR News*. Vol. 8, no. 1 (January): 1.

Bradford, Michael. 1988. "Day-Care Firm Sued Over Loss of Cover." *Business Insurance*. 22 (October 24): 2, 12.

Bredekamp, Sue, ed. 1984. *Accreditation Criteria and Procedures of the National Academy of Early Childhood Programs*. Washington, DC: National Association for the Education of Young Children.

⸻ ed. 1987. *Developmentally Appropriate Practice in Early Childhood Programs Serving Children from Birth Through Age 8*. Washington, DC: National Association for the Education of Young Children.

⸻ 1989. *Regulating Child Care Quality: Evidence from NAEYC's Accreditation System*. Washington, DC: National Association for the Education of Young Children.

Bremner, Robert H. 1956. "Scientific Philanthropy, 1873-93." *Social Service Review* 30 (June): 168–172.

Bridgman, Anne. 1985a. "Day-Care Centers Rocked by Rising Insurance Costs: High Premiums, Cancelled Policies May Close Many." *Education Week* (May 29): 1, 13.

⸻ 1985b. "Day Care: Tightening Insurance Squeeze." *Education Week* (September 11): 1, 14.

⸻ 1985c. "Early-Childhood Education: States Already on the Move." *Education Week* (October 16): 1, 14–15.

Brooke, Rev. Stopford. 1881. "Child Life in Christ." *Barnard's Journal of Education* 6 (July): 281–288.

Brooks, Andree. "Rules for Condo Owners Can Pre-empt Litigation." *The New York Times* (April 8), p. Y34.

Brooks, Angeline. 1887. "A Mission Kindergarten." *Lend Hand* 2 (July); 415–419.

Brown, Caroline F. 1901. "Elizabeth Peabody House: The Kindergarten Settlement of Boston." *Kindergarten Review* 12 (October): 63–67.

Brown, Hank, and Ron Haskins. "The Day-Care Reform Juggernaut." *National Review* (March); pp. 40–41.

Brown, Kate L. 1887. "Application of Froebel's Principles to the Primary School." *Journal of Proceedings and Addresses of the National Education Association*, pp. 338–350.

Browning, Lucy E. 1906. "A Discussion of the Training of Kindergartners Under Differing Conditions." *Proceedings of the Thirteenth Annual Meeting of the International Kindergarten Union*, vol. 13, pp. 45–48.

Brozan, N. 1972. "Day Care in Crisis: Without the Money, Ideals Are in Peril." *New York Times* (November 17), p. 54.

Bureau of National Affairs, Inc. 1984. *Employers and Child Care: Development of a New Employee Benefit.* A BNA Special Report. Rockville, MD: Bureau of National Affairs, Inc.

——— 1987a. "BNA Special Survey Shows Few Employers Provide More Than Referrals for Day Care." *Daily Labor Report.* No. 59 (March 30), pp. C-1–C-4.

——— 1987b. "BNA Survey." *Labor Relations Reporter* (April 6), pp. 224–228.

——— 1989. "Liability Risks Prompt Employers to Be Wary of On-Site Day Care Centers." Department of Labor Relations Report No. 217 (November 13), A-2–A-5.

——— 1990a. "House Gives Approval to Democrats' Compromise Legislation on Child Care." (March 30).

——— 1990b. "States Take Multifaceted Role in Child Care Services Development." Department of Labor Relations Report No. 131 (July 9), pp. A-15–A-16.

——— 1990c. "Employers' Group Provision in House Bill Could Discourage Child Care Programs." BNA, Department of Labor Report No. 83 (April 30), p. A-9.

Burk, Frederic and Caroline Frear Burk. 1899. *A Study of the Kindergarten Problem in the Public Kindergartens of Santa Barbara, California, for the Year 1898-1899*. San Francisco: Whitakerand Ray Co.

Burud, Sandra and Pamela Aschbacker, and Jacquelyn McCrosky. 1984. *Employer Supported Day Care: Investing in Human Resources*. Boston: Auburn House.

Bush Center in Child Development and Social Policy. *The School of the Twenty-First Century*. New Haven: Yale University Press.

Butler, Susan Lowell. 1987. *The National Education Association: A Special Mission*. Washington, DC: National Education Association.

Caldwell, Bettye M. 1971. "A Timid Giant Grows Bolder." *Saturday Review*, (February 20), pp. 47-53ff.

—— 1986. "Day Care and the Public Schools—Natural Allies, Natural Enemies." *Educational Leadership* (February): 34-39.

—— 1989a. "All-Day Kindergarten—Assumptions, Precautions, and Overgeneralizations." *Early Childhood Research Quarterly* 4 (June): 261-266.

—— 1989b. "A Comprehensive Model for Integrating Child Care and Early Childhood Education." *Teachers College Record* 90 (Spring): 404-414.

Caldwell, Wilhelmina T. 1895. "Mothers' Meetings Among the Poor." *Kindergarten News* 5 (October): 283-285.

"California Makes Business a Partner in Day Care." 1987. *Business Week* (June 8), p. 100.

Campbell, Bertha D. 1987. "From National Debate to National Responsibility." In *Early Schooling*, ed. by Sharon L. Kagan and Edward F. Zigler, pp. 65-82. New Haven: Yale University Press.

Carmody, Deirdre. 1989. "More and More, Kindergarten Means a Full Day." *The New York Times* (October 4), p. 20.

Carnes, Kevin, and Connie Hine. 1990. "Have Child Care...Will Travel." *Kids and Company Update* [Lakeshore Curriculum Materials Company] (Spring), pp. 3–4.

Carroll, C. F. 1899. "Place of the Kindergarten in the Common School." *Journal of Pedagogy* 12 (May): 126–136.

Cary, Alice Dugged. 1900. "Kindergartens for Negro Children." *Southern Workman* 29 (August): 461–463.

Celis, William. 1990a. "Backlash on Schools Unrealized." *The New York Times* (November 14), p. B9.

——— 1990b. "State Plan for Choice of Schools Is Voided." *The New York Times* (November 14), p. B9.

Center for Law and Social Policy. 1989. "Child Care and the Family Support Act." *Family Matters* 1, no. 3 (Spring): 1–14.

——— 1990. "Transitional Child Care: Eligibility Issues Unresolved." *Family Matters* 2, no. 2 (April): 1–14.

"Charity Kindergartens in the United States." 1881. *American Journal of Education* 31: 651–653.

Child Care Action Campaign. 1988. *Child Care: The Bottom Line. An Economic and Child Care Policy Paper.* Prepared by Barbara Reisman, Amy J. Moore, and Karen Fitzgerald. New York: Child Care Action Campaign.

Child Care Coalition. n.d. "Child Care Coalition Recommendations On Federal Child Care Legislation."

"Child Care and Development Block Grant." 1990. Summary provided by Children's Defense Fund (October 16).

"Child Care/Early Education Focus Continues in Congress." 1989. *Young Children* [Washington update] (March): 38.

Child Care Employee Project. 1989. *Who Cares? Child Care Teachers and the Quality of Care in America.* Report of the National Child Care Staffing Study. Oakland, CA: Child Care Employee Project.

"Child Care Grows As a Benefit." 1981. *Business Week* (December 21), pp. 60–61.

Child Care Law Center. 1990. "Update of *Day Care Licensing and Religious Exemptions*," (July 9).

Child Welfare League of America. 1988. Reprint of Testimony Presented by Joyce Strom on H.R. 3660, The Act for Better Child Care (February 25).

––––– 1989. "Child Welfare League Calls for Passage of Child Care Bill." News Release (October 3).

––––– 1990. "Child Care Bill Still in Conference: White House Hopes for a Bill President Can Sign. Rally, Press Conference, Demonstrate Growing Support for Child Care Bill." *Children's Voice* 6, No. 6 (July–August): 1–2.

Children's Advocacy Committee. n.d. "A Profile of Child Care Across the Episcopal Church." *The Children's Advocate.* New York: The Episcopal Center, Office of Social Welfare.

Children's Defense Fund. 1982. *Employed Parents and Their Children: A Data Book.* Washington, DC: Children's Defense Fund.

––––– 1983. *A Corporate Reader: Work and Family Life in the 1980s.* Washington, DC: Children's Defense Fund.

––––– 1986. *A Children's Defense Budget: An Analysis of the FY 1987 Federal Budget and Children.* Washington DC: Children's Defense Fund.

––––– 1990a. Alert (The Hawkins/Dodd/Hatch Agreement and the Downey Alternative) (January 10).

––––– 1990b. Memorandum. (January 17).

––––– 1990c. Memorandum. (July 30).

———— 1990d. "CDF Study Finds Enormous Gaps in State Child Care Quality Assurances and Enforcement," (September 4).

———— 1990e. "Children's Defense Fund Hails New Child Care Law as Historic Step: Children Get off on Right Foot in the New Decade." Press Release (October 29).

———— 1990f. "Summary of Additional Child Care Provisions in the Reconciliation Act" (October 31).

———— 1990g. "Child Care Legislation— A Chronology: January 1989–June 30, 1990."

———— 1990h. *S.O.S. America! A Children's Defense Budget.* Washington DC: Children's Defense Fund.

———— 1990i. *Children 1990: A Report Card, Briefing Book, and Action Primer.* Washington DC: Children's Defense Fund.

———— 1990j. Update (The Act for Better Child Care: S. 5, H.R. 3, and the Dodd-Hawkins-Hatch Compromise) (January).

———— 1990k. Memorandum. (July 26).

———— 1990l. "Beyond Loaning Books, Libraries Stimulate Children's Learning and Development." *CDF Reports*, 12 (October) 6–8.

———— 1990m. "Child Care and Development Block Grant." Summary, (November 5).

———— 1990n. "Child Care and Development Block Grant." Summary, (October 16).

Church, George. 1986. "Sorry, Your Policy is Canceled." *Nation* (March 24), pp. 16–26.

"Church, State and Child Care Policy: The ABC Bill Spells Disaster." 1988. *Church and State* (July–August), p. 13.

"Churches and Child Care: The ABC Bill and Religious Discrimination." 1988. *Church and State* (July–August), p. 4.

Clark, Lillian M. 1915. "Kindergarten Legislation in California: How We Secured It and Some of Its Results." *Journal of Proceedings and Addresses of the National Education Association*, 632–637.

Claxton, Philander Priestly. 1900. "Kindergartens in the South." *Kindergarten Magazine* 13 (October): 81–88.

Clifford, Richard M., and Susan D. Russell. 1989. "Financing Programs for Preschool-Aged Children." *Theory into Practice* (Winter): 19–27.

Clinton, Hillary Rodham. 1990. "In France, Day Care Is Every Child's Right." *The New York Times* (April 7), p. 15.

Coalition of Labor Union Women. 1984. *Child Care Resolution*. CLUW Resolution No. 3.

——— 1985. "Bargaining for Child Care: Contract Language for Union Parents." New York: Coalition for Labor Union Women; revised 1989.

——— 1988a. "Child Care" and "Health Care" in brochure for American Family Day Celebration (May 14).

——— 1988b. "Child Care." (February).

——— 1988c. "National Health Care." (March).

Cohen, Abba. 1990. Letter to author (October 24).

Cohen, Abby J. 1986. Testimony for the Child Care Law Center before the Joint Investigative Hearing—Department of Insurance/Legislative Task Force on Child Care Liability (File No. RH -248). Los Angeles (June 25).

Cohen, Deborah L. 1990a. "Parents as Partners." *Education Week* (May 9): 13–21.

——— 1990b. "Program Draws Grassroots Support from the Start." *Education Week* (May 9): 18.

——— 1990c. "Coaching Parents to Perform in Their Natural Role as Teacher." *Education Week* (May 9): 15.

——— 1990d. "Helping Families Build a Foundation for Learning." *Education Week* (May 9): 13, 14, 16, 17, 19, 20.

——— 1990e. "Tulsa Business Official Leading Drive for Citywide School-Based Child Care." *Education Week* (October 10): 5.

——— 1990f. "Child Care Accord Improves Chances for Bill's Passage." *Education Week* (October 24): 1.

Cohen, Nancy, ed. 1990. *Highlights of The National Family Day Care Project.* New York: National Council of Jewish Women.

Cohen, Sol. 1964. *Progressives and Urban Reform.* New York: Bureau of Publications, Teacher's College, Columbia University.

Collins, Glenn. 1988. "Wooing Workers in the 90's: New Role for Family Benefits." *The New York Times* (July 20), p. A14.

Committee of Nineteen, authorized by the International Kindergarten Union. 1924. *Pioneers of the Kindergarten in America.* New York: London: Century Co.

The Conference Board. 1989. "Prevalence of Employer-Supported Child Care." The Conference Board's Work and Family Information Center (June).

——— 1990. "Work and Family Policies: The New Strategic Plan." Conference Summary Sheet.

Congressional Research Service. 1988. *Child Day Care: Summaries of Selected Major Bills in the 100th Congress*, prepared by Sharon Stephan, Karen Spar, Anne Stewart, and Marie E. Morris (April 19).

——— 1989a. *Child Care: An Analysis of Major Issues and Policy Options Considered by the 100th Congress*, prepared by Anne C. Stewart (January 17).

—— 1989b. Constitutionality of Possible Amendment to S. 5 Removing Certificates From Section 19(a), prepared by David M. Ackerman of the American Law Division. Washington, DC: The Library of Congress; May 9. Printed in the *Congressional Record*, Senate (June 22).

—— 1990a. *Child Day Care*, (CRS Issue Brief, Major Planning Issue), prepared by Anne C. Stewart (April 10).

—— 1990b. *Summary Comparison of H.R. 3, as Passed by the House and as Passed by the Senate: Child Care and Other Provisions*, (CRS Report for Congress), prepared by Anne Stewart, Marie Morris, and David Ackerman (May 8; revised May 23).

Conliff, Maud. 1909. "A Bohemian Kindergarten in Baltimore." *Home Mission Monthly* 23 (January): 73

Conn, Joseph L. 1988. "Churches and Child Care: Will the ABC Bill Underwrite Religious Discrimination at Taxpayers' Expense?" *Church and State* [Boston] (July–August), p. 4–5.

Cooper, Mary Anderson. 1987. "The Alliance for Better Child Care." *Prepare* [National Impact Education Fund]. (November): 3.

—— 1988. "Church-State Issues in 'The Act for Better Child Care Services'." *Impact* [National Council of Churches] (June).

—— 1989a. "The Bush Administration Plan." *Mark-Up* [National Council of Churches] 18 (April): 1,2.

—— 1989b. "Child Care: It's up to the House." *Mark-Up* [National Council of Churches] 18 (July–August): 1–3.

—— 1989c. "Welfare 'Reform' Revisited." *Mark-Up* [National Council of Churches] 18 (June): 1–3.

—— 1989d. "Act for Better Child Care Services." *Mark-Up* [National Council of Churches] 18 (June): 5–6.

—— 1990a. "Child Care Legislation: The Final Stages." *Mark-Up* [National Council of Churches] 19 (April): 1–3.

—— 1990b. "Child Care." *Mark-Up* [National Council of Churches] 19 (August): 6.

—— 1990c. "Child Care." *Mark-Up* [National Council of Churches] 19 (October–November): 3-5.

—— 1990d. "At last! House Child Care Action." *Mark-Up* [National Council of Churches] 19 (March): 1-3.

Cooper, Sarah B. 1882. "The Kindergarten as a Child-Saving Work." *Proceedings of the National Conference on Charities and Corrections*, pp. 130–138.

—— 1885. "The Kindergarten as Character Builder." *National Conference on Charities and Corrections Proceedings*, pp. 222–228.

—— 1889. "Free Kindergartens: Practical Results of Ten Years' Work." *National Conference on Charities and Corrections Proceedings*, pp. 186–194.

Council of Chief State School Officers. 1988. *A Guide For State Action: Early Childhood and Family Education*. Washington, DC: Council of Chief State School Officers.

Cremin, Lawrence Arthur. 1961. *The Transformation of the School; Progressivism in American Education*. New York: Knopf.

Croft, Nancy L., and Carol Dilks. 1986. "Child Care: Your Baby?" *Nations Business* 74 (December): 16–22.

Cross, Ermine. 1898. "The Work of the Chicago Free Kindergarten Association." *The Kindergarten Magazine* (April): 509–515.

Culiff, Maud M. 1906. "Little Foreigner in Baltimore." *Home Mission Monthly* 20 (August): 251–252.

Dahrendorf, Rolf. 1959 (originally published 1957). *Class and Class Conflict in Industrial Society*. Stanford, CA: Stanford University Press.

Dahrendorf, Rolf. 1962. "Toward a Theory of Social Conflict." In *The Planning of Change: Readings in the Applied Behavioral Sciences*, ed. Warren G.

Bennis, Kenneth D. Benne and Robert Chin. New York: Holt, Rinehart and Winston.

Dahrendorf, Rolf. 1968. *Essays in the Theory of Society*. Stanford, CA: Stanford University Press.

Daley, Suzanne. 1990. "Besieged Urban School Chiefs Are Dropping Out." *The New York Times* (December 26), pp. 1, 13.

Davis, Lorraine. 1981. "New Public Utility? (Child Care Facilities)." *Vogue*. Vol. 171 (July), p. 71.

"Day Care Bill Advances Despite Church-State Disagreement." 1988. *Church and State* (September), p. 14.

"Day Care: The Boom Begins." 1970. *Newsweek* (December 7), pp. 92–96.

"Day-Care Firm Moves Further into Financial Services Market." 1987. *American Banker* (June 26), p. 2.

"Day-Care Network Takes on Unusual Charge and Young Family Market with Thrift Merger." 1987. *American Banker* (February 10), pp. 2–3.

"Day-Care Poll Results Mixed: Ohio's Laws Found Weak in Some Areas, Strong in Others." 1990. *The Plain Dealer* [Cleveland] (September 5), p. 6-C.

"The Debate Begins: Should Schools Take on Child Care?" 1985. *Education U.S.A.* (January 28), pp. 172–173.

Democratic Study Group. 1990a. "Child Care." Fact Sheet No. 101-26 (March 27).

——— 1990b. "Child Care Group Positions." Supplement to DSG Fact Sheet No. 101-26 (March 28).

——— 1990c. "Reconciliation Update." Fact Sheet No. 101-61S (October 30).

——— 1990d. "1990 Budget Reconciliation Act." Fact Sheet No. 101-62 (November 9).

DePalma, Anthony. 1990. "As a Need for Day Care Collides with Zoning." *The New York Times* (November 8), p. A12.

Dermott, Maureen. 1989. Testimony for Kinder-Care Learning Centers, Inc. Before the Committee on Finance United States Senate. Hearing on Child Care Proposals (April 19).

Dervarics, Charles. 1990a. "Tax Provision Could Force Companies to Drop Dependent Care Programs." *Report on Preschool Programs* 22 (May 23): 103.

———— 1990b. "Few Workers Have Access to Work-Site Child Care." *Report on Preschool Programs* 22 (May 23): 110.

Deutsch, Claudia H. 1990. "Saying No to the 'Mommy Track'." *The New York Times* (January 28), p. F29.

Dewey, John. 1900. "Froebel's Educational Principles." *The Elementary School Record* 1 (June): 143–151.

DeWitt, Karen. 1990. "Debate on School Choice Continues." *The New York Times* (November 14), p. B9.

Dobbin, Sheila L., and Andrew J. McCormick. 1980. "An Update on Social Work in Day Care." *Child Welfare* 59 (February): 97–102.

Dodd, Christopher J. 1988. "Should the Congress Adopt the Proposed 'Act for Better Child Care Services of 1988'?" *The Congressional Digest.* 67 (November): 264, 266.

Dozier, C. P. 1908. "History of the Kindergarten Movement in the United States." *Educational Bi-Monthly* 2 (April): 352–361.

Dublin, Thomas. 1979. *Women at Work: The Transformation of Work and Community in Lowell Massachusetts, 1826-1860.* New York: Columbia Press.

Duncklee, Helen L. 1899. "The Kindergartner and Her Mothers' Meetings." *Kindergarten Review* 10 (September): 12–15.

Eaton, William J. 1990a. "Democrats Near Child-Care Accord." *The Los Angeles Times* (March 20), p. A16.

―――― 1990b. "Child-Care Bill Moves Ahead." *The Phoenix Gazette* (March 20), p. A6.

Ebb, Nancy, Sherrie Lookner, Jodie Levin–Epstein and Mark Greenberg. 1990. *Transitional Child Care: State Experiences and Emerging Policies Under the Family Support Act.* Washington, DC: Children's Defense Fund and Center for Law and Social Policy.

Economic Policy Council of UNA-USA. 1985. *Work and Family in the United States: A Policy Initiative.* A Report of the Family Policy Panel. New York: United Nations Association of the United States of America.

Ecumenical Child Care Newsletter. 1985. New York: National Council of the Churches of Christ in the U.S.A.

Edelman, Marian Wright. 1988a. Memorandum to ABC members. (February 12).

―――― 1988b. "Should the Congress Adopt the Proposed 'Act for Better Child Care Services of 1988'?" *The Congressional Digest* 67 (November): 274, 276, 278, 280, 282.

―――― 1989. "Turf, Not Toddlers, the Issue." *The Plain Dealer* [Cleveland] (December 21), p. 7-B.

―――― 1990. Letter to Members of Alliance for Better Child Care (October 31).

Education Commission of the States. "State Characteristics: Kindergarten." Denver: Education Commission of the States, March.

Eitzen, Stanley. 1986. *Social Problems.* 3rd ed. Boston: Allyn and Bacon, Inc.

Elardo, Phylis T., and Bettye M. Caldwell. "The Kramer Adventure: A School for the Future?" *Childhood Education* 50 (January): 143–152.

Elkind, David. 1986. "Formal Education and Early Childhood Education: An Essential Difference." *Phi Delta Kappan.* (May): 631–636.

—— 1987a. *Miseducation: Preschoolers at Risk.* New York: Alfred J. Knopf Publishers.

—— 1987b. "Early Childhood Education on Its Own Terms." In *Early Schooling*, ed. Sharon L. Kagan and Edward F. Zigler, pp. 98–115. New Haven: Yale University Press.

Ellis, Katherine, and Rosalind Petchesky. 1972–73. "The Politics of Day Care." *Social Policy* (November–December/January–February): 14–22.

Engardio, Pete. 1986. "Kinder-Care Will Mind your Money, Too." *Business Week* (June 9), pp. 34, 35.

Englade, Kenneth F. 1988. "The Bottom Line on Kinder-Care." *Across the Board* (April), pp. 45–53.

Euben, Donna. 1988. "Baby Boon or Boondoggle: Politics in 1988." *Child Care Action News* 5, no. 5 (September–October): 1, 7–9.

Fandetti, Donald J. 1976. "Day Care in Working Class Ethnic Neighborhoods: Implications for Social Policy." *Child Welfare* 55 (November): 618–626.

Featherstone, Joseph. 1970. "The Day Care Problem: Kentucky Fried Children." *The New Republic* (September 5)pp. 12–16.

Feldman, Diane. 1989. "Prices and Perks of Parenting." *Management Review* (January): 7–10.

Fenn, Donna. 1983. "Day Care Chains (Child-Care Centers Run By Chain Organizations). *Working Woman* (August), pp. 104–105, 108.

—— 1987. "Kid Stuff: How to Create Affordable Alternatives to On-Site Day Care." *INC.* (September), pp. 127–130.

Fernandez, John P. 1986. *Child Care and Corporate Productivity: Resolving Family/Work Conflicts.* Lexington, MA: Lexington Books.

"Few Workers Have Access to Work-Site Child Care." 1990. *Report on Preschool Programs.* 22 (May 23): 110.

Fisher, Laura. 1905. "The Kindergarten." *Report of the Commissioner of Education for the Year 1903*, vol. 1 Chapter 16, Washington, DC: Government Printing Office. pp. 689–719.

Fishhaut, Erna H., and Donald Pastor. 1977. "Should the Public Schools Be Entrusted with Preschool Education: A Critique of the AFT Proposals." *School Review* 86 (November): 38–49.

Fishman, Walda Katz. 1987. "The Struggle for Women's Equality in an Era of Economic Crisis: From the Morality of Reform to the Science of Revolution." *Humanity and Society*, 11 no. 4: 519–532.

Fiske, Edward B. 1986. "Early Schooling Is Now the Rage." *The New York Times* (April 13), Education Life Supplement, pp. 24–30.

——— 1989. "Historic Shift Is Seen in School Financing." *The New York Times* (October 4), p. B9.

——— 1990a. "With Bright National Goals for Schools Set, Governors Puzzle Over How To Attain Them." *The New York Times* (February 28), p. B7.

——— 1990b. "Starting Over." *The New York Times* (April 8), Education Life Supplement, pp. 34–35.

——— 1990c. "Starting with a Center for Child Care, a School Welcomes Social Services for Families." *The New York Times* (January 17), p. 21.

Fitzpatrick, Frank. 1892. "What Shall the State Do Toward the Education of Children Below the School Age?" *Journal of the Proceedings of the National Educational Association*, pp. 626–636.

Foos, Charles S. 1909. "Kindergartens." *Reading, Pennsylvania Board of Education, Biennial Report, 1907–1909*, pp. 503–513. Reading: Eagle Book and Job Press.

Ford Foundation. 1989. *Early Childhood Services: A National Challenge*. New York: Ford Foundation.

Foster, Mary J. Chisholm. 1894. *The Kindergarten of the Church*. New York: Eaton and Mains.

Freligh, Becky. 1987. "Former Directors Defend Kinder-Care Centers Here." *The Plain Dealer* [Cleveland] (April 26), p. 4-G.

Fried, Mindy. 1987. *Babies and Bargaining: Working Parents Take Action.* Southeastern Massachusetts University, Arnold M. Dubin Labor Education Center, November.

Friedan, Betty. 1981. *The Second Stage.* New York: Summit Books.

Friedman, Dana E. 1985a. "Taking Care of the Kids: The Corporate Role in Providing Child Care." *PTA Today,* (April), 11–13.

——— 1985b. *Corporate Financial Assistance for Child Care.* New York: The Conference Board, Inc.

——— 1987. *Family-Supportive Policies: The Corporate Decision-Making Process.* New York: The Conference Board, Inc.

Fromberg, Doris Pronin. 1989. "Kindergarten: Current Circumstances Affecting Curriculum." *Teachers College Record* 90 (Spring): 392–403.

Fullerton, Howard N., Jr. 1989. "New Labor Force Projections, Spanning 1988 to 2000." *Monthly Labor Review* (November): 3–12.

Futrell, Mary Hatwood. 1988. "Should the Congress Adopt the Proposed 'Act for Better Child Care Services of 1988'?" *The Congressional Digest* 67 (November): 268, 270, 272, 274.

Galinsky, Ellen. 1989. "A Parent/Teacher Study: Interesting Results." *Young Children* (November): 2–3.

——— 1990. "I Have Seen the Beginnings of a Transformation in Attitudes." *Young Children* (September): 1, 76.

Gallagher, James J. 1989. "The Impact of Policies for Handicapped Children on Future Early Education Policy." *Kappan* 71 (October): 121–124.

Gard, Willis L. 1924. "The Influence of Kindergarten on Achievement in Reading." *Educational Research Bulletin* 3 (April 2): 135–138.

Garland, Mary J. 1924. "Elizabeth Palmer Peabody." In *Pioneers of the Kindergarten in America*, ed. the Committee of Nineteen, pp. 19–25. New York: Century Co.

Gesell, Arnold. 1926. "The Downward Extension of the Kindergarten." *Childhood Education* 2 (October): 53–59.

Giddings, Margaret. 1908. "The Relative Advantages and Disadvantages of Having One Supervisor of Kindergartens and Primary Work in the City-School System." *The Seventh Yearbook of the National Society for the Study of Education,* vol. II, Part II, pp. 50–60. Bloomington, IL: Public School Publishing Company.

Gilder, Richard Watson. 1903. "The Kindergarten: An Uplifting Social Influence in the Home and the District." *Journal of Proceedings and Addresses of the National Educational Association*: pp. 391–394.

Gnezda, Terry. 1987. "State Fiscal Policies for Child Care and Early Childhood Education." *State Legislative Report* 12, no. 7 (October). Denver: microfiche reproduction by Eric Documents Research Service, ED 292 542.

——— and Catherine Sonnier. 1988. "Recent State Early Childhood Initiatives." In *Shaping the Future for Early Childhood Programs* pp. 36–41. Ypsilanti, MI: High Scope Press.

Goldman, Joyce E. 1975. "From the Folks Who Brought You Fast Food, Nursing Homes and Mini–golf... Vacuum–Packed Day Cares." *Ms.* (March), pp. 80–83.

Good, Harry G., and James D. Teller. 1973. *A History of American Education,* 3rd ed. New York: Macmillan Co.

Goodman, Irene F., and Joanne P. Brady. 1988. *The Challenge of Coordination: Head Start's Relationship to State-Funded Preschool Initiatives.* Executive Summary. Newton: Education Development Center, Inc., May.

Graeff, Virginia E. 1898. "The Elizabeth Peabody Kindergarten Settlement." *Kindergarten Review* (May): 605–606.

Granger, Robert C. 1989. "The Staffing Crisis in Early Childhood Education." *Kappan* 71 (October): 130–134.

Gray, Wendy. 1979. "Day Care As A Social Service Strategy: 1890 to 1946." Ph.D. dissertation, Brandeis University.

——— 1980. "The Social Work Profession and Day Care Services: Social Policy Issues, 1890 to 1990." Paper presented at the First National Conference on Social Work with Women, Washington, DC, September 15.

Greenman, James. 1978. "Day Care in the Schools? A Response to the Position of the AFT." *Young Children* 33, 4: 4–13.

Gregory, Benjamin C. 1908. "The Necessity of Continuity Between the Kindergarten and the Elementary School." *National Society for the Study of Education.* Vol. II, seventh yearbook, Part II, pp. 22–34. Chicago: University of Chicago Press.

Griffin, Clifford S. 1967. "Religious Benevolence as Social Control, 1815–1860." In *Ante-Bellum Reform*, pp. 81–96. ed. David Brion Davis, New York: Harper and Row.

Grubb, W. Norton. 1987. *Young Children Face the States: Issues and Options for Early Childhood Programs.* New Brunswick: Rutgers, the State University of New Jersey.

——— and Marvin Lazerson. 1977. "Child Care Government Financing and the Public Schools: Lessons from the California Children's Centers." *School Review* 86 (November): 5–37.

——— and Marvin Lazerson. 1982. *Broken Promises: How Americans Fail Their Children.* New York: Basic Books.

"A Half-Baked Day-Care Plan." 1990. *Pittsburgh Post-Gazette* (July 24), p. 6.

Hailmann, William N. 1872. "The Adaptation of Froebel's System of Education to American Institutions." *Journal of Addresses and Proceedings of the National Education Association*: 141–149.

—— 1890. "Schoolishness in the Kindergarten." *Journal of Addresses and Proceedings of the National Education Association*: 565–573.

Hanckel, Marion S. 1911. "New Fields for the Kindergarten in the South." *Kindergarten-Primary Magazine* 23 (June): 282–285.

Hansen, Dora. 1904. "Luzerne Kindergarten for Foreign Speaking Children." *Home Mission Monthly* 18 (May): 154–156.

Harris, Phyllis Braudy. 1987. "Leadership and Quality of Patient Care in Nursing Homes: A Path-Goal Model of Leadership Effectiveness." Ph.D. dissertation, Case Western Reserve University.

Harris, William T. 1889. "Kindergarten Methods Contrasted with the Methods of the Primary School." *Journal of Addresses and Proceedings of the National Education Association*: 448–453.

Harrison, Elizabeth. 1903. "The Scope and Results of Mothers' Classes." *Journal of Proceedings and Addresses of the National Education Association*: 400–405.

Harvey, Reverend Thomas J. 1990a. Letter to President Bush (September 10).

—— 1990b. Letter to Representative Thomas S. Foley [Catholic Charities Position Statement] (March 27).

Haskins, Ron. 1988. "What Day Care Crisis?" *AEI Journal on Government and Society* (March–April): 13–21.

Hatch, Orrin G. 1982. "Families, Children, and Child Care." In *Day Care: Scientific and Social Policy Issues*, ed. Edward F. Zigler and Edmund W. Gordon, pp. 255–259. Boston: Auburn House Publishing.

Haven, Caroline T. 1908. "The International Kindergarten Union: Why It Was Organized." *IKU, Proceedings of the Fifteenth Annual Meeting*: 115–119.

Hawkins, Augustus. 1990. Press Release (October 16).

Hayes, Cheryl D., John L. Palmer and Martha J. Zaslow eds. *Who Cares for America's Children? Child Care Policy for the 1990s*. Washington, DC, National Academy Press.

"Head Start: A Program that Works." 1990. *Child Care Information Exchange*. (September–October): 13–15.

Hochschild, Arlie, and Anne Machung. 1989. *The Second Shift: Working Parents and the Revolution at Home*. New York: Viking Penguin.

Hofer, Amalie. 1892. "The Christ in Education." *Kindergarten Magazine* 4 (December): 194–195.

——— 1895. "The Social Settlement and the Kindergarten." *Kindergarten Magazine* 8 (September): 47–59.

Hofer-Hegner, Bertha. 1901. "A Story of a Settlement Garden." *Kindergarten Magazine* 13 (May): 483–488.

Holcomb, Desma. 1990. Telephone conversation with author, (October 12).

Holden, Francis Cooke. 1905. "Does Kindergarten Training Prepare the Child for the Primary School? The Teacher's Point of View." *Kindergarten Magazine* 17 (March): 389–396.

Holland, Ernest O. L. 1913. "The Effect of Kindergarten Work on Children in the Grades." *Journal of Proceedings of the National Education Association*: 452–458.

Holloway, Clyde C. 1988. "Should the Congress Adopt the Proposed 'Act for Better Child Care Services of 1988'?" *The Congressional Digest* 67 (November): 265.

Holmes, Steven A. 1990a. "In House, Day Care Becomes a Church-State Issue." *The New York Times* (March 22), p. A13.

——— 1990b. "House, 265-145, Votes to Widen Day Care Programs in the Nation." *The New York Times* (March 30), p. 1.

Horton, Paul B. and Chester L. Hunt. 1984. *Sociology*. 6th ed. New York: McGraw-Hill.

Hufford, Lois C. 1899. "Free Kindergarten Work in Indianapolis. Twenty Years of Character Building." *Kindergarten Magazine* 2 (January): 305–313.

Hughes, James L. 1899. "The Relation of the Kindergarten to the Public School System." *Kindergarten Magazine* 6 (June–July): 750–757.

Hull House Bulletin 1896. 1, no. 6 (October 15).

Humphrey, Greg. 1990. Telephone conversation with author (September 19).

"The Impact of the Federal Regulations in the ABC Bill." 1988. *Child Care Review*. (April–May): 5–8.

Independent Sector. 1990. *Government Relations Info and Action* 13, no. 9 (October 31).

"Investment Banker Offers to Buy Kinder-Care Firm." 1989. *The Plain Dealer* [Cleveland] (November 4), p. 3-E.

Jacobson, Carolyn J. 1986. "Women at Work: Meeting the Challenge of Job and Family." Reprint *AFL-CIO American Federationist* (April 5): 1–16.

Jameson, E. J. 1890. "The City Waif." *The Kindergarten* 3 (September): 19–20.

Jenkins, Elizabeth. 1930–31. "How the Kindergarten Found Its Way to America." *Wisconsin Magazine History* no. 14: 48–62.

Joe, Hollis L. T. 1981. *Polemics on Day Care*. Toronto: Williams-Wallace International.

Johnson, Julie. 1989. "Child Care Shortage Clouds Future of Welfare Program." *The New York Times* (November 12), pp. 1, 12.

Johnston, Bertha. 1900. "The Chicago Kindergarten Institute." *Kindergarten Magazine* 12 (June): 573–581.

Johnston, David. 1989a. "Child Care Bills Near Completion." *The New York Times* (October 10), pp. 1, 12.

—— 1989b. "Congress Plans to Put Off Action on Child Care Because of Impasse." *The New York Times* (November 17), p. 10.

Jones, Jacqueline. 1982. *To Get Out of This Land of Suffering: Black Migrant Women, Work and the Family in Northern Cities, 1900-1930.* Wellesley College, Center for Research on Women, Working Paper No. 91.

—— 1983. *Hardest Times: Black Women, Work, and the Family in the Great Depression.* Wellesley College, Center for Research on Women, Working Paper No. 109.

Kagan, Sharon L. 1987. "Early Schooling: On What Grounds?" In *Early Schooling*, ed. Sharon L. Kagan and Edward F. Zigler, pp. 3–26. New Haven: Yale University Press.

—— 1989a. "Early Care and Education: Beyond the Schoolhouse Doors." *Kappan* 71 (October): 107–112.

—— 1989b. "The Care and Education of America's Young Children: At the Brink of a Paradigm Shift?" *Caring for America's Children: Proceedings of the Academy of Political Science* 37: 70–83.

—— 1989c. "The New Advocacy in Early Childhood Education." *Teachers College Record* 90 (Spring): 465–473.

—— and Theresa Glennon. 1982. "Considering Proprietary Child Care." In *Day Care: Scientific and Social Policy Issues*, ed. Edward F. Zigler and Edmund W. Gordon, pp. 402–412. Boston: Auburn House.

—— and James Newton. 1989. "For-Profit and Nonprofit Child Care: Similarities and Differences." *Young Children* (November): 4–10.

—— and Edward F. Zigler. 1987a. "Early Schooling: A National Opportunity?" In *Early Schooling*, ed. Sharon L. Kagan and Edward F. Zigler, pp. 215–230. New Haven: Yale University Press.

———— and Edward F. Zigler. 1987b. *Early Schooling: The National Debate.* New Haven: Yale University Press.

Kahn, Alfred, and Sheila Kamerman. 1987. *Child Care: Facing the Hard Choices.* Dover: Auburn House Publishing Company.

Kamerman, Sheila B. 1980. "Child Care and Family Benefits: Policies of Six Industrialized Countries." *Monthly Labor Review* 23, no. 6 (November).

———— 1989. "An International Overview of Preschool Programs." *Kappan* 71 (October): 135–137.

———— and Alfred Kahn. 1979. "The Day-Care Debate: A Wider View." *The Public Interest* 54 (Winter): 76–94.

———— and Alfred Kahn. 1981. *Child Care, Family Benefits, and Working Parents: A Study in Comparative Policy.* New York: Columbia University Press.

———— and Alfred J. Kahn. 1989. "The Possibilities for Child and Family Policy: A Cross-National Perspective." *Caring for America's Children: Proceedings of the Academy of Political Science* 37: 84–98.

Kantrowitz, Barbara. 1986. "Changes in the Workplace; Child Care Is Now an Item on the National Agenda." *Newsweek* (March 31) p. 57.

Kessler-Harris, Alice. 1981. *Women Have Always Worked: A Historical Overview.* Old Westbury, NY: The Feminist Press.

Keyserling, Mary Dublin. 1972. *Windows on Day Care: A Report on the Findings of Members of the National Council of Jewish Women on Day Care Needs and Services In Their Communities.* New York: National Council of Jewish Women.

Kidwell, Mary. 1990. Letter to author (October 16).

Kilpatrick, William H., ed. 1933. *The Educational Frontier.* New York: The Century Co.

"Kinder Care Makes Employers into 'Uncles'." 1982. *Sales and Marketing Management* (January 18) 52–54.

Kinder-Care. 1989a. "Perry Mendel Remembers." *The Centerline.* 12 (July–August): 1.

——— 1989b. "1,000,000!!!." *The Centerline* 12 (October): 1.

——— 1989c. "20 Years of Caring." *The Centerline* 12 (July–August): 4–5.

——— 1990. "Kinder-Care at Work." *The Centerline* 13 (February): 1.

"The Kindergarten in America." 1902. *Outlook* 71 (May 10), pp. 107–108.

"Kindergarten Work in Baltimore." 1900. *Kindergarten Magazine* 12 (April): 456–457.

Klemmack, David L. and Lucinda Lee Roff. 1985. "Employers' Responsibility for Social Services: Public Perceptions." *Social Work* 30 (September–October): 445–447.

Kornblum, William; Joseph Julian and Carolyn D. Smith. 1989. *Social Problems.* 6th ed. Englewood Cliffs; N.J.: Prentice Hall.

Kurtz, Barbara. 1990. Personal communication with author (December 15).

"La Petite Academy, Inc." 1988. *Fortune* (May 9), p. 70.

Lake, Alice. "The Day-Care Business: Which Comes First the Child or the Dollar?" 1970. *McCall's* (November), pp. 60–61, 96–97.

Langzettel, Marion B. 1903. "Discussion." *Journal of Proceedings and Addresses of the National Educational Association Annual Meeting*: 405.

"Latest Benefit to Employes: Day Care for Their Children." 1972. *U.S. News and World Report* (December 11), pp. 64–66.

"Laws on Child Care Centers Rapped." 1990. *Plain Dealer* [Cleveland] (September 4), p. 8–A.

Lawson, Carol. 1989. "Seven Employers Join to Provide Child Care at Home in a Crisis." *The New York Times* (September 7), p. 1.

———— 1990a. "In Missouri, Schools Open Their Doors to Day Care." *The New York Times* (October 4), pp. B1, B5.

———— 1990b. "Effort to Mobilize Parents Starts Anew." *The New York Times* (November 22), p. L C5.

Lazerson, Marvin. 1971. *Origins of the Urban School; Public Education in Massachusetts.* Cambridge, MA: Harvard University Press.

———— 1972a. "Historical Antecedents of Early Childhood Education." *Education Digest* 38 (November): 24–27.

———— 1972b. "The Historical Antecedents of Early Childhood Education." *Early Childhood Education: The Seventy-first Yearbook of the National Society for the Study of Education*, Part 1, pp. 33–53. Chicago: University of Chicago Press.

Lehrman, Karen. 1985. "While You Count the Toilets, Do You Mind Watching My Kids? Day Care Rules Hurt Those They're Supposed to Help." *The Washington Post* [national weekly ed] (November 25), p. 25.

Levitan, Sar, and Elizabeth A. Conway. 1988. *American Child Care: Problems and Solutions Special Report #12* by, Bureau of National Affairs. Washington DC: Buraff Publications.

Leviton, Joyce. 1977. "As Little Red Schoolhouses Dot the Land, Perry Mendel Becomes the Colonel Sanders of Day Care." *People* (August 8), pp. 72, 75.

Lewin, Tamar. 1989. "Small Tots, Big Biz." *The New York Times Magazine* (January 29), pp. 30, 89-91.

Lewis, Neil J. 1990. "Lobbyist's Bitter Attack on Congressmen Reverberates From 60's to the 90's." *The New York Times* (January 5), p. 11.

Liekweg, John. 1989. "The Establishment Clause Does Not Prohibit the Participation of Religious Providers in Federal Child Care Legislation: Unrestricted Vouchers Are a Constitutional Alternative That Deserves

Serious Consideration by Congress." Paper photocopied by the United States Catholic Conference.

Lightfoot, Sara Lawrence. 1978. *Worlds Apart: Relationships Between Families and Schools*. New York: Basic Books.

Lindner, Eileen W., and Mary C. Mattis, and June R. Rogers. 1983. *When Churches Mind the Children: A Study of Day Care in Local Parishes*. Ypsilanti, MI: High/Scope Press.

Linkins, Karen. 1990. Telephone conversation with author, (October 22).

Logan, Mary. 1986. "Child Care: Slow Progress, Pitiful Funding." In *Work and Family (AFL-CIO)*; Reprint of (March 22): 3–11.

Louis Harris and Associates, Inc. 1989. *The Philip Morris Companies Inc. Family Survey II: Child Care*. New York: Louis Harris and Associates, Inc., 1989.

Lynn, Larry. 1978. "Father Goose in Day Care: A Southern Entrepreneur Institutionalizes Day Care and Moves in on a Southern and National Trend." *The South Magazine* (August), pp. 18–19.

Mabie, Hamilton W. 1905. "The Free Kindergarten." *Harper's Magazine* (October), pp. 649–657.

Macchiarola, Frank J. 1989. "Schools That Serve Children." *Caring for America's Children: Proceedings of the Academy of Political Science* 37: 170–181.

MacKenzie, Constance. 1886. "Free Kindergartens." *Proceedings of the National Conference on Charities and Corrections*: 48–53; (November 1908): 37–41.

MacLear, Martha. 1914. "A Study of the Work Done By Kindergarten Children in the First Grade." *Educational Review* (May): 512–517.

Magid, Renee Y. 1983. *Child Care Initiatives for Working Parents: Why Employers Get Involved*. New York: American Management Association.

Magnet, Myron. 1983. "What Mass-Produced Child Care Is Producing." *Fortune* (November 28), pp. 157–174.

Mahoney, Kathleen. 1985. "Day Care and Equality in Canada." *Manitoba Law Journal* 14 no. 3: 305–340.

Maley, Lucie. 1898. "Benefit of the Kindergarten to the Indian Children." *Kindergarten Magazine* 10 (March): 438–441.

Manson, Elizabeth E. 1908. "The Ideals of a Kindergarten Settlement." *Kindergarten Review* 19 (November): 136–144.

Marriott, Michel. 1990a. "A New Road to Learning: Teaching the Whole Child." *The New York Times* (June 13), pp. A1, A10.

——— 1990b. "Dropout Fight Is Retooled for Grade Schools." *The New York Times* (November 14), pp. B1, B9.

Marrison, Benjamin. 1990. "Tenants Face Eviction if Board Reopens School." *Plain Dealer* [Cleveland] (September 20), p. 1-C.

Martin, Edwin. 1977. "Public Policy and Early Childhood Education: A Buddhist Garden." In *Early Childhood Education*, ed. L. Golubchick and B. Persky, pp. 17–19. Wayne: Avery Publishing Group.

Martin, Patricia Yancey, Sandra Seymour, Myrna Courage, Karolyn Godbey, and Richard Tate. 1988. "Work-Family Policies: Corporate, Union, Feminist, and Pro-Family Leaders' Views." *Gender and Society* 2, no. 3 (September): 385–400.

Massengill, Douglas and Donald J. Peterson. 1988. "Childcare Programs Benefit Employers, Too." 65 (May): 58–62.

McCartney, Kathleen; Phillips, Deborah; and Sandra Scarr. 1989. "Dilemmas of Child Care in the United States: Employed Mothers and Children at Risk." *Canadian Psychology* 30, no. 2: 126–139.

McCarty, Stella. 1898. "Charity and the Kindergarten." *The Charities Review* 7 (January): 946–950.

McEntee, Gerald W. 1988. "Should the Congress Adopt the Proposed 'Act for Better Child Care Services of 1988'?" *The Congressional Digest* 67 (November): 284, 286.

McGill, Douglas C. 1989. "Kinder-Care to Separate Operations." *The New York Times* (May 30), pp. D-1, D9.

McKenny, Charles. 1908. "The Contributions of the Kindergarten to Elementary Education." *Kindergarten-Primary Magazine* 21 (November): 37–41.

McMinn, Martha. 1897. "Problems of Mothers Lacking Wealth." *Kindergarten Magazine* 10 (November): 157–163.

Meisels, Samuel J. and L. Steven Sternberg. 1989. "Quality Sacrificed in Proprietary Child Care." *Education Week* (June 7): 36.

Mercer, Elizabeth. 1989. "Women, Work and Child Care: The Need." Fact Sheet of National Commission on Working Women of Wider Opportunities for Women, May.

Merrill, Jenny. 1898. "Twelve Hundred and Fifty Children in New York Public Kindergartens: Complete Report of the Forty-Three Kindergartens by the Supervisor." *Kindergarten Magazine* 11 (October): 105–110.

——— 1907. "Kindergarten Progress in the Public Schools of New York." *Kindergarten Review* 17 (April): 468–471.

——— 1908. "Ways and Means for Securing Organic Continuity Between the Kindergarten and the Primary School in the Development of the Child." *National Society for the Study of Education Seventh Yearbook, Part 2*, pp. 9–21. Bloomington, IL: Public School Publishing Co.

Merton, Robert K. 1968. *Social Theory and Social Structure*. New York: The Free Press.

——— 1976. *Sociological Ambivalence and Other Essays*. New York: The Free Press.

———— 1978. "A Paradigm for Functional Analysis." In *Contemporary Sociological Theories*, ed. Alan Wells, pp. 13–17. Santa Monica: Goodyear Publishing Co.

Micheli, Robin. 1986. "The Perk of the Eighties." *Working Woman* (June), pp. 132–133.

Miller, Annie E. 1904. "Practical Plans Bring Speedy Success." *Home Mission Monthly* (May), pp. 152–153.

Miller, Darla. 1989. *First Steps Toward Cultural Difference: Socialization in Infant/Toddler Day Care*. Washington, DC: Child Welfare League of America.

Miller, Dorothy D. 1989. "Poor Women and Work Programs: Back to the Future." *Affilia* 4, no. 1 (Spring): 9–22.

Mitchell, Anne, Michelle Seligson and Fern Marx. 1989. *Early Childhood Programs and the Public Schools: Between Promise and Practice*. Dover, MA: Auburn House Publishing Co.

Modigliani, Kathy. 1988. "Twelve Reasons for the Low Wages in Child Care." *Young Children* (March): 14, 15.

Monahan, Frank J. 1990a. Memorandum to State Catholic Conference Directors and Other Interested Parties, United States Catholic Conference (March 30).

———— 1990b. Memorandum to Bishops, State Catholic Conference Directors and Other Interested Parties, United States Catholic Conference. (November 2).

Montgomery, David. 1987. *The Fall of the House of Labor: The Workplace, the State and American Labor Activism, 1865–1925*. Cambridge and New York: Cambridge University Press.

Mooney, Barbara. 1988. "Area Day-Care Centers Feeling Pinch." *Crain's Cleveland Business* (October 17), pp. 19, 24.

Moore, Evelyn. 1975 "Black Concerns." In *One Child Indivisible*, ed. J. D. Andrews. Washington, DC: National Association for the Education of Young Children.

————— 1987. "Child Care in the Public Schools: Public Accountability and the Black Child." In *Early Schooling*, ed. Sharon L. Kagan and Edward F. Zigler, pp. 83–97. New Haven: Yale University Press.

————— and Carol Brunson Phillips. 1989. "Early Public Schooling: Is One Solution Right for All Children?" *Theory into Practice* (Winter): 58–63.

Morado, Carolyn. 1989. "State Government Roles in Schooling for 4-Year--Olds." *Theory Into Practice* (Winter): 34–40.

Morgan, Gwen. 1977. *The Trouble with Title XX: A Review of Child Day Care Policy*. Washington, DC: Day Care and Child Development Council of America, Inc.

————— 1985. "Programs for Young Children in Public Schools? Only If...." *Young Children* (May): 54.

————— 1989. "Stalemate or Consensus? Barriers to National Policy." *Theory into Practice* (Winter): 41–46.

Morrison, Frederick J. 1989. "Child Care for the 21st Century: An Overview and Commentary." *Canadian Psychology* 30, no. 2: 148–151.

Morton, John. 1969. "Nursery Schools Will Be Opened by Chicken Chain." *The National Observer* (February 17), pp. 1, 20.

Murray, Anna. 1900. "A Plea for Kindergartens in the Southland." *Kindergarten Magazine* 13 (November): 117–121.

Murray, Kathleen A. "Child Care and the Law." *Santa Clara Law Review* 25 (Spring/Summer, 1985): 261-302.

Muscari, Ann. 1988. Testimony for Kinder-Care Learning Centers, Inc. Committee on Finance. United States Senate. Hearing on the Federal Role in Child Care. September 22.

————— 1990a. Telephone conversation with author, (February 13).

————— 1990b. Letter to author (February 19).

Nash, Nathaniel C. 1990. "Tax Credit of Many Stripes Reborn as Child Care Tool." *The New York Times* (October 21), p. 17.

National Association for Child Care Management. 1984a. Testimony for the Record of the Select Committee on Children, Youth and Families (April 4).

———— 1984b. Testimony presented by Carole M. Rogin before the Senate Finance Committee. Subcommittee on Taxation and Debt Management (July 27).

National Association for the Education of Young Children. 1989. "State Policies on Kindergarten." Washington DC: National Association for the Education of Young Children, April.

———— 1990. "Child Care Legislation: Success at Last!" *Young Children* (November): 61.

National Association of State Boards of Education. 1988. *Right from the Start: The Report of the NASBE Task Force on Early Childhood Education.* Alexandria, VA: National Association of State Boards of Education.

National Black Child Development Institute, Inc. 1985. *Child Care in the Public Schools: Incubator for Inequality?* Washington, DC: National Black Child Development Institute, Inc.

———— 1987. *Safeguards: Guidelines for Establishing Programs for Four-Year-Olds in the Public Schools.* Washington, DC: National Black Child Development Institute, Inc.

National Child Care Association. 1990a. "NCCA Will Issue National Teacher Credential—The Certified Childcare Professional (CCP)." *National Focus* (July): 1.

———— 1990b. "NCCA Child Care Professional Recognition Forms Mail in August!" *National Focus* (July): 1.

———— 1990c. "New NCCA Affiliate Associations for Teachers and Parents Moving Ahead." *National Focus* (July): 2-3.

———— 1990d. "National Child Care Association Sets Programs and Policies for the Nation's Private Child Care Community." Press Release, Atlanta (August).

———— 1990e. Because Child Care is More Than Child's Play. (brochure).

National Cooperative Bank, and its affiliate NCB Development Corporation. 1990. Letter to Barbara Kurtz (August 3).

National Council of the Churches of Christ. 1984. "Policy Statement on Child Day Care," (November 7).

National Council of Churches. 1989a. "In the Pipeline: Act for Better Child Care Services." *Mark-Up* 18 (June): 5–6.

———— 1989b. "Church-State Issues Threaten Child Care Bill." (May 31).

———— 1990a. "Perspective I: At Last! House Child Care Action." *Mark-Up* 19 (March): 1–2.

———— 1990b. "Child Care." *Mark-Up* 19 (September): 7–8.

———— 1990c. "In the Pipeline: Child Care." *Mark-Up* 19 (October–November): 3–4.

National Council of Jewish Women. 1988. "Employer Supports for Child Care." (Summary of Mothers in the Workplace Study). New York: Center for the Child, (August): 2–6.

———— 1990a. "Highlights of the NCJW National Family Day Care Project." April. New York: National Council of Jewish Women.

———— 1990b. "Innovative NCJW Public/Private Partnership Focuses on Work/Family Issues." *News* (November): 1–2.

National Education Association. 1989. "Enlisting Parents as Partners in Schooling." *Doubts and Certainties* 3, no. 7 (March): 1–3.

———— 1990a. "The Danforth Foundation Links Four National School-Based Projects." *Doubts and Certainties* 4, no. 10 (June): 4.

———— 1990b. *Early Childhood Education and the Public Schools*. Washington, DC: National Education Association.

National Impact. 1989. "Support HR 3 and the Act for Better Child Care Services." *Action* (September 22).

National Parent Teacher Association. 1988a. Letter to all members of the Congress (January 4).

———— 1988b. "Alternatives to Vouchers for Child Care in Private Institutions." Washington DC: National PTA.

———— 1988c. Testimony presented by Arlene Zielke before the Subcommittee on Human Resources on Education and Labor U. S. House of Representatives regarding Child Care and Early Childhood Education Programs (April 21).

National Society for the Study of Education. 1907. *The Kindergarten and Its Relation to Elementary Education*, sixth yearbook. Bloomington, IL: Public School Publishing Society.

———— 1908. *The Coordination of the Kindergarten and the Elementary School*, seventh yearbook. Part 2. Bloomington, IL: Public School Publishing Society.

National Women's Law Center. n.d. "Budget Reconciliation Bill Expands Earned Income Tax Credit" (released November).

"NCCA Launches New Initiatives." 1990. *Child Care Information Exchange*. (September–October): 11.

Nelson, John R., Jr. 1982. "The Politics of Federal Day Care Regulation." In *Day Care: Scientific and Social Policy Issues*, ed. Edward F. Zigler and Edmund W. Gordon, pp. 267–306. Boston: Auburn House Publishing Co.

Neugebauer, Roger. 1989. "Child Care 1989: Status Report on For Profit Child Care." *Child Care Information Exchange* (February): 19–23.

———— 1990a. "How's Business? Status Report #6 on For Profit Child Care." *Child Care Information Exchange* (February): 31–34.

—— 1990b. "Status Report #1 on Non Profit Child Care." *Child Care Information Exchange*. (April): 20–24.

"A New Builder Amenity: Day-Care Centers." 1986. *Professional Builder* 51 (February): 158–161.

Newton, Rev. R. Heber. 1881. "The Free Kindergarten in Church Work." *American Journal of Education*, no. 30: 705–730.

—— 1886. "The Bearing of the Kindergarten on the Prevention of Crime." *Proceedings of the National Conference on Charities and Corrections*: 53–58.

Norgren, Jill. 1981. "In Search of a National Child Care Policy: Background and Prospects." *Western Political Quarterly* 34, no. 1: 127–142.

"Notes of Progress Among the Kindergartens." 1903. *Kindergarten Review* 13 (February): 381–384.

Nye, Barbara A. 1990a. "President's Update: ACCCI Continues to Develop and Grow." *The Associate* [Association of Child Care Consultants International](Spring): 1.

—— 1990b. "The Politics and Reality of Family Care in Corporate America." *The Associate* [Association of Child Care Consultants International]. (Spring): 1.

O'Grady, C. Geraldine. 1911. "The Kindergarten Situation in the Southern Mills." *Kindergarten Review* 22 (October): 130–131.

Oakes, Maribeth. 1990. Telephone conversation with author (September 14).

Oliver, Valeri. 1990. "Marriott Deal Helping Boost Corporate Child Care Growth." *Nashville Business Journal* (September 3–7): 1, 20.

Olsen, Deborah. 1989. "Problems with the All-Day Kindergarten: Presumed or Real?" *Early Childhood Research Quarterly* 4 (June): 267–270.

—— and Edward Zigler. 1989. "An Assessment of the All-Day Kindergarten Movement." *Early Childhood Research Quarterly* 4 (June): 167–186.

On-Site Day Care: The State of the Art and Models Development. 1980. Albany: New York State Committee on the Work Environment and Productivity. A Joint Committee of the Governor's Office of Employee Relations.

Orcutt, Hortense May. 1907. "The History of the Kindergarten in the New York Public Schools." *Kindergarten Magazine* 19 (March): 434–441.

——— 1910. "The Kindergarten and the Family of the Little Foreigner." *Kindergarten Magazine* 23 (November): 86–87.

Parker, Marcia. 1988. "Consolidations Make Day Care Intelligent Bet." *Pension and Investment Age* (October 17): 52–53.

Parsons, Talcott. 1978. "The Concept of Society: The Components and Their Interrelations." In *Contemporary Sociological Theories*, ed. Alan Wells, pp. 18-32. Santa Monica: Goodyear Publishing Co.

Pave, Irene. 1985. "The Insurance Crisis That Could Cripple Day-Care." *Business Week* (June 17), pp. 114, 116.

Payne, Bertha. 1908. "How Can the Training of Kindergartners and Primary Teachers Contribute to Economy in Education of Children?" *The Seventh Yearbook Part 11 of the National Society for the Study of Education.* vol. 2, pp. 35–49. Bloomington, IL: Public School Publishing Co.

Peabody, Elizabeth P. 1875. *Lectures on the Nursery and Kindergarten*, 2nd ed. Pittsburgh: J. S. Travelli.

——— 1882. "The Origin and Growth of the Kindergarten." *Education II* (May–June): 507–527.

——— 1896. "The Connection of the Kindergarten with the School." In *The Kindergarten and the School*, ed. Anne Page. (Publisher unknown.)

Pear, Robert. 1990. "House and Senate Pass Budget Bill; Bush Is 'Pleased': Most Americans Will Feel a Shift in Social Policy." *The New York Times* (October 28), pp. A1, A14.

Pease, Don J. 1989. "No, Funding the Bottom Line." *The Plain Dealer* [Cleveland] (December 21), p. 7–B.

Perry, Sara Kathryn Sean. 1978. "Survey and Analysis of Employer-Sponsored Day Care in the United States." Ph.D. dissertation, University of Wisconsin—Milwaukee.

Philip Morris Companies, Inc. 1989. *The Philip Morris Companies Inc. Family Survey II: Child Care—the Executive Summary Report.* New York: Philip Morris Companies.

Phillips, Deborah A. 1987. "Whither Churches That Mind the Children? Current Issues Facing Church-Housed Child Care." *Child Care Information Exchange*, (May): 35–38.

——— and Edward Zigler. 1987. "The Checkered History of Federal Child Care Regulation." In *Review of Research in Education*, ed. Ernest Z. Rothkopt, vol. 14, pp. 3–41. Washington, DC: American Educational Research Association.

Pierce, William. 1975. "Profiting From Day Care." In *Rationale for Child Care Services: Programs vs. Politics*, vol. 1, ed. S. Auerbach. New York: Human Sciences Press.

——— 1976. "Prospects for National Day Care Legislation." *Washington Social Legislation Bulletin* 23, no. 47 (December 13): 185–188.

Preston, Anne E. 1988. "The Effects of Property Rights on Labor Costs of Nonprofit Firms: An Application to the Day Care Industry." *Journal of Industrial Economics* 36 (March): 337–349.

Putnam, Alice H. n.d. "The Use of Kindergarten Material in Primary Schools." *The Kindergarten and the School*, ed. Anne Page, pp. 94–107.

Quinn, Jane Bryant. 1983. "Federal Help on Day Care Shifted from Poor to Middle Class." In *A Corporate Reader: Work and Family Life in the 1980s*, compiled by The Children's Defense Fund, pp. 159–160. Washington, DC: Children's Defense Fund.

Radest, Howard B. 1969. *Toward Common Ground: The Story of the Ethical Societies in the United States.* New York: Frederick Ungar.

Rasky, Susan F. 1989. "House Endorses Tax Credits and Grants for Child Care." *The New York Times* (October 6), p. 10.

——— 1990a. "Aides Say Bush Faced Choice: A Deal on Taxes, or a Fiasco." *The New York Times* (October 25), pp. A1, A10.

——— 1990b. "The Budget Battle Reflects the Strains in the System." *The New York Times* (October 28), p. 4-1.

Read, Katherine and June Patterson. 1980. "The Nursery School and Kindergarten," In *History and Theories Influencing Contemporary Ideas in Early Education*, pp. 41–63. New York: Holt, Rinehart and Winston.

Recken, Roberta. 1989. "Who Gets Accredited?" *Young Children* (January): 11–12.

Rector, Robert. 1988. "Should the Congress Adopt the Proposed 'Act for Better Child Care Services of 1988'?" *The Congressional Digest* 67 (November): 275, 277, 279, 281, 283, 285, 287.

Reese, C. 1982. "Bringing Children to Work: A Hospital Day Care Center." *Children Today* 11 (July–August): 16–21.

Report of the Educational Commission of the City of Chicago. 1898. Appointed by the Mayor Carter B. Harrison. Chicago: The Lakeside Press, R. R. Donnelley and Sons Co.

Rice, Joseph Mayer. 1893. *The Public School System in the United States.* New York: Century Co.; reprint edition New York: Arno Press, 1969.

Rimer, Sara. 1990. "A School in the Bronx That Somehow is Making It." *The New York Times* (March 12), pp. A1, A13.

Roberts, Josephine E. 1942. "Elizabeth Peabody and the Temple School." *New England Quarterly* 15: 497–508.

Roby, Pamela, ed. 1973a. *Child Care—Who Cares? Foreign and Domestic Infant and Early Childhood Development Policies*. New York: Basic Books, Inc.

——— 1973b. "Young Children: Priorities or Problems? Issues and Goals for the Next Decade." In *Child Care—Who Cares? Foreign and Domestic Infant and Early Childhood Development Policies*, ed. Pamela Roby, pp. 123–156. New York: Basic Books.

"Rocking Horse Child Care Centers of America, Inc." *Philadelphia Business Journal* 7 (December 12): 26–27.

Rose-Ackerman, Susan. 1983. "Unintended Consequences: Regulating the Quality of Subsidized Day Care." *Journal of Policy Analysis and Management* 3: 14–30.

——— 1986. "Altruistic Nonprofit Firms in Competitive Markets: The Case of Day-Care Centers in the United States." *Journal of Consumer Policy* 9 (September): 291–309.

Rosenbaum, David E. 1990a. "Bush Drops Fight for a Lower Tax on Capital Gains." *The New York Times* (September 30), pp. A1, A17.

——— 1990b. "House Approves Democratic Plan to Reduce Deficit." *The New York Times* (October 17), pp. A1, A14.

——— 1990c. "Senate Overcomes Final Obstacles to a Budget Bill." *The New York Times* (October 19), pp. A1, A10.

——— 1990d. "President's Aides Quit Budget Talks in Tax Stalemate." *The New York Times* (October 22), pp. A1, A10.

——— "White House and Congress on Verge of Tax Deal." *The New York Times* (October 23), pp. A1, A11.

——— 1990f. "Leaders Reach a Tax Deal and Predict Its Approval; Bush Awaits Final Details." *The New York Times* (October 25), pp. A1, A10.

——— 1990g. "House and Senate Pass Budget Bill; Bush Is 'Pleased': Relief Is Visible." *The New York Times* (October 28), pp. A1, A15.

Rosenbaum, Sara. 1990. "Child Health and Poor Children." Paper presented at the Armington Symposium on the Impact of Poverty on Children, Case Western Reserve University, March 2, pp. 1–24.

Rosenberg, Mark L. 1988. "Should the Congress Adopt the Proposed 'Act for Better Child Care Services of 1988'?" *The Congressional Digest* 67 (November): 267, 269, 271.

Rosewater, Ann. 1989. "Child and Family Trends: Beyond the Numbers." *Caring for America's Children: Proceedings of the Academy of Political Science* 37: 4–19.

Ross, Elizabeth Dale. 1976. *The Kindergarten Crusade: The Establishment of Preschool Education in the United States*. Athens: Ohio University Press.

Rothman, Barbara Katz. 1989. "Women as Fathers: Motherhood and Child Care Under a Modified Patriarchy." *Gender and Society* 3, no. 1 (March): 89–104.

Rothman, Sheila M. 1973. "Other People's Children: The Day Care Experience in America." *The Public Interest* 30 (Winter): 11–27.

Rowland, Mary. 1986. "The Liability Crisis Hits Home." *Working Woman* (June), pp. 104–106, 136–137.

Rubin, Karen. 1987. "Whose Job is Child Care?" *Ms.*, (March), pp. 32–44.

Ruopp, Richard R. 1979. *Children at the Center: Final Report of the National Day Care Study: Executive Summary/Richard R. Ruopp*. Cambridge, MA: Abt Books.

——— and Jeffrey Travers. 1982. "Janus Faces Day Care: Perspectives on Quality and Cost." In *Day Care: Scientific and Social Policy Issues*, pp. 72–101. Boston: Auburn House Publishing.

Rural Education Division. 1927. United States Bureau of Education. "A Manual of Educational Legislation." Bulletin, 1926, No. 22. Washington, DC: Government Printing Office.

Russell, James. 1904. "The Kindergarten Outlook." *Teachers College Record* 5 (November): 407–411.

Rust, Frances O'Connell. 1989. "Early Childhood in Public Education: Managing Change in a Changing Field." *Teachers College Record* 90(Spring): 452–464.

Ryan, Mary Tuohy. 1953. "A Garden Where Children Grow." *Wisconsin Journal of Education* 86 (November): 6–9, 27.

Sallee, Alvin L. 1986. *Corporate Sponsored Child Care: Options and Advantages*. Las Cruces: New Mexico State University, pp. 2–22.

Sanger, Carol. 1983. "Day Care Center Licensing and Religious Exemptions: An Overview For Providers." San Francisco: Child Care Law Center.

Schaeffer, Mary Frances. 1906. "Conservatism Versus Radicalism in the Kindergarten." *Education* 27 (September): 37–44.

Schlafly, Phyllis. 1988. "Should the Congress Adopt the Proposed 'Act for Better Child Care Services of 1988'?" *The Congressional Digest* 67 (November): 271, 273, 275.

Schlossman, Steven. 1976. "Before Home Start: Notes Toward A History of Parent Education in America, 1897–1929." *Harvard Educational Review* 46: 436–467.

Schorr, Lisbeth, and Daniel Schorr. 1988. *Within Our Reach: Breaking the Cycle of Disadvantage*. New York: Doubleday; paperback, Anchor Books, 1989.

Seligman, Daniel. 1984. "Jailbird Rights." *Fortune* (October 1), pp. 161–162.

"Senate, White House Agree on Child Care." 1990. The Plain Dealer [Cleveland] (October 17), p. 17A.

Service Employees International Union, AFL-CIO. n.d. "SEIU Child Care Activities."

——— 1989a. *The Service Economy: Portrait of a New Workforce*. Washington, DC: Service Employees International Union.

———— 1989b. "Child Care and Family Leave: Workplace and Community Initiatives." *Work and Family*.

———— 1989c. "Summary of Union Child Care Activities." *Work and Family*.

———— 1989d. "Who's Minding the Children?" *Work and Family*.

"Settlement and Settlement Kindergartens in New York City." 1907. *The Kindergarten Magazine and Pedagogical Digest* (May): 610–615.

Shanker, Albert. 1974. "Early Childhood Education is a Job for the Public Schools." *The New York Times* (September 8), p. E11.

———— 1977. "Public Schools and Preschool Programs: A Natural Connection." In *Early Childhood Education*, ed. L. Golubchick and B. Persky. Wayne: Avery Publishing Group Inc.

———— 1987. "The Case for Public School Sponsorship of Early Childhood Education Revisited." In *Early Schooling*, ed. Sharon L. Kagan and Edward F. Zigler, pp. 45–64. New Haven: Yale University Press.

———— 1989. "Leave Well Enough Alone...Restore the Old ABC Bill." *The New York Times* (June 25).

Shannon, W. V. 1972. "Radical Direct, Simple Utopian Alternative to Day Care Centers." *New York Times Magazine* (April 30), pp. 13ff. (discussion May 21, pp. 96–97).

Shapiro, Michael Steven. 1983. *Child's Garden: The Kindergarten Movement from Froebel to Dewey*. University Park: Pennsylvania State University Press.

Sheldon, Rev. Charles M. 1898. "The Central Church Kindergarten, Topeka." *Kindergarten Review* 8 (February): 355–357.

Shepard, Irwin. 1890. "The Effects of the Kindergarten Training on the Primary School." *Journal of Proceedings of National Educational Association*: 554–560.

Shinn, M. W. 1890. "Charities for Children in San Francisco." *Overland Monthly* 15 (January) Second Series: 78–101.

Sidel, Ruth. 1974. "But What About the Children?" *Ms.* (March), p. 38.

Silverman, Suzann. 1989. "When It Comes to Child Care, Hospitals May Be Setting the Pace for Much of the Nation." *Journal of the American Medical Association* (April 7): 1857, 1861.

Simon, Barbara Levy. 1988. "Social Work Responds to the Women's Movement." *Affilia* 3, no. 4 (Winter): 60–68.

Smith, Geoffrey. 1979. "Perry Mendel's Golden Diapers: Kinder Care Learning Centers." *Forbes* (June 25), pp. 67-69.

Smith, Nora A. 1898a. "The Kindergarten in Home and Neighborhood Work." *The Ladies Home Journal* (November), pp. 20–21.

——— 1898b. "The Kindergarten Gifts." *The Ladies Home Journal* (December), pp. 34–35.

——— 1899a. "The Kindergarten Possible in Every Home and Village," (five part series). *The Ladies Home Journal* (November–March 1899).

——— 1899b. "The Kindergarten Occupations." *The Ladies Home Journal* (January), pp. 16–17.

——— 1899c. "Stories and Story-telling." *The Ladies Home Journal* (February), pp. 22–23.

——— 1899d. "The Kindergarten Songs and Games." *The Ladies Home Journal* (March), pp. 28–31.

Smith, Timothy L. 1957. *Revivalism and Social Reform: In Mid-Nineteenth Century America*. New York and Nashville: Abingdon Press.

——— 1961. "Progressivism in American Education: 1890–1900." *Harvard Educational Review* 31: 168–193.

Snider, William. 1990a. "U.S. Programs Recognize Parent Contributions." *Education Week* (November 21): 17.

——— 1990b. "Parents as Partners." *Education Week* (November 21): 11–13, 16–20.

——— 1990c. "'Choice and 'Voice' Acknowledge Parents' Key Role in Education Process." *Education Week* (November 21): 20.

——— 1990d. "Role of Parents in School Decisions Long Debated." *Education Week* (November 21): 13.

——— 1990e. "Power of Parents Put to the Test in Chicago Reform Experiment." *Education Week* (November 21): 14–15.

Snyder, Thomas D. 1988. "Trends in Education." *Principal* 68 (September): 26–30.

Social Justice and Peacemaking Office. 1989. Letter to Members of the U. S. House of Representatives (June 26).

Spakes, Patricia. 1989. "Reshaping the Goals of Family Policy: Sexual Equality, Not Protection." *Affilia* 4, no. 3 (Fall): 7–24.

Spencer, Anna G. 1910. "The Changing Population of Our Large Cities." *Kindergarten-Primary Magazine* 23 (November): 65–71.

Standard and Poor's Corporation. 1990. "Kinder-Care Learning Centers." Standard OTC Stock Reports. Vol. 56, No. 11, Sec. 16 (January 26), p. 4357V.

Steiner, Gilbert Y. 1971. "Day Care Centers: Hype or Hope?" *Transaction* 8 (July–August): 51.

——— 1976. *The Children's Cause*. Washington, DC: The Brookings Institution.

Steinfels, Margaret O'Brien. 1973. *Who's Minding the Children? The History and Politics of Day Care in America*. New York: Simon and Schuster.

Strasser, Susan M. 1980. "An Enlarged Human Existence? Technology and Household Work in Nineteenth-Century America." In *Women and Household Labor*, ed. Sarah Fenstermaker Berk. Beverly Hills: Sage Publications.

Streuer, Erika. 1973. "Current Legislative Proposals and Public Policy Questions for Child Care." In *Child Care—Who Cares? Foreign and Domestic Infant and Early Childhood Development Policies*, ed. Pamela Roby, pp. 49–70. New York: Basic Books.

Sturges, Jannette L. 1901. "Our Work for Foreigners in Chicago." *Home Mission Monthly* 15 (August), pp. 236–238.

Sugarman, Jule M. 1989. "Federal Support Revisited." *Caring for America's Children: Proceedings of the Academy of Political Science* 37: 99–109.

——— Ed Martin, and Ted Taylor. 1975. "Who Will Deliver Education to Preschool Children?" In *One Child Indivisible*, ed. National Association for Young Children, pp. 97–133. Washington, DC: NAEYC.

Suro, Roberto. 1990. "Courts Ordering Financing Changes in Public Schools." *The New York Times* (March 11), pp. 1, 13.

Sweeney, John and Karen Nussbaum. 1989. *Solutions for the New Work Force*. Bethesda, MD: Seven Locks Press.

Tanner, Daniel and Laurel Tanner. 1990. *History of the School Curriculum*. New York: Macmillan Publishing Co.

Temple, Alice. 1937. "The Kindergarten in America-Modern Period." *Childhood Education* 13 (April): 358–363.

Tentler, Leslie Woodcock. 1979. *Wage-Earning Women: Industrial Work and Family Life in the United States, 1900–1930*. New York: Oxford University Press.

Tietze, Wolfgang and Karin Ufermann. 1989. "An International Perspective on Schooling for 4-Year-Olds." *Theory into Practice* (Winter): 69–77.

Tolchin, Martin. 1990. "Negotiations on Child Care Bill Arouse Anger." *The New York Times* (March 5), p. A-10.

Tomkins, Calvin. 1989. "A Sense of Urgency: Marian Wright Edelman." *The New Yorker* (March 27), pp. 48-74.

Tribe, Laurence H. 1988. *American Constitutional Law*, 2nd ed. New York: The Foundation Press, Inc.

Troen, Selwyn K. 1972. "Operation Headstart: The Beginnings of the Public School Kindergarten Movement." *Missouri Historical Review* (January): 211-229.

—— 1975. *The Public and the Schools: Shaping the Saint Louis School System: 1838-1920*. Columbia: University of Missouri Press.

Trost, Cathy. 1989. "Few Use Credits For Child-Care Plans, Study Finds." *The Wall Street Journal* (November 14).

Turner, Jonathan. 1982. *The Structure of Sociological Theory*, 3rd ed. Homewood, IL: The Dorsey Press.

"Twenty-Five Years of Head Start—the Commitment Lives On." *Child Care Information Exchange* (September–October): 16-18.

Tyack, David B. 1974. *The One Best System: A History of American Urban Education*. Cambridge, MA: Harvard University Press.

Weber, Evelyn. 1969. *The Kindergarten: Its Encounter with Educational Thought in America*. New York: Teachers College.

United States Catholic Conference. 1989. "Child Care." Washington, DC: United States Catholic Conference.

—— 1990. Letter to House/Senate Conference Committee conferees by Frank J. Monahan (June 13).

Value Line Investment Survey. 1987. Part 3, Ratings and Reports, 2nd ed. (July 3), pp. 343, 354.

Vandewalker, Nina Catherine. 1908. "Kindergarten Legislation in the United States." *American School Board Journal* 37 (October): 3, 20.

——— 1923 [1908]. *The Kindergarten in American Education*. New York: The Arno Press.

Viteritti, Joseph P. 1989. "Urban Governance and the Idea of a Service Community." *Caring for America's Children: Proceedings of the Academy of Political Science* 37: 110–121.

Waite, Mary G. 1926. *The Kindergarten in Certain School Surveys*. United States Bureau of Education Bulletin No.13. Washington, DC: Government Printing Office.

Waldo, Eveline A. 1900. "Second Annual Meeting of Kindergarten Department, Southern Educational Association." *Kindergarten Magazine* 12 (February): 334–341.

——— 1904. "Kindergartens in the Southern States and in Some of the Countries South of the United States." *National Education Association Journal of Proceedings and Addresses*: 411–415.

Walsh, Daniel J. 1989. "Changes in Kindergarten: Why Here? Why Now?" *Early Childhood Research Quarterly* 4 (September): 377–392.

Warger, Cynthia, ed. 1988. *A Resource Guide to Public School Early Childhood Programs*. Alexandria, VA: Association for Supervision and Curriculum Development.

"Washington Update." 1988a. *Young Children* (May): 56.

"Washington Update." 1988b. *Young Children* (September): 59.

Waterman, Mary H. 1907. "New York Kindergarten Association." *Kindergarten Review* 17 (April): 461–467.

"A Week in the Hampton Kindergarten." 1907. *Southern Workman* 36 (October): 537–544.

Wells, Amy Stuart. 1990. "Lawsuit Adds New Twist to Tuition Voucher Case." *The New York Times* (December 19), p. B8.

Wesley, Edgar B. 1957. *NEA: The First Hundred Years*. New York: Harper and Brothers.

Wheelock, Lucy. 1894. "Ideal Relation of Kindergarten to Primary School." *Journal of Addresses and Proceedings of the National Education Association*: 702–703.

——— 1915. "Kindergarten Clubs and Parent Teachers Associations." *Kindergarten Review* 26 (December): 261–263.

——— 1942. "From the Kindergarten to the Primary School." *Childhood Education* 18 (May): 414–416.

White, Lynn. 1990. Telephone conversation with author (September 27).

Whitney, Laura. 1906. "Christmas in a Jewish Kindergarten." *Kindergarten Magazine* 18 (December): 193–198.

"Why Should the Kindergarten Be Municipalized?" 1897. *Kindergarten Magazine* 9 (March): 507–516.

Wiggin, Kate Douglas. 1888. "The Relation of the Kindergarten to Social Reform." *Proceedings of the National Conference on Charities and Corrections*: 247–258.

——— 1892. *Children's Rights*. Cambridge, MA: The Riverside Press of Houghton, Mifflin and Co.

——— ed. 1892b. *The Kindergarten*. New York: Harper and Brothers Publishers.

——— and Nora Archibald Smith. 1896. *Kindergarten Principles and Practice*. Cambridge, MA: The Riverside Press.

Wilk, Danny. 1973. "'Save the Children': Implications of Day Care." *The Black Scholar*. (May–June): 14–20.

Willer, Barbara A. 1988a. *The Growing Crisis in Child Care*. Washington, DC: National Association for the Education of Young Children.

——— 1988b. "Summary of Key Early Childhood Bills Now Before Congress." Washington, DC: National Association for the Education of Young Children, March 3.

——— 1989a. "A Comparison of Early Childhood/Child Care Bills Introduced in the 101st Congress." Washington, DC: National Association for the Education of Young Children, January 3.

——— 1989b. "A Comparison of Selected Early Childhood–Child Care Bills Before the House Education and Labor–Senate Labor and Human Resources Committees in the 101st Congress." Washington, DC: National Association for the Education of Young Chilren, March 31.

——— 1989c. "A Comparison of ABC as Passed by the Senate and H.R.3–ABC as approved by the House Education and Labor Committee." Washington, DC: National Association for the Education of Young Children, July 29.

——— 1990a. "Federal Comprehensive Child Care Legislation: Much Success in 1989 but More Work Ahead in 1990." *Young Children* (January): 25–27, 49.

——— 1990b. "A Comparison of ABC as Passed by the Senate and H.R. 3 as Passed by the House." Washington, DC: National Association for the Education of Young Children, April 2.

Yans-McLaughlin, Virginia. 1981. *Family and Community: Italian Immigrants in Buffalo, 1880–1930*. Chicago: University of Illinois Press.

Yelaja, Shankar A. 1978. "What is Social Policy? Its Assumptions, Definitions and Uses." In *Canadian Social Policy*, pp. 3-23. Wilford: Laurier University Press.

Zigler, Edward F. 1987a. "Formal Schooling for Four-Year-Olds? No." In *Early Schooling*, ed. Sharon L. Kagan and Edward F. Zigler, pp. 27–44. New Haven: Yale University Press.

——— 1987b. "Formal Schooling for Four-Year-Olds? No." *American Psychologist* 42, no. 3 (March): 254–60.

——— 1987c. "A Solution to the Nation's Child Care Crisis: The School of the Twenty-first Century." Paper presented at the tenth anniversary of the Bush Center in Child Development and Social Policy, New Haven, Connecticut, September 18, and at the National Health Policy Forum, Washington, DC, September 23.

——— 1988. "The School of the 21st Century: A Bush Center Fact Sheet." New Haven: The Bush Center in Child Development and Social Policy.

——— and Pamela Ennis. 1988. "Child Care: A New Role for Tomorrow's Schools." *Principal* (September): 10–13.

——— and Pamela Ennis. 1989. "Child Care: Science and Social Policy the Child Care Crisis in America." *Canadian Psychology* 30: 116–125.

——— and Matia Finn-Stevenson. 1989. "Child Care in America: From Problem to Solution." *Educational Policy* 3, no. 4: 313–329.

——— and Jody Goodman. 1982. "The Battle for Day Care in America: A View from the Trenches." In *Day Care: Scientific and Social Policy Issues*, ed. Edward F. Zigler and Edmund W. Gordon, pp. 338-350. Boston: Auburn Publishing House.

——— and Edmund W. Gordon. 1982. *Day Care: Scientific and Social Policy Issues*. Boston: Auburn House Publishing Co.

——— and Jean Valentine. 1979. *Project Head Start: A Legacy of the War on Poverty*. New York: The Free Press.

II. GOVERNMENT DOCUMENTS

Act for Better Child Care Services of 1989, S. 5. 1989. 101st Congress, 1st session.

Child Care and Development Block Grant. 1990. Senate Labor and Human Resources. Subcommittee on Children, Families, Alcoholism and Drugs (October 22).

Congressional Quarterly. (CQW and CQA cited in text only).

Early Childhood Education and Development Act of 1989, H.R. 3. 1989. Presented before the House of Representatives January 3, 1989. 101st Congress, 1st session, Union Calendar No. 152. Presented before the Senate April 2, 1990. 101st Congress, 2nd session, Calendar No. 500.

Family Support Act of 1988, 1988. PL 100-485, 102 Stat. 2343.

"Highlights of Labor Committee Conference Agreements on Child Care." 1990. Senate Labor and Human Resources Subcommittee on Children, Family, Drugs and Alcoholism (June).

Nixon, Richard. 1971. "Veto of Economic Opportunity Amendments of 1971." In *Weekly Compilation of Presidential Documents*. vol. 7, pp. 1634-1636. Washington, DC: Government Printing Office.

Omnibus Budget Reconciliation Act of 1990. 1990. Report 101-964. Conference Report to Accompany H.R. 5835. 101st Congress, 2nd session (October 27).

U.S. Bureau of Education. 1872. *The Kindergarten*. Washington, DC:Government Printing Office, July.

———— 1914. *Kindergartens in the United States: Statistics and Present Problems*. Bulletin no. 6 (whole number 577), Washington, DC: Government Printing Office, pp. 5-133.

U.S. Congress. Committee on Children, Youth and Families (House). 1988. *Children and Families: Key Trends in the 1980s.* 100th Congress, 2nd session (December).

——— Committee on Education and Labor (House). 1968. *Trust Funds for Educational Scholarships and Child Care Centers. Hearings Before a Special Committee on Labor of the House Committee on Education and Labor on H.R. 14314.* 90th Congress, 2nd session (March 27).

——— Committee on Education and Labor (House). 1989. *Report on Early Childhood Education and Development Act of 1989 Together with Dissenting, Additional, and Individual Views Presented Before the House of Representatives by Mr. Hawkins to accompany H.R. 3/ Report 101-190.* 101st Congress, 1st session, July 27.

——— Committee on Education and Labor (House). 1969–1970. *Comprehensive Preschool Education and Child Day-Care Act of 1969. Hearings Before the Select Committee on Education of the House Committee on Education and Labor on H.R. 13520.* 91st Congress, 1st and 2nd sessions, November 18 and 20; December 1–4, 9–11, and 16; February 25 and 26; March 2–4; February 21 and 23.

——— Committee on Education and Labor (House). 1988. *Report on Act for Better Child Care Services of 1988 together with Dissenting, Additional, and Individual Views presented before the House of Representatives by Mr. Hawkins. To accompany H.R. 3660/Report 100-985 part 1.* 100th Congress, 2nd session, September 27.

——— Committee on Education and Labor (House). 1989. *Hearings on Child Care. Hearings Before the Committee on Education and Labor House of Representatives.* 100th Congress, 1st session, February 9, March 6, and April 5.

——— Committee on Finance (Senate). 1971. *Child Care. Hearings Before the Senate Committee on Finance on S.2003.* 92nd Congress, 1st session, September 22, 23, 24.

——— Committee on Finance (Senate). 1976. *Data and Materials on Proposals Relating to Federal Child Care Standards. Prepared by the Staff for the Use of the Senate Committee on Finance.* 94th Congress, 2nd session.

——— Committee on Finance (Senate). 1977. *Child Care: Data and Materials. Prepared by the Staff for the Committee on Finance.* 95th Congress, 1st session.

——— Committee on Human Resources (Senate). 1977–1978. *Child Care and Child Development Programs, 1977-78. Hearings Before the Subcommittee on Child and Human Development of the Senate Committee on Human Resources on Examination of How Best to Shape Future Federal Legislation Involving Child Care and Child Development.* 95th Congress, 1st and 2nd session, 2 parts: November 25; December 12; February 8 and 20.

——— Committee on Labor and Human Resources (Senate). 1979. *Hearings Before the Subcommittee on Child and Human Development of the Senate Committee on Labor and Human Resources on S. 4.* 96th Congress, 1st session, February 6 and 21.

——— Committee on Labor and Human Resources (Senate). 1987. *A Bill for a Federal Program for the Improvement of Child Care, and for Other Purposes.* S. 1885, 100th Congress, 1st session, November 19.

——— Committee on Labor and Human Resources (Senate). 1988. *Hearings before the Subcommittee on Children, Family, Drugs, and Alcoholism of the Committee on Labor and Human Resources on S.1885 (Act for Better Child Care Services of 1987).* 100th Congress, 2nd session, March 15 and June 28.

——— Committee on Labor and Public Welfare (Senate). 1968. *To Allow Employer Contributions to Funds for Scholarships and Day-Care Centers Under Section 302 of Taft-Hartley Act. Hearings Before the Subcommittee of the Senate Labor and Public Welfare Committee on S. 2704.* 90th Congress, 2nd session, (February 16).

——— Committee on Labor and Public Welfare (Senate). 1971. *Comprehensive Child Development Act of 1971. Joint Hearings Before the Subcommittee on Employment, Manpower, and Poverty and the Subcommittee on Children and Youth of the Senate Committee on Labor and Public Welfare on S. 1512.* 92nd Congress, 1st session, 3 parts. May 13 and 20; May 25 and 26; May 27; and June 16.

——— Committee on Labor and Public Welfare (Senate). 1974. *Child And Family Services Act, 1974. Joint Hearings Before the Subcommittee on Children and Youth of the Senate Committee on Labor and Public Welfare and the Select Committee on Education of the House Committee on Education and Labor and the Subcommittee on Employment, Poverty, and Migratory Labor of the Senate Committee on Labor and Public Welfare on S. 3754.* 93rd Congress, 2nd session, August 8 and 9.

——— Committee on Labor and Public Welfare (Senate). 1975. *Child and Family Services Act, 1975. Joint Hearings Before the Subcommittee on Children and Youth and the Subcommittee on Employment, Poverty, and Migratory Labor of the Senate Committee on Labor and Public Welfare and the Subcommittee on Select Education of the House Committee on Education and Labor on S. 626 and H.R. 2966.* 94th Congress, 1st session, 9 parts: February 20; February 21; March 12–14; April 25 and 26; June 5, 16, 19; and 20; and July 15.

——— Committee on Ways and Means (House). 1989. *Report on Early Childhood Education and Development Act of 1989 Presented Before the House of Representatives by Mr. Rostenkowski together with Additional and Dissenting Views. To accompany H.R. 3/Report 101-190 part 2.* 101st Congress, 1st session, September 12.

——— (House). *Labor-Employer Contributions to Trust Funds for Scholarships, Etc.* 1969. House Report No. 91-286. *Congressional Record,* vol. 115, pp. 1159-1162.

——— (Senate). 1988. *Report on Act for Better Child Care Services of 1989 Together with Additional Views Presented before the Senate by Mr. Kennedy. To Accompany S. 1885/Report 100-484.* 100th Congress, 2nd sess., August 1.

——— (Senate). 1989. *Report on Act For Better Child Care Services of 1989 before the Senate Together with Additional and Minority Views. To Accompany S. 5.* 101st Congress, 1st session, January 3.

——— (House). 1990. *Report on Augustus F. Hawkins Human Services Reauthorization Act of 1990 Conference Report. To accompany H.R. 4151/Report 101-816.* 101st Congress, 2nd session, October 5.

———— Select Committee on Children, Youth, and Families (House). 1985. *Child Care: The Emerging Insurance Crisis. Hearings Before the Select Committee on Children, Youth, and Families.* 99th Congress, 1st session, July 18 and 30.

———— Select Committee on Children, Youth, and Families (House). 1986. *A Report on the Activities of the Select Committee on Children, Youth, and Families, Together with Dissenting Minority Views. U.S. House of Representatives.* 99th Congress, 2nd. session; reproduced by EDRS in microfiche, ED 269 158.

———— Select Committee on Children, Youth, and Families (House). 1987. *U.S. Children and Their Families: Current Conditions and Recent Trends, 1987. A Report Together with Additional Views of the House Select Committee on Children, Youth, and Families.* 100th Congress, 1st session, March.

———— (Senate). 1987. Senator Hatch speaking for S. 1678. A bill to establish a block grant program for child care services, and for other purposes, the Child Care Services Improvement Act. 100th Congress, 1st session, September 11. *Congressional Record*, vol. 137.

———— Subcommittee on Children, Family, Drugs and Alcoholism (Senate). 1989 *Hearings on Child Care Quality.* January 24.

———— Subcommittee on Human Resources (House). 1989. *Hearings before the subcommittee on Human Resources of the Committee of Ways and Means. How to Help the Working Poor; and Problems of the Working Poor.* 100th Congress, 1st session, February 28, March 21, and April 27.

U.S. Department of Commerce. Bureau of the Census. 1982. *Child Care Arrangements of Working Mothers: June 1982.* Current Population Reports. Special Studies Series P-23, No. 129.

———— 1987. "Where the Children Are." Statistical Brief-4-87, October.

U.S. Department of Health, Education and Welfare. 1967. Social and Rehabilitation Service. Children's Bureau. U.S. Department of Labor. Wage and Labor Standards Administration. Women's Bureau. *Child Care Arrangements of Working Mothers in the United States.*

—— 1970. *A Statement of Principles*.

—— 1975. Office of Human/Development Research and Evaluation Division. *Child-Care Programs in Nine Countries*. Publication 30080.

—— 1977. Office of the Assistant Secretary for Planning and Evaluation. Prepared by the Center for Systems and Program Development, Inc. *Policy Issues in Day Care: Summaries of 21 Papers*. Washington, DC: Center for Systems and Program Development, Inc.

U.S. Department of Health and Human Services. Office of Human Development Services Administration for Children, Youth, and Families. 1985. *Head Start Research Since 1965: Head Start Synthesis Project*. Washington, DC: U.S. Government Printing Office.

—— 1989. Head Start Bureau. "Project Head Start Statistical Fact Sheet." January.

U. S. Department of Labor. 1988. "BLS Reports on Employer Child-Care Practices." *News* [Bureau of Labor Statistics] (January 15).

—— Children's Bureau. 1922. *Industrial Homework of Children*. Study Made in Pawtucket and Central Falls, RI. Bureau Publication No. 100.

—— Women's Bureau. 1930. *The Immigrant Woman and Her Job*. By Caroline Manning. Bulletin of the Women's Bureau, No. 74.

—— Women's Bureau. 1972. Employment Standards Administration. *Federal Funds for Day Care Project*.

—— Women's Bureau. 1989. *Employers and Child Care: Benefiting Work and Family*.

Index